The Golden Age of
maritime maps

**When Europe
Discovered the World**

Under the direction of
Catherine Hofmann
Hélène Richard
Emmanuelle Vagnon

The Golden Age of maritime maps

When Europe Discovered the World

FIREFLY BOOKS

A FIREFLY BOOK

Published in English by Firefly Books Ltd. 2013

First published in France under the title *L'Âge d'or des Cartes Marines* © Éditions du Seuil, 2012.

First printing

Publisher Cataloging-in-Publication Data (U.S.)
A CIP record for this title is available from Library of Congress.

Library and Archives Canada Cataloguing in Publication
A CIP record for this title is available from Library and Archives Canada.

Published in the United States by
Firefly Books (U.S.) Inc.
P.O. Box 1338, Ellicott Station
Buffalo, New York 14205

Published in Canada by
Firefly Books Ltd.
50 Staples Avenue, Unit 1
Richmond Hill, Ontario L4B 0A7

Printed in China

Cet ouvrage a bénéficié du soutien des Programmes d'aide à la publication de l'Institut français.

Exhibition

Commission
Catherine Hofmann, Hélène Richard,
Jean-Yves Sarazin and Emmanuelle Vagnon

Production
Exhibition services of the National Library
of France, under the direction of
Ariane James-Sarazin

General Coordination
Anne Manouvrier

Registry of Works
Vincent Desjardins

Technical Registry
Serge Derouault, assisted by François Sorlin,
Nathalie Grassi, Paul Roth and Charlie Thicot

Framing and Mounting
Éric Vannereau, Éric Rousseau, Christine Julien,
Olivier Paitreault, Caroline Bruyant and the Atelier Pinson

Displays
Atelier des 3 Coups

Graphics
LD Publicité

Exhibit Providers

France

Archives départementales des Alpes maritimes, Nice
Association des "Amis du Musée de la marine de Rouen"
Bibliothèque à vocation régionale de Marseille
Bibliothèque de l'Assemblée nationale, Paris
Bibliothèque de l'Institut de France, Paris
Bibliothèque municipale, Dijon
Bibliothèque municipale, Lyon
Bibliothèque Sainte-Geneviève, Paris
Château-Musée, Dieppe
Fondation Calouste Gulbenkian, Paris
Mobilier national et manufactures nationales des Gobelins,
    de Beauvais et de la Savonnerie, Paris
Musée de la Marine, Paris
Musée du Conservatoire national des arts et métiers, Paris
Musée du Louvre, département des Peintures, Paris
Musée du Nouveau Monde, La Rochelle
Musée national de la Renaissance, Écouen
Musée du Quai Branly, Paris
Musée Guimet, Paris
Service historique de la Défense, Vincennes
Société de géographie, Paris

Europe

British Library, London
Biblioteca Medicea Laurenziana, Florence,
Biblioteca Nazionale Marciana Venezia, Venise

Private Collection

Mr. Hubert Clayens

Publishing

Editorial direction
Pierrette Crouzet (National Library of France)
Claude Hénard (Seuil)

Editorial Oversight
Jacqueline Michelet (National Library of France)

Oversight and Coordination of Illustrations
Laurianne Bossis, Céline Delétang, Caterina D'Agostino,
    Frédérique Savona (National Library of France)

Graphic Design and Page Layout
Volume Visuel / Cyril Cohen

Acknowledgments

We extend our thanks first to the patrons of the exhibit, the Fondation d'enterprise Total and ESRI France, who, through their generosity, made possible the outstanding success of "The Golden Age of Maritime Maps."

The exhibit is also indebted to the research support from MeDIan (Les societies méditerranénnes et THE INDIAN OCEAN). Financed by the agence nationale de la Recherce from 2010 to 2013 (ANR-09-SSOC-050) in partnership with the University of Rheims, the Maison de l'Orient et la Méditerranée de Lyon and the laboratoire Islam medieval (UMR 8167), this agency brought important support, both financial and scientific, not only in preparation for but also in the production of the exhibit. The organizers also thank Didier Marcotte, Françoise Micheau, Éric Vellet, Jean-Charles Ducéne, Patrick Gautier-Dalché and Henri Bresc. A partnership with the University Al-Iman of Ryad, the Saudi cultural office in Paris and the Saudi ministry of higher Education, the dialogue des cultures chair of the université Paris 1 Pantheon-Sorbonne, provided support during 2012.

The exhibit is also indebted to internal research support from the National Library of France between 2010 and 2012, which had three components: an inventory, description and digitization of all portolan maps kept in public collections in France. We are especially grateful to Nicole Da Costa, Thierry Pardé and Olivier Jacquot of the Research and Strategy Division for their support of the project, to Laurent Manœvre, Thierry Claërr, Florent Palluault and Cécille Souchon for their help with the national survey, to Arnaud Beaufort, director of the Department of Services and Networks, for considering the many specific technical requirements of such a program, to Aline Girard, Frédéric D. Martin, Cécille de Becdelièvre, Sylvie Damase and Catherine Brial, from the Department of Cooperation, for launching and promoting this program nationally. We thank all technical services of the National Library of France for partaking in the digitization, specifically Isabelle Dussert-Carbone, Dominic Maillet, Nathalie Leborgne, Annie Bonnaud, Bernard Dulac, Alain Terrienne, Franck Bardon, Patrick Bramoullé, Philippe Salinson, Alain Puigbo, Sébastien Rat. Nor do we wish to forget all the librarians and research assistants in the Department of Maps and Plans, who compiled or added to the metadata of this huge body of information: Emmanuel Pavy, Françoise Boucard and Cécile Conduché.

This exhibit would not have seen the light of day without the determination and strong support of Bruno Racine, president of the National Library of France, and of Jacqueline Sanson, the director general. At the core of the leadership team, we thank Marc Rassat, communications delegate, Kara Lennon Casanova, patronage delegate, and Thierry Grillet, cultural distribution delegate, and to their very many collaborators in charge of exhibits, publications, multimedia and educational efforts, who, through joint action, led to the successful public appreciation of the exhibit. We are indebted to Françoise Juhel, chief of multimedia publications, for assembling this team, and especially to Emmanuelle Bérenger for so effectively showcasing this exhibit online through the National Library of France website.

This exhibit includes numerous pieces from departments that oversee the National Library of France collections. We thank Denis Bruckmann, director of collections, for his support in this effort, and Jean-Yves Sarazin, director of the Department of Maps and Plans, for his unfailing engagement in the project. We are also indebted to all the department directors who loaned us items and to their colleagues who provided their scientific expertise and technical aid in document selection. They include: Charlotte Denöel, Marie-Pierre Lafitte, Isabelle Le Masne de Chermont, Anne Mary, Nathalie Monnet, Jean-Pierre Riamond, Annie Vernay-Nouri from the Department of Manuscripts; Sylvie Aubenas, Barbara Brejon de Lavergnée, Caroline Bruyant, Séverine Lepage and Marie-Hélène Petitfour from the Department of Prints; Bruno Blasselle, Nathalie Coilly, Ève Netchine and Séverine Pascal from the Arsenal Library; Antoine Coron, Geneviève Guilleminot-Chrétien and Fabienne Le Bars from the Rare Book Reserve; Michel Amandry and Mathilde Avisseau-Brouste from the Department of Coins, Medals and Antiques.

Numerous documents are on display from both French and foreign institutions. We wish to express our gratitude to those in charge of those collections and to their personnel for their kindness, for their timely assistance and for loaning their documents, which made this exhibit so successful. Our recognition is extended to the institutions and personnel listed below:

In France
Archives départementales des Alpes Maritimes: Jean-Bernard Lacroix, Hélène Cavalié, Laurence Lachamp
Bibliothèque de l'Institut: Gabriel de Broglie, Hélène Carrère d'Encausse, Mireille Pastoureau
Bibliothèque municipale de Lyon: Gilles Éboli, Pierre Guinard, Sylvie Bouteille
Bibliothèque municipale de Marseille: Christian Laget, Brigitte Blanc
Bibliothèque municipale de Dijon: Marie-Paule Rolin, Nadia Harabasz
Bibliothèque de l'Assemblée nationale: Éliane Fighiera, Pierre Jouin
Bibliothèque Sainte-Geneviève: Yves Peyré, Yannick Nexon
Château-musée de Dieppe: Pierre Ickowicz, Martine Gatinet
Club des maquettistes du musée maritime de Rouen: Marc Bonnans
Fondation Calouste Gulbenkian: Arlette Darbord
Musée du Quai Branly: Stéphane Martin, Yves Le Fur, André Delpuech, Hélène Joubert, Laurence Dubaut
Musée Guimet: Olivier de Bernon, Jean-Paul Desroches, Céline Morisseau

Musée du Louvre: Henri Loyrette, Stéphane Loire, Blaise Ducos, Sébastien Allard
Musée des Arts et métiers: Serge Chambaud, Cyrille Foasso, Aminata Zerbo
Mobilier national: Bernard Schotter, Arnaud Brejon de Lavergnée, Marie-Odile Klipfel, Françoise Cabioc'h
Musée national de la Marine: Jean-Marc Brûlez, Marjolaine Mourot
Musée national de la Renaissance — château d'Écouen: Thierry Crépin-Leblond
Musée du Nouveau Monde (La Rochelle): Annick Notter
Service historique de la Défense: François Gasnault, Karine Leboucq, Alain Morgat, Sylvie Yeomans, Martin Barros, Véronique de Touchet
Société de géographie: Jean-Robert Pitte, Michel Dagnaud

Outside of France
British Library (London): Lynne Brindley, Peter Barber, Andrea Clarke, Lesley Thomas
Biblioteca Medicea Laurenziana (Florence): Vera Valitutto, Anna Rita Fantoni
Biblioteca Nazionale Marciana (Venice): Pietro Falchetta, Maurizio Messina, Annalisa Bruni, Maria Letizia Sebastiani

We also thank the entire team of the Exhibition services, who under the direction of Arianne James-Sarazin, were with us every step of the way in putting together this exhibit. We are grateful to Vincent Desjardins, Serge Derouault and especially to Anne Manouvrier, who was in charge of the exhibits. Her efficiency, patience and advice never failed us, despite many hurdles to overcome. Setting up the many items of this display greatly involved the exhibits preparation studio, led by Éric Vannereau, and the Large Format Division of the Department of Maps and Plans was under the direction of Alain Roger. They all deserve our warmest thanks.

Finally, during its many months of preparation, this exhibit depended on the savoir-faire and talents of the curators of the Large Format Division, which among others included Alain Roger, Isabelle Suire, Evelyne Cabourg, Sandy Dupuet and their many trainees. We are very grateful to them collectively, and to our colleague Benoît Cote-Colisson, chief of communications and conservation of Maps and Plans, and the entire teams of warehouse people of the department, whose job it was to retrieve our precious portolan maps from their storage cabinets.

A well-planned exhibition is not complete without a well-crafted and illustrated catalog, in order to help insure its permanence. We sincerely thank all those at Editions du Seuil, under the guidance of Claude Hénard, and at the National Library of France, under the direction of Jocelyn Rigault, who contributed to this large undertaking. They include Pierrette Crouzet, chief of Book Publishing Services, Jacqueline Michelet, in charge of publishing, and Céline Delétang, iconographer. Finally, we owe a special debt to Cyril Chen, our talented graphic designer.

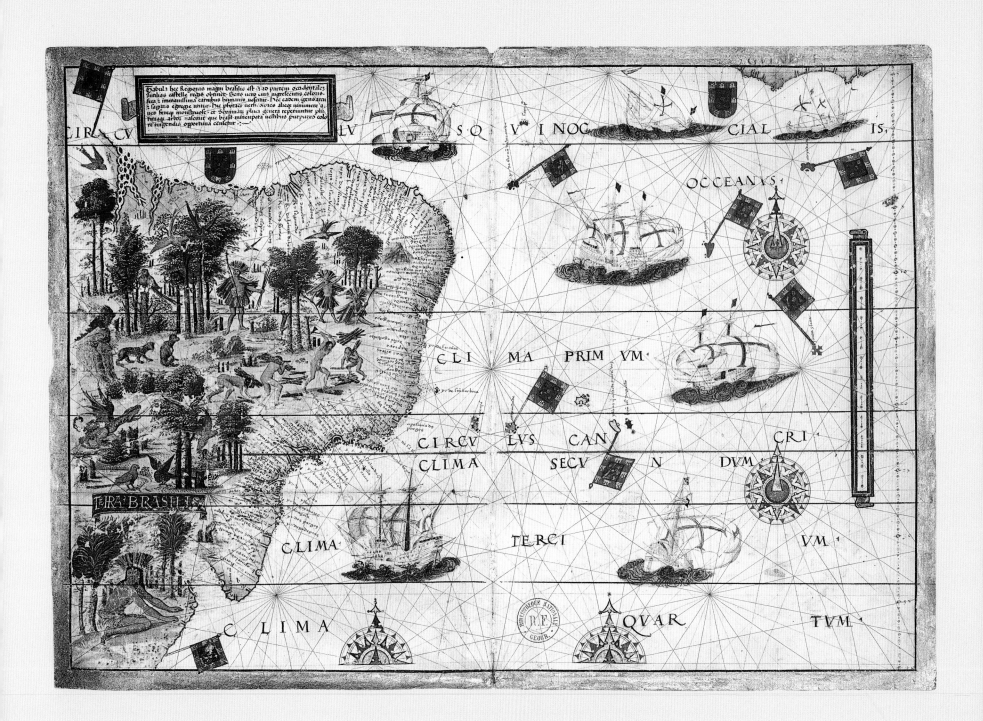

TABLE OF CONTENTS

9   Foreword
Bruno Racine

10   Oceanic Overture
Frank Lestringant

18   The Fascination of Portolans:
Historiography and Collections
Catherine Hofmann

30   How Portolan Maps Were
Made and Used Through
the Centuries
Catherine Hofmann,
Hélène Richard,
Emmanuelle Vagnon

42   *Catalonian Atlas*

The Mediterranean

58   The Mediterranean:
The Cradle of Portolan Maps
Emmanuelle Vagnon

60   Navigational Maps:
The First Widely
Distributed Maps
Ramon J. Pujades i Bataller

72   Mediterranean Cartographers
of the 16th and 17th Centuries
Corradino Astengo

86   Antique, Medieval and
New World Cities on
Portolan Maps
Jean-Yves Sarazin

90   Insular Maritime Cosmography
and European Expansion During
the Renaissance
Georges Tolias

98   *Nautical Planisphere*
Nicolò de Caverio

Wide Open Spaces

108   The Challenge of the Oceans
Hélène Richard

110   The Exploration and Geopolitical
Stakes of Iberian Cartography
(15th and 16th Centuries)
Luisa Martín-Merás Verdejo

126   From the Mediterranean to
the Ocean: New Problems,
New Solutions
Joaquim Alves Gaspar

136   Norman Hydrographers
(16th and 17th Centuries)
Sarah Toulouse

148   *Universal Cosmography*
Guillaume Le Testu

160   The Iconography of
the New World
(15th–17th Centuries)
Surekha Davies

174   Hydrographers along the Thames
(16th and 17th Centuries)
Sarah Tyacke

180   *The Miller Atlas*

The Indian Ocean

196   The Distribution of Knowledge
Emmanuelle Vagnon

198   Medieval Cartography of the
Indian Ocean: The Imagined Ocean
Emmanuelle Vagnon

216   Nautical and Humanist
Cartography of the Indian Ocean
(16th and 17th Centuries)
Zoltán Biedermann

228   Cartography of the Dutch East
India Company's Far East Routes
Hans Kok

240   *Map of the Pacific Ocean*
Hessel Gerritsz.

Appendixes

248   Bibliography

249   Glossary

250   List of Exhibit Pieces

252   Index of Names

254   The Authors

256   Photographic Credits

FOREWORD

Of the maritime maps produced in the West, the sumptuous, rare charts of the Mediterranean region — which first appeared in the 13th century, with their abundance of gold, decorations and ornamentation — have undoubtedly inspired the most interest, since their original design and construction are still shrouded in mystery. The National Library of France (NLF), which has holdings of some 500 of these maps, mainly in the Maps and Plans Department, can boast of having a collection of exceptional quality, covering nearly all of the world and representing all the schools of cartography up to the 18th century. The library is undertaking a full census of these maps as well as taking stock of all rare maps in national public collections in France, so as to establish the value of this incalculable heritage, which is still largely unknown. Initial results are already available through its online library, *Gallica*, which shows all the holdings of the NLF, as well as those of the Historical Service of Defense. The NLF also wanted to open for public viewing a large exhibit of the most exceptional originals and the most representative examples of such documents. These were produced after the big discoveries by European navigators, and they provided Westerners the first glimpses of faraway lands and their people. These documents also underscored the dreams that fueled those extraordinary enterprises.

In this book, the library also offers a synthesis, in high-color resolution, of the accumulated knowledge — thoroughly updated over the last 20 years — of a cartography that was imbued with vitality and exceptional longevity. Originating in the ports of Majorca, Genoa or Venice, this cartography was embraced by Portuguese mariners who faced the challenges of transoceanic crossings. This also proved to be a valuable navigational tool for the European maritime powers of the time and was used until the end of the 18th century. The basis of the present work, a collaboration of about 15 European experts, was enriched by the results of research undertaken by the Mediterranean societies and of the Indian Ocean (MeDIan), financed by the National Research Agency and supported by the Department of Maps and Plans of the National Library of France. The program focuses on the exchange of knowledge between civilizations, and it has allowed us to showcase the role of these exchanges in the design and construction of a cartographic image of the Indian Ocean, from antiquity until the 18th century. Benefitting these blended approaches, *The Golden Age of Maritime Maps* provides a broad look at these rare maps and, through them, at the voyages, ideas and knowledge that led to a common view of the image of our modern world.

Bruno Racine
President of the National Library of France

OCEANIC OVERTURE

Frank Lestringant

1.

1

**Jacques de Vaulx, Frontispice
of *Premières Œuvres***
Le Havre, 1583

The *Premieres Œuvres* of the Norman captain
Jacques de Vaulx is a treatise on navigation,
lavishly illustrated and dedicated to the duke
of Joyeuse, a French admiral. The frontispiece
shows, in the small medallions, the hydrographer
at work along with his main tools: book, map,
spheres, compass, hourglass, astrolabe, crossbow,
etc. The citation of a verse from psalm 107 exalts
the nobility of this craft, through which are
revealed the "works of the Lord."

NLF, Paris, Manuscripts, French 150.
Manuscript printed on velum, 11 × 17¾ inches (28 × 45 cm)

FROM EMPTY TO FULL: UNDERSTANDING THE WORLD THROUGH PORTOLAN MAPS

Sea navigation begins with a sense of wonderment — a
wonderment that, in turn, mirrors another. "Those
who travel the seas in ships, are called to witness the
Lord's work."[1] In quoting this verse from Psalm 107
at the beginning of his *Premières Oeuvres*, a treatise on
hydrography, Jacques de Vaulx, captain of the Havre
and probable protestant, has two messages. He praises
the glory of God while at the same time praising the
breadth and nobility of His creations. In paraphrasing
this Psalm, he could have just as well cited the poet
Clément Marot:

Those who within the galleys
Above the seas journey,
And in large salty bodies of water
Conduct many travels

Those witnesses from God
Marvelous works,
On the deep center
Of perilous waves[2]

These words seem to echo the *Traicté en forme
d'exhortation, contenant les merveilles de Dieu et
de la dignité de l'homme* (Treatise in the form of
exhortation, concerning God's marvels and the
dignity of man) by Jean Parmentier, a sailor and poet
born in Dieppe who died in Sumatra in 1529:

Who shall know the marvels of the sea,
The horror of perishing there
Of emotional and troubling waves beyond measure?
Who shall witness her roiled by heavy winds,
Shoved, roiled, sublimated and destroyed,
And then suddenly tranquil, without breaks?
Who will know his place in nature's plan?
But who can say: "I have lived such and such an
adventure,"
And who but can sail above of it?
This one can very well state, without any doubt,
"Oh marvelous and terrible workmanship
Of the marvels that live beneath"![3]

The sea has long belonged to the domain of the
marvelous, with its horrific storms, formidable
creatures, unpredictable gusts of wind and fearsome,
uniform calm. Our ancestors considered death at sea to
be the ultimate curse. However, once they conquered
their fears, the sea offered humans unlimited expanses,
where they could freely trace their own course.
Considered a hostile environment, the sea nevertheless

remained an undifferentiated and unified space, where
theory most closely equated with practice.

In his nautical instructional manual entitled *Art de
naviguer* (The art of navigation), which was in use all
over Europe from the Renaissance, Pierre de Medina
notes, "It is a large subtlety when a man bearing a
compass and a protractor would know how to navigate
the entire world."[4] This is the challenge posed by the
nautical map, which guides the mariner across "a
thing that is so vague and so spacious, such as the sea,
where there is neither a roadway nor a outline." The
sea, among other things, has neither color nor contour,
again according to Pierre de Medina, "since our
perspective does not stop at the surface of the water,
but delves much deeper: and when we look at the sea
from afar, she sort of has the color of the sky; and
when winds trouble her, she takes on many different
colors."[5] From then on, what is most striking, even
more so today than in the past, is how disproportionate
the "means" are from the "ends"; the means are the
rather pitiful map and compass, while the end results
are world exploration, a broadening of understanding
of the known world and, finally, full acquaintance with
the circumscribed globe.

Maritime maps were also known as "portolan
maps" or simply, "portolans." Although simple in
appearance, these maps were nevertheless quite
detailed and of admirable quality.

We are aware that all maps consist of three main
components: drawings, written text and measurement
scales. In other words, maps have an image, whole or
in part, of the world, with legends and instructions
and finally, measurable quantities. The portolan —
an old maritime map on parchment or, more rarely,
on paper — is foremost a spiderweb of fine lines
radiating from focal points on the map's background.
In short, it's an abstract schematic over which coastal
outlines are superimposed and which are labeled in
perpendicular fashion with names of ports, harbors,
capes and islets. These maps are — at the most
basic level, as shown in the Pisane Map or Pietro
Vesconte's atlas, which contains some of the simplest
maps known — a network of geometric lines and
linear designs without surfaces, except when they are
reduced to the cramped and circumscribed islands.
While showing little more than contours, coastlines
and the undulating or broken lines of beaches and
capes, these maps were mostly empty spaces and
silent, similar to the representations of Chinese
lettering, and, like Chinese letters, combining written

AV · HAVRE · DE · GRACE ·

· LAN · M. D. LXXXIII. ·

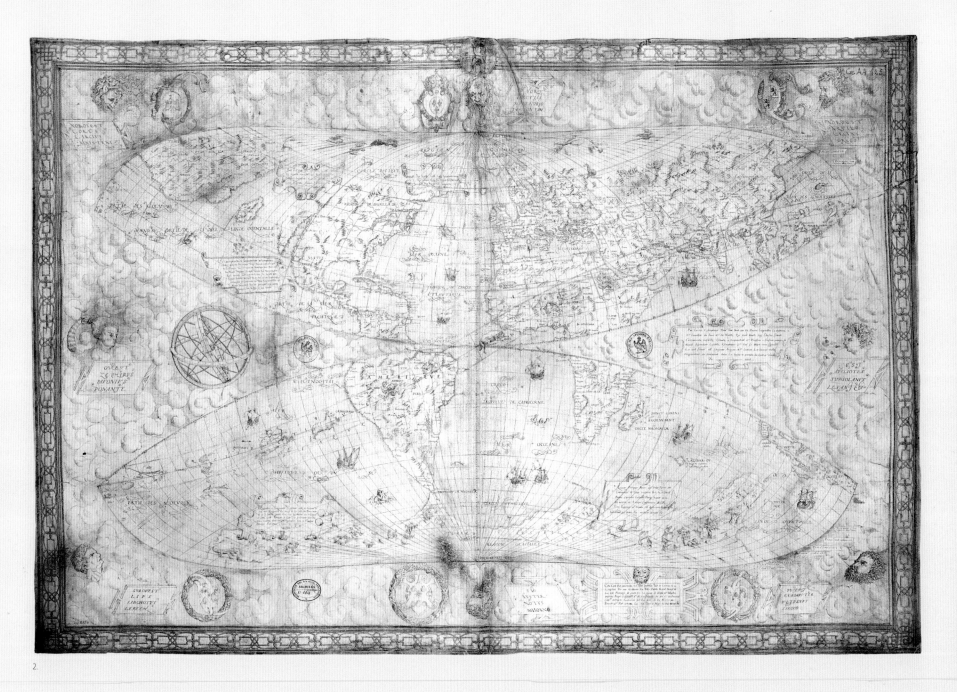

2.

lines with drawn lines on a background of rising fog and blinding whiteness.[6]

This graphic map system, which combined wind roses and rhumb lines corresponding to compass directions, enabled sailors to orient themselves and to mark their location while also recording the distance they estimated having traveled in any given direction. The maps of the first marine navigators thus provided an index of directions one should follow between marked points. Initially, such maps served merely as a system of projected estimates and did not provide a true distance scale.

Portolan maps never cease to fascinate us or to raise many questions. They are perhaps the most vibrant part of the medieval cartographic heritage, as compared to the far too simplistic theological cartography of world maps in the shape of "TO," signifying Christ on the cross (the "T") inscribed within the terrestrial globe (the "O"). These presented the space between the three sections of the then known world, Europe on the left, Africa on the right and Asia above them, in relation to the East, where paradise was thought to be. Maps like these were the scholarly works of monks and abbots and were kept in monasteries and among books, the opposite of the open, free-flowing maritime cartography, based not on any particular school of thought or religious beliefs.

In that it was based on practice and experience, which Aristotle himself referred to as the "mistress of all things" (*omnium rerum magistra*), portolan cartography was constantly evolving. It was progressive and imperceptibly directed toward the advance to new worlds. At first glance this may appear paradoxical. While portolan cartography was initially constrained to seas and waterways near shorelines and dedicated primarily to coastal navigation and direction finding, it also extrapolated boldly toward oceanic islands, new territories and unknown continents. At the onset of the 16th century, it included the Mediterranean coastline as well as those of faraway America and the Indian Ocean. The growth of portolan maps paralleled that of the "insular" or *insolario* atlas, which consisted entirely of island maps and complemented portolans by beginning at the Aegean Sea, the ancestral archipelago, before conquering the entire world.

Through this, portolan maps were adapted to first incorporate latitude scales and then by taking into account magnetic declination and sometimes even a longitude scale, as shown by Le Testu in 1566 on his velum planisphere (see illustration 2).

It has been said that this kind of cartography totally ignores a system of projections and that it was entirely empirical. This unfairly criticizes the mariners of the time, who, not being in a position to develop a theoretical world system, nevertheless had a fairly precise concept thanks to celestial observation. This empirical type of cartography was not without external influences. For Asia, for instance, it brings to mind Marco Polo and how he gathered geographical information and the toponymy of the peoples he encountered. It also readily delves into whatever information is readily available, including academic cartography, the science of the cabinet geographers. When Ptolemy's *Geography* was newly accessible in the West at the onset of the 15th century, it provided some help, with its grid of parallel lines and meridians, its division into climatic zones and representation of the then known world. Ptolemy also mentioned the celestial influences on the world, the character and mores of its inhabitants and, quite simply, the length of a day.

Portolans are sea maps and maps to navigate by. Yet they were often left behind, on land. For example, at the beginning of Rabelais' *Le Quart Livre* (The fourth book), the hero Pantagruel, leaving his father, Gargantuan, to visit the oracle of the Bouteille Bacbuc to drink, who was near Cathay, in upper India, gives him a "large and universal Hydrographie" on which he has marked his route.[7] This hydrography is nothing more than, according to Rabelais' proper definition, a "maritime map"[8] on which the sedentary father could follow his son's long journey, as he received information by the return flights of carrier pigeons.

But why would mariners not have carried such maps aboard the ships themselves? Surely this is where they would have served their best purpose, as we are reminded in the pages of Ramon Pujades.[9] Undoubtedly, they were not willing to expose such ornate and detailed maps to water, but their unsatisfying copies, reduced to a bare minimum and made in series by patrons in workshops, were at best inferior reproductions.

MAPS OF GOLD

Portolan maps were essentially partial maps and, consequently, extendable. They were full of gaps, bare drafts, continental interiors tagged as *terrae incognitae* and tumultuous expanses of oceans showing drownings and sea monsters. These empty spaces begged to be

2

Guillaume Le Testu,
***Mappemonde* (World Map)**
1566

Guillaume Le Testu, royal captain at Havre from 1556, combined his taste for maritime expeditions (Brazil, Mexico, etc.) with cosmographical speculations, as is shown in this world map in a Bonne projection. Was he hoping to show his supporters, the Admiral of Coligny and Vice-Admiral Charles de la Meilleraye, that he was both a cultured man as well as a scientist?

NLF, Paris, Maps and Plans, GE AA 625 (RES). Manuscript on parchment, 46½ × 3⅛ inches (118 × 79 cm).

3
Lopo Homem, *Atlas Miller*
Pedro and Jorge Reinel, António De Holanda
Portugal, 1519

Done for King Manuel the Fortunate of Portugal, the *Miller Atlas*, which carries the name of its last owner, reflects the Portuguese vision of the world at the dawn of Magellan's voyage. Among the lands allocated in 1494 by the Treaty of Tordesillas, which split the world between the two Iberian sovereigns, this map only represents those that were allocated to Portugal.

NLF, Maps and Plans, GE-D 26179 (RES), f. 1.
Illuminated manuscript on velum, 23¼ × 16¼ inches (59 × 41.5 cm).

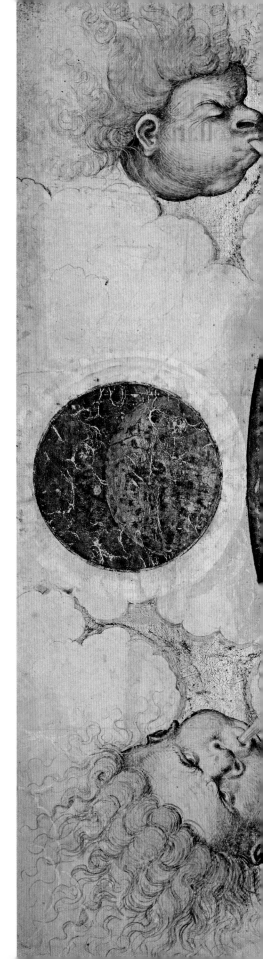

filled. Almost abstract at the beginning, over centuries many users enriched portolans with iconography that even today makes us dream. Born from mathematics and geometry, such maps were soon opened up to imaginations and poetry. These are precisely the reasons why serious scientists and geographers demeaned them and why bibliophiles and antiquarians avidly collected them.

Continental interiors, which were shown largely as empty spaces on marine maps, were populated by mythical animals like unicorns, griffons as well as by monsters described by geographers and naturalists of antiquity, such as Pliny and Solin. These included giants, pigmies, cyclopes, amazons, headless Blemmies with faces in the middle of their chests and Sciapods, whose unique and gigantic foot served as a parasol when they lay on their backs. With regard to the ocean crisscrossed with rhumb lines, it contained multicolored archipelagos with islands in gold, scarlet or deep red. Also shown are naval battles, sinking ships and monstrous whales and other marine creatures huffing and puffing among the chaos and belching forth columns of salt water on unfortunate sailors. No doubt the artist's intent had less to do with the divine game of creation than with humor.

Some of the portolan maps are genuine pictorial compositions. The *Miller Atlas*, a Portuguese atlas produced around 1519, shows Brazil as a country populated by feathered Indians, parakeets and flying dragons. Florida, under the legend "Terra Bimene" holds a terrestrial paradise with rock gardens and cascades, luxuriant vegetation and birds in the open sky. Stags, foxes and bears cohabitate comfortably. This world, as painted and represented there, is not totally mythical however. In the case of Brazil, the map shows such colonial realities as trading of wood that has been cut, trimmed and transported on the backs of bare brown-skinned aboriginals (see illustration 105i).

The portolan scenography reaches new heights in what is known as the Dieppe School, a Norman school of cartography ensuing from and informed by the Portuguese tradition. In the *Vallard Atlas*, of 1547, the map of Brazil serves as a pretext to highlight a bartering scene between Norman sailors and coastal aboriginals: battle-axes and trinkets against monkeys and parakeets held graciously by three nude aboriginal maidens, as beautiful as the Three Graces. The captain's gesticulation as he holds a mirror at arm's length invites the feathered chieftain and the shy aboriginal maidens — all as if captured in a drawing done on site. The same natural and detailed

ethnography appears in the *Boke of Idrography* by Jean Roze (also knows as John Rotz), a Scotsman who lived in Dieppe. His map of Brazil offers a vivid image of alliances between the French and the Tipinamba aboriginals through joint warfare, camping close to one another and consolidating the trade of Brazilian wood. Nothing is omitted in this velum painting, not the "sounds," the grill pan with human limbs or the village square surrounded by stockades showing open cabins with suspended hammocks. (see illustration 4).

The *Cosmologie universelle* (Universal cosmology) of Guillaume Le Testu, an atlas on paper drawn in 1556 for the benefit of the French Admiral Gaspard de Coligny by the royal captain of Le Havre, is the most complete portolan map of the world as well as the most richly illustrated. It is unique in devoting nearly a quarter of its regional maps — a dozen out of 50 — to the mythical Austral lands, a hypothetical fifth continent that is linked with the Land of Fire, or the "Big Java," and becomes the southern counterpoint of northern Eurasia. In order to justify what is in effect fiction, Le Testu, in his commentaries, calls upon the "imagination," a prospective imagination that tries to anticipate future progress in geography. No falsehoods were attributed to this vast green continent, such as indigenous peoples dressed in feather skirts prancing amid an improbable fauna. Rather, it is a future projection that extrapolates from the meager landmarks spotted by Portuguese and Spanish navigators in the 1520s.[10]

In portolan cartography, practical usage does not exclude symbolic functionality.[11] The belief is that a map will not be less accurate or useful if it is beautiful. Ornamental aspects do not impede such maps from being of political use. The *Universal Cosmography* (see illustrations on pages 148–159) by Le Testu at Coligny, is a richly illustrated work and proposes to King Henry II, the French admiral and sovereign, the dream of an empire. However, as shown clearly in the accurate description of the coastal regions of Canada and Brazil, this dream is largely based on their most recent discoveries. While this atlas is somewhat correct, it also contains much extrapolation. When fashioned in the image of its author, be that navigator and cartographer or pirate and courtier, a portolan atlas like this met many needs; it flattered while also teaching, pleased the eye and, through its assemblage of data, prepared for the future. At once complex in its origin and multifaceted in its development, the portolan map is nevertheless diverse in its goals.

Frank Lestringant

Works Cited

1. *Les Premieres Œuvres de Jacques Devaulx*, Le Havre, 1583, title page citing verses 34 and 24 of psalm 107.

2. Clément Marot, *Œuvres poétiques*, Paris, Bordas, coll. "Classic Garnier," 1993, t. II, 665.

3. Jean Parmentier, "Traicté en forme d'exhortation, contenant les merveilles de Dieu et la dignité de l'homme," XVII, v. 154-165, in *Le Discours et navigation de Jean et Raoul Parmentier de Dieppe*, ed. par Charles Schefer, Paris, E. Leroux, 1883, p.122. Cf. Jean Parmentier, *Œuvres poétiques*, ed. Françoise Ferrand, Geneva, Droz, 1971, 96–97.

4. Pierre of Medina, *L'Art de naviguer*, Lyon, G. Rouillé, 1561, f.°3 ro. Cited by Frank Lestringant, *L'Atelier du cosmographe ou l'Image du monde à la Renaissance*, Paris, Albin Michel, 1991, p. 30.

5. Ibid.

6. On the other hand, it is necessary to discard the hypothesis of a possible Chinese influence that was raised, according to Joseph Needham and Nichel Nollat, in Monique de la Roncière and Michel Mollat du Jourdin's *Les Portulans. Cartes marines du XIIIe au XVIIe siècle*, Fribourg/Paris/Office du Livre/Nathan, 1984, "Introduction" p. 17.

7. Rabelais, *Quart Livre*, chap.1, in *Œuvres complètes*, ed. Mireille Huchon, Paris, Gallimard, coll. "Bibliothèque de la Pléiade," 1994, p.537.

8. Rabelais, "Briefve Declaration d'aulcunes dictions plus obscures contenües on quatriesme livre des faicts et dicts Heroïcques de Pantagruel," ibid., p.705.

9. See pages 60-66.

10. Roger Hervé, *Découverte fortuite de l'Australie et de la Nouvelle-Zélande par des navigateurs portugais et espagnols entre 1521 et 1528*, National Library/CTHS, Paris, 1982.

11. Margriet Hoogvliet, *Pictura et Scriptura. Textes, images et herméneutique des Mappae Mundi (xiiie-xvie siècles)*, Turnhout, Brepols, coll. "Terrarum orbis" (7), 2007, p.248 : "A map destined for practical use can also be the starting point of hermeneutic activities."

4

Jean Roze, *Boke of idrograpy* (Book of Hydrography)

1542

Jean Roze, the Dieppian captain of Scottish origin who was also known as John Rotz, was in the service of the British King Henry VIII from 1542 to1546, to whom he dedicated his work *Boke of idrography*, composed of a world map and 11 regional maps. From a very young age, he participated in his father's activities and experienced firsthand navigations to faraway lands like New Guinea and Brazil (the latter is shown in the illustration here). Several scenes that illustrate these maps appear to have been sketched in situ.

British Library, London, ms 20 IX, f. 27 v0-28. Illuminated manuscript on parchment, 16 leaflets, 30¼ × 23½ inches (77 × 59.5 cm).

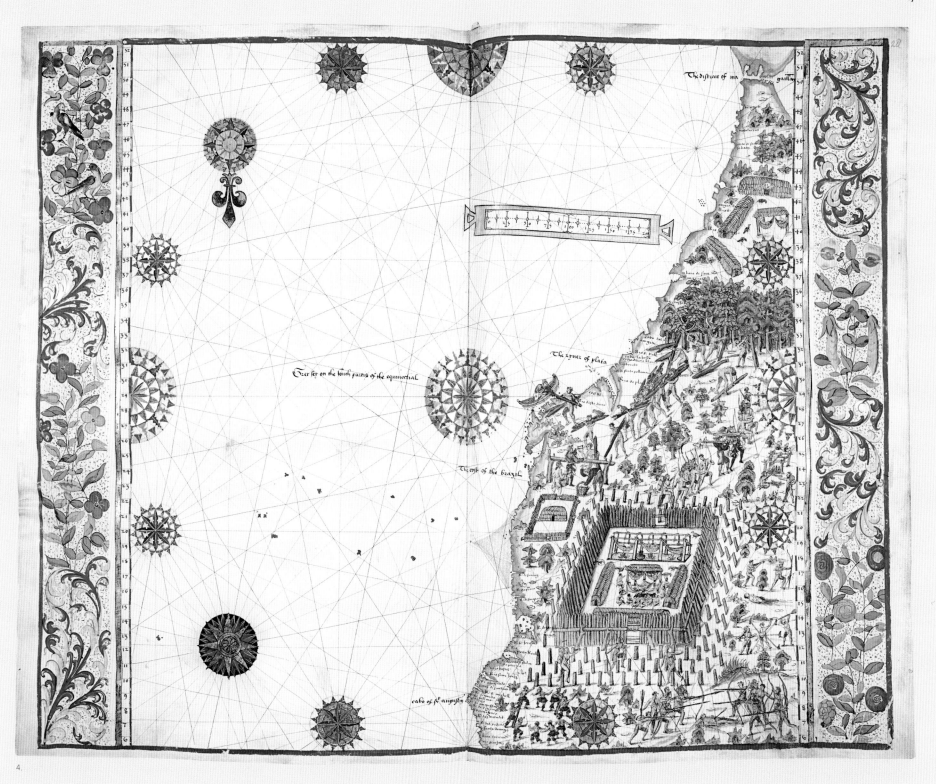

The distrait of ma... gaillan

The zyuer of plata

Neer ser on the south parts of the equinoctial

The cost of the brazil

cabo of st augustin

THE FASCINATION OF PORTOLANS

HISTORIOGRAPHY AND COLLECTIONS

Catherine Hofmann

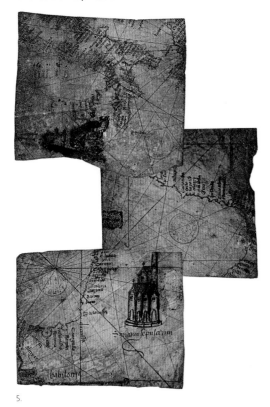

5.

5

Fragments of a Map of the Mediterranean
Majorca, early 15th century

These fragments, about 4 inches (10 cm) square, represent southern mainland Italy and Sicily as well as a portion of the Black Sea and the Near East. They are probably from a Catalonian map from the early 15th century. They served as bookmarks in the notes of a journal belonging to the notary of Perpignan.

NLF, Paris, Maps and Plans, GE D 3005 (RES).
Manuscript on parchment, 6 fragments each measuring about 4 × 4 inches (10 × 10 cm).

6

Augustin Roussin, Map of the Atlantic Coastline and the Strait of Gibraltar
See page 22 for the full caption and map.

Judging from the extreme case of a map being used as bookmarks in the journals of the notary of Perpignan during the 16th century (see illustration 5),[1] portolans were not always considered priceless treasures. In fact, it is still possible to discover, during a restoration, fragments of maps that were used on the covers of notary or parish registers from the 16th and 17th centuries. Nevertheless, with respect to the most luxurious maps produced, they have long been sold as prized objects "for the mighty and the curious." This despite the fact that the geographic information on them was sometimes limited, as indicated by the geographer Pierre Duval in the 17th century: "I feel obliged to warn those that use these maritime maps, that they will find manuscripts, ever so brilliant in gold, silver, azure and many other beautiful colors. Despite the fact that these books often have their place on the shelves of the noble and curious; these maps are nevertheless incorrect as they have themselves been copied from other astonishingly erroneous maps that were made more than a hundred years ago."[2] Soon, however, portolan maps became status symbols among bibliophiles and were often ready-made for the armories of an eminent commander who collected them. As examples, we can cite a 14th-century travel journal with a wooden binding that is engraved and painted with the coat of arms of the Cornaros, an illustrious Venetian family who procured a doge in the republic from 1365 until 1368 (see illustration 8),[3] and the atlas of the Provençal Augustin Roussin, which features a dedication to Cardinal de Richelieu engraved in gold lettering on the binding (see illustration 9).[4]

SUBJECTS OF RESEARCH...

The notion of gathering these maps and atlases in the form of collections did not emerge until the middle of the 19th century, at a time when theses antique maps were being given renewed consideration. Benefitting from the development of new disciplines like geography and historical sciences like archeology and philology, portolan maps were subsequently considered as archeological artifacts from which historical information might be gleaned.[5] Therefore, in the first academic study on the *Catalonian Atlas* (done in 1841), the expression "restoration of the monument" was used to designate the identification stage of toponyms (place names). With their romantic views of the Middle Ages, the historians of the time naturally produced the first compendium of ancient map facsimiles, which appeared in the 1840s and 1850s (Santarém, Jomard, Lelewel, Kuntsmann[6]) and included medieval world maps and portolans.

Why then did many cartographical historians so desire portolans? Several factors account for this. Since they were from the Middle Ages, such maps helped provide a coherent image of the Mediterranean relative to modern evaluation criteria, and so historians considered them to be the very first "works of positive geography" — as underscored by Vivien de Saint-Martin in 1873 — unlike other world maps whose symbolism generated so much confusing information. Consequently, this reinvigorated and engaged a whole generation of geographers and inspired them to discover the origins of these maps.

Handwritten and thought to be unique, portolan maps generated more interest than the older engraved productions, which seemed to lack any "major individual character." Since they were often collectors and preservers of essential information, the earliest historians focused their research efforts on issues of rarity and esthetics, in line with the example of Marie Armand Pascal d'Avezac (1799–1875), who gave herself the title of "bibliophilic geographer."

Toward the middle of the 19th century, another more powerful force explains what caused a surge in the demand for portolan maps: they were considered primary sources to study the history of exploration and discoveries. Through their geographical characteristics and lists of location names, portolan maps provided records of voyages and their timelines. They could also be used in multiple ways, combining the teaching of the new science of geography and national interests. For instance, the famed viscount of Santarém (1791–1856), a Portuguese historian and diplomat who had been well schooled in Parisian scientific institutions, published a work titled *Atlas composé de cartes des XIV, XV, XVI, et XVII* (Atlas composed of maps from the 14th, 15th, 16th and 17th centuries) in Paris in 1841, with the support of the Portuguese government. This atlas, as the title implies, was intended to show the preexistence of Portuguese discoveries in West Africa. In this way, the colonial interests of Portugal were defended during a time of diplomatic conflict with France over the Casamance region in present-day Senegal.

... AND OBJECTS OF COLLECTION

The very rich collection of ancient maps in the National Library of France, which today comprises nearly 500 items, can be attributed to the appreciation and spirited curiosity they inspired in 19th-century historians and collectors.[7] Up until the French Revolution, the library held very few maps and portolan atlases, with the

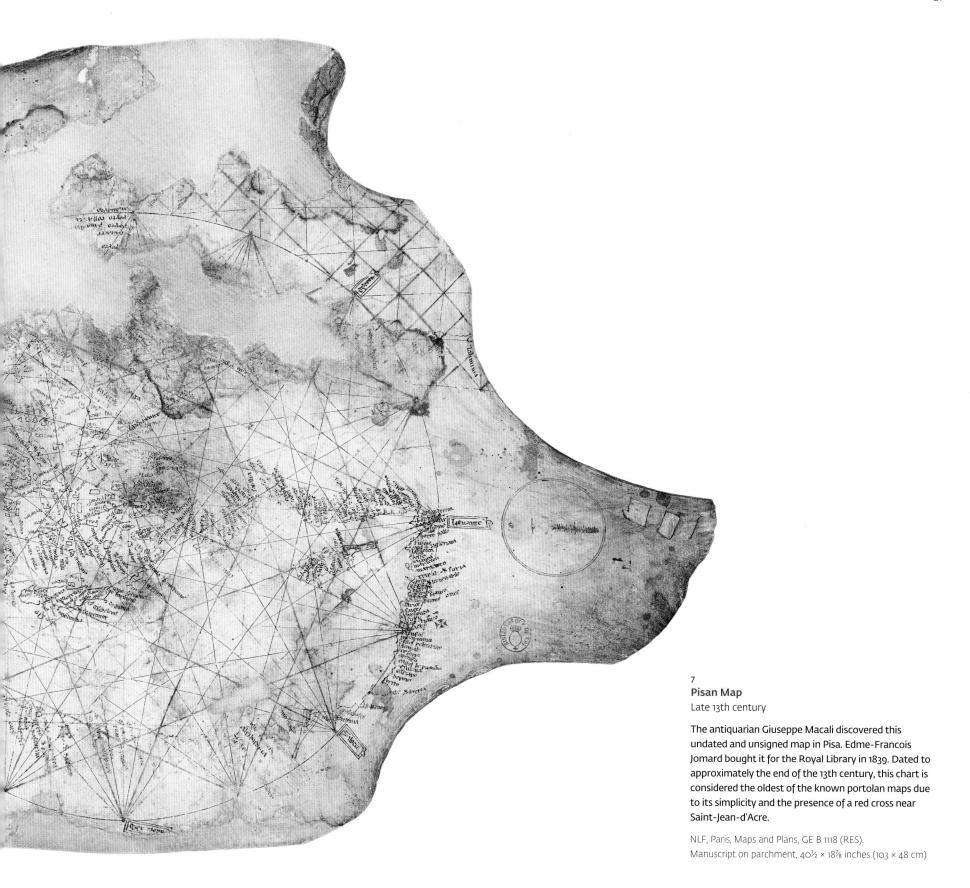

7
Pisan Map
Late 13th century

The antiquarian Giuseppe Macali discovered this undated and unsigned map in Pisa. Edme-Francois Jomard bought it for the Royal Library in 1839. Dated to approximately the end of the 13th century, this chart is considered the oldest of the known portolan maps due to its simplicity and the presence of a red cross near Saint-Jean-d'Acre.

NLF, Paris, Maps and Plans, GE B 1118 (RES).
Manuscript on parchment, 40½ × 18⅞ inches (103 × 48 cm)

8

Atlas of the Mediterranean on the Coat of Arms of the Cornaro Family
Venice, 2nd quarter of the 14th century

Composed of four maps delicately drawn and decorated in the corners with emblems of evangelists, animals and monsters, this anonymous atlas covers the entire Mediterranean. The flat portions of the binding were painted with the coat of arms of the Venetian Cornaro family, topped by a feminine silhouette, undoubtedly from the crest on a casket.

Municipal Library of Lyon, Ms. 179. Binding.

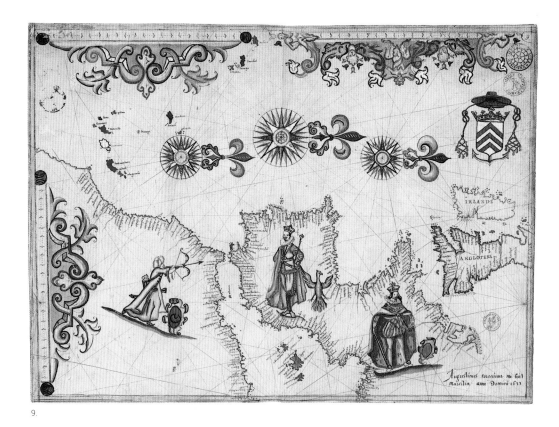

9.

8.

9

Augustin Roussin, Map of the Atlantic Coastline and of the Strait of Gibraltar
Marseille, 1633

This map belongs to a Mediterranean atlas drawn by a Marseillian hydrographer. It bears the coat of arms of Cardinal Richelieu, superintendent of the navy from 1626, who was in charge of maintaining the security of the French provincial coastline. The images of sovereigns are King Philippe IV of Spain and King Louis 12th of France, indicating the powers of the times.

NLF, Paris, French Manuscripts 20122, f. 2 v0-3. Illuminated manuscript on parchment, 20¼ × 13¾ inches (51.5 × 35 cm)

10

Joris Carolus, Map of the Northern European Coastline
Enkhuizen, 1614

A sumptuous trompe-l'oeil frame is labeled at the top with the coat of arms of the House of Orange-Nassau and a the bottom with those of the city of Enkhuizen. The projected polar map illustrates the search for the northeast passage to China by Dutch navigators while circumventing Asia to the north.

NLF, Paris, Maps and Plans, GE SH ARCH7 (RES). Illuminated manuscript on parchment, 31⅞ × 29¾ inches (81 × 75.5 cm).

exception of a few prestigious pieces, like the celebrated *Catalonian Atlas*, which had been offered to King Charles V and had been a part of the royal collections since 1380.

The core of the first French portolan collection was established by Edme-François Jomard, the first conservator of the Maps and Plans Department and who, between 1828 and the time of his death in 1862, assembled a group of 52 maps (of which 46 were bought and six donated), which included some of the rarest and most renowned specimens. Among those were four famous examples: the Pisane Map (see illustration 7), long considered the oldest portolan map, which was acquired in 1839 for 245 francs, and the map of the Catalonian Jew Mecia de Viladestes (1413), which was acquired in 1857 for 800 francs. The map said to belong to Christopher Columbus was bought in 1848 for 250 francs, and the very beautiful nautical atlas of Diogo Homem (1559) was obtained in 1842 for 80 francs. Jomard also created facsimiles by copying these documents by hand. In 1843, four maps preserved in the archives of the Bavarian army and containing some of the earliest examples of Portuguese hydrography from the era of European exploration were signed by Pedro and Jorge Reinel. They were drawn by Otto Progel, a Bavarian officer, and the library bought these copies for 950 francs (see illustration 11). Since the originals disappeared during World War II, only these Parisian facsimiles can attest to the existence of the original documents. Toward the end of the 19th century, the National Library of France's collection was further enriched through donations as well as significant purchases. In 1897, a grouping of maps was acquired from the widow of the collector Emmanuel Miller, maps directly derived from the viscount of Santarém and containing the famous *Atlas Miller* (1519), one of the department's treasures.

At the beginning of the 20th century, after the centralization of the national library's administration, the supply chain became more institutionalized, because the institution was then recognized as the obvious recipient of such marine documents. That resulted in the transfer of fragments of maps from the departmental archives of the Vaucluse and the Ardèche, exchanges of maps with the national archives, a transfer of maps held by the Ministry of External Affairs and the Geographic Society, and, especially, transfers of some 269 maps through funds from the hydrographic service of the navy. Without

delving too deeply into details of these acquisitions, we must emphasize the importance of this latter acquisition. It came from an organization that has been producing maps since 1720 and allowed the national library to obtain a collection representing all centers of production, without neglecting the 17th and 18th centuries, which were less valued by the first fans of portolan maps. The National Library of France now conserves more than 90 Dutch maps, coming mainly from the Dutch East India Company (1602–1799) and withdrawn in 1810 from the Dutch archives by order of Napoleon to enrich the French navy's consignments (see illustration 10).[8] The totality of these collections was described in a 1963 catalog,[9] and that catalog is currently being converted and enriched in the National Library of France's general online catalog.

OBJECTS OF DESIRE... AND OF PIRATING

Several Portolan maps are neither signed nor dated and remain shrouded in mystery. Some are attributed to several authors and dates, by which they're variously known in the specialized literature, which has resulted in vigorous debates between experts, like a map that was attributed to Christopher Columbus and dated from 1492 by Charles de la Roncière in the 1930s (see illustrations 12 and 13).[10]

Several questions regarding the origin, manufacture and usage of portolan maps during the Middle Ages have yet to be answered uncontestedly, mostly due to a lack of relevant documentation. Generations of historians have demonstrated their ingenuity, sometimes even becoming obsessed with their hypotheses, not to mention the ulterior motives of nationalists. In the context of the 1920s and 1930s, a controversy arose between Italians and Spanish experts on the question of which "country" invented portolans, which continued until the 1960s due to the longevity of the opponents.,

Portolan maps also inflamed the spirits of smaller nations, as shown by the passion of Norman historians toward the end of the 19th and the beginning of the 20th century concerning the nationality of hydrographers from Dieppe and The Hague.[11] A certain artist, Miss Tissot, commanded high prices for her copies of manuscripts drawn on parchment paper while leaving faithful reproductions in Dieppe, evidence of the Norman history that was spread throughout the world.[12]

Finally, the passion associated with making a big discovery was at times a poor counselor. A group of some 13 world maps in the style of portolans that are dated from 1509 to 1528, and signed though not documented by authors purported to be Venetians, was recognized in 1944 by David Howard as forgeries created at the turn of the 19th and 20th centuries.[13] Some of these had unfortunately been acquired by prestigious institutions!

Rearranged artificially by historians to suit their subjects of research and debate, portolan maps were not called that prior to the 19th century. Instead, they were called different things depending on the function they served and the places and times they were from. They were called navigator maps, *pro navigandi* and *mappe maris* during the Middle Ages, hydrographical maps by the Normans, and *kaarten* in the United Provinces. Indeed, it was not until they were deemed of historical importance and collectable objects, which gave rise to this field of study, that they were named portolan maps. Adopted in the 1890s by historians,[14] this name underscored the presumed complementary link between these maps and the *portolani*, which were the written descriptions of coastlines and the method of entering a port that also appeared in the Middle Ages. Though still contested, the designation portolan received a partial consecration in 1987 by Tony Campbell, author of a remarkable synthesis of the subject that appeared in the first volume of a major history of cartography published by the University of Chicago Press.[15] Twenty years later, in 2007, a young Catalan historian, Ramon Pujades i Bataller, devoted his thesis to a new analysis of medieval map production,[16] and in 2009 an American researcher, Richard Pflederer, undertook the first international census of the genre, covering all eras and all production sites.[17] The National Library of France itself undertook a program in 2010 to make a census and catalog all national collections. Two hundred years after its beginning, it appears that the passion for these maritime maps has remained intact, and they are still considered at once as navigation tools, carriers of advanced technologies and cultural objects laden with past dreams and imagination.

Catherine Hofmann

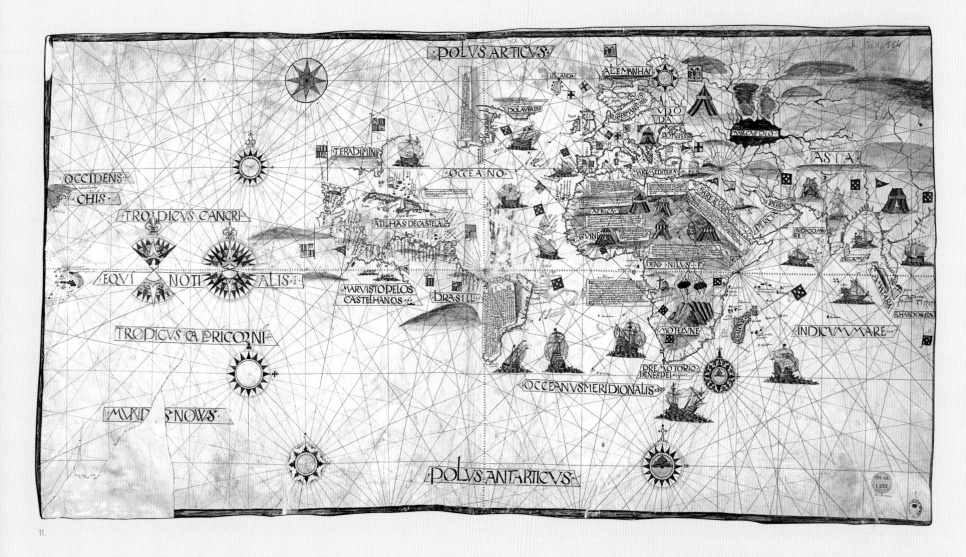

11.

11

Jorge Reinel (?), World Map
1519 (1843 facsimile)

This manuscript copy was created in 1843 by a Bavarian officer, Otto Progel, from an original previously conserved in the Bayerische Armeebibliotek of Munich and lost since 1945. Attributed to the Portuguese cartographer Jorge Reinel and dated to 1519, it is thought that Magellan used the original to prepare for his voyage.

NLF, Paris, Maps and Plans, GE AA 564 (RES).
Illuminated manuscript on parchment, 48¾ × 25½ inches (124 × 65 cm).

Works Cited

1. NLF, Paris, Maps and Plans, Ge D 3005 Rés. See Ernest Théodore Hamy. "Note sur des fragments d'une carte marine catalane du XVIe siècle ayant servi de signets dans les notules d'un notaire de Perpignan (1541–1556)," *Bulletin du CTHS. Section de geographie historique et descriptive*, No. 1, 1897, 21–31.

2. Pierre Duval, *La carte générale et les cartes particulières des costes de la mer Méditerranée*, Paris, at the author's, 1664, preface.

3. Municipal Library of Lyon, Ms. 179.

4. NLF, Paris, French Manuscripts, 20122.

5. See Gilles Palsky, "L'esprit des cartes : approches historiques sémiologiques et sociologiques en cartographie" (diploma in ability to guide research activities), vol. 2, 18–36 ("I. Fondation. L'histoire de la cartographie comme archéologie et généalogie").

6. Manuel, Vicount of Santarém, *Atlas composé de mappemondes, de portulans et de cartes hydrographiques maps depuis le VIe siècles jusqu'au XVIIe siècle*. Paris, 1842–1853; Edme-François Jomard. *Les Monuments de la géographie. Recueil d'anciennes cartes européennes et orientales, accompagnées de sphères terrestres et célestes, de mappmondes et tables cosmographiques, d'astrolabes et autres instruments d'observation, depuis les temps les plus reculés jusqu'à l'époque d'Ortelius et de Gérard Mercator*, Paris, 1842–1862; Joachim Lelewel, Géographie du Moyen-Âge, Brussels, 1848–1857, and Atlas, 1849; Friedrich Kuntsmann, *Die Entdeckung Amerikas, nach den ältesten Quellen geschichtlich dargestellt von Friedrich Kunstmann*, Munich, A. Asher, 1859 (151 p. and an Atlas).

7. Mireille Pastoureau, "Histoire d'une collection : les "portulans" de la Bibliothèque nationale," *Académie de marine. Communications et mémoires*, academic year 1990–1991, No. 3, April–June 1991, 61–71.

8. Kees Zandvliet, *Mapping for money: maps, plans and topographic paintings and their role in Dutch overseas expansion during the 16th and 17th centuries*, Amsterdam, De Bataafsche Leeuw, 1998, p.267-269.

9. Myriem Foncin, Marcel Destombes et Monique de La Roncière, *Catalogue des cartes nautiques sur vélin conservées au département des Cartes et Plans*, Paris, National Library, 1963, xv–315.

10. NLF, Paris, Maps and Plans. Ge AA 1562. See Monique Pelletier, "Peut-on encore affirmer que la BN possède la carte de Christopher Columb ?" *Revuede la Bibliothèque nationale de France*, No. 45, Fall, 1992, 22–25.

11. The Abbott Albert Anthiaume. *Cartes marines, constructions navales, voyages de découverte chez les Normands, 1500–1650*. Paris, E. Dumont, 1916, 2 vol.

12. Ambrose Milet, Catalogue of the Dieppe Museum, Dieppe, 1904, 103.

13. David Woodward, "Could These Italian Maps Be Fakes?" *The Map Collector*, No. 67, summer 1994, 2–10.

14. First verified usage in English: Adolf Erik Nordenskjöld, in *Report of the Sixth International Geographical Congress*, London, John Murray, 1896, 694.

15. Tony Campbell, "Portolan Charts from the Late Thirteenth Century to 1500" in John Brian Harley and David Woodward (ed.), *Cartography in Pre-historic Ancient and Medieval Europe and the Mediterranean*, series "The History of Cartography," vol. 1, Chicago/London, University of Chicago Press, 1987, 371–463.

16. Ramon J. Pujades I Bataller, *Les cartes portolanes : la representació medieval d'una mar solcada*. Barcelona. Institut Cartogràphic de Catalunya / Institut d'Estudis Catalans / Institut europeu de la Mediterrània, 2007, 526.

17. Richard Pflederer, *Census of Portolan Maps & Atlases*, 2009.

12

Map Said to Belong to Christopher Columbus (detail)
See page 28 for the full caption and map.

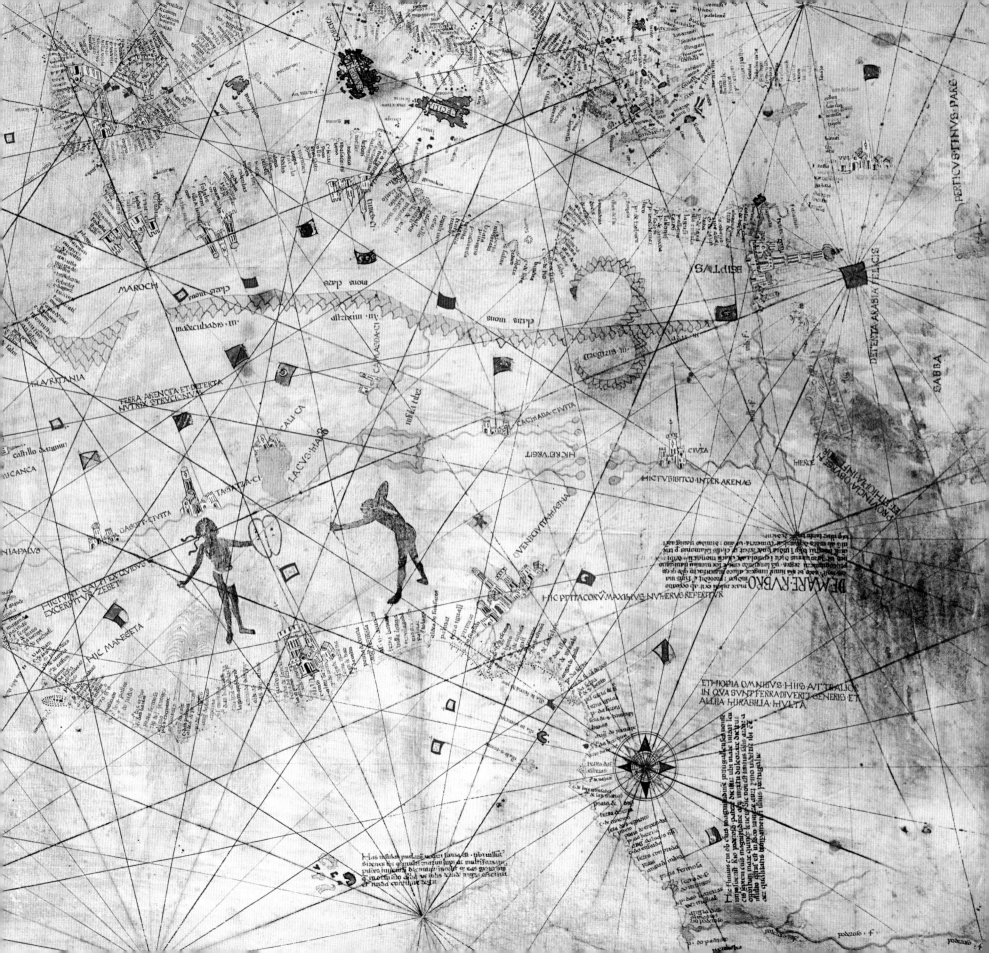

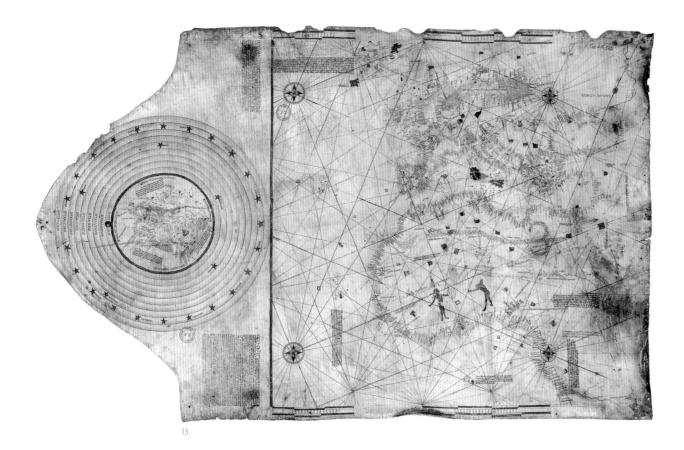

13.

13

Map said to belong to Christopher Columbus
Genovese writing, after 1488

This map juxtaposes a maritime map of the Mediterranean — which includes the lands the Portuguese discovered in Africa up to the gulf of Guinea — with a circular world map that is surrounded by seven celestial spheres. The circular map shows the Cape of Good Hope, discovered by Bartholomee Diaz in 1488. Its attribution to Christopher Columbus by Charles of the Roncière is responsible for much ink.

NLF, Paris, Maps and Plans, Ge AA 562 (RES).
Illuminated manuscript on parchment, 44 × 27½ inches (112 × 70).

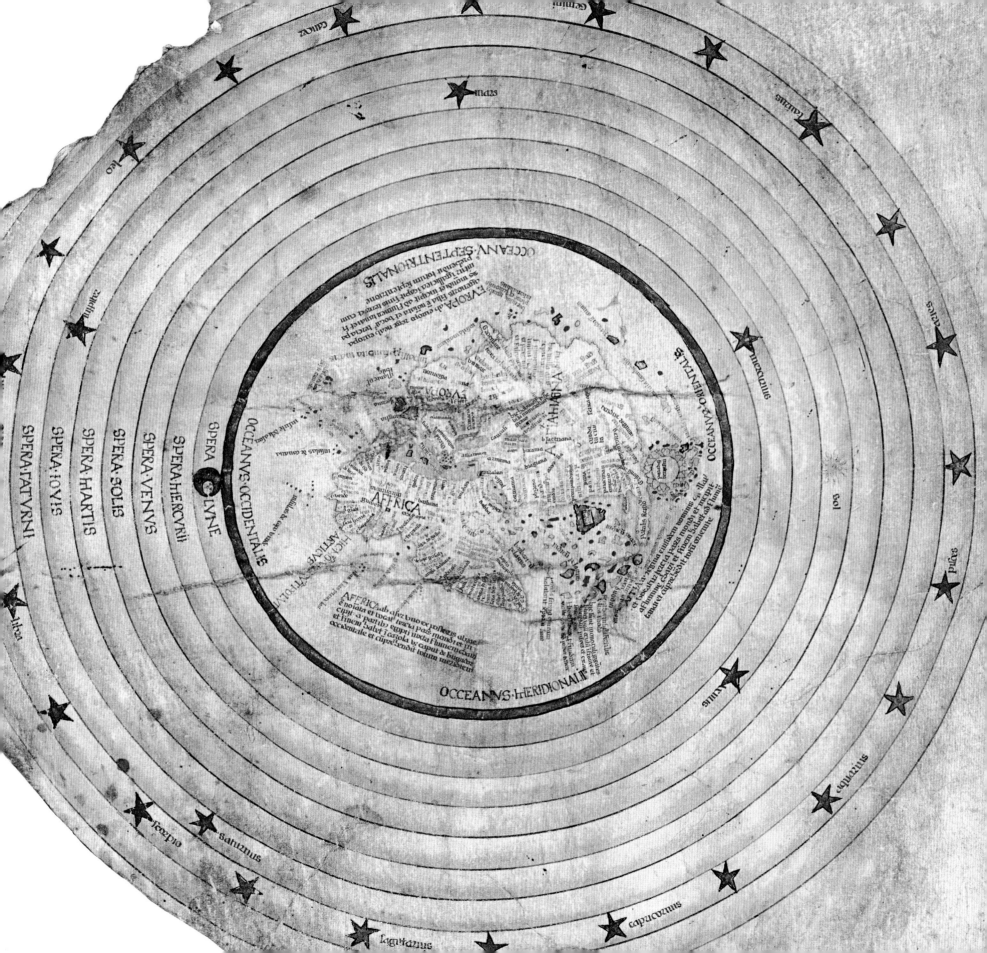

HOW PORTOLAN MAPS WERE MADE AND USED THROUGH THE CENTURIES

Catherine Hofmann
Hélène Richard
Emmanuelle Vagnon

In the middle of the 19th century, the first historians of cartography considered maps describing maritime regions as mere curiosities or monuments. Semantically derived from the term *portolano*, which were instruction manuals that described accesses to ports and harbors, they were often quite spectacular, drawn on parchment and entangled with lines, and widely associated with grand adventurers who sailed the oceans to discover the world. This body of work, which geographers have amassed during the last two centuries, represents not only documents mapping everything from the entire world to just nearby islands but also historical records that the mapmakers would not have made otherwise. Therefore the term portolan, as used here, refers to a large-scale map rather than a simple road map, which we show here through images that have been assembled in various libraries and that constitute a collection of historical works.

According to the oldest known sources, portolan maps originated in Western Europe during the Crusades, in maritime cities of the Balearic Islands and in northern Italy. They featured a very specific and original cartographic style that was linked with progress in navigational technology and European maritime expansion. Although opinions differ among historians, there is no evidence or established lineage between portolans and cartographies prior to the 13th century, namely those originating from ancient journeys, Roman world maps and Greek or Arabic geographies. Nevertheless, despite the differences among these many styles of cartography, they do share many features. Portolan maps were also impacted by scientific discoveries of the times that were not directly tied to nautical knowledge. They are consequently scholarly maps associated with advances in map projection methods as well as to the actual dimensions of the known world.

PORTOLAN CHARACTERISTICS

Portolan maps were produced over a period spanning more than 500 years, from the 13th to the 18th centuries. They were primarily maritime maps or "sea charts" designed to show the size of the seas and their boundaries: ports, coastlines, islands and other obstacles to navigation. While the principal outlines in such maps delineated continental coastlines, cartographers also included continental interiors and islands with varying degrees of descriptive details. Although they initially dealt mainly with the Mediterranean and Black Seas, portolan maps eventually became regional charts and included all areas discovered or explored by navigators, whether truly seen or just imagined.

For the most part these maps were hand drawn on parchment or animal skins, but eventually they were also produced on sheets of velum paper, which were then either cut and combined into larger maps or bound to make an atlas. Some portolan maps, however, were also drawn on paper as it existed at that time, as well as being printed on parchment.

The toponymy (place names) were inscribed perpendicular to the coast line (see illustrations 15 and 16), regardless of their actual orientation, meaning that the maps had to be laid flat and turned in order to read some names. The labels of the principal ports were shown in red, while those of secondary harbors were in black.

Decorative elements were less systematically applied and varied considerably from one chart to another and from one era to another. These included various colors and silver underscoring of islands and estuaries as well as banners, city descriptions, wind vanes, vegetation, people, animals of the region and sometimes even ships sailing the waves.

14.

14

Pietro di Versi (based on Michel de Rhodes)
Portolan of Spain
Venice, 1444

The map reproduced here illustrates the coast of Spain. This is part of *La Raxion de marineri*, a navigation manual written by the Venetian Pietro di Versi, who cites word for word part of a treatise by Michel de Rhodes. It deals with several methods of measurement useful to navigators and for portolan maps, particularly written descriptions of coastlines without an actual map.

Marciana Library, Venice, Cod. Marc. Ital. IV. 170 (5379), f. 50 v° -51. Manuscript on vellum, 5 ½ × 8 inches (14 × 20.5 cm).

15

Grazioso Benincasa, Map of the British Isles, France and the Iberian Peninsula
(detail)
See page 32 for the full caption and map.

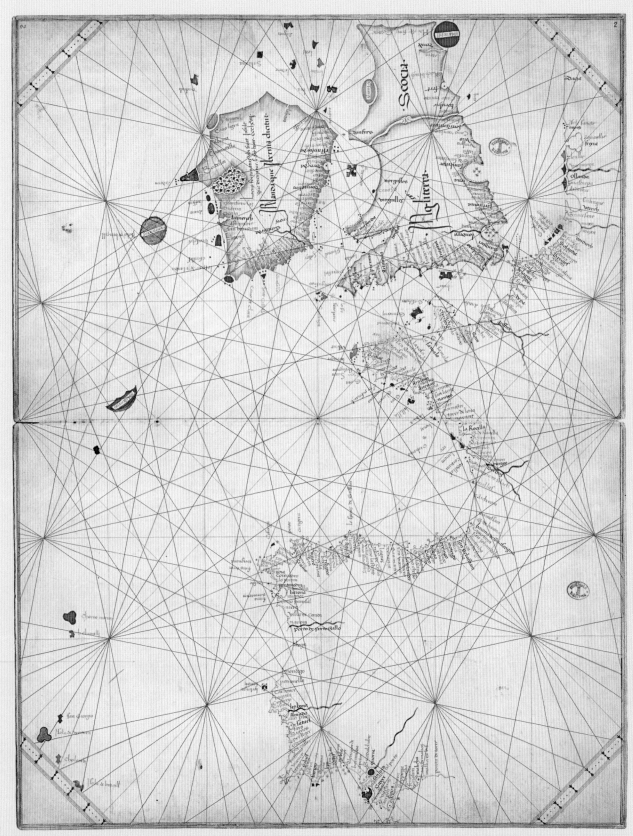

16.

16

Grazioso Benincasa, Map of the British Isles, France and the Iberian Peninsula
Rome, 1467

Benincasa, an ancient patron of ships, signed a large number of atlases and maps produced in Venice and Rome during the second half of the 15th century. In addition to depicting the Mediterranean and Black Seas, these maps also showed the coastlines and islands of the Atlantic Ocean from England (shown here) to the shores of Africa, which had recently been explored by Portugal (the Cape Verde Islands). This cartographer's restrained but gracious style was frequently imitated.

NLF, Paris, Maps and Plans, GE DD 988 (RES), f2.
Manuscript on velum, 8⅞ × 13¾ inches (22.5 × 35 cm).

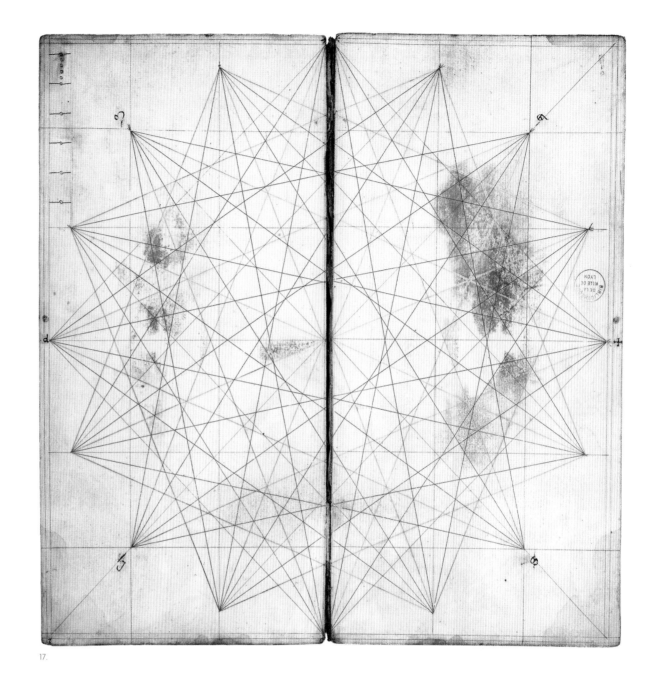

17.

17

Pietro Vesconte, Atlas of the Mediterranean Sea
Venice, 1319

This atlas of the Mediterranean, signed and dated, contains seven maps glued together as double pages on wooden planks. The wind rose forms a polygon into which each map was placed. Shown here is a preparatory canvas that shows the wind lines and internal compartments without any names or geographic details.

Municipal Library of Lyon, MS. 175, f.2 V0 -3.
Manuscript on velum, 11⅜ × 11½ inches (29 × 29.2 cm).

Portolan maps were drawn on a background of wind rose lines positioned in relation to the cardinal points. Radiating from a central point, eight principal lines and several secondary lines established 16 or 32 angles within a circle. The intersection of these lines with the circle formed new centers from which additional intersecting lines, in black, red or green, radiated (see illustration 17). According to historians, the names of these lines varied. The proposed French term "marteloire," is derived from the Italian *marteloggio*, but it is not quite suitable because it refers to sets of numerical tables used to quickly determine the position of a ship when planning a voyage.

The term "rhumb" appeared at the end of the Middle Ages to refer to the angular areas that separate each one of the 32 directions of a compass (see illustration 18). This eventually led to the term "rhumb lines." The word "loxodromy" refers to lines that define a uniform direction on the surface of a sphere and was not used until Mercator's innovation was created. In effect, had the spherical shape of the Earth been known since antiquity and throughout the Middle Ages, portolan maps would be considered as "flat charts," in other words they were drawn without taking into consideration a projection system that incorporates the curvature of the Earth. As long as use of such maps was confined to the Mediterranean and to other limited maritime areas, the absence of such projections was of no consequence. With the beginning of sailing over much greater distances in the 16th century, however, portolan maps had to be modified to incorporate such new elements as latitudes, which was quickly followed by a second scale to keep track of magnetic declination and, finally, by the use of the Mercator projection in the following century.

While these characteristics define portolan maps, there are many other types of charts that, though not part of the same class of documents, are very similar. As with other works, at that time the rules governing cartography were not strict, and the final product often reflected the artist's initiatives and the wishes of the clients. In addition, there were many interrelated influences between scholarly cosmography, nautical cartography and books describing islands, terrestrial atlases and illuminated manuscripts.

THE MANUFACTURE AND USE OF PORTOLAN MAPS

Not much is known about the manufacture of maps during medieval times; documents become more numerous and more accurate in modern times. Parchment was chosen because it provided the necessary space and could accommodate the scale required. The background of wind lines was often done prior to the depictions of the coastlines. The latter were based on more detailed models and often revealed landform details. Nomenclature and ornamentation were added subsequently and might well have been done by a different person. It is known that during the Middle Ages, there were shops that specialized in the production of nautical maps. Maps, atlases and world maps (also known as *mappemonde*) were produced in numerous reproductions and signed by the master of the studio.

During the era of the great sea explorations, far more than during the preceding centuries, the designs of world maps became affairs of state. La Casa de contratación (house of contracts) in Spain and l'Armazém in Portugal were the official administrators of information on and analysis of the new worlds discovered by navigators. The compilation of the results of this study led to the construction of the famous *padrón real* (royal patron), which were models validated by the nation's sovereign that in principle, were to serve as prototypes for all maps to be used by sailors (see illustration 69). In practice, however, production of the padrón real was complex and irregular, and efforts to ensure conformity of all new maps proved to be futile. Since the 19th century, some have fantasized about the supposed "secrets" surrounding these royal Portuguese maps that spies allegedly sought. The world map of Cantino (today housed in Modena) and the great map of Caverio (conserved in National Library of France) are actually Italian copies of the great Iberian maps that showed for the first time the explorations of southern Africa and the contours of the new American continent. The rules of secrecy were nevertheless applied in a limited manner to two main objectives. One was to reduce competition among cartographers by limiting production of such maps to a few "master cartographers" who were deemed qualified. The second reason was to protect sensitive geographic information, such as the discovery of Brazil by Cabral in 1500, and thereby prevent territorial competition among nations.

Portolan maps are not primarily land charts but reflections of first-hand experiences of sailors. At this stage in portolan development, we are well into what, in the modern age, is called "consultant hydrography." This refers to the practice of starting with an accepted marine chart and then updating it frequently with additional information provided by

18
Sea compass Made by Manoel Ferreira
Lisbon, 1744

This marine compass, which points to the magnetic north pole to help pilots maintain their course, was made in Lisbon by Ferreira, many of whose other navigational instruments were also preserved. The wind rose decor, consisting of 32 rhumb lines (separated by about 11°), is very similar to those on marine charts.

Maritime Museum, Paris, 1 NA 10.
Wood, metal and paper, L: 16¾ inches (42.5 cm), W: 16⅛ inches (41 cm), H: 10 inches (25.5 cm).

18.

navigators and ship captains. They are the actual sailors and navigators and the experts in approaching ports, often with their own detailed sketches of where accidents have occurred and other dangers in the coastal regions that they know by heart.

In reality, for trips along the coast or short crossings, especially in the Mediterranean, it was not essential to use maps aboard ships. There was no need, especially during good weather, to analyze the trip or change course; the mariner's experience was enough. Nonetheless, from the 13th century on, general mention is made in stories and archives that charts were on board ships. These were the property of the ship's captain or of certain sailors, and they included nautical charts and other reference instruments. These were kept in a locker among personal belongings but taken out when stormy weather made steering the ship difficult.[1]

However, for more distant voyages, maps quickly became indispensable.[2] This is evident from the many navigation treatises outlining how to use them. In the middle of 17th century, Father Fournier explained how to use rhumb lines (see illustration 22): the pilot outlines his route on the map using two dry point compasses (see illustration 20), in order to keep track of the path followed from the point of departure and measuring the distances traveled according to the latitude the ship has traveled.[3] Fournier also specified that there were several kinds of marine maps, underscoring that these were based on cartographic models that were derived using techniques of varying degrees of accuracy.[4] It is for this reason that maps made by route and which only served for nearby destinations, as in the Mediterranean, do not mention either latitude or longitude. He further cites charts based on latitude and by route that show neither the meridian nor longitude, and only a single distance measure is applied to the entire map. He further mentions "common" charts (or plates), which show parallels and meridians through perpendicular lines forming equal-sided squares. Lastly he talks about "reduced" maps, inspired by the Mercator projection (see illustration 21), were parallels are placed at curved intervals as one recedes from the equator. These made it possible to trace loxodromic routes that cut across all meridians at the same angle.

Portolan map production, which basically relied on the use of the compass, continued to the end of 18th century. Pilots continued to prefer rhumb lines and maps that were "covered with an infinity of such lines."[5] (see illustration 19). It was not until the last third of the 18th century that longitude measures came into general use, thanks largely to a new type of instrumentation (marine chronometers, the circle of Borda, etc.), and, as additional scientific information became available to navigators, the use of portolan maps inevitably declined.

Despite being used for several centuries, portolan maps that have survived to this day — despite the hazards of conserving ancient documents — only rarely show traces of actually having been used at sea. Far more often they are signed documents that are very valuable and have been kept in libraries or archives more as reference maps than actual instruments of navigation. Maps that were actually used were less beautiful, usually drawn on paper and easily damaged and then destroyed when no longer useful. Consequently, what helped make portolan maps so rich and beautiful was that they have been treasured since the Middle Ages for their decorative value and their ability to stimulate the imagination. Some of the most beautiful examples, like the *Catalonian Atlas* from the Middle Ages and Guillaume Le Testu's *Cosmographie* from the 16th century, are objects for book lovers and, often, works of art produced for an influential ruler. Not only are the coastal outlines shown in these documents, there are also illustrations of the continents that demonstrate a growing familiarity with their geography. These are indicative of the ambitions and conflicts of the great European powers and their visions of new lands and increasing fascination with the immensity of the world yet to be discovered.

Catherine Hofmann
Hélène Richard
Emmanuelle Vagnon

19
Denis Rotis, Map of the North Atlantic Ocean
1674

The Northwest Passage, the supposed route to China bypassing the Spanish empire, is shown to lie north of the Saint Laurence River on to this map drawn by a pilot on the Saint-Jean-de-Luz. Derived from the map Reinel produced 150 years earlier, this map is an example of one "scribbled with an infinity of lines," as decried by Father Fournier in *Hydrographie*.

NLF, Paris, Maps and Plans, GE SH ARCH 21.
Manuscript on parchment manuscript, 34⅝ × 17 inches
(88 × 43.4 cm).

19.

Works Cited

1. See pages 60–71.

2. See pages 126–135.

3. Georges Fournier, *Hydrographie contenant la theorie et la practique de la navigation*, Paris, J. Dupuis, 1667, vol. XXVII, chapter XIII.

4. Ibid, vol. XV, chapter XV.

5. Ibid, vol. XVII, chapter Vi

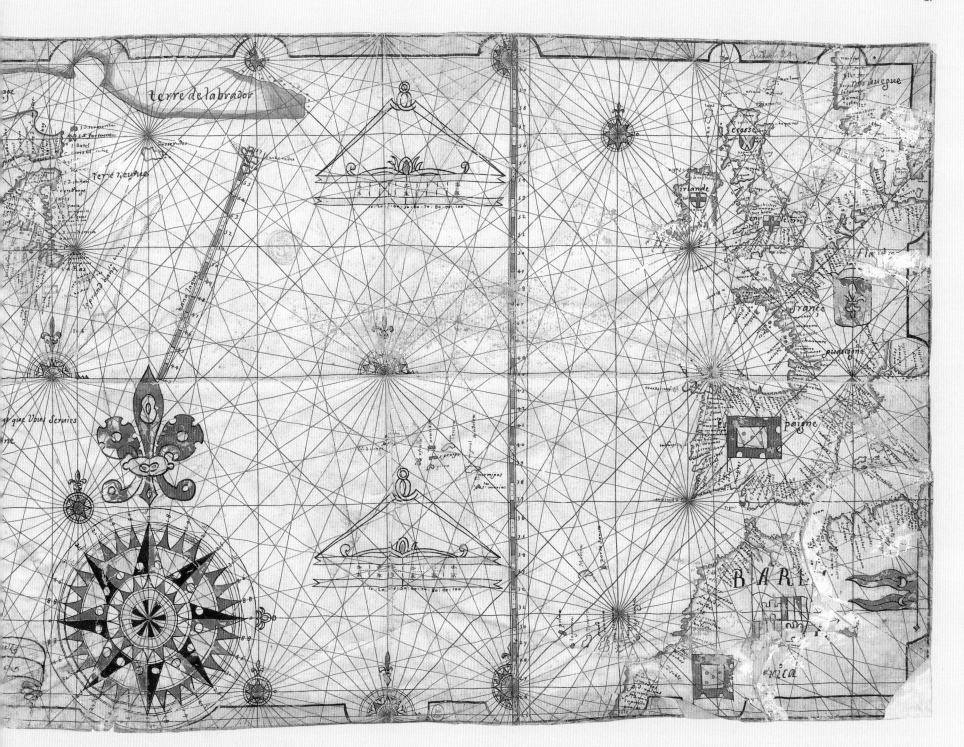

20

Pierre de Vaulx, Map of the Atlantic
(detail)
The Hague, 1613

This details shows a dry point compass atop a graphic distance scale. The dry point compass was the first cartographic instrument, useful in constructing maps but also for sailors, who could use it to log the distances they traveled on maps to scale. Norman hydrographers like Pierre de Vaulx often included a depiction of this basic instrument of cartographers and navigators on their maps. See page 141 for the full map.

NLF, Paris, Maps and Plans, GE SH ARCH 6 (RES).
Illuminated manuscript on parchment, 37¾ × 27 inches (96 × 68.5 cm).

21

Guillaume Le Vasseur, Map of the Atlantic Ocean
(detail)
Deippe, 1601

This canvass by Guillaume Le Vasseur shows crossing latitudes. Le Vasseur, the author of a very comprehensive treatise on geography (see page 140), was the first Norman hydrographer to use the Mercator projection, known as crossing latitudes, in his charts. In signed and dated cartridges containing maps that were brought to Latin America, he indicates a framework from oo latitude (equator) to 60°.

NLF, Paris, Maps and Plans, GE SH ARCH 5 (RES).
Illuminated manuscript on parchment, 39 × 29¼ inches (99 × 74.5 cm).

22

Georges Fournier, *Hydrographie contenant la théorie et la pratique de toutes les parties de la navigation* (Hydrographie containing the theory and practice of all aspects of navigation)
Paris, Soly, 1643

This is the original edition of the first French maritime encyclopedia, re-edited in 1667 and 1679. The chapters that George Fournier assigned to different maps and their usage display the author's relationship with the Norman school of hydrography, showing in particular the importance of the works of Guillaume Le Vasseur.

NLF, Paris, Arsenal, FOL-S 1295.
Book printed in folios.

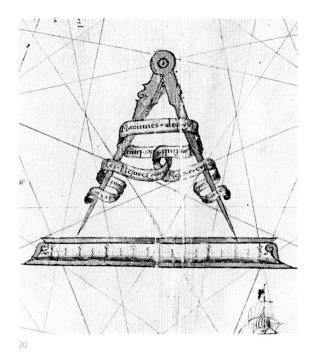

20.

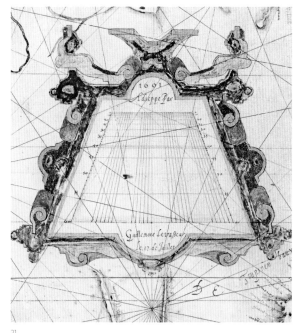

21.

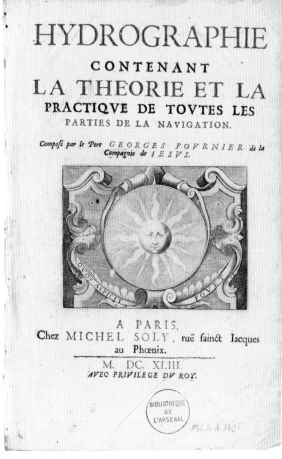

22.

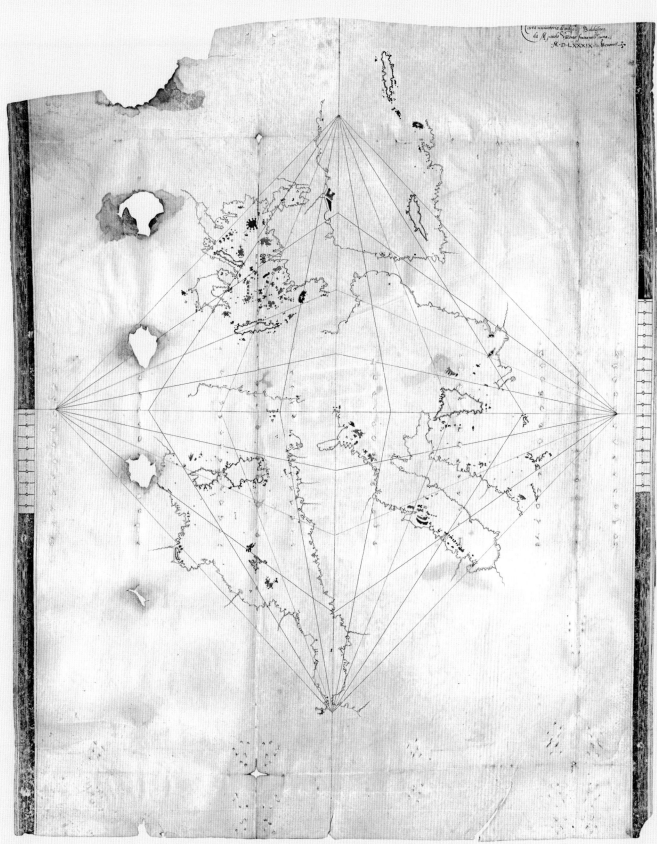

23

**Baldasaro da Maïolo Visconte,
Mute map of the Mediterranean**
Genoa, 1589

Dated and signed by a member of the
Maggiolo family (holders of the Genovese
map monopoly), this puzzling map shows
the Mediterranean divided into four basins,
without any names or regular orientation
indicated. The lines shown are also not the
usual wind lines. Could this have been a device
to make map reproduction easier?

Departmental Archives of the Maritime Alps,
Nice, 1Fi 1534.
Manuscript on parchment, 27⅛ × 22 inches
(69 × 56 cm).

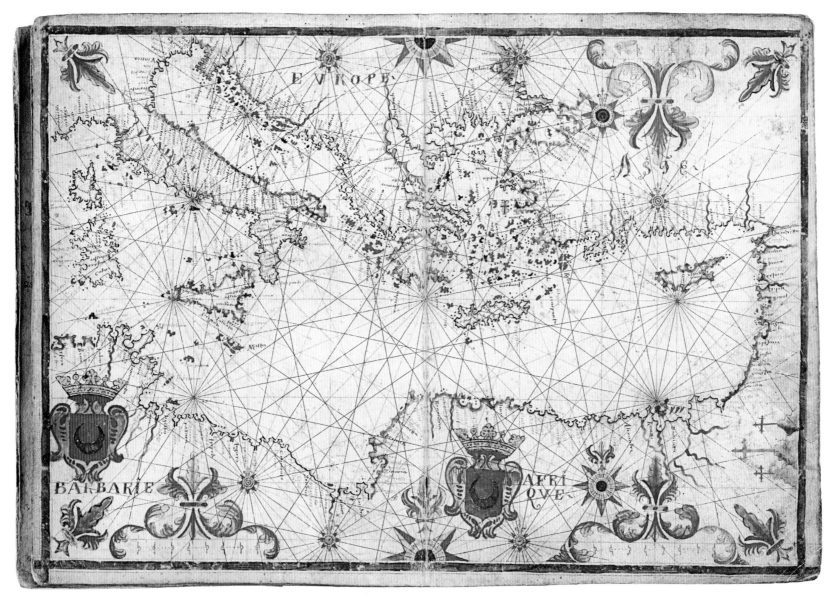

24 a.

24

François Ollive Studio,
Atlas of the Mediterranean
Marseille, circa 1660

The studio of François Ollive, which was active
from about 1646 to 1662, was extremely productive.
This atlas included both the western and eastern
Mediterranean. The second edition shows the grid
system used to facilitate the reproduction and
enlargement these maps. This system was outlined
in the 16th century by the Spanish mathematician
Martin Cortés, in his treatise *Breve compendio de la
Esfera y de la arte de navigar* (A brief summary of the
Sphere and the art of navigation; Cadiz, 1551).

24 a
Map of the eastern Mediterranean with
the wind lines, the names of locations and
decorations. (f.3)

24 b
Mute map of the eastern Mediterranean
showing an orthogonal grid. (f.5)

Alcazar Library, Marsellie, Ms. 2104, f. 3 and 5.
Illuminated manuscript on parchment, five sheets glued
back to back.

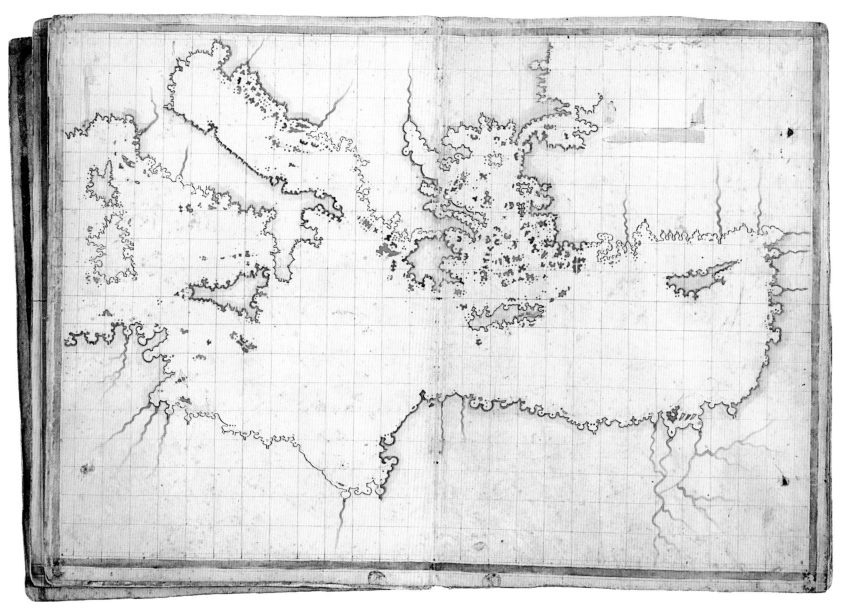

24 b.

CATALONIAN ATLAS

25

Catalonian Atlas attributed to Abraham Cresques
1375

The document known as the *Catalonian Atlas* is a compendium of six maps and annotated schematics, drawn on parchment paper and glued onto each side of a protective wooden plank that is higher than it is wide (9⅞ × 25¼ inches / 25 × 64 cm). In time, the sheets of velum that serve to bind the work split.

The first two planks carry a translation, in Catalan, of the *imago mundi* by Honorius Augustodunensis, with a description of the widespread world of the Middle Ages, and a large circular calendar as well as astrological signs. The next planks, lined up end to end, comprise a representation of the world in four maps, two for the Orient, from China to the Persian Gulf, and two for the Western Mediterranean, from the Black Sea to England. The reading direction, from east to west, is the same as that of large circular world maps of the 13th century, like Ebstorf's world map, which is oriented with the east upward. The contents of the map, notably the toponymy in the Asian section, stem from ancient texts as well as from Marco Polo's accounts and Arabian sources. The maps' structures, crisscrossed with wind lines even over the continental areas as well as the Mediterranean, European and African toponymy, all correspond to the Catalonian portolan maps of that era.

According to its calendar, we know that the *Catalonian Atlas* dates back to 1375, and thanks to the 1380 inventory, we know that it was housed in the Charles V library. And yet, a letter of November 5, 1381, from the Infant of Aragon demands that a world map of this kind be sent to the new King of France, Charles VI, while requesting a consultation with its author, Cresques the Jew from Majorca, to further clarify it.

E. V.

NLF Manuscripts, Spanish 30.
Illuminated manuscript on parchment; 12 half-sheets each measuring 9⅞ × 25¼ inches (25 × 64 cm).

25 a
Central Asia

Inspired by Marco Polo, this detail of a map is evocative of the Silk Road: a merchant's caravan with dromedaries and horses crossing the Lop Nor desert.

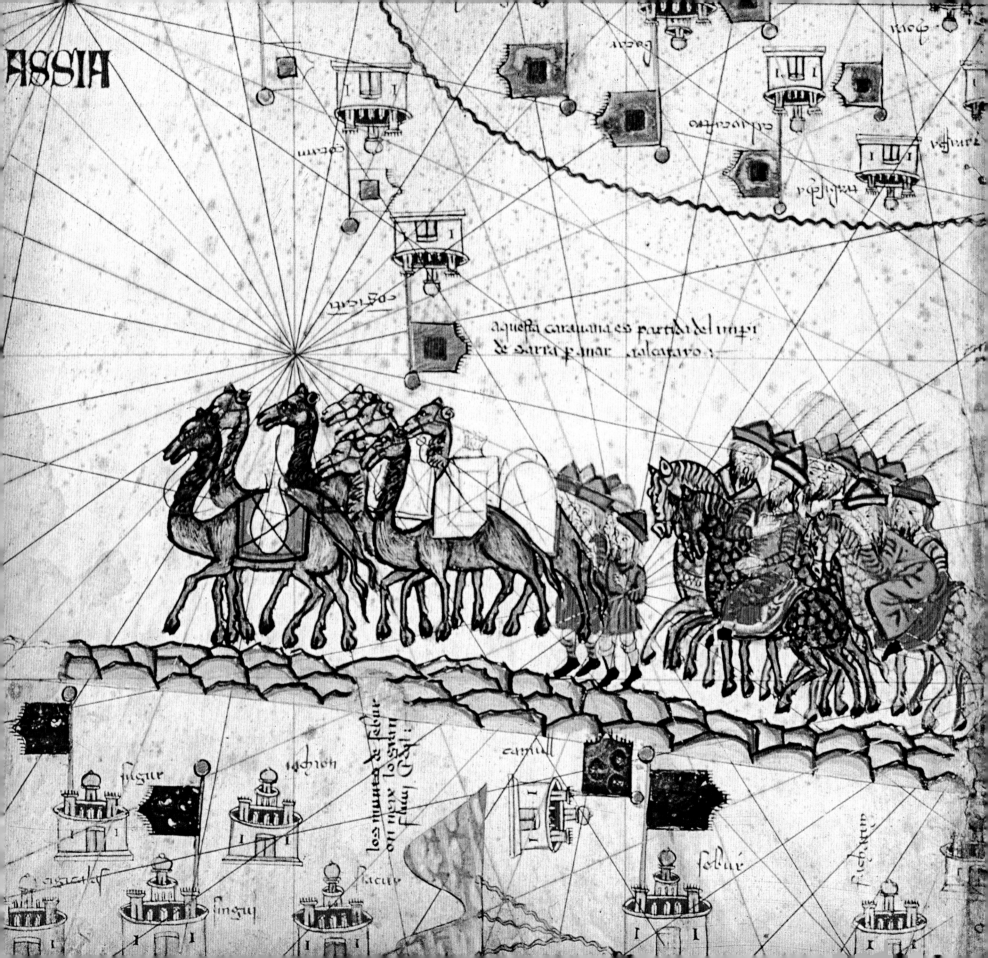

25 b
Cosmographical Calendar for 1375

See pages 46–47 for close-ups and
page 42 for full caption.

25 c
**Cosmographical Schematics and Description
of the World (in Catalan)**

See page 42 for full caption.

25 b.

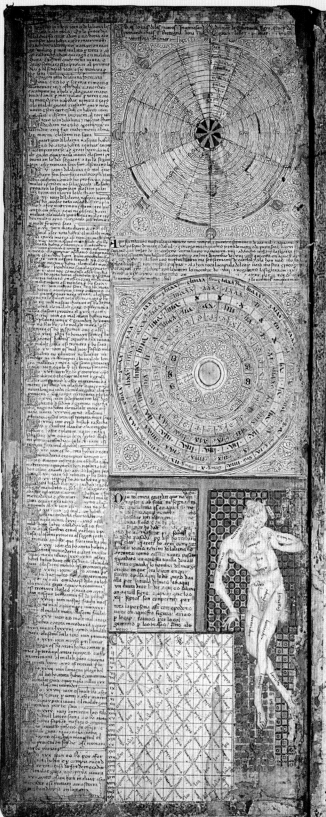

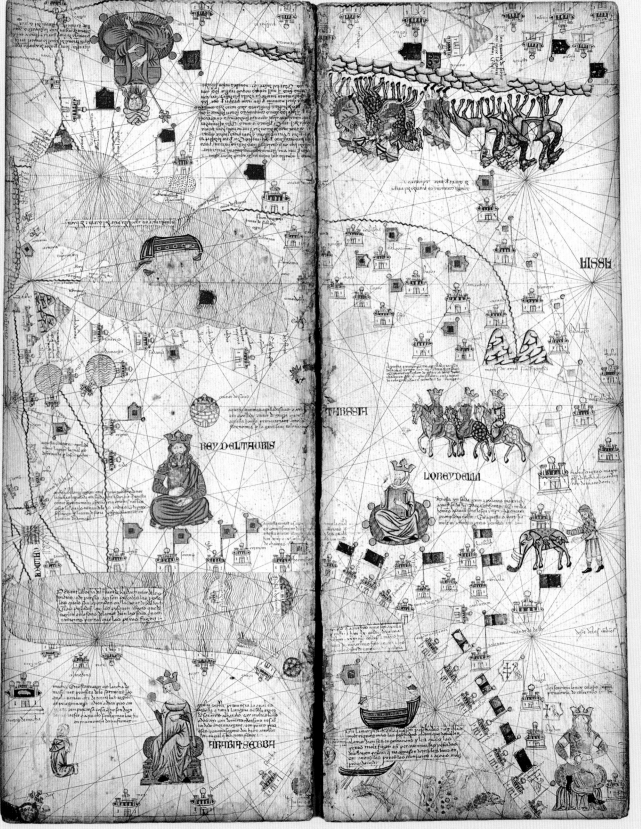

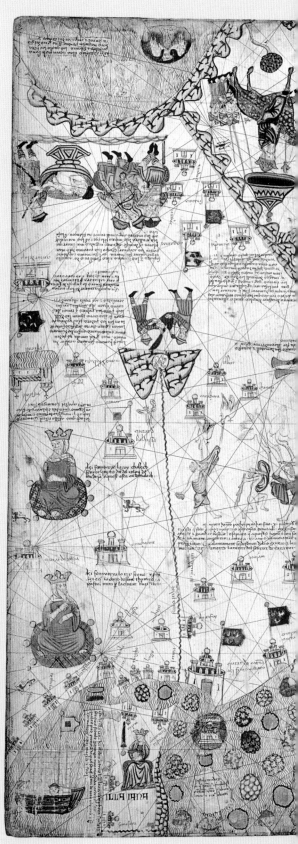

25 d.

25 e.

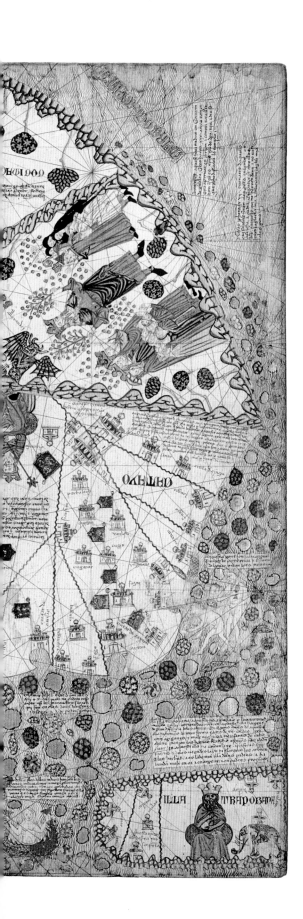

25 d
Western Asia: Caspian Sea and Persian Gulf

See page 42 for full caption.

25 e
Eastern Asia and China Sea

See page 42 for full caption.

25 f
Asia

Set in the Far East, this is a representation of the Last Judgment in a garden-like paradise next to the kingdom of Gog and Magog.

See pages 50–51 and page 42 for full caption.

laquatta ro

lo gran seyor princep de gog e de
magog aquest exira en lo temps
dante xpist ab molta gent

GOG IMAGOG

ara carta

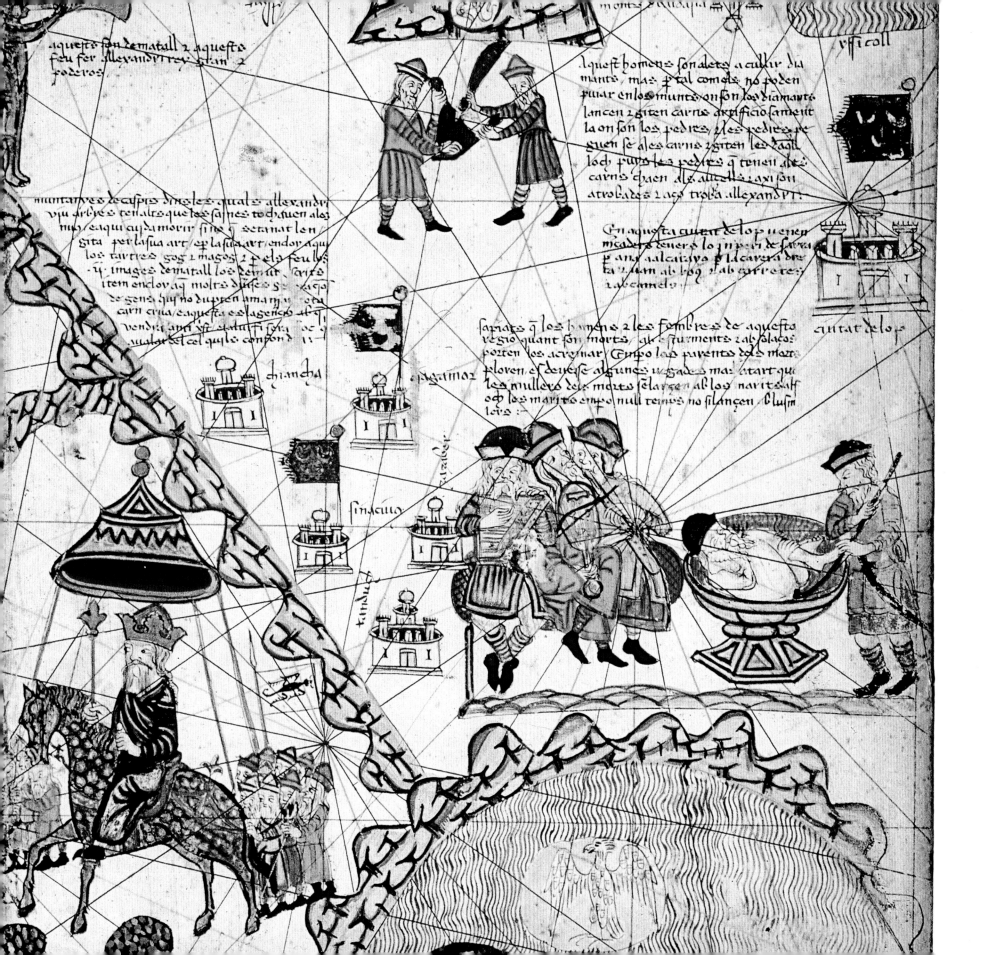

25 g
Western Mediterranean and Atlantic Ocean

See page 42 for full caption.

25 h
Eastern Mediterranean and Black Sea

See page 42 for full caption.

25 i
Western Africa and Atlantic Ocean

The ship on this detail evokes the explorations of Catalan Jaime Ferrer along the African coasts in 1346. A nomad on a dromedary en route to Mecca is also shown.

See pages 54–55 and page 42 for full caption.

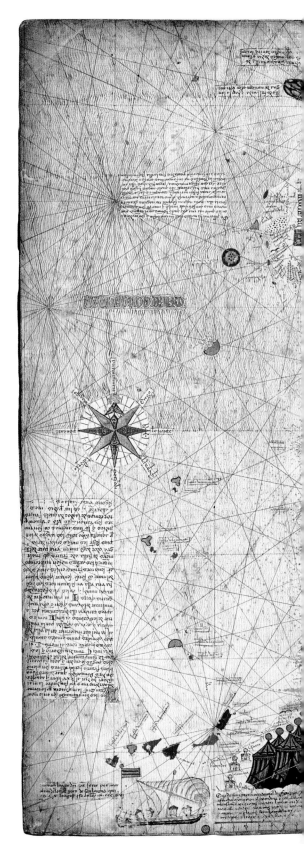

25 g.

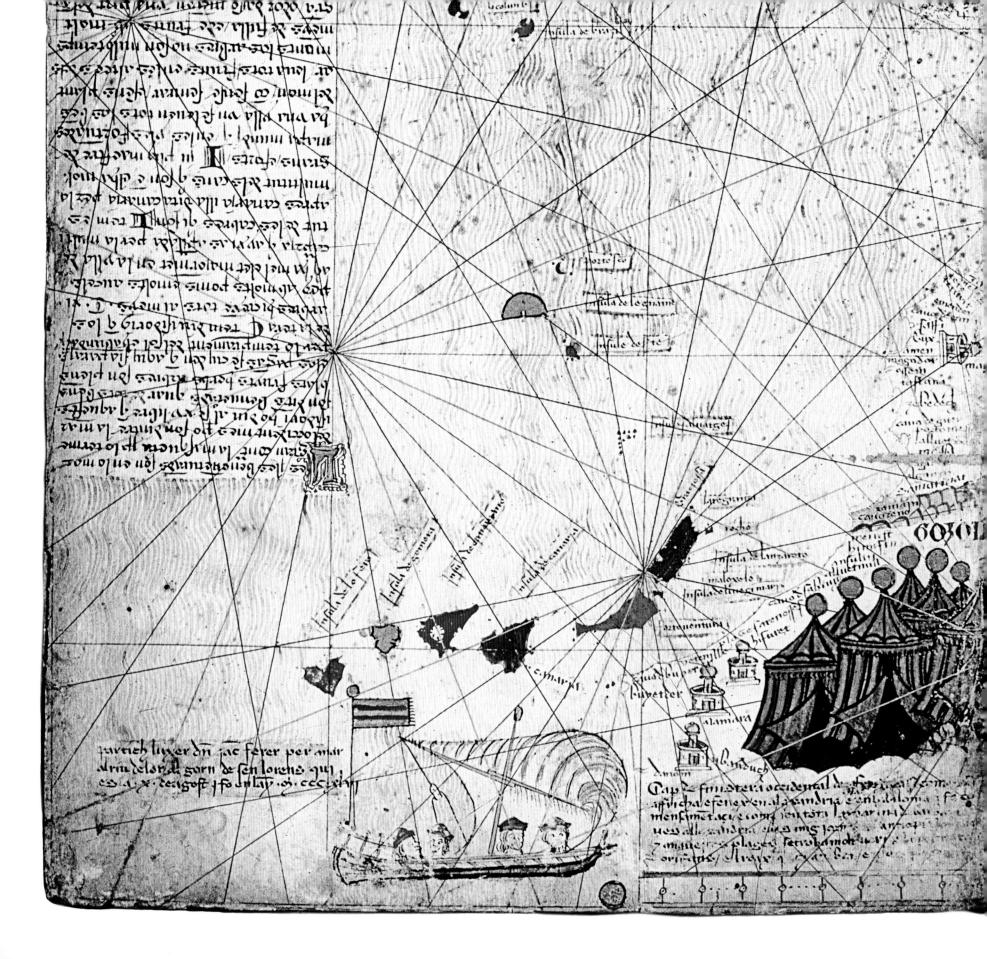

THE
MEDITERRANEAN

THE MEDITERRANEAN: THE CRADLE OF PORTOLAN MAPS

Emmanuelle Vagnon

In his founding work on the history of portolan maps, the historian Nordenskiöld proposed that when medieval marine maps were first developed, they were based on a model or matrix that gave rise to all others. He tried to establish the shape and contours of this original source, calling it the "original portolan" and basing it on the oldest charts and texts, notably the *Carte Pisane* and the *Compasso da navigare*, both thought to date to the late 13th century. According to him, the original marine maps were limited to the Mediterranean basin and the Black Sea and bordered in the west by the Strait of Gibraltar and in the east by the Darnadelles or the confines of the Greek empire. This expanse encompassed the economic realm governed by the maritime city-states and reflected their expansion. Consequently, the first portolan maps, produced principally in Genoa, Venice and Majorca, placed the Mediterranean, whose main outlines were established by the end of the 14th century, at their center. The Mediterranean Sea also served as the center of the grid of wind lines that radiated toward points in the Balearic Islands and Italy. Other seas were placed at the margins all around and were often shown in different colors, for example wavy blue lines for the Baltic Sea or the Persian Gulf and scarlet for the Red Sea. The Mediterranean and Black Seas, on the other hand, were almost never shown in color; however, their islands, like jewelry, were highlighted in green, red, gold or silver. The Mediterranean and its islands were the main focus of these maps, while the continents were limited to the naming of their shores, the flows of the rivers and the estuaries, coastal swamps and lagoons.

These speculative grids, which could be extended or shrunk to different horizons, were also placed on the most prestigious, richly illuminated maps. Such lavish decorations provided supplementary information about the people and economic resources of the coastal regions shown. There too, the Mediterranean was at the center of it all. Trade sections and frontier regions, which both united and divided Christian and Muslim people, east and west, were indicated. The charts also specified the borders of Venetian and Genovese colonies of the Aegean and Black Seas, indicating both rivalries and alliances among local residents. The geopolitical aspects of the countries that bordered the Mediterranean remained relevant well beyond the Middle Ages, even as many portolan maps were being extended to more distant maritime horizons, into larger expanses and indeed into the whole world.

Portolan maps of the Mediterranean Sea continued to be produced during the 16th century, at a time when the Ottoman Empire was threatening Venice and the Holy Roman Empire directly and when the French kingdom was beginning dangerous liaisons with the Ottoman government. These maps were valued into the late 17th century, even though by then they were deemed as archaic and obsolete. By that time, the banners shown on the cities and the clothes on the people were well out of date. What is more important, however, is that the nomenclature in this well-known region did not change much, and so portolan maps of the Mediterranean Sea, just like larger-scale atlases of the region, retained their honorable pedigree at a time when printed maps had become common. In this subtle manner, portolans remained part of the canon of a style of cartography that had become traditional.

26
Alvise Gramolin, Map of the Aegean Sea
(detail)

See page 80 for full caption and map.

NAVIGATIONAL MAPS: THE FIRST WIDELY DISTRIBUTED MAPS[1]

Ramon J. Pujades i Bataller

At the start of 1990 all historians interested in the maps we call "portolans" became aware of a striking contradiction. On the one hand, the number of surviving portolan maps (including about 180 examples that were dated before 1500) and the fact that they were found among the belongings of Italian and Catalan merchants and sailors, as well as numerous references written in both Latin and vernacular languages, indicated that such maps were widely available, at least in the large coastal cities that were engaged in international maritime commerce. However, most scholars studied portolan maps in isolation, as though they were treasures for collectors, and considered them to be costly and relatively exotic items made with little scientific precision, concluding that they could not have been very useful nor much used for navigation. It was also often asserted that these maps were made by knowledgeable cartographers who were experts in geography and astronomy but who worked primarily to satisfy the intellectual curiosity of princes, prelates and the rich.[2] But can we really conclude anything from the limited samples we have today? From a quantitative and qualitative point of view, do these form a statistically representative sample of the cartographic production of the late Middle Ages?

We will not find the answers to this question simply by studying the charts and atlases that have survived. It is necessary to determine their essential characteristics and then compare the results with information gleaned from secondary or indirect sources. Such sources include inventories of deceased individuals, auction sales, notary contracts, commercial and institutional correspondence, military orders, complaints, judicial records seeking compensation for losses due to attacks by pirates, scientific and technical reports, sailing logs and poems.[3] After assessing these lists of documentary evidence, which is really only the start, it seems clear that portolan maps were circulated among people involved in maritime commerce because they served as navigational aids. It is also apparent that maps intended for practical purposes, those always used with a pair of *sestes*, or divider, and compass, were not the very ornate or magnificent atlases that have been preserved to this day; as utilitarian objects, they were excluded from conservation in libraries. On the contrary, these maps, hardly decorated or not decorated at all, were copied quickly and efficiently based on available models by special painters, who were artist-copyists without much expertise and who either worked only on this task or were involved with other mercantile and marine activities. These were authentic navigational tools, sold for less than a Lira

before the Black Death in 1348 and, after the epidemic raised prices and salaries,[4] for a bit more than two Genovese or Majorcan Lira. This price, which at the time was the equivalent of half the monthly salary of a Mediterranean sailor, was sometimes reduced by as much 75 percent for *per marinieri* maps, which were handed down after extensive use on ships.

I will focus here on two recently discovered documents of extraordinary importance. In combination with the documents on the list I have already published,[5] they help to account for the navigational maps circulated by the thousands from the last years of the 13th century to the end of the 15th century.

The first document, discovered in Genoa, concerns the Catalan navigator Francesc Solanes, who was attacked during a popular uprising in Genoa in March 1393.[6] In addition to two compasses and an hourglass calibrated for half hour intervals (the property of the Majorcan navigator Nicolau Andreu), the following items were also on board his ship: the *carta a navigando* and *busolam unam*, belonging to the Valencian sailor Lluís de Collbató, as well as the *carta pro navigando* and *unam busolam* of Jaon Serra, also from Valencia. In addition, as the testimony of Jaume Ciribert makes clear, the Barcelonan merchant and co-owner of the ship, Bernat Oliva, brought with him several course-plotting maps and other goods stolen by the assailants. This was further corroborated and expanded in the account of Bartomeu Tornil. According to his deposition, Bernat Oliva *habebat cartas pro navigando, causa venderi, sex vel septem* (he brought six or seven maps that he intended to sell). They were still in his possession at the time of the attack since he had not had the time to sell any of them (*quia nulla vendiderat*). He estimated their Genovese market value at about 18 Florentine Florins.[7] According to the exchange rates at the time, that represented 260 Barcelona cents, or about 40 cents per map. Apparently Catalonian maps imported into Genoa were about 20 percent costlier than the locally produced maps.

These documents also mention another merchant vessel in which at least two crewmen had navigation maps and compasses. Like many of the other references already published, this evidence supports the idea that a large proportion of the merchant ship officers involved in maritime commerce had navigation maps and, consequently, that it was rare for any ship, big or small, even simple fishing boats, not to have one on board.[8] Such documentation also shows that the six export orders for maps received by the Barcelonan merchant

27
Mecia de Viladestes,
Marine Map of the Mediterranean
(detail)

See pages 68–69 for full caption and map.

Domingo Pujol in 1390–1392 (numbers 18–20 and 23–25) were nothing unusual. In fact, six months later, another Barcelonan merchant took the initiative and brought six or seven other maps that he intended to sell on his business trip. What is important to note is the coincidence of the dates, locations and prices, which, through the good fortune of documentary conservation, allows us to demonstrate that at least 33 navigation maps were exported during a period of only two and a half years, between October 1389 and March 1392. Moreover, this was done by only two merchants who came from a city for which there is no evidence that dependable cartographic studios existed. All indications are that the articles sold by these two Barcelonans were maps obtained from the island of Palma de Majorca, a common stopover for such voyages.

Majorca not only satisfied the needs of the multitude of ships that called at its port, it also exported its maps directly. This is proven through the *carteggio* of the agents of the Datini company, which operated on the island and exported at least five other articles (numbers 98, 99 and 100) between March 1395 and June 1938, and three letters dated February 1408, which refer to the exportation of two more maps. This clearly shows that such activity was not sporatic but constant (number 104).[9] The maps mentioned in the *carteggi* of the Datini agents, which were decorated with flags and vignettes of cities, cost two to four times more than ordinary maps. This does not necessarily mean that the Datini agents were making an exception by exporting more decorated than utilitarian maps, but as they have explained themselves, decorated maps had to be ordered well in advance and were consequently discussed more frequently in business correspondence. The more utilitarian maps were purchased directly in bulk from specialty shops, where they were produced in lots of three to seven units. Since such maps were not part of the official ship cargo, and where instead more general merchandize sold directly by sailors and merchants, they were not usually mentioned unless a misadventure befell their owners and they had to list their personal inventories while seeking compensation. All this has been much to the delight of historians today.

The data show us that, contrary to what had been assumed to date, several thousand portolan maps were actually produced, sold and used during the late Middle Ages. This is further substantiated by the fact that different types of maps may have been found on board the same ship, at different time periods and from one end to the other of the Mediterranean Sea.

In one document dated 1433, we see that the studio of the Majorcan Gabriel de Vallseca paid a debt during a delivery of four maps they had previously borrowed and then promised to provide 24 more maps in the coming six months. In my opinion, this evidence is unlikely to be an unusual situation, as recently suggested by Tony Campbell.[10] Indeed, as we just explained, four centuries earlier, the 33 maps sold in only two and a half years by just two Barcelonan merchants were in addition to those sold by local merchants and Italian agents working on the island, who exported more maps in order to satisfy the demand in the great port of Majorca. Clearly, this illustrates the following facts: such maps were in constant production, in series, including utilitarian maps produced in lesser but significant quantities, moderately ornate maps with coats of arms and views of cities as well as the occasional production of sumptuously decorated charts and world maps. We can conclude this by considering the fact that, to our knowledge, only three active mapmaking shops operated in Majorca at the same time during the last decades of the 14th century. These included the studio of Jafudà Cresques, a.k.a. Jaume Ribes, a Jewish convert who was in Barcelona in service of the court in 1394; the studio of his ex-apprentice, Samuel Corcós, a.k.a. Marcià de Viladesters, who became independent in 1390; and the studio of the Christian Guillem Soler and his son Joan.[11] Correspondence in 1408 between Datini agents indicates that no other cartographic studios existed on the island at that time because, after the departure of the Cresques, alias Ribes, to Barcelona, one of the two remaining studios ceased production temporarily at the start of the year for reasons that are not clear, thereby leaving only one active business. This brought about a decrease in the supply of maps, which was followed by an increase in the price of 66 percent over a very short period of time, showing that the demand for maps was constant and not just sporadic. Like all other medieval artisan shops, in order to survive, portolan mapmakers often contacted their clients as to their needs and wishes, even if that slowed their production flow at different stages of development. Such developments might someday provide us with documents showing that a universe of associations existed among mapmakers, their under-studies and provisional associations that were just as complex as those of paint studios for instance, a form of art closely related to cartography. At least four of the known Majorcan cartographers also worked as painters and miniaturisers.[12] That could give us pause to reflect further on the value of economic scrutiny, which tends to formulate general rules that only apply in unstable and very relative ways.

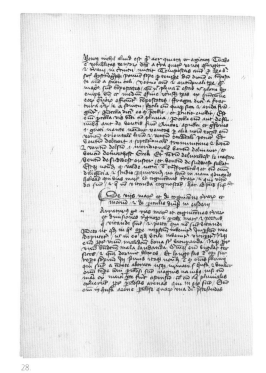

28.

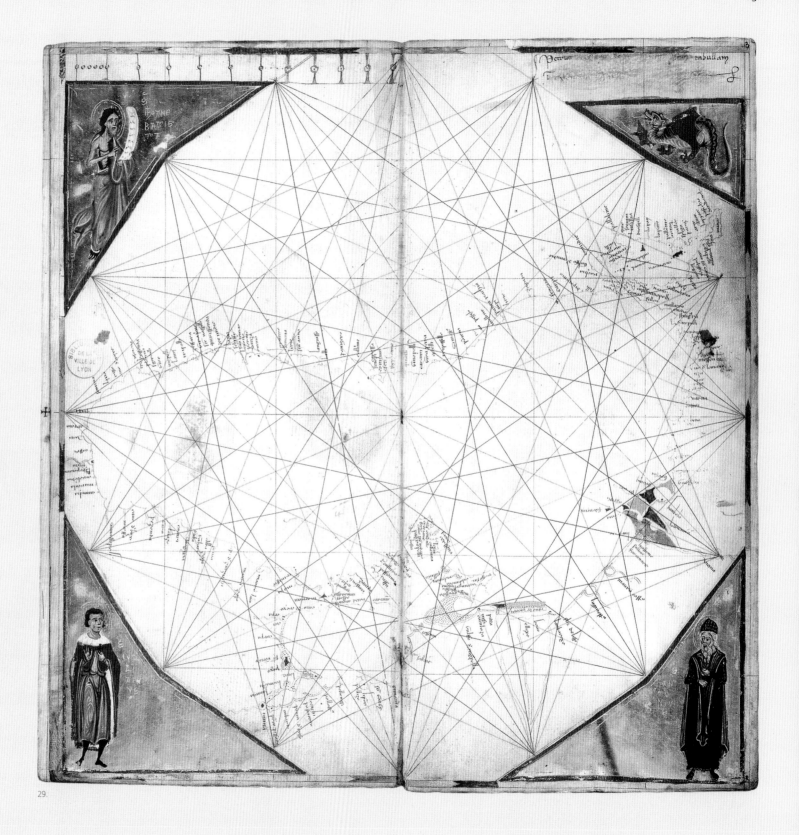

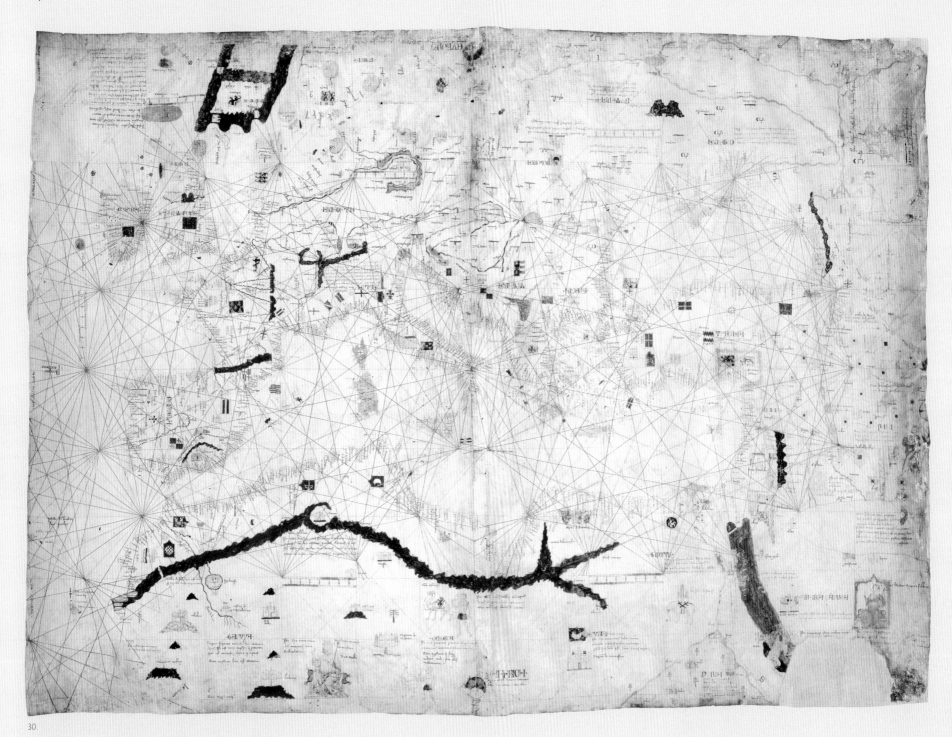

I shall end by offering a document dated September 2, 1405, a letter written in Sicilian and kept in the archives of the Aragon kingdom. Rogerio di Camera, the fleet physician under the command of Martin the Younger of Sicily, explains to King Martin I the circumstances of the return of his son to Sicily, recounting in a very detailed manner one part of this intricate expedition (see pages 66–67).[13]

After several days of forced sailing against the wind, despite the best efforts of the sailors there was no sight of land and supplies were becoming short. The ship's officers conferred over maps and compasses to get a sense of where the ship was in relation to some known point of reference.

The text clearly shows that warships were also equipped with navigational maps. When the officers met, each brought his own navigational instruments, notably the *carti a falsi cumpassi* (these refer to dividers), which they used to determine the position of the fleet and the direction it should take. However, this was only possible when some feature of the coastline was visible, whereby they could realistically gauge the ship's position. Indirectly, the text also helps us understand why there were maps on board the vast majority of ships during the Middle Ages, even though these maps were not as accurate as today's navigational maps, and why each flag officer personally owned one or more maps. Alicudi, Filicudi, Vulcano and Ustica, islands situated north of Sicily, and Milazzo, the highest cape of northern Sicily, were points of reference they could identify before reaching the Sicilian coast. After leaving Cagliari, the ship's navigators were concerned about keeping the cape in view in spite of the unfavorable winds. They were consequently not as lost as one might think. They discussed the limited options open to them within the defined geographic region, being under the impression of already having lost their "direction," that is, the location of their ship. The orientation indicated on their compass and their estimation of the distance they had already traveled allowed them to deduce that they were close to the northern coast of Sicily. Their navigational maps reminded them of the many possibilities they had to consider before they could be sure of their position, since their maps had wide margins of error, up to a day and a half.

With their lists of toponyms that were directly linked to the drawings, which were really more mnemonic devices rather than realistic descriptions of the coastline, portolan maps helped their owners a lot, not only to infer the position of their ship but also to help them keep in mind the coastal features, be they natural or manmade, that they might come across and need to identify. Such maps were also a mariner's personal tool to help him remember and identify what he had seen. That is why the vast majority of captains, merchants, co-owners of ships and officers whose job it was to physically navigate a vessel, whether mercantile or military, possessed and used such maps through the two centuries of the late Middle Ages. It is not surprising, therefore, as explained in the 15th century by Benedetto Cotrugli in his *De navigatione*, that navigators had to demonstrate their ability to use maps in order to obtain public validation as a competent sailor.[14]

There is no doubt that Middle-Age documents and literature will continue to provide new evidence concerning the large-scale production and ownership of navigational maps. In this way, even the greatest skeptics will gradually cease to believe that portolan maps were not widely distributed among marine merchants and various other sailors who resided in the principal cities of the western Mediterranean to the end of the Middle Ages.

Ramon J. Pujades i Bataller
Original text translated by Laurent Bury

30
Angelino Dulcert,
Marine Map of the Mediterranean
Majorca, 1330

This is the oldest map produced in Majorca, signed and dated. Drawn on a double network of lines, it extends from the Canary Islands to the Persian Gulf and from Scandinavia to the Kingdom of Mali. The shapes being indicated in relief, the hydrography and the descriptions of the cities and rulers are typical of the Catalonian style of the end of the 15th century.

NLF, Paris, Maps and Plans, GE B-696 (RES).
Manuscript on velum, 40⅛ × 29½ inches (102 × 75 cm).

Works Cited

1. This article was written as part of a research project financed by the Spanish Ministry of Science and Innovation and titled "La Corona de Aragón en le Mediterráneo bajomedieval. Interculturalidad, mediación, integración y tranferencias culturales (HAR2010-16361)".

2. Tony Campbell, "Census of Pre-sixteenth Century Portolan Charts," *Imago Mundi*, 38, 1986, 67–94, and "Portolan Charts from the Thirteenth Century to 1500," in John Brian Harley and David Woodward (eds.), *Cartography in Pre-historic, Ancient and Medieval Europe and the Mediterranean* series, "The History of Cartography," vol. 1, Chicago/London, University of Chicago Press, 1987, 370–463. These two works were extensively revised and extended for the electronic version (http://www.maphistory. info/portolan.html).

3. Ramon J. Pujades i Bataller, *Les Cartes portolanes, la representació medieval d'una mar solcada/Portolan Charts: The Medieval Representation of a Ploughed Sea*, Barcelone, Institut Cartogràfic de Catalunya/Institut d'Estudis Catalans/Institut Europeu de la Mediterrània, 2007, 60–125 and 423–451.

4. Paolo Malanima, *Pre-modern European economy: One Thousand Years (10th–19th Centuries)*, Leyde/Boston, Brill, 2009, 252–292.

5. Ramon J. Pujades i Bataller, "References to Nautical Cartography in Medieval Documentation," in Ramon J. Pujades i Bataller *op. cit.*, 428–439.

6. Giovanna Petti Balbi, "I Catalani nella Genova tardomedievale," in *La Presència catalane a l'espai de trobada de la Mediterrània medieval. Noves fonts, recerques i perspectives*," proceedings of the international colloquium, Barcelona, May 13–16, 2009, to appear.

7. Gênes, Archivio di Stato di Genoa, *Notai antichi*, cart. 463, f.1-12 vo and 35–39.

8. Apart from the diverse documents attesting to the presence of maps aboard small ships, already indexed in the first list I published, we can cite *La mige carte de naveguar* (a half-sized navigation map) belonging to the Majorcan fisherman Rafel Garbi in 1458. Majorca, Arxiu del Regne de Mallorca, Protocols 1-134, f. 6–9. Transcription of a document published in Maria Barceló and Guillem Rosselló, *La Casa gòtica a la ciutat de Mallorca, Majorca*, Lleonard Muntaner, 2009, 118.

9. This confirms another letter from Valencia, dated December 3, 1397, in which Valencian representatives from the Datini company sent the following request from their Majorcan colleagues: *Avisateci se trovassi da conperare uno bello [m]appamondo e quello costerebe.* (Please let us know if you can find a nice world map for sale and what the price is.) See Angela Orlandi, *Mercaderies I diners : la correspondència datiniana enter València i Mallorca (1395–1398)*, Valence, Universitat de València, 2008, 142–143.

10. The documents, commentaries and English translation can be consulted in Ramon J. Pujades i Bataller, *Les Cartes...*, op.cit., 273–278 (Catalan)/497–498 (English). Campbell's interpretation can be read at http://www.maphistory. info/PortolanAttributions. html#contract.

11. Ramon J. Pujades i Bataller, *La Carta de Gabriel de Vallseca de 1439/Gabriel de Vallseca's 1439 Chart*, Barcelona, Lumenartis, 2009, 70–87 (Catalan)/308–316 (English).

12. Matilde Miquel Juan, *Retablos, prestigio y dinero. Talleres y mercado de pintura en la Valencia del gótico internacional*, Valencia, Universitat de València, 2008.

13. Barcelona, Arxiu de la Corona d'Aragó, *Cartes reial de Martí I*, appendix No. 148.

14. Ramon J. Pujades i Bataller, *op. cit*, 446.

31

The Use of a Map After a Storm
Letter in the Sicilian dialect, dated September 2, 1405

At the start of the 15th century, Sicily belonged
to the Aragonian crown. In this letter the royal
fleet physician, Rogerio di Camera, reports to King
Martin I regarding the return trip from Sicily of his
son, the prince. He explains how mariners used
maps to determine the position of the ship after
a storm.

Barcelona, Arxiu de la Corona d'Arago,
Cartes reials de Martí I, appenice no° 148.

31.

And when the weather improved, we rowed a course for Sicily, and after being about a hundred miles out at sea, we ran into unfavorable winds, the kind all sailors were in favor of turning back from. However the mentioned nobleman, since he was the nobleman, decided by himself to carry on, regardless of the misgivings of the sailors and their captain until it became possible to tack, saying that the wind would ease and the weather would improve, he argued like a sailor and expert such that the sailors did not know what to answer and began to tack. And so they tacked all day Wednesday and part of Thursday, and because of this manner of sailing, two galleons, that of the city of Valencia and the one from Mathieu di lu Re, became separated and lost from the rest of the fleet. But after the wind dropped we were able to advance by rowing throughout the day and the following night, such that by Friday morning the sailors thought that we were close to land. When daylight came and after three more hours had passed, no land could be seen and we were already short of water, such that we only had enough water for another day, and it was so fetid that the lord king had to add vinegar to the water to remove the bad taste, and virtually all other supplies were running short, except the biscuits. The lord king held a meeting with all the mariners in order to discuss our location and where we might be. One maintained that we were 50 miles in line from the swamps, another said that we were close to the islands of Alicudi and Filicudi, another said near Vulcano, and another near Milazzo. All indicated their doubts with their maps and compass. In the end, the lord king, seeing their lack of agreement, ordered that we row straight south, which was bound to bring us to one part or other of Sicily. This was done for the whole day, rowing with as much force as possible until the end of the afternoon, just before sunset. We did not see any sign of coastline and were in total confusion, such that the confused sailors said we had lost the arbitration. At that point the captain of the Castille galleon appeared and began to shout "Oh my good men, you are going there! You are going straight to Barbary! We have already left Sicily in the north!" Consequently, seeing such perilous discord, we feared greatly getting lost because we doubted that we could approach the coast of Sicily, which we were moving away from, and lacking water we were going to our demise. We continued to be greatly confused. Amid these debates someone started to cry "Land, land!," saying that he had seen it in the distance. And while one said that it was land, another said it was a thick cloud. Finally, as we drew near, we found that it was the island of Ustica. How happy we were at that point!

Text originally translated by Ramon Pujades and Emmanuelle Vagnon from the original Sicilian text shown opposite.

E abonantzatu lu tempu ni partemmu vocandu versu Sichilia, e essendu ben chentu miglia a mari ni incontrau ventu contrariu, per modu ki tutti li marinari acordavanu di tornari. Ali quali, lu dittu signuri comu signuri sforzu su sulu resistiu, comandando ki si tenissiru in mari quantu potissiru volaiandu, ca lu ventu si miteva o y abonantziria; pero ki era statu assignandu supra zo varii raxuni e comu marinaru e comu philosofu, ali quali li marinari, non sapendu rispunderi, incommenzaru a volaiari. E cussì andaru volaiandu lu di mercuri e parti di lu di iovi, in lu quali volaiare due galei, zoè quella di Valentia e di Matheu di lu Re, si sperderu di nui altri, e in quistu lu ventu abonazau, e per forza di remi voccamu avanti lu dittu iornu e la notte sequenti, per modu ki lu di venneri li marinari si credianu esseri apressu terra per la matina. E vinendu lu iornu e essendu ia terza passata, di nulla parti si vidia terra, e ia ni era mancata l'aqua, per modu ki non di haviammu si non per quellu iornu, e quella pocu fetia, per modu ki bisognava a lu signuri re biuri di lu achitu in l'aqua, per levanrindi lu mal sapuri, e quasi omni altra victualla ni era mancata excepto biscoctu ki haviamu. Lu signuri re fichi teneri consiglu a tutti li marinari ki arbitrasseru undi potiamu esseri. E l'unu dichia ki eramu a rassu di lu maresmu L miglia, e l'altru dichia ki eramu in derittu di li issuli di Arcudi e Filicudi, e l'altru di Bulcanu, e l'altru di Milatzii, mostrando loru dubii carti e falsi cumpassi. Allu fini lu signuri re, videndu loru discordii, comandau ki vocassimu avanti derittu per mezuiornu, ki per certu in alcuna parti di Sichilia prenderiamu. E fu ffattu tuttu lu iornu vocandu a grandi arigatta fini ala sera, a xxii huri, e per nulla banda vidiammu terra, e allura tutti fommu confusi, in tantu ki li marinari tutti confusi dichianu ki haviamu perduto lu arbitru. E par cussì vocandu avanti lu comitu di la galea di Castella; incomenzau a cridari "O, boni homini, undi andati! Ca vui andati in Barbaria! Ca ia ni havimu lassata Sichilia per tramuntana!" Allura nui, videndu tanti periculusi discordii appimu grande pagura di perderini, pero ki dubitavamu non volendu acustari in Sichilia indi allongassimu, e per deffetu di aqua ni perdissimu, e stavamu in grandi confusiuni. E standu in quisti dibati unu incomenzau a cridari terra, terra!, dicendu ki la vidia. E cussì pocu paria ki l'unu dichia ki era terra, l'altru ki era nebulatu. Allu fini, acustandusi, acordanu ki era la isula di Ustica. Comu e allura fomu tutti allegri!

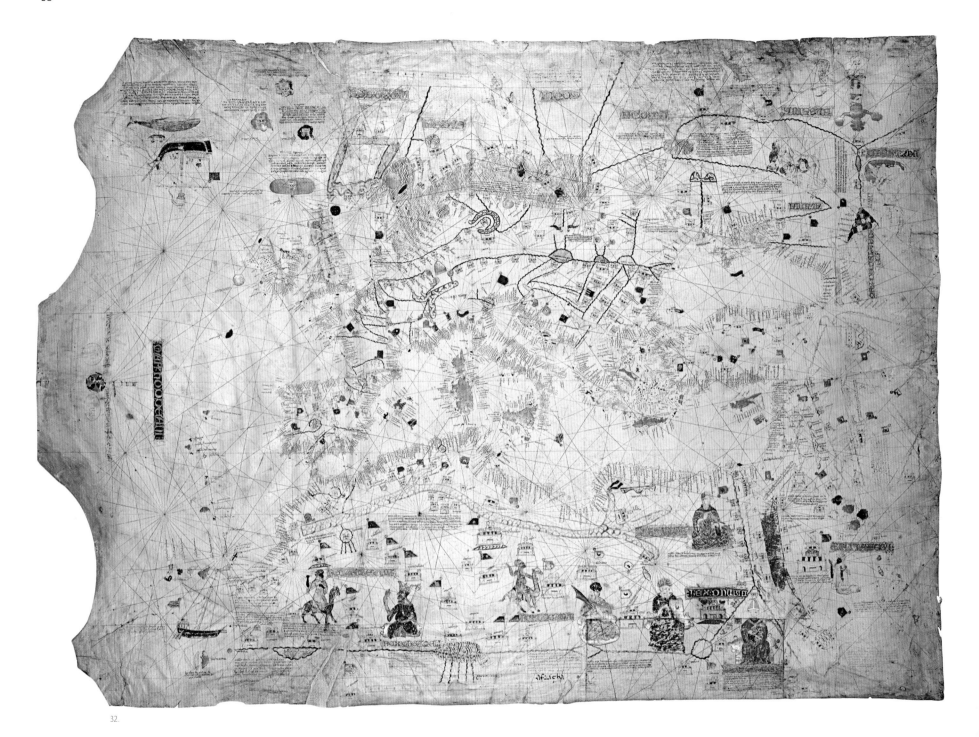

**Mecia de Viladestes,
Marine Map of the Mediterranean**
Majorca, 1413

Ordered by the prior of the nunnery of Valdemosa in Majorca, this luxurious Catalonian map is richly decorated with people and animals and describes the commercial routes of Africa (for ivory) and of the Persian Gulf (for gold and spices) as well as the transport of merchandise as far as Northern Europe. One can also see south of the Nile, with a picture of the priest John, the mystical Christian sovereign of Ethiopia, who is shown in bishop's garments.

NLF, Paris, Maps and Charts, GE AA-566 (RES).
Manuscript on velum, 46½ × 33¼ inches (118 × 84.5 cm).

33
Ethiopian Processional Cross
Ethiopia, region of Addis-Abeda, 15th century

During the 14th and 15th centuries, European Christians formed a military alliance with Ethiopian Christians against the powerful sultan of Egypt, in order to establish ties with their ruler, the "priest" Jean. The core of this magnificent processional cross is embossed on both sides by icons. One side shows the Virgin Mary and the infant Jesus, while the other side has three protector saints, the abbots Salama, Abreha and Asbeha.

Quai Branly Museum, Paris, Inv.74. 1994.9.1.
Copper alloy, 8⅞ × 12¼ inches (22.5 × 31.2 x cm).

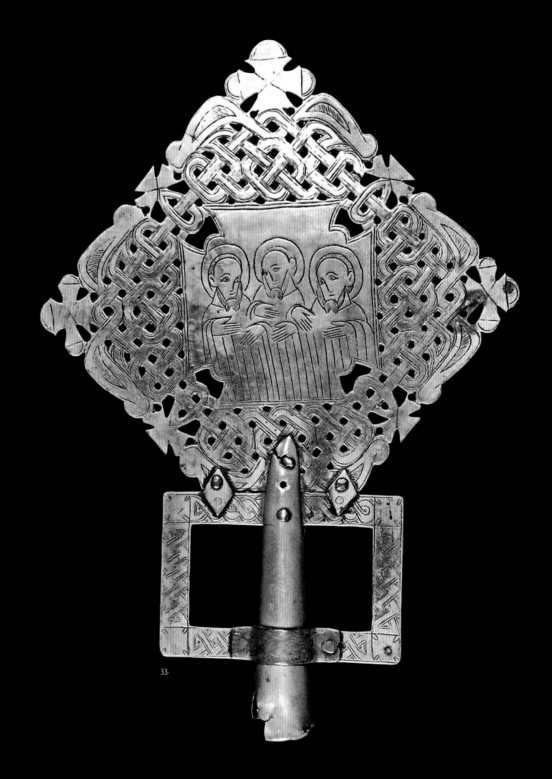

33.

34.

34
Sailor's Trunk
Nuremberg, 17th century

Since the Middle Ages, sailors have carried their personal belongings in trunks. These generally contained such documents as lists for after death, a list of contents, some clothes, a few personal belongings, and sometimes navigational instruments, such as maps and compasses. This common type of strongbox, made in Nuremberg during the 17th and 18th centuries, was used by ship captains to preserve important papers, precious objects and money.

Château Museum, Dieppe, Inv. 964.4.1.
29⅛ × 13 inches (74 × 33 cm) without handles, or 13⅜ inches (34 cm) with handles.

35
Grazioso Benincasa,
Map of the Central Mediterranean
Rome, 1467

The author's signature, his initial decorated with a golden watermark, can be seen above a map of Italy displaying the city of Ancone, his native town. Such very limited maps, which do not show continental details, are splendidly crafted, with alternating colors and meticulous calligraphy. The distance measures are placed at the corners.

NLF, Paris, Charts and Plans, GE DD-1988 (RES), f.5.
Manuscript on vellum, 8⅞ × 13¾ inches (22.5 × 35 cm).

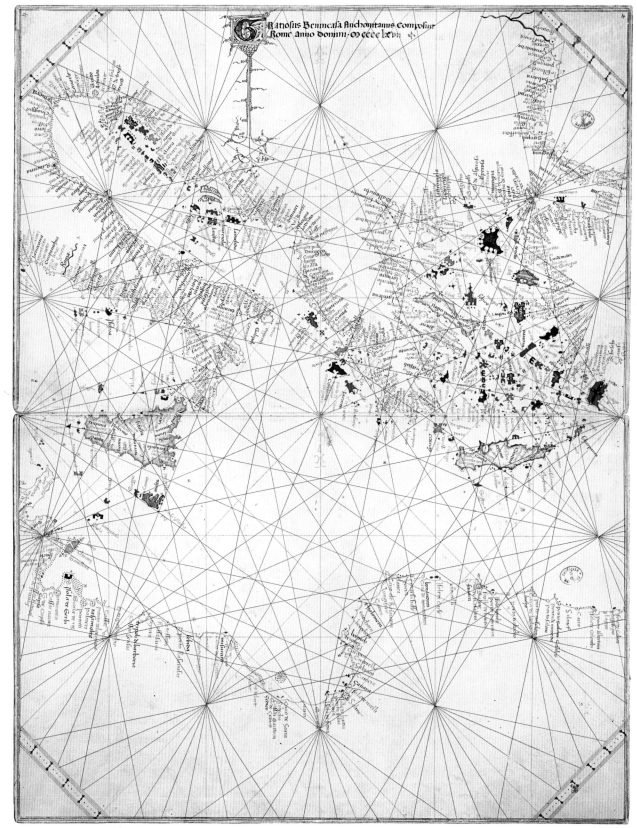

MEDITERRANEAN CARTOGRAPHERS OF THE 16TH AND 17TH CENTURIES

Corradino Astengo

36

Angelus, Virgin and Child
Marseille, 1575

Protective religious figures such as these (Christ, the Virgin, saints, etc.) often figured prominently on the "neck" of a parchment map and at the beginning or end of the volume of a parchment atlas. These figures are usually associated with the signature of the cartographer. On the example below, the name of the first owner is also shown, Cristol Viguié, who is undoubtedly from Marseille but was not an important individual, simply the owner of the ship.

NLF, Paris, Manuscripts, French 9669, f.11 v°.
Illuminated manuscript on parchment, 7½ × 10⅝ inches
(19 × 27 cm).

36.

During the era of European maritime exploration of the oceans and the new worlds, Mediterranean portolan map production continued for the most part along traditional lines. Moreover, the progress in astronomical navigation, which had been in use since the 16th century for long voyages over great distances along oceanic routes,[1] had little effect on the practices of Mediterranean sailors. As outlined in the work of Benedetto Cotrugli (1464) and later authors, sailors continued to navigate by dead reckoning and by estimating a ship's position through coastal reference points.[2] Nevertheless, some changes in the construction of maps are obvious, evidence of some interest in the scientific advances of the times, while the chart's decorative elements catered more to the tastes and artistic developments of the Renaissance.

However, demand for portolan maps remained strong and resulted in a large production in some big Mediterranean ports, particularly by smaller, family-run artisan studios, which were passed on from father to son. Among those documents that have survived to this day, portolan maps and atlases produced during the 16th and 17th centuries are about four times more plentiful than those dating to the 14th and 15th centuries. More maps are being discovered all the time in libraries and in private hands, to the point where over 800 examples are known. The wide range of owner's marks on these maps suggests that the pool of interested buyers had expanded considerably and, in addition to nobility, prelates and high officials, included captains and pilots for whom they no doubt represented souvenirs of entire lives spent at sea (see illustrations 36 and 37).

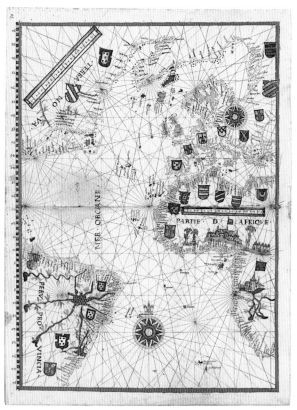

37.

37

Angelus, Map of the Atlantic Ocean
Marseille, 1575

One of the first nautical atlases produced in Marseille contains this richly illuminated map, which shows La Mina and Manicongo (Portuguese possessions in Africa), as well as the Amazon River, proof that Mediterranean cartographers were not just interested in the Mediterranean region. Curiously, in the north, a portion of Terra Nova is shown reattached to Europe.

NLF, Paris, manuscript in French 9669, f.9 v°- 10.
Illuminated manuscript on parchment, 14¾ × 10¾ inches
(37.5 × 27.4 cm)

38

François Ollive,
Special Map of the Mediterranean Sea
(detail)

See pages 84–85 for full caption and map.

ISTRIA

DALMACIE·

ALBANIE

POMANIE

DESTROIT DE COSTANTINOPLI

MER ADRIATIC VE·

GRECIA

ARMANIA

ROMAGNIE

SCLAVONIE

GOLFE·DE·VENISE·

NATOLIE

TOSCANE

LIA

NAPOLI

NIGROPONTI

ACHAIE

GALIFOLI

CALABRIA

CIPRE

ME

DI

L'ARCHIPELAGE·

S

CANDIA

NEE

MALTA

TER

RA

GOLFE·DE·LA·SIDRA

LIBIA·DISERTA

L'EGYPTE

TRIPOLI

BARCA·DISERTA

CAURO

AFRI
CA

L'FENIL

B
A
R
I
A

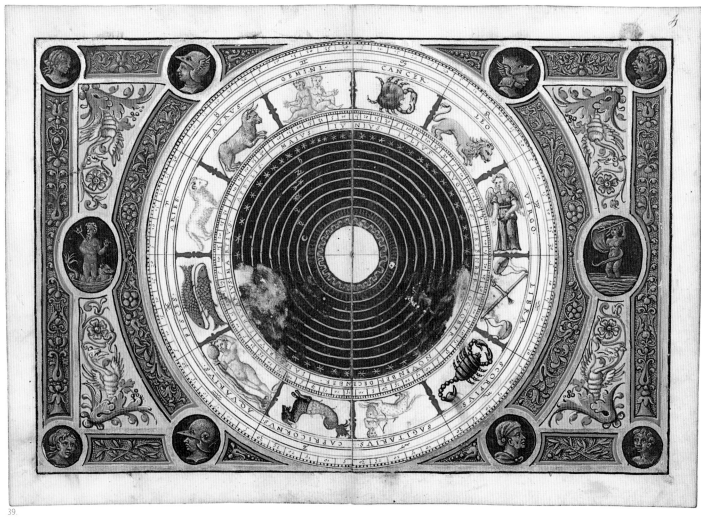

39.

39

Battista Agnese(?), Geocentric Cosmographic Representation with Signs of the Zodiac
Venice, circa 1550

This prolific and high-quality work is attributed to Battista Agnese, a Genovese hydrographer who lived in Venice. Atlases from his studio were often supplemented with hydrographic maps and calendars, world maps and representations of the systems of the world, underscoring the connection between cartography and cosmology.

NLF, Paris, Manuscripts, Latin 18249, f.3. v°-4
Illuminated manuscript on parchment, 12½ × 8¾ inches
(31.7 × 22.2 cm)

40

Carte de la Méditerranée faictte par Roussin sur le dessain de Jasques Collomb et Jaques Anthoine Ollandois (Map of the Mediterranean Done by Roussin, Based on the Design of Jasques Collomb and Jaques Anthoine Ollandois)
Marseille, 1672

Of the four maps of the Mediterranean included in this atlas, three were drawn up using English or Dutch hydrographic sources, including the one shown here, while the fourth conformed to the older Italian and provincial designs. The first three maps show the centerline of the Mediterranean correctly, placing Gibraltar at approximately the same latitude as Cyprus (35–360), while the latter, following medieval tradition, placed Gibraltar at the latitude of Alexandria.

NLF, Paris, Manuscripts, NAF 1465, 5ᵉ carte.
Illuminated manuscript on parchment, 31⅛ × 21⅞ inches
(79 × 55.5 cm)

40.

EVROPE

CARTE

Faicte Par Roussin Sur
Le Dessain De Iasques Collomb
et Iaques Anthoine Ollandois
1672.

SAVOYE   VENIZE

ITALIE   DALMATIE   POLONIE

PROVENCE   ESCLAVONIE   MER

CATALOGNE   GRECE   NOIRE

ASIE

TVNNIS

ALGER

BA   SVRIE

TRIPOLI

RIE

AFRIQVE   Echele Des Lieües

41
Jacopo Maggiolo,
Marine Map of the Mediterranean
Genoa, 1563

Jacopo Maggiolo, the official cartographer of the Genovese Republic, added some very rich iconography to this profuse map, which is adorned with gold, including vignettes of cities, images of European rulers sitting on thrones at the entrances of tents in Africa, ships in the Atlantic with unfurled sails and the Virgin and Child at the "neck" of the parchment.

NLF, Paris, Maps and Plans, Geographic Society, SG Y 1704 (RES).
Illuminated manuscript on parchment, 40⅜ × 33½ inches
(102.5 × 85 x cm).

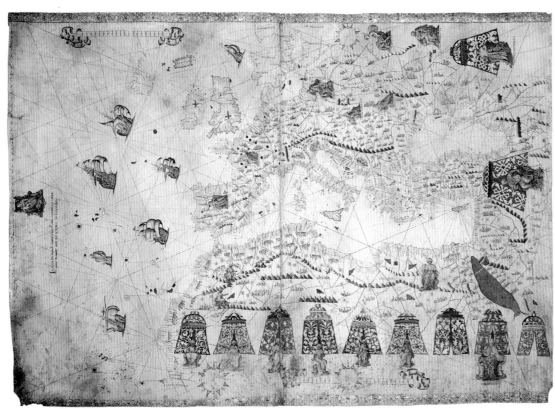

41.

MAP CONSTRUCTION AND DECORATION

The chief characteristics of portolan maps from the Middle Ages remained unchanged throughout the 16th and 17th centuries. Charts and atlas were always drawn on parchment, a valuable and very resilient material. The wind rose lines were coded in colors (black for the eight primary winds, green for half-winds and red for the 16 quarter-winds) and the positions of the toponyms never varied.

On the other hand, technical innovations also appeared in the 16th century, with regard to the orientation of the Mediterranean Sea and the use of detailed scales. Traditional portolan maps invariably showed the Mediterranean misaligned along its east-west axis; it was always shown between 8° and 11°15' higher in a counterclockwise direction, such that the Strait of Gibraltar appeared at the same latitude as the Nile delta. This error is attributed to problems in determining the correct magnetic declination.[3] In all likelihood sailors knew that Crete and Cyprus were more or less at the same latitude as the Strait of Gibraltar, and the misrepresentation evident on portolan maps did not relate except in such a way that north coincided with the direction indicated by a compass.

A latitude scale was introduced on some maps of the Mediterranean during the first half of the 16th century. Centered in the Atlantic Ocean, it indicated a latitude of about 36° north for the Strait of Gibraltar, but it was not valid for the central or western Mediterranean. During the second half of the century, we see several attempts to correct this error. One of the first examples is shown in an anonymous portolan atlas held in the French National Library.[4] In addition to adding latitude scales on all his maps, the author divides the Mediterranean onto two pages and sets the eastern portion further south relative to the western portion in such a way that Crete and Cyprus are on a latitude that is approximately correct, between 35° and 36° north. However, there is no continuity between these two maps, and this lone adjustment method did not seem to have provided an effective solution.

This problem was accentuated when the western magnetic declination, which had varied between 8° and 11° from the 12th to the 15th centuries, began to diminish at the beginning of the 16th century and ceased completely in the middle of the next century. At that point positions on traditional maps did not even coincide with compass directions. During the 17th century, several cartographers attempted to correct this error by simply printing maps in which the Mediterranean Sea's axis was rotated in the opposite direction, thereby placing Crete and Cyprus once again at the same latitude as the Strait of Gibraltar. Consequently we see that Giovanni Oliva, François Ollive, Giovanni Battista and especially Giovan Fancesco Monno corrected their maps so that sailing in the Mediterranean could be done using astronomical navigation.

In order to compete with the rise in printed map production, the shops of principal mapmakers, including those of Battista Agnese in Venice, Joan Martines in Messina and Giovanni Battista Cavallini in Livorno, started to produce atlases supplemented with tables and also with terrestrial maps that show the whole world, including the continents, regions and islands. While the sources for these maps in the Mediterranean and Europe remained the nautical tradition, in the rest of the world maps became more heterogenous, going from insular maps and Ptolemy's Geography to the contemporary printed maps and atlases.

Decorative elements were of prime importance in the production of Mediterranean maps, most of which were destined for work cabinets and libraries. Ornamental wind roses, small depictions of cities, images of rulers, plants and animals, real or imagined, were copious, and in the 16th century they often indicated the work of expert artisans (see illustration 42). We also see with increasing frequency depictions of religious figures, the Virgin Mary, Jesus Christ or saints on the "neck" on such maps (which corresponds to the neck of the animal whose skin was used for the parchment) or the frontispiece of atlases. The quality of decorative elements declined during the 17th century, and miniatures were often replaced by printed images that were glued to the parchment.

DYNASTIES, STUDIOS AND THE PROFESSION OF CARTOGRAPHY

Because they signed their maps and atlases, we know of about 80 names of authors from the 16th and 17th centuries, to which must be added those of the cartographers who are known only through written sources that indicate their profession.

Through archival documentation, we know of the Maggiolo family in Genoa and their opposition, Battista Agnese (see illustration 39), a Genovese working in Venice. Numerous documents have allowed us to reconstruct the lineage of the Maggiolo family and follow the trials and tribulations of their lives in managing the studio *approvato e privilegiato*, which was active in Genoa from 1518 and enjoyed a position of dominance and profited from public support. For Agnese, in contrast, and despite the operation's extensive production, archival records have revealed nothing, to the point where it is even difficult to determine how long he was active. This might well indicate the difference between shops that enjoyed a semi-public status and ones that were an entirely private business.

Such reasons no doubt explain why unsigned maps attributed to Maggiolo are very rare, with only two or three known examples in total, so much so that we can conclude the missing signature was simply due to an oversight on his part. Conversely, more than half of the works attributed to Agnese lack signatures. According to Baldacci, such anonymous copies were most likely made by the shop's employees, with or without authorization from the owner, and then sold at considerably lower prices.[5] Such practices may have been possible in a private studio, but not in a public or semi-public establishment, which was more controlled.

The profession of cartography is hard to characterize, and we have to look at it more as an individual undertaking. The distinction between professional and occasional cartographers is also blurred. In case of the former, the owners of genuine studios were active full time and used them as their principal source of income. As a prime example one must point out the Genovese cartographer Battista Agnese, without a doubt the most productive mapmaker, who manufactured more than 80 maps and atlases between 1536 and 1564.[6] His Venice studio typically subdivided various tasks among cartographers, copyists, designers and illuminators, resulting in an organizational structure that guaranteed continuous production. For example, in 1542, a series of atlases signed on May 15, June […], June 28 and September 25 was produced.

We can also categorize as professionals the father and son studio of Pietro and Jacopo Russo, who were active from 1508 to 1588 in the port city of Messina, as well as Giovanni Battista and Pietro Cavallini, also father and son, who worked in Livorno from 1635 to 1688. Even more important was the shop of Vesconte and Jacopo Maggiolo (see illustration 41), who, under the title of *magister cartarum pro navigando*, received official sanction from the Republic of Genoa. However, the level of production that has survived to this day does not seem to us as a sufficient criterion to categorize someone as professional. Other members

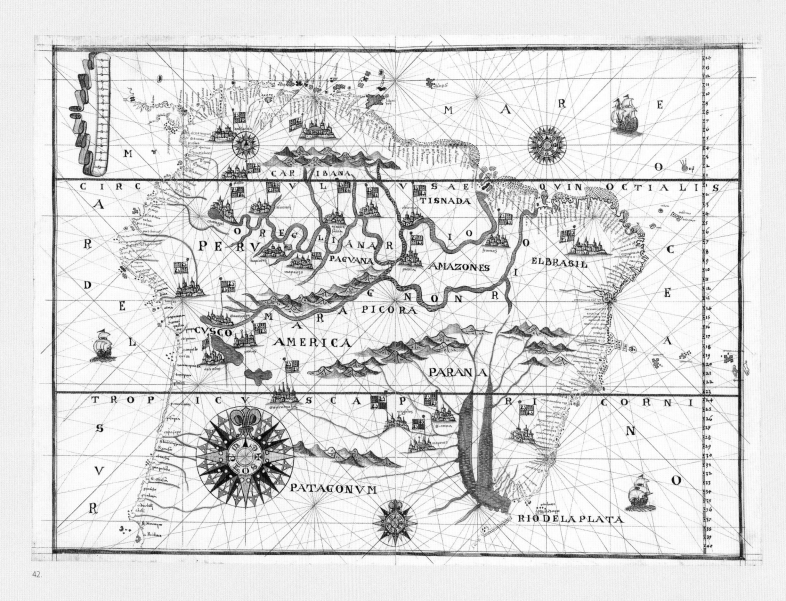

42.

42
Joan Martines,
Map of South America and Adjacent Oceans
Messina, 1583

Of Catalonian origin but working in Messina, Joan Martines is the author of a luxurious world atlas, profusely ornate and illuminated. European seats of power, fortified cities, sinuous rivers, mountains and hills, wind roses, etc., all contributed to his maps often being bound in precious collections, such as this one, which dates from the 18th century and belonged to the marquis de Paulmy.

NLF, Paris, Arsenal, Ms. 8223, 3rd map (right part).
Illuminated manuscript on parchment, 22⅞ × 16 (58 × 40.5 cm).

43.

Works Cited

1. See pages 126–135.

2. Benedetto Cotrugli, *De navigatione liber*, Italian manuscript, 1464, Yale University, Beinecke Rare Book and Manuscript Library, M5 557; Pantero Pantera, *L'Armata navale*, Rome, Egidio Spada, 1614, and Giovan Francesco Monno, *Arte della vera navegatione*, Italian manuscript, 1633, Genoa, Biblioteca Universitaria, MSS.F. VII.4.

3. See glossary.

4. Corradino Astengo, "Tradition et innovation dans la cartographie nautique manuscrite : l'atlas Rés Ge EE 5610 de la Bibliothèque nationale de France," *Le monde des cartes*, 2005, No. 184, 23–30.

5. Osvaldo Baldacci, *Introduzione all studio delle geocarte nautiche di tipo mediavale e la raccolta dell Biblioteca Comunale di Siena*, Florence, Olschki, 1990, 71.

6. There is also a portolan that is dated 1514 and signed "Baptista Januensis" and is attributed to him. If this attribution is correct, his active life lasted 50 years.

7. Secondary centers were located in Albissola, Alexandria, Barcelona, Civitavecchia, Crete, Malta, Palermo, Pisa, Rome, Safed, Sienna and Toulon.

8. The circumstance of Joan (or Giovanni) Oliva are typical: He lived in Messina from 1592 to 1599, in Naples from 1601 to 1603, followed by a first return to Messina from 1606 to 1608. He then lived in Malta in 1611, in Marseille from 1612 to 1614, a second return to Messina in 1614, a return to in Marseille in 1615, and, finally, he moved to Livorno in 1616, where he seemed to settle permanently, as he was still there in 1643.

43

Alvise Gramolin,
Marine Map of the Aegean Sea
Venice, 1624

The Greek archipelago, which has been thoroughly explored by sailors for thousands of years, has been an area of dispute and often received special attention from marine cartographers. The tents, shields and crescent moon on this map underscore the Ottoman Empire's dominance in the region, but the cross atop the Island of Rhodes and the view of Troy, in Asia Minor, suggest that this was not always the case.

NLF, Paris, Maps and Plans, GE B 550 (RES).
Illuminated manuscript on parchment, 25½ × 42⅛ inches
(65 × 107 cm).

of the Maggiolo family who also earned the official designation of cartographers, namely Cornelio, Nicolò and Cornelio II, were also professionals even though they left us no maps. And let us not forget, as indicated in the Maggiolo family archives, that these enterprises not only manufactured maps but also compasses and hourglasses and that they repaired such instruments.

Among part-time cartographers, sea-faring men were foremost, such as the Greek Antonio Millo, pilot and port master of Candie and Zante, and Admiral Marco Fassoi. For the latter, mapmaking was probably a secondary activity that he undertook without financial gain. Conversely, Millo was exceedingly productive, so it is hard to determine what his primary activity was. Some unexpected professionals were also involved with cartography. For instance, Giovan Francesco Monno of Monaco listed himself as a surgeon in the most important of his works, *L'Arte della vera navegatione*. With respect to Bartolomeo Crescenzio, Francesco Maria Levanto and Battista Testa Rossa, they seem more like savants than cartographers, since the few maps they did produce served almost exclusively to support theories they espoused in their works. Finally we must also include religious men who usually only left us one very meticulous work that was likely the result of extended studies; Nicolò Guidalotti from Mondavio, the author of an atlas that required five months to complete, from the month of December to May 1646, is an example.

PRODUCTION CENTERS

We have identified at least 20 centers of portolan map production that were active in the Mediterranean region between the 16th and 17th centuries. Among these, eight were very productive, thereby indicating that several professional studios had a stable and prolonged presence. It seems the dozen or so other centers only occasionally engaged in map production.[7] An important aspect of that era was that cartographers exhibited a remarkable degree of mobility and migrated from one port to another, in search no doubt of the best opportunities or more favorable working conditions.[8] Some of the more open-minded political locales, like Venice, Livorno and Marseille, readily accepted foreigners who brought new energy and knowledge. By contrast, in Genoa, the effective monopoly of the Maggiolo family, which established itself in 1519 and continued for some 130 years, excluded foreign cartographers and forced other Genovese cartographers, like Battista Agnese and Giovanni Battista Cavallini, to immigrate in order to practice their trade.

Some of the most productive cartographic centers were already active during the Middle Ages. These included Palma de Majorca, Genoa, Venice and Ancône. In Majorca, marine cartography began in the early 16th century during a time of decline, but it then flourished again, this time beyond the island of Majorca, thanks to the Olives family, who expanded to other Mediterranean ports. The founder of this veritable dynasty was Bartomeu Olives, who left Palma to establish himself first in Venice then Messina and then Palermo. We know of at least 13 cartographers from this family. In Italy they changed their name to Oliva and in Marseille to Ollive. In Venice, geographic maps were always seen as tools to control and manage territorial possessions by different regimes. However, these regimes did not seems to be very interested in portolan maps, which were so important for commerce and navigation. Production of portolans was left entirely to private initiatives and in large measure in the hands of foreigners, like the aforementioned Genovese Battista Agnese and the Greeks Johannes Xenodocos, Antonio Millo and Giorgio Sideri, known as the Callapoda. Production of portolan maps did not last long in Ancône. During the second half of the 15th century, after having worked in Genoa, Venice and Rome, Grazioso Benincasa, without a doubt the most important cartographer of his era, returned to establish himself in Ancône, his native city, where he practiced his profession and was later followed by his son Andrea and by Comte and Angelo Freducci, another father and son. Local demand for maps, however, seems to have declined significantly by then, and it eventually ceased altogether in the 17th century, probably because of a lack of innovation.

During the 16th and 17th centuries, the cities of Naples, Messina, Livorno and Marseille all became major medieval capitals due to the enormous growth in marine traffic. In Naples, a very populated and prosperous city, marine cartography did not develop until the second half of the 16th century, with the arrival of members of the Olives-Oliva family, namely Jaume, Domingo and Juan Riczo, father, son and grandson, respectively. At the end of the century, the Calabrasian Domenico Vigliarolo also worked in Naples and later immigrated to Seville, where he changed his name to Domingo de Villaroel and became *cosmógrafo del Rey* in the Casa de contratación. In any case, around 1620, all cartographic activity seems to have halted in Naples. The port of Messina also experienced great growth, thanks to its central location in the Mediterranean

and its control of the Strait of Messina. The first cartography studio was opened there at the beginning of the 16th century by Pietro Russo, and it continued under his son Jacopo. A little later, Joan Martines, who was probably Catalan, arrived and left a rich collection of portolan maps and atlases. He was followed by other members of the Oliva family, including Placidus Caloiro and Oliva, a family that dominated mapmaking in the 17th century (see illustration 44), at least from a quantitative standpoint, having left us some 30 works. In Livorno, the prosperity of cartographers was basically due to the Grand Duke of Tuscany's interest in marine matters and the presence of the order of the knights of Saint Stephen. This religious order of knights was created in 1561 to protect the Mediterranean against the Turks and pirates from Barbary. Most of the cartographers who worked there were foreigners, like Vicko Volcic, alias Vincenzo Volcio, from Ragusa; Giovanni Oliva, a member of the Olives dynasty; and Giovanni Battista and Pietro Cavallini, from Genoa. It was in Marseille that marine cartography developed last, with close ties to the Oliva family, first Giovanni then Salvatore and finally François, who changed his name to Ollive (see illustrations 38 and 45). Two members of the Roussin family, Augustin and Jean-François (though we do not know how they were related), also worked in Marseille, as did Estienne and Jean-André Brémond, who were active in the late 17th century, at the point when production was declining.

In conclusion, although the most important clients of portolan mapmakers were members of the ruling classes who lived in the economic and cultural capitals of their times, Rome, Florence, Paris, etc., map production centers were in the major port cities, since these were crucial links between manufactured products and the practical reality of navigation. Nevertheless, toward the end of the 17th century, undoubtedly because of prices being too high and changes in preferences among partners, map production declined and the workshops where they were manufactured disappeared completely. Only Marseille remained active, since traditional cartographic practices were adapted to new market demands and mapmakers switched to printed maps. Jean-André Brémond teamed up with Henry Michelot to commercialize printed marine maps that incorporated new cartographic features. That was the beginning of modern hydrography.

Corradino Astengo

44
Francesco Oliva,
Marine Map of the Mediterranean
Messina, 1603

Francesco Oliva was from the Oliva family, who were originally from Majorca. He shows here the geopolitical regions of the Mediterranean at the beginning of the 17th century, featuring 11 rulers, in the northern Mediterranean with their armor and sword, and in the south with long robes and scimitars, either facing or ignoring one another. Horses, elephants, camels and palms form a contrasting background.

NLF, Paris, Charts and Plans, GE C 5093 (RES).
Illuminated manuscript on parchment, 21¼ × 35½ inches (54 × 90 cm).

44.

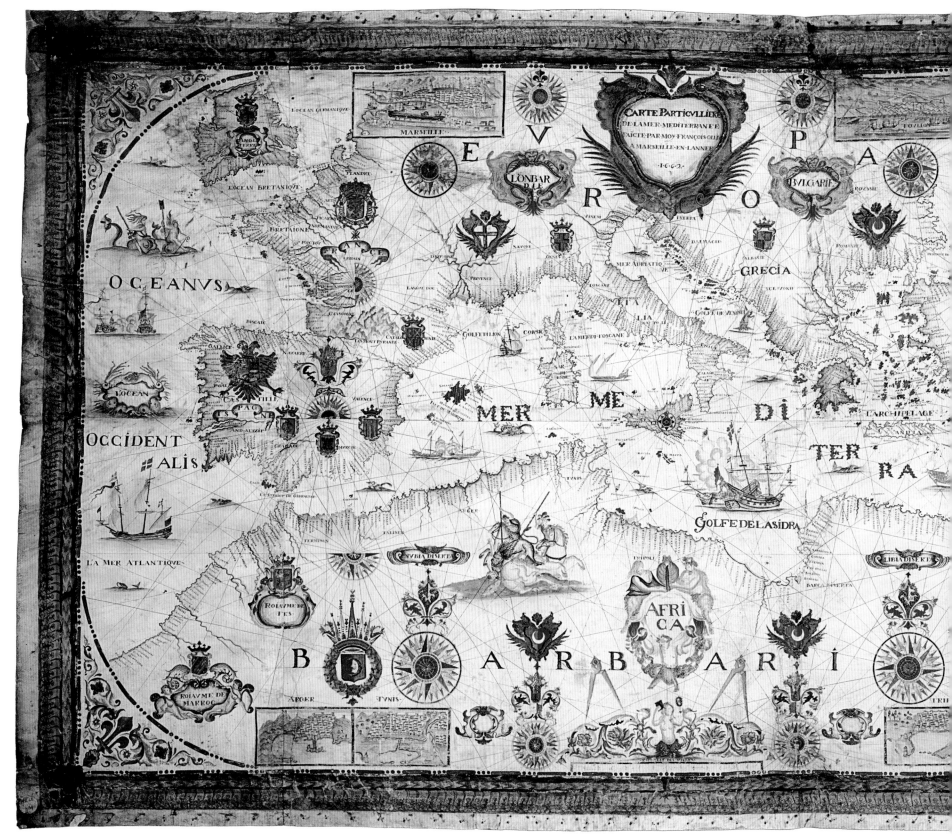

45
François Ollive,
Special Map of the Mediterranean Sea
Marseille, 1662

Made of six combined skins, this map is the work of a prolific hydrographer from Marseille who was knowledgeable about color palettes and had a taste for abundant iconography. Inserted into a tromp l'oeil–style frame, it unfolds into a tableau of hunting scenes in Africa, naval battles near Crete, views of cities (Marseille, Toulon, Algiers, Tunis, Tripoli, Alexandria), sites of Christian and Muslim saints — many travel invitations in time and space.

ANTIQUE, MEDIEVAL AND NEW WORLD CITIES ON PORTOLAN MAPS

Jean-Yves Sarazin

La carta dello navigator la quale è universal guida al nostro proposito, è signa de tri cose principali, cioè venti, migla et nome delli lochi.

The navigational map, which is for us a universal guide, shows us three principal things: the winds, the miles and the names of places.

Benedetto COTRUGLI,
De navigatione, f. 61 vº. This
navigation treatise by Benedetto
Cotrugli was dedicated to the
Venetian Senate in 1464 (Yale
university, Beinecke Rare Book
and Manuscript Library, Medieval
and Renaissance Manuscripts,
MS 557).

Portolan maps can be distinguished from other representations of the world through some particular graphic elements, including wind, or rhumbs, lines, distance scales in miles and toponyms. Indeed, some of the most plain portolans — notably those of Petrus Vesconte — depict the area between the Strait of Gibraltar and the Black Sea without any beautifying images on the shoreline. Ports and shelters along the coastline are identified by a series of colored names written in red or black if not in gold. Beginning in the 14th century, however, cartographers began to supplement the coastlines with sketches outlining urban centers. On maps like these, regardless of which continent was being depicted, a coherent and repeated system was used to designate cities. These included antique cities now long gone (Troy, Nineveh, Susiana, and Persepolis);

contemporary maritime city-states (Genoa, Venice); mercantile cities (Vicina, at the mouth of the Danube, Damascus, Cairo [Babylon]; African cities (Timbuktu, Mogadishu (see illustration 49); and Asian cities (Aden, Hormuz, Peking). What was the reason for showing portraits of such cities on portolan maps, be they coastal ports or inland centers?

In 1339, Angelino Dulcert in Majorca inserted, in the form of vignettes, images of the main cities of his time on his maps (see illustration 47). Not limiting himself to coastal cities, he also included those further inland, including Paris, Rome, Salamanca, Bologna, the hanseatic cities of Lübeck and Stettin, the African cities of Fez and Tilimpsen, and the caravan centers Segelmese and Timbuktu. Dulcert did not try to reproduce the topography of these distant cities, which he undoubtedly had not visited. Instead, he tried to establish a simple method that could be applied to all territories and all latitudes. Soleri, Cresques (the presumed author of the *Catalonian Atlas*) and Viladestes (see illustration 32) followed his example and marked important Mediterranean ports, both northern and southern, including Alexandria, Cairo (see illustration 52), Tripoli, Tunis, Bougie, Algiers, Cerceli, Oran, Ceuta, Salé and Zamora. Between 1375 and 1550, portolan mapmakers showed the importance of coastal sub-Saharan cities in Africa. These proved to be of key importance in commercial circles and were attractive locations for Genovese, Venetian and Aragonian merchants trafficking in gold, people, ivory and salt with traders coming on camelback from southern Africa. Apart from the *Catalonian Atlas*, which stood out through its exceptional coverage of Asia, most portolan mapmakers focused their attention on Africa as the world beyond Europe and included its cities, people, fauna and flora, uneven grounds, waterways and resources along with descriptive vignettes of buildings, topographic descriptions and various legends.

The parchment sheets of the *Catalonian Atlas* are cluttered with urban images of military and religious buildings, which are readily recognized by their conical roofs topped by a cross or dome (see illustration 46), depending on whether they are in Christian or Muslim countries. Cities are depicted by enclosures that might be crenate and covered with blemishes and a gate with rising tower that occasionally frame two similarly crenate turrets. The latter rise up to form two or three circular, overlapping shapes of decreasing size, thereby forming successive terraces of sorts. There is a

distinct hierarchy regarding the choice of shape, size and number of these symbols, which were used to depict cities of varying importance. For cities crossed by a body of water, two symbols are shown (e.g., Peking) or even three, as with Paris (see illustration 46), where two vignettes are displayed on opposite sides of the Seine, as well as a red one in the middle of the river, representing the Île de la Cité.

At the beginning of the 16th century, Portuguese conquests were indicated on the great world planispheres by symbolic representation of their fortresses. For example, in 1445 Arguin is shown facing Senegal, and in 1471 Elmina is indicated on the coast of Ghana. In 1591, the producer of the illuminated *Miller Atlas* identifies Arab cities (Aden, Hormuz) and cities in Persia (Suse and Persepolis), India (Pundranagara in Bengal) and Burmu (Aracam or Garmana, ancient names of Rangoon) in similar ways. Looking at the outlines of these vignettes, we see that cities placed in relief (Tekour, Aden, Potosí, Quito) are opposed to those on flattened fields (Timbuktu, Mogadishu). The authors always show the former cities with monumental and military characteristics and the latter with religious or commercial features. The Dulcert example was followed for a long time with respect to Africa, in order to help map readers differentiate Christian and Islamic areas, by using bell towers and crosses for Christian territories and domes and crescents for Muslim territories.

In the 17th century, it was no longer as important to represent political or religious capitals as it was to designate commercial centers, vital to European economies in Africa, the Americas and Asia. These served as European and indigenous trading centers. In the Indian Ocean, we note cursory views or vignettes of Sofala, Mozambique, Mombasa, Socotra, Hormuz, Goa, Muscat as well as the fortress of Diu. In South America, Lima is indicated (Cidade de los Reis, see illustration 50), while in Asia minor, the cities of Troy (Trogia), Burnoa are shown, as is Securio, on the Asia minor plateau, close to the coast of the Sea of Marmara.

Regarding the Mediterranean world, for the portolan maps made by François Ollive (working in Marseille from 1643 to 1664), which constitute the *terminus ad quem* of our discipline, the author sets aside a part of the margins for simple depictions of the big provincial French ports, Marseille and Toulon; Italian ports, Genoa and Naples; and North African ports, Algiers, Tunis, Tripoli and Alexandria (see illustration 45). Such city portraits became part of the tradition of cavalier depictions in the 15th century and were widely distributed through printing the following century. On one map from 1662, Marseille is highlighted by the Fort of Saint Nicholas, which was built in 1660 by order of the young King Louis XIV; in addition the jetty of Genoa is also clearly shown. This was undoubtedly done to emphasize the maritime powers of the Mediterranean, favoring commerce during peacetime.

Some of the more prestigious maps show images of major world cities, maritime powers, commercial capitals, mythical or long-disappeared cities as well as trading centers established by Europeans in Africa and Asia. Over the course of centuries, these provided iconographic pretexts for a maritime cartography for which the geographic content seemed to be supplanted in favor of purely decorative elements. In doing so these maps reveal a codification that is at once political, geographic, economic and at times religious (for cities like Mecca, Rome or Jerusalem). Cartographers and illuminators of portolan maps had developed a European, highly schematic way of portraying urban centers, and they applied this model to Indian, African and American cities along more imaginary than realistic lines. Consequently, deliberately or not, they drew European-style medieval urban landscapes, as if towered buildings surrounded by walls had become some sort of international urban standard.

Jean-Yves Sarazin

46
Catalonian Atlas
(detail)
Majorca, 1375

The four maps from the *Catalonian Atlas* show African, European and Asian cities by the hundreds as a kind of pictogram from which rise fortified buildings, which are indicative of their political affiliations. See pages 48–49 and 52 for the full panel.

NLF, Paris, Manuscripts, Spanish 30 (RES).
Illuminated manuscript on parchment, 12 half-sheets, 9⅞ × 25¼ inches (25 × 64 cm).

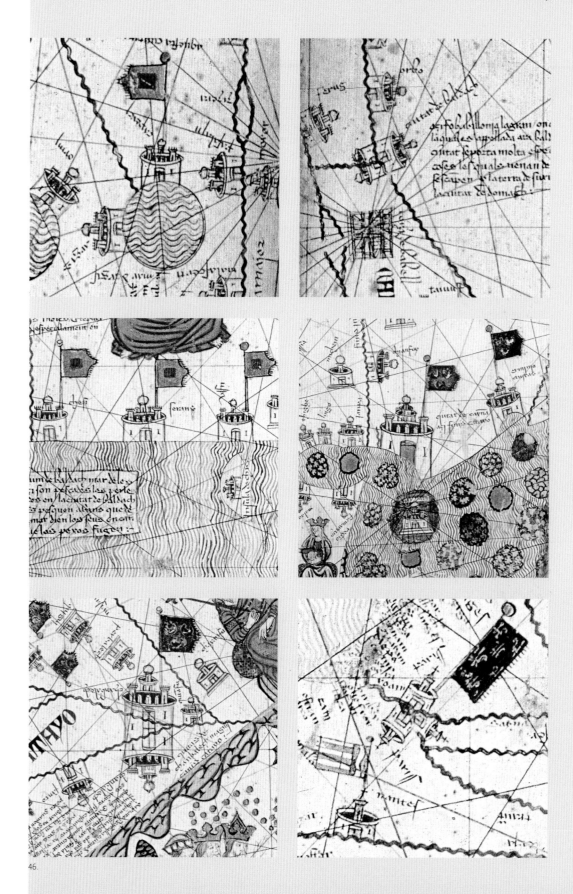

46.

47.

48.

49.

50.

51.

52.

47
Angelino Dulcert,
Marine Map of the Mediterranean
(detail)
Majorca, 1339

The southern portion of this atlas is labeled terra nigrorum. Angelino Dulcert broke new ground by showing the mercantile cities lining the trans-African trade routes — including Sidjilmassa (Sigelmessa) in Morocco and Bouda (Buda) and Tabelbalat (Taberbert) in Algeria — along which Sudanese gold reached North African ports. See page 64 for the full map.

NLF, Paris, Maps and Plans, GE B 696 (RES).
Manuscript on velum, 40⅛ × 29½ inches (102 × 75 cm).

48
Mecia de Viladestes,
Marine Map of the Mediterranean
(detail)
Majorca, 1413

It is impossible to recognize Venice's distinctive cityscape in this depiction by Mecia de Viladestes, since he uses the same graphic codes for every great city near a body of water, using the "urban" symbol on both sides of a river. He also likens a lagoon to a river! See entire map on page 68.

NLF, Paris, Maps and Plans, GE AA 566 (RES).
Manuscript on velum, 46½ × 33¼ inches (118 × 84.5 cm).

49
Miller Atlas
(detail)
Lisbon, 1519

Mogadishu (Mogadoxo) was definitely one of the most active ports on the African coast, although the richness of its merchants did not help to enhance its architecture, as was the case in the mercantile cities of Europe. See entire map on pages 182–183.

NLF, Paris, Maps and Plans, GE DD 683 (RES), f.3.
Illuminated manuscript on parchment, 23¼ × 16½ inches (59 × 42 cm).

50
Map of the Atlantic Ocean
(detail)
Portugal, circa 1550

Lima was founded by Francisco Pizarro in 1535 under the name of Cidade de los Reis and was at the core of the Spanish colonial domain — and it has never looked more flamboyant than on this map. At the same time, the depiction of the Indian city of Quito on the slopes of Pichinda owes much to mapmaker's imagination. See entire map on page 135.

NLF, Paris, Charts and Plans, GE B 1148 (RES).
Illuminated manuscript on parchment, 34⅝ × 28¾ inches (88 × 73 cm)

51
François Ollive,
Map of the Mediterranean
(detail)
Marseille, 1662

We see here two standardized images of the ports of Algiers and Tunis in the mid-17th century that bear some resemblance to the actual cities. See page 40 for full map.

NLF, Paris, Maps and Plans, GE A 850 (RES).
Illuminated manuscript on parchment, 77⅛ × 48 inches (196 × 122 cm).

52
Gabriel de Vallseca,
Marine Map of the Mediterranean
(detail)
Majorca, 1447

Gabriel de Vallseca depicts Cairo (*Babylonia*), the commercial metropolis of Abdalwadides, as a walled city with many high towers. He thereby helped to promote the perception of Western urbanization as being universal.

NLF, Paris, Maps and Plans, GE C 4607 (RES).
Illuminated manuscript on parchment, 37 × 23¼ inches (94 × 59 cm).

INSULAR MARITIME COSMOGRAPHY AND EUROPEAN EXPANSION DURING THE RENAISSANCE

Georges Tolias

The insular, that is, a book about islands (from *insularium* in Latin or *isolario* in Italian), is a type of geographic literature that bloomed during the age of great discoveries. This literature was focused on a new type of nautical cosmography, an eclectic encyclopedia of island cartography that offered a novel way of representing the oceanic space beyond continental coasts, which typical portolan maps described.

Islands have always been associated with notions of travel, exploration and territorial expansion. The inventor of this style of cartography, the Florentine monk Cristoforo Buondelmonti, provides a good example of the underlying basis of insular geography.[1] His book *Liber insularum Archipelagi*, written in Rhodes or Constantinople around 1420, contains descriptions and maps of the islands of the Ionian and Aegean Seas, as well as important coastal locations like Constantinople, Gallipoli, Attica and the straits of the Black Sea (see illustration 55).[2] At this time, the Ottoman Turks defied the rulers of Venice, Genoa and France and were threatening their colonies in the eastern Mediterranean and adjoining feudal centers established after the dissolution of the Byzantine Empire, following the fourth crusade, in 1204. Buondelmonti proposed a scholarly and historical revival of the Greek Orient by way of a collection of the Latinate past and present of the archipelago's islands. His primary source, like a traveling companion if not his guide, was Virgil, whose poetry alluding to these regions he cited as often as he could. This omnipresent echo from the past transformed *Liber insularum Archipelagi* into a kind of geographic documentary of the travels of Aeneas amid the Greek islands and promoted an image of the archipelago as an area that shared an ancient Roman heritage.

By combining geographic descriptions of maritime regions with a novel-like narrative, Buondelmonti did not border the seas by their coastlines as was done on portolan maps. Instead, *Liber insularum* focused more on the contents of the seas, which were both insular and fragmented. It is therefore not surprising that, during this time of expanding marine horizons, his work was imbued with a rich tradition. Dozens of editions of this treatise in various languages were disseminated during the 15th century. In some versions, the large Mediterranean islands were also included, namely Sicily, Sardinia and Corsica. The atlas of the Greek islands gradually became an atlas of the entire Mediterranean. This progress of transformation of Buondelmonti's *Liber insularum* led to *Insularium illustratum*, which was drafted in Florence between 1480 and 1490 by Henricus Martellus Germanus, a scholarly German who was equally known for his extravagant copies of Ptolemy's *Geography* as for his modern maps. In his insular, Martellus emphasized the geopolitics of the times by adding a map of Cyprus, which had only recently come under Venetian control, as well as plans for such Latin bastions as the Archipelago, Rhodes (Knights of Saint John) and Chio (ruled by Genoa). In addition to Buondelmonti's maps, the *Insularium illustratum* included maps of the larger Mediterranean islands, the British Isles, Ireland, Ceylon and Japan (see illustration 56) as well as the four Mediterranean peninsulas, namely Spain, Italy, the Balkans and Asia Minor. It also featured Scandinavia, Palestine, France and Germany and included three marine maps, namely the Atlantic coast of Europe, the Mediterranean and the Black and Caspian Seas, as well as an atlas of the world's islands. Thus, the *Insularium illustratum* constitutes a cartographic summary of the evolution of the view of the world at the dawn of great discoveries and an indication of what was to come from explorations then underway.

Due to the rapid development in the exploration of the world's oceans, insulars progressively shifted their focus toward the west, as shown by the Portuguese mapmaker Valentim Fernandes. He was a merchant and Moravian printer who was attracted to Lisbon at the end of the 15th century by the Portuguese discoveries and by the commercial prospects opened up through maritime expansion. The king of Portugal made Fernandes, who represented the German company Welser, a spices trade agent with Germany. When he was a printer, Fernandes published primarily religious books but also books about the voyages of Marco Polo and Nicolò de' Conti (1502). His book about islands, in which Fernandes introduces Lisbon as the future capital of international maritime commerce, was sent to the great German humanist Konrad Peutinger, along with other documents about exploration, including *roteiros*[3] and outlines of Portuguese discoveries and their expansion overseas. This collection, compiled in 1507 under the title of *As ilhas do mar oceano* and renamed by Peutinger *De insulis et peregrimatione Lusitanorum*, contained 31 maps and descriptions of Atlantic islands, grouped into two sections, the Canary Islands and the Cape Verde Islands.

The influence of the insular style is also evident in Mediterranean portolan production during the 16th century, be it Western or Ottoman. Nautical atlases produced by the Venetians Battista Agnese,

53
Anonymous Map of the Aegean Sea
(detail)

See page 92 for full map.

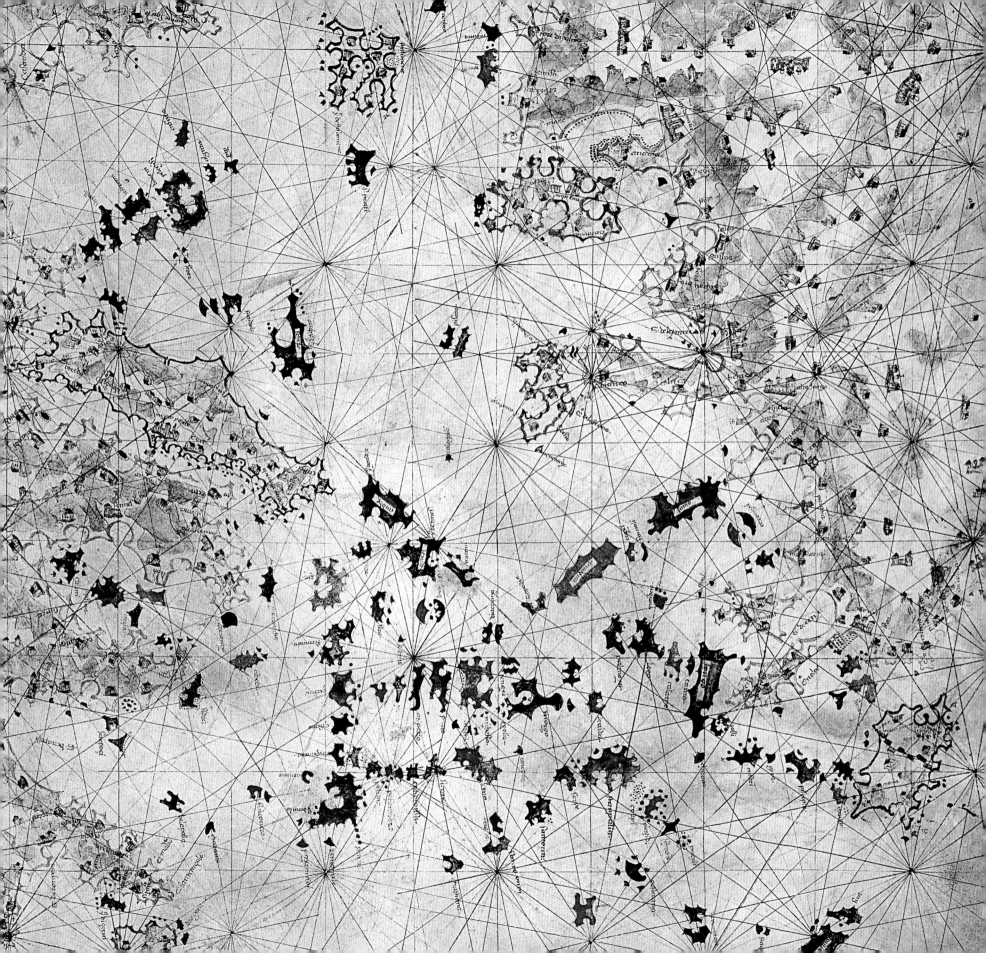

54.

C. 18777

54
Anonymous Map of the Aegean Sea
16th century

The Aegean archipelago, described in the first insular maps, occupies all the space in this large, detailed map. The many islands extending from southern Greece (starting at Peloponnese, at left) to Turkey (at right) are highlighted in vibrant colors; Crete is shown near the map's "neck."

NLF, Paris, Maps and Plans, GE AA- 567 (RES).
Manuscript on velum, 41 × 28¾ inches (104 × 73 cm)

Giorgio Sideri, Diogo Homen (see illustration 57) or Antonio Millo, included many maps of islands,[4] while Pirî Reis, the great Ottoman cartographer, adopted the insular model for his *Kitâb-i bahriyye* (Book of navigation), written in the year 1520. The analytical presentations of the Mediterranean in the Kitâb (see illustration 58) contain brief geographic descriptions that are illustrated with charts. There are 130 of these in the short version of the atlas and 220 in the long version, which depict and map islands, peninsulas, coastal cities, coastlines and deltas.

Images of maritime and oceanic regions, and the world as a whole, still had to be refined and incorporated in the "universal" *isolarii* that were proposed by two major cosmographers of the 16th century, the Spaniard Alonso de Santa Cruz and the Frenchman André Thevet. Santa Cruz was an essential cartographer of Spanish expansionism during the 16th century. His *Islario general de todas las islas del mundo* (General insular of all the islands of the world), published in 1545, followed the concepts of the seas and oceans developed by the cosmographer serving King Phillip II.[5] The first part of this work featured eight large numbered portolans representing the principal seas explored to that time. Next came 102 maps, mainly of islands but also of peninsulas and coastal regions, including 11 maps of northern and Western Europe, 60 of the Mediterranean, 13 of Africa and Asia, and lastly 18 of the Pacific and the Americas. The *Islario general* underlined Spain's worldwide supremacy: more than 40 maps are devoted to Spanish possessions in the Mediterranean, in western Europe and in America.

The *Grand insulaire et pilotage* (The great insular atlas and piloting) by André Thevet (see illustration 59), a colossal work that was to cover at least 263 islands from around the world, was one of the French cosmographer's last. It remained only in manuscript form because of the political instability in the country, the absence of patrons and financial setbacks. Nonetheless, Thevet was able to have most of his maps engraved by the printer Thomas de Leu in Flanders, most likely around 1586. His project of a complete atlas of the seas and oceans was confirmed in the preface of the book, which Thevet presented as the complement that would make his cartographic works "a comprehensive cosmographic body."

Printed insulars provided the public at large with images of maritime routes dotted with islands and, through that, visions of oversea exploration and expansion. As a result, this type of publication became very fashionable. One of the first printed insulars, the *Navigation insulaire*,[6] published by Bartolomeo da li Sonetti in Venice around 1485 or 1486, was a book about the islands of the Aegean Sea and Cyprus, all true to the descriptions of Buondelmonti. The expressive sonnets that accompanied the island maps were encircled by a compass arrow (see illustration 60), thereby generating an aura of adventure and romance. In 1528, the *Libro […] de tutte l'isole del mondo*, a work by Benedetto Bordone, a Paduan miniaturist, engraver and astrologer, appeared in Venice. This work included three introductory maps: Europe with the Mediterranean, the Levant and an oval map of the world as depicted by Francesco Roselli. These were followed by 107 small wood etchings in three separate sections. The first consists of maps of the islands and peninsulas of the Atlantic Ocean that are encountered after leaving the European coast when sailing toward America and then returning via the Canaries and Azores up to Cadiz. The second section contains the islands of the Mediterranean, particularly those of the Greek archipelago, the heart of the Venetian maritime empire. The third section holds eight maps of island in the Pacific and Indian Oceans. In order to highlight the most recent discoveries, Bordone adopted the model used for the western Mediterranean. This model, featuring an arrangement of neighboring islands and their capital cities (Venice and Constantinople), was applied to Spanish possessions in America. The "great city of Temixtitan" (Mexico City) appears like a city on an island lagoon similar to Venice, after the recently discovered archipelagos.

We are indebted to Bordone for the term *isolario*[7] as well as for the beginning of a fervent public interest in this type of publication. With his book and that of Bartolomeo da li Sonetti, the printing of insulars was established in Venice, where it became a sort of adoptee. As an island-city, the capital of a vast colonial island empire in the eastern Mediterranean and a major center of cartography during the 16th century, Venice was definitely the best place for the development of this type of cartographic center and, effectively, most 16th-century insulars were printed there, leading most cartographic historians to perceive the genre as a local specialty. And yet, as we have seen, much of the evolution of insulars took place elsewhere, and such maps were not produced solely in Venice until the end of their popularity. In fact, they shared a common fate with Venice and experienced a progressive decline before disappearing. This decline was reflected in the insulars that were distributed after Lèpante (1571), to let people know about the victories and losses in the Levant,[8] and in a best-seller of the time, *L'Isole piu famose del mondo* (The most famous islands in the world), published in Venice in 1572. In this anthology of islands, written by the scholar Thomaso Porcachi and illustrated with maps engraved on copper by Girolamo Porro, the maritime regions are split up and the geography is shrunk, leaving them to history and wonderment.

Insulars were a product of the beginning of modern geographic thinking and the Renaissance. They could not, however, survive the Age of Enlightenment without progressing further toward descriptive geography and cartography. Despite the efforts of Boschini and Coronelli to revive this Venetian tradition during the latter half of the 17th century, insular mapmaking must be viewed as a transitional form. This history also serves to illustrate the hit-and-miss progress of our understanding and perception of maritime regions during an era of rapid expansion and radical change in the way the world was conceived.

Georges Tolias

Works Cited

1. A simple insular work, without maps, had already been proposed by the learned Florentine Domenico Silvestri around 1390 in his work *De insulis*, a dictionary of islands and peninsulas, similar to Boccace's *De mondibus, silvis, fontibus*.

2. Here, "Archipelago" designates all the Greek islands.

3. This refers to roadmaps or descriptions of maritime itineraries.

4. Instead of limiting themselves to coasts, the great nautical atlases, particularly those from Battista Agnese's workshop, included maps of Sicily, Crete, Cyprus, Lesbos, Chio, Rhodes or Malta.

5. Santa Cruz took part in Sébastien Cabot's expedition of 1526 to 1530 and was named royal cosmographer in 1536. He was responsible to the *padrón real* (royal patronage) for the official marine map produced by the Casa de contratación.

6. Since the first edition had no official title, the incipit title *Periplus nison nel qual se contiene* was used.

7. This was effectively the title of the second edition (1534).

8. These were the information insulars published in Venice by Francesco Camocio and the brothers Bertelli and Simon Pinargenti between 1565 and 1575.

spirat: quibus in locis ampla pandebatur planities. Si aut ad triorem accedes sil
uam et am brachium suum offendes: ad orientem denicz insule mnulte propa
lantur: in quibus olim habitauere patres: nunc tandem pp insidias pyrcataruz
ad desolationem deuenere ·

oriens

Ambrachius
sin̄g
Silua
mata
S. nico
laus
mñt ·80·
s. maur
opidi
leucata
panaya
planiciet fertiliss̄
Leuchate:
Sca maura
3

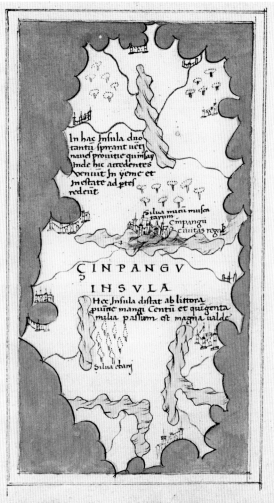

In hac Insula duo
tantu spirant uen̄
naues prouincie quinsay
Inde hic accedentes
ueniut In yeme et
In estate ad ptes
redeut

Silua mini musa
rarum
Cinpangu
ciuitas regia

CINPANGU
INSVLA
Hec Insula distat ab littora
puine mangi Centu et quiqenta
mila passum est magna ualde

Silua chang

56.

Ostendimus Leucatum nunc ad dulichias t̄ransimus que oli̅ itacha et nunc
tha Idecompare nominatur· altis rupib; circumsepta que montuosa et
inutilis: nisi in medio exiquus planus aliquib; arborib; casisq; habetur: et ei̅c
cum circa portuosa satis deoriente ad ocicidium p·xp· et in latitudine ·y·mñt.
amphiatur: cuius quidem duo extrema induobus aperiuntur cornib; a nautis in
nocte periculosis: fuit enim hin· ut asserciut ille eloquentissim̄ gigrorum Vlysses

57.

55

Cristoforo Buondelmonti,
Liber insularum Archipelagi
Italy, circa 1465–1475

In this guide illustrating the Greek islands, there are 92 maps painted in gouache, and three supplemental maps at the end that show Crete, Sicily and Corsica with Sardinia. We also see the island of Leucate, with tree-covered mountains along with its plains and main fortified cities.

NLF, Paris, Maps and Plans, GE FF-9351 (RES). F.3 v°.
Manuscript on paper manuscript, 8 × 11½ inches (20.5 × 29 cm).

56

Henricus Martellus Germanus,
Insularium illustratum
Florence, circa 1489

This preparatory manuscript for a more luxurious guide assembled the text and maps of Ptolemy, Buondelmonti and more recent sources. It describes all the islands of world that were known to Europeans. The Japanese island of Cipangu, however, is largely imagined.

Biblioteca Medicea Laurenziana, Florence, XXIX-25, f.76.
Manuscript on parchment, 8½ × 11½ inches (21.5 × 29 cm).

57

Diogo Homem, Map of the Aegean Sea
Lisbon, 1559

This luxurious atlas contains eight maps of the Mediterranean and oceanic European coastlines. The map of the Aegean Sea is drawn at a larger scale and allows one to distinguish the islands. The names of Turkey and Greece, buildings and fortifications stamped with crescents, underline the Ottoman Empire's domination of this region.

NLF, Paris, Maps and Plans, GE DD- 2003 (RES), f.10.
Illuminated manuscript on velum, each sheet is 23 × 17⅜ inches (58.6 × 44 cm).

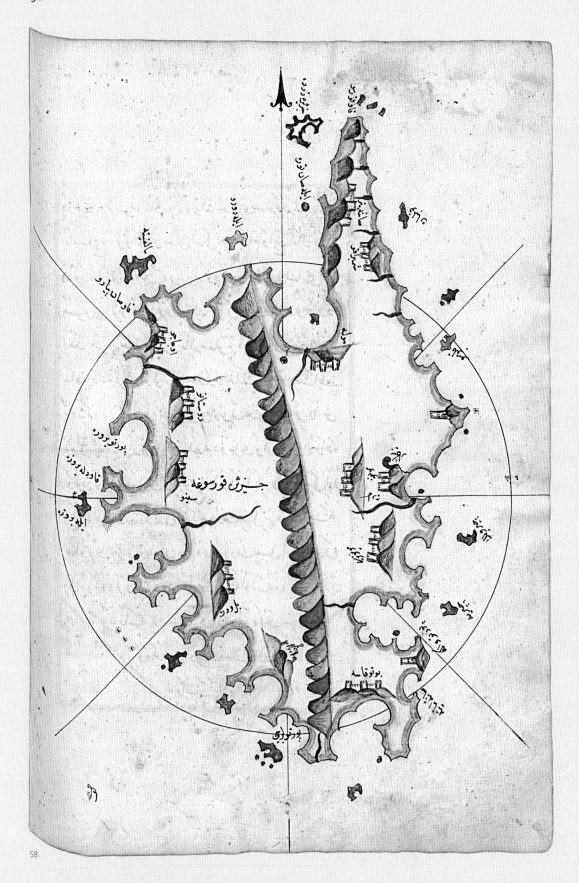

58.

58

Pirî Reis, *Kitâb-i bahriyye*
(Book of the Sea)
1525–1526

Pirî Reis, a Turkish admiral, distinguished himself in the Indian Ocean in service of the Ottoman Empire. His cartographic work of the Mediterranean Sea and its islands, inspired by Italian portolans, was seen as the most complete at the time. He used the Arab alphabet for the nomenclature on his maps, which were delicately highlighted with vibrant colors.

NLF, Paris, Manuscripts, suppl. turc 956, f. 266 v°.
Manuscript on paper, 9 × 13¾ inches (23 × 35 cm).

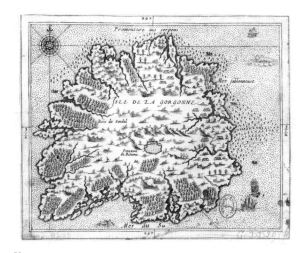

59.

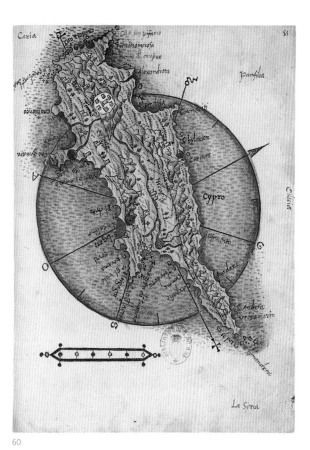

60.

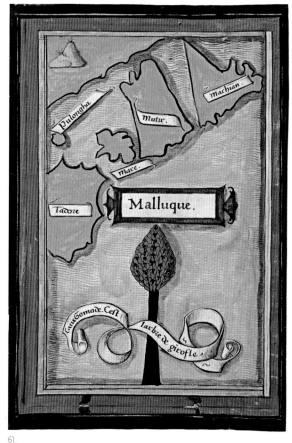

61.

59
André Thevet, Gorgona Island
Circa 1586

This plate comes from the *Grand Insulaire et Pilotage d'André Thevet Cosmographe du Roy. Dans lequel sont contenus plusieurs plants d'Isles habitées et deshabitées et description dicelles* (the Great insular and navigation atlas by André Thevet, cosmographer to the king, which contains several plans of inhabited and non-inhabited islands and descriptions of the these). As the author of universal cosmography, Thevet extended the insular map style to the whole world. This Pacific island is close to Colombia.

NLF, Paris, Maps and Plans, GE DD-2987 (9298).
Copper engraving printed on paper, 7½ × 6 inches (19 × 15 cm).

60
Bartolomeo da li Sonetti,
Map of the Island of Cyprus
Venice, 1485

Bartolomeo da li Sonetti was a ship's officer and master of a Venetian ship as well as a geographer and poet. He was inspired by Buondelmonti in composing his *Isolario*, the first printed collection of geographic maps exclusively dedicated to islands; the islands were described in sonnet-like verses. The printed maps are enhanced with colors and carry compass direction lines.

NLF, Paris, Maps and Plans, GE-DD 1989, f. 55 v°.
Maps printed on paper, 6¾ × 9½ inches (17 × 24 cm).

61
Antonio Pigafetta, *Navigation et discovrement de la Indie supérieure* (The Navigation to and Discovery of Upper Indonesia)
16th century

Antonio Pigafetta, who traveled with Magellan, was one of the few survivors of this first trip around the world, which was undertaken to find a maritime route via the Malay Archipelago. His written account, illustrated with summary maps of the new islands, was not widely distributed after his return in 1522. This map shows a clove tree, which was much-coveted spice.

NLF, Paris, Manuscripts, French 24224, f. 73 v°.
Illuminated manuscript on parchment, 7¼ × 10⅞ inches (18.5 × 27.6 cm).

NAUTICAL PLANISPHERE
NICOLÒ DE CAVERIO

NICOLÒ DE CAVERIO

62

Nicolò de Caverio, Nautical Planisphere
Genoa, circa 1505

This great planisphere, consisting of 10 parchment pages, is the work of the Genovese cartographer Nicolò de Caverio. Like many world maps from the early 16th century, it is very similar to a copy of the Portuguese *padrón real* (royal patronage), known as "the map by Cantino" and dated 1501. Caverio nonetheless included in his planisphere discoveries made up to 1505, and his work undoubtedly served as a source of the famous world map by Martin Waldseemüller of 1507.

Based on a system of rhumb lines 35½ inches (90 cm) in diameter centered in Africa, along with 16 secondary centers, his network of lines is completed by another concentric system about 71 inches (180 cm) in diameter, of which only three centers are shown on each side. The world map lies at the core of this network. It is surrounded by celestial spheres and has a latitude scale on the left border. Under its somewhat crude guise, Caverio's work offers many meticulous decorations: vignettes of cities; tents, including that of "Magnus Tartarus"; many Portuguese and Spanish buildings with a cross; birds and wild animals; people; forests; and outlines of the countryside.

The African coastline is shown with remarkable precision and a rich toponymy that indicates the ports of call on the route to India. On the southern coast of Africa, which was discovered between 1484 and 1499, six stone columns are shown, called *padraos*. Labeled with the Portuguese coat of arms, these were planted every time a new territory was claimed by a navigator, all the way from Cape Lopez to Malindi. Two Portuguese trading centers — Arguin, founded in 1445 and facing Senegal, and Elmina, founded in 1471 on the coast of Ghana — are easily recognized thanks to their symbolic representation as fortresses. The empty areas of the continent's interior are packed with the "big three" wild animals, the lion, giraffe and elephant, the latter being guided by a Moor. There is also an imposing mountain named Moon Mountain, which Ptolemy and other geographers traditionally placed at the source of the Nile. This representation of the African contours, labeled by the author with names in Portuguese, strongly influenced Renaissance cartography. We also note the presence of Madagascar, discovered in 1500 by an associate of Cabral, which is shown here too far south in relation to the continent.

J.-Y. S. et C. H.

NLF, Maps and Plans, GE SH ARCH 1 (RES).
Manuscript on parchment, 10 bound pages,
88½ × 45¼ inches (225 × 115 cm).

62 b
The Full Map

62 c
Western Africa

62 d
Indian Ocean
See pages 102–103.

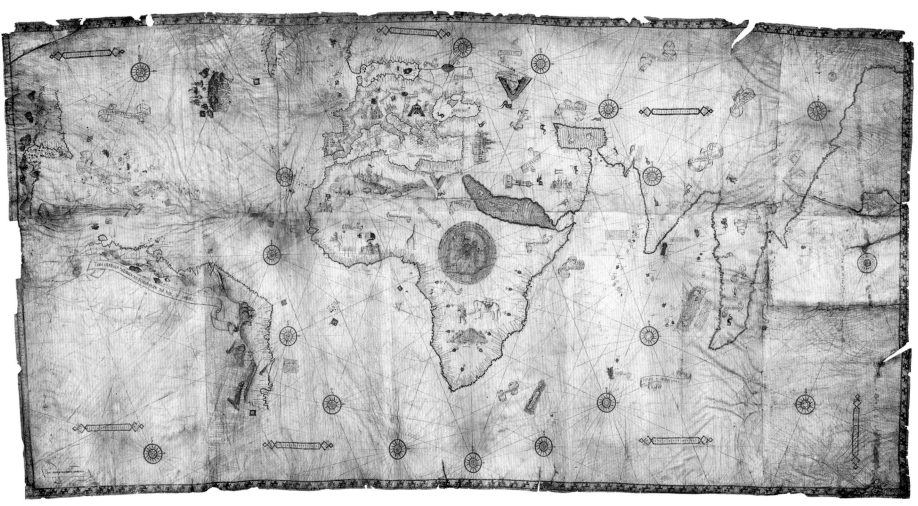

62 b.

MARE MEDITERANEVM

BARBARIA

REGNVM NVBIE

REGNVM OROVENE

REGNVM MVSAMELI
DE GINOIA

MARE MEDITERANEVM

BARBARIA

EGIPTVS

·EGIPTVS·

RECNVM·NVBIE

ENE

·EPTIOPIA·

ARABIA

Mecha

MARE·RVBRVM

NINOTORA·REGIO

SINVS·BARBARICVS

·PERSICVS·

GEMINIS · CANCER · LEO
TAVRVS · SATVRNVS · VIRGO
ARIES · IVPITER · MARS · LIBRA
PISCIS · MERCVRIVS · SCORPIVS
AQVARIVS · CAPRICORNVS · SAGITARIVS

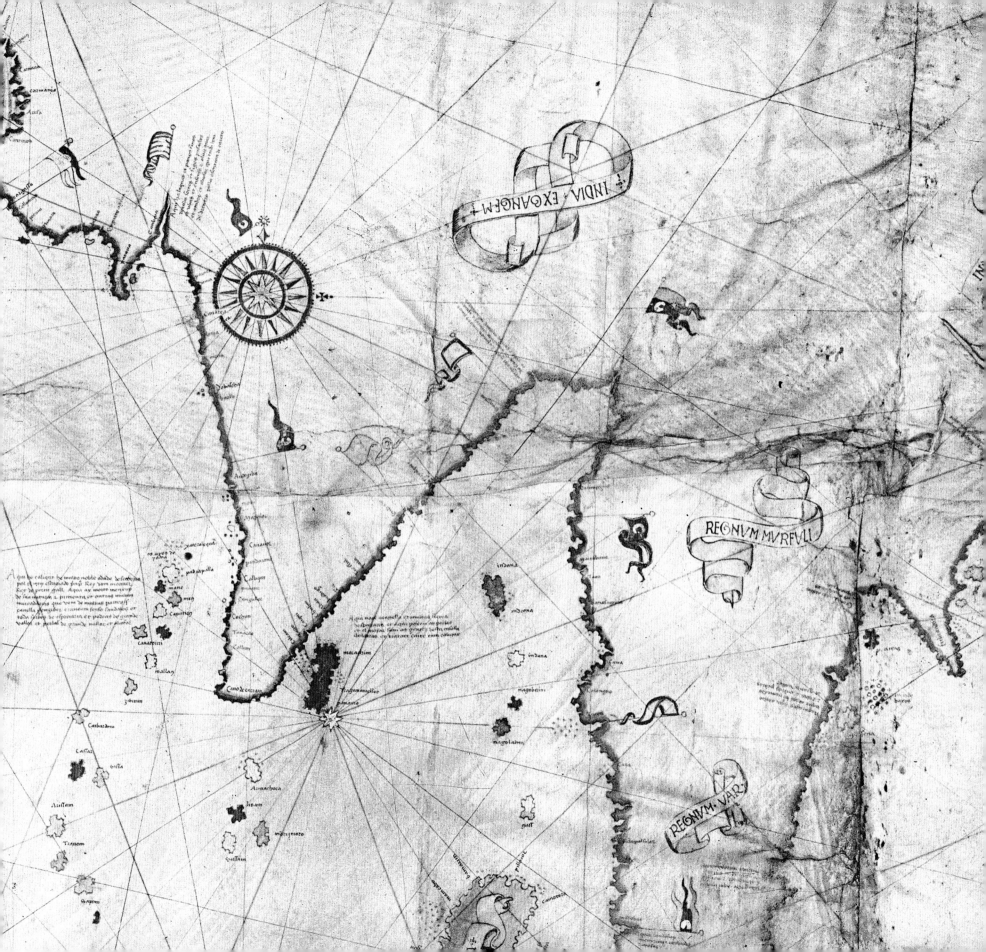

EPTIOPIA

mons lune

MARE·PRASSODVM

MADAGASCAR

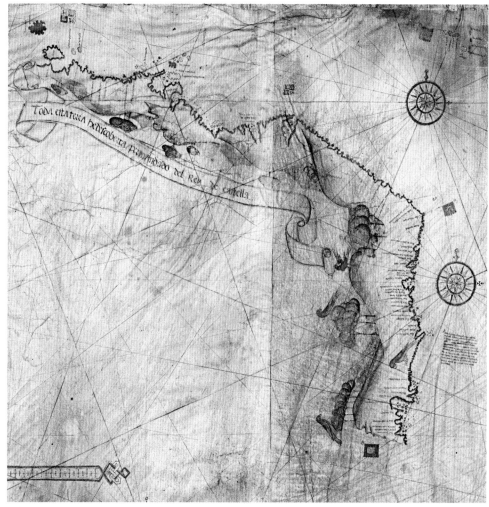

62 f.

62 f
Eastern Coast of South America

62 e
Southern Africa

WIDE
OPEN
SPACES

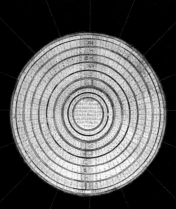

THE CHALLENGE OF THE OCEANS

Hélène Richard

When Europeans began large-scale exploration of the oceans toward the end of the Middle Ages, it resulted in a complete turnaround in how the world was represented. One of the best indicators of this revolution is the portolan maps that were produced during this period, which bore witness to the progress in maritime technology and the horizons beyond the Mediterranean. Voyages became more frequent and longer, moving toward destinations that no one could have previously envisioned.

The maps show the progressive discovery of new lands whose contours became gradually defined and completed with the names of ports and harbors. We can also see the outlines of Africa, discover the Americas and venture into the Pacific Ocean and areas ever closer to the poles. These portolans also show the technical problems that confronted these sailors once it became impossible for them to navigate based on compass directions and their estimates of the distances they had traveled. The appearance of latitude measurements, the improvements provided by map projections, which took into account the curvature of the Earth, and constraints imposed by keeping angles small in order to follow a coastline were all technical innovations brought about by navigators accessing wide open spaces.

However, portolans also reflect political expansions, namely those associated with the growth of European empires. By the start of the 16th century, portolans no longer represented the various European, African and Asian kingdoms solely with unrealistic figures. Cartographers also used ruler-drawn lines to indicate the borders between Portuguese and Spanish domains in the Atlantic Ocean, South America and, on the other side of the world, the Pacific Ocean, where it became essential to determine who controlled the Maluku Islands and the precious spices found there.

The most richly decorated portolans made room for supplemental information that was useful to voyagers and, perhaps more importantly, to those who had to make decisions regarding military and commercial enterprises. The maps did show information that was useful to sailors, indicating the dangers they might face near land as well as the water and wood resources they might need in order to continue the journey, but they mostly provided information about places that were rich in vegetation, fauna and precious minerals. One could also glean information regarding the relationships that could be established with the inhabitants of the regions and whether they were friendly or dangerous, or even cannibalistic. Such relations would determine the success of a colony and the viability of a trading post.

Portolans, however, also indicated unknown regions and imaginary lands, as well as their supposed resources, which were sometimes inspired by tales of medieval voyages, sometimes adventurous conjectures. These unknown lands fueled political and commercial ambitions, igniting the imaginations of rulers and adventurers. Despite the efforts of the Iberian powers to establish monopolies in the newly discovered territories, from the 16th century onward, other European nations, such as France, the Netherlands and England, were launching their own colonial conquests. Portolan maps also reflect these broader European ambitions to become scientific, political and commercial masters of the world.

63
Jacopo Maggiolo,
Marine Map of the Mediterranean
(detail)

See pages 76–77 for full caption and map.

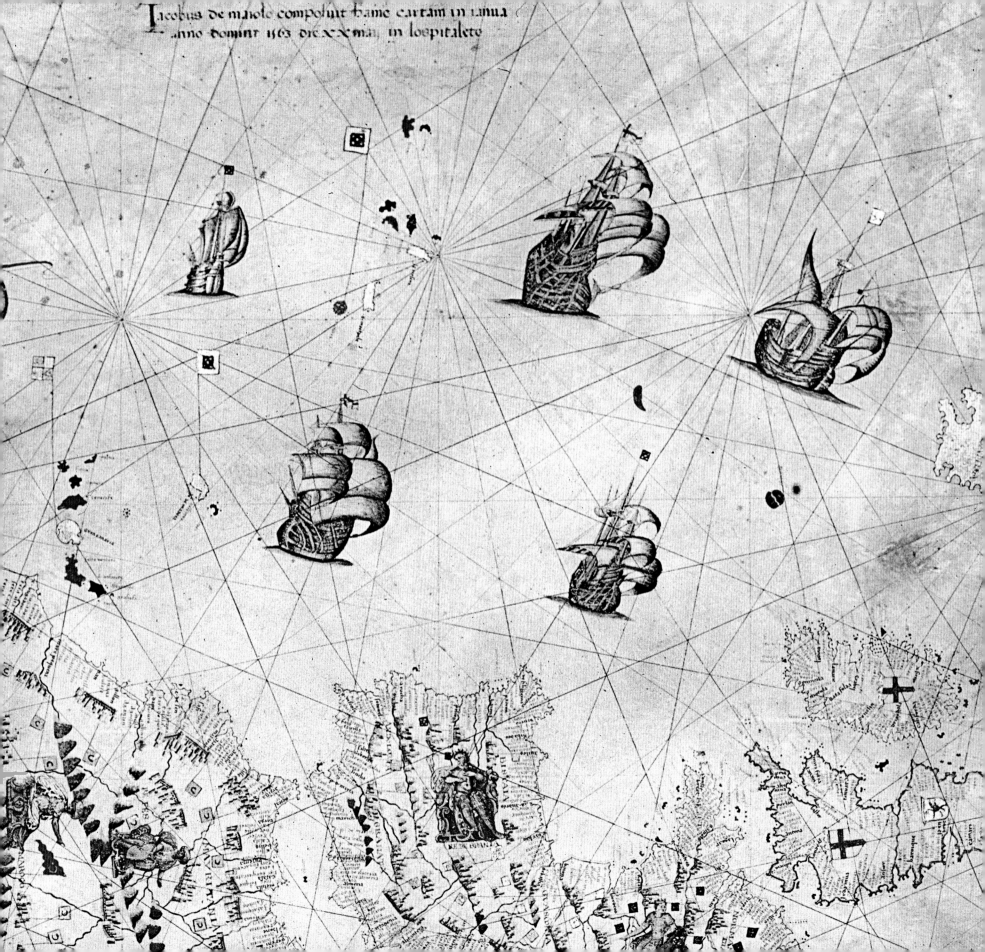

THE EXPLORATION AND GEOPOLITICAL STAKES OF IBERIAN CARTOGRAPHY
15TH AND 16TH CENTURIES

Luisa Martín-Merás Verdejo

Nautical Planisphere
Known as Salviati's Map
(detail)

See pages 118–119 for full caption and map.

SPAIN AND PORTUGAL: THE ATLANTIC FRONTIER

The Portuguese launched their enterprise of exploration with the intention of reaching Asia by traveling eastward. They sought to procure for themselves the spices and other precious goods that were not readily available in Europe. Land routes to Asia had not been re-established after the fall of Constantinople and the closure of the eastern Mediterranean by the Turks. In addition to trade, one can also add various other reasons to travel eastward, including scientific curiosity and political and religious designs.

The Portuguese began their expedition by circumnavigating Africa, since they believed that, according to the theories of Claudius Ptolemy and Pomponius Mela, who greatly underestimated the size of the African continent, travel toward India would be simpler and shorter via that route. After several geographic discoveries, by 1488 Bartolomeu Dias had traversed the entire southern Atlantic and rounded the Cape of Good Hope, ahead of the Spaniards, who were also trying to establish Atlantic routes. Whereas Portugal was at peace and enjoying a period of social and economic stability during the second half of the 15th century, in Spain, Castile was immersed in a successional war and had yet to reach the last stage in its war to recapture the Muslim kingdom of Grenada (1482–1492).

The war to determine who would succeed Henry IV — his sister, Isabella, or his daughter, Jeanne — was further aggravated by an international conflict that also involved Portugal, who favored Jeanne. This confrontation allowed Isabella to challenge the Portuguese Atlantic monopoly; however, her efforts to disrupt commerce with Guinea faced strong resistance from the Portuguese flotilla. Following the Treaty of Alcáçovas (1479–1480), which ended the war, distinct zones of influence were established: north of the Canary Islands went to Castile and the south went to Portugal.

Hence, Spain was not able to dedicate itself to the exploration of the Atlantic at the same time as Portugal, though the Portuguese were well acquainted with Spain's plans for conquest and colonization. Even though several Sevillian noblemen proposed a plan to conquer the Canary Islands in 1402, it was the Spanish kings who, in 1477, ordered the conquest of the three remaining Canary Islands, namely Gran Canaria (in 1480), La Palma (in 1492) and Tenerife (in 1496). This was done to prevent Portuguese intervention in light of the treaty. Because of its very strategic location, the Canary archipelago was the first stop for ships on their way to America.

To increase the effectiveness of their Atlantic explorations, the Portuguese perfected the caravel, a type of ship whose design was better adapted to this new type of navigation. They also experimented and implemented astronomical navigation, a system of navigation that was better suited to the high seas and was quite different from the estimation methods used in the Mediterranean.

JURIDICAL BATTLES: THE PAPAL BULLS

Since the Portuguese direct route to the east was closed to Spain, the Castillian crown was forced to find a different route. It was Christopher Columbus who proposed an alternate route, which he followed in 1492. Columbus was relying on two geographical principles:
— if the Earth is round, one can reach the east in just a few days by sailing toward the west;
— by resting on certain ocean islands, it would be possible to reach the land of spices faster than the Portuguese.

These were, in fact, sound geographic concepts based on the notion that the Earth was round. However, since the plan was unlikely to have any immediate practical consequences, there was strong opposition to it, mostly based on the prejudice that it is impossible to navigate westward.

Columbus's discoveries provoked a political conflict between Spain and Portugal. King Jean II maintained that the expedition had violated the territory placed under his jurisdiction by the Treaty of Alcáçovas, and he consequently lodged a complaint with the Spanish court and the Pope. In 1493, however, the Spanish kings managed to convince Pope Alexander VI to issue a series of bulls favorable to them. As a result, the bull *Inter æctera* granted Spain possession of all western discoveries that were not previously the possession of another Catholic sovereign. This bull established a line of demarcation that passed 100 miles (160 km) to the west of Cape Verde, thereby contradicting the Treaty of Alcáçovas, which had granted all lands south of the Canary Islands to Portugal. Another papal bull, the *Dudum siquidem*, which was pronounced in September of the same year, allocated all lands and islands to the south, east and west of the Indies to Spain, thereby annulling the Portuguese prerogative. Spain was

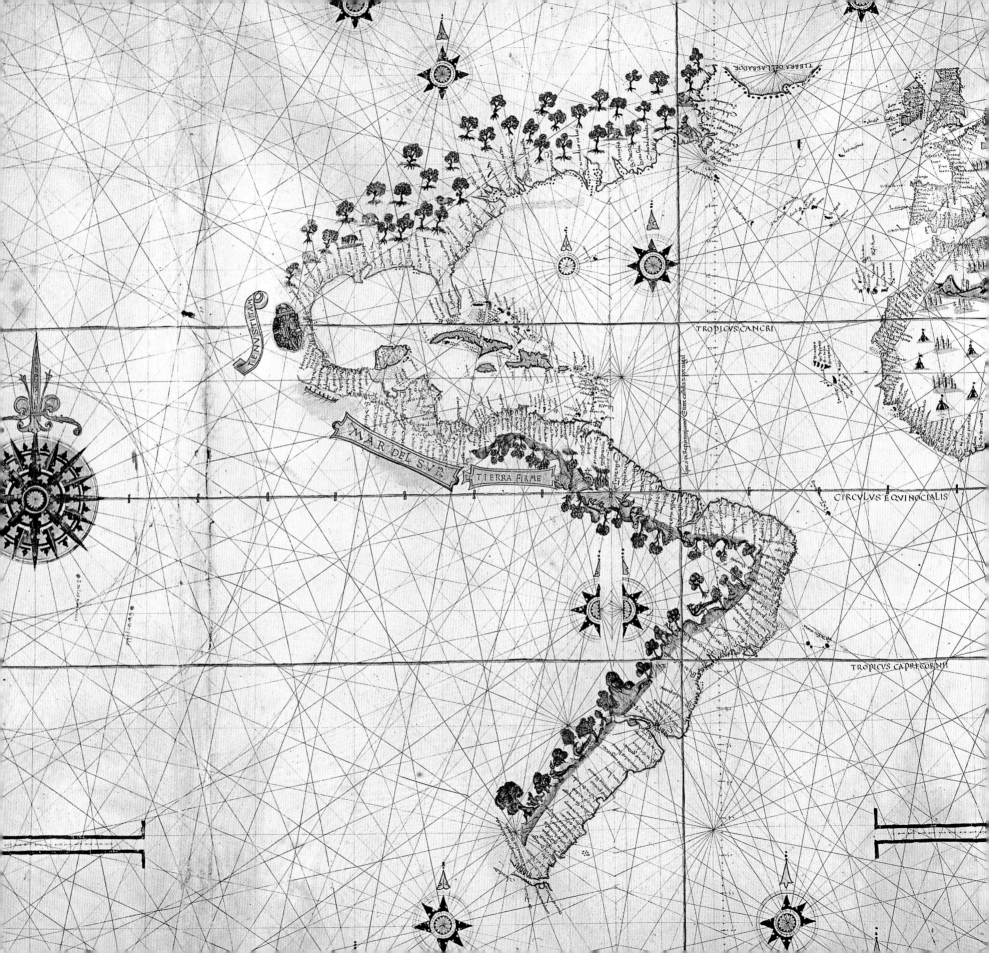

TIERRA DEL LABRADOR

TROPICVS CANCRI

TENVSTITAM

MAR DEL SVR

TIERRA FIRME

CIRCVLVS EQVINOCIALIS

TROPICVS CAPRICORNII

thereby free to explore via the western route any lands that Portugal had not yet discovered nor occupied via the eastern route. As a result, the Castilian–Portuguese rivalry was once again resolved in favor of the Spanish. The Portuguese countered by complaining that the 100-league (about 354 miles/555 km) distance was too narrow of a corridor for their ships coming from Saint George of the Mine (the Gulf of Guinea) and did not allow them to profit from favorable trade winds and currents. This led to the signing of the Treaty of Tordesillas on June 7, 1494, which established a dividing line from one pole to the other some 360 leagues (about 1,243 miles/2,000 km) to the west of Cape Verde. This began the Castilian expansion into the Atlantic, all within the limits established by the Treaty of Torsedillas, which delineated all explorable territories and seemed to satisfy both kingdoms.

THE WESTWARD EXPANSION OF CASTILE: COLUMBUS AND THE ANDALUSIAN VOYAGES

Following Columbus's first voyage, there was a series of expeditions to the newly discovered lands, which can be classified into several phases, based on their politico-geographic objectives.

The first phase, which comprises the voyages immediately undertaken after Columbus's first expedition, spans the years 1494 to 1503, when the Casa de contratación de las Indias was established in Seville.[1] From a geographic standpoint, the goal of these voyages was to ascertain that newly discovered territories were indeed the archipelago that, according to Ptolemy, preceded the Asian continent. From a political standpoint, the goal was to confirm that the new lands were located well within the zone of influence established by the Treaty of Tordesillas. These first-phase voyages were directed toward the Caribbean and the north coast of South America. We must also consider voyages undertaken by other nations, who had underestimated Columbus's plans. England would go on to send John Cabot on expeditions in 1497 and 1498; he was pushed by the Labrador Current and discovered Nova Scotia and Cape Hatteras. Portugal quickly dispatched the Corte-Real brothers to the same areas, and they arrived on the coasts of Labrador and Nova Scotia in 1498 and 1502, and the Álvares Cabral flotilla reached Brazil in 1500.

The most representative map of this era is the universal map of Juan de La Cosa (see illustration 66), dated 1500, which instated the prototype of the *pardón real*, the official

and secret reference map of the Casa de contratación, where new discoveries were listed relative to the rest of the world.[2] This map was followed around 1502 by the Cantino Planisphere, which included information concerning Portuguese discoveries in Brazil.[3] Nicolò de Caverio's map, dated around 1504, also appears to be of Portuguese origin.[4] Pirî Reis's map (see illustration 65), which closes this period, describes the state of discoveries in 1503,[5] though it might actually be dated to 1513.

THE SEARCH FOR A PASSAGE: MAGELLAN'S EXPEDITION

The second phase of Spanish discoveries spans from 1504 to 1513, when the realization that a new continent had been found had begun to take hold. The terms *Quarta pars* (the fourth part) and *mundus novus* (new world) emerged after Vespucci's voyage in service of the Portuguese in 1502, and this notion became widespread among the more enlightened minds of Europe. In addition, as Europeans began to consider the entirety of the information obtained from the Spanish and Lusitanian explorers, the extent of the eastern coast of South America was becoming clearer, making it difficult to cling to Columbus's theories.

From a geographic standpoint, the goal of the new expeditions was to find a passage to the Indies. The Antilles, Central America and the south coast of the Americas were targeted for this search. Pesaro's universal map (circa 1506) illustrates this second phase.[6] The universal map by Count Ottomano Freducci (see illustration 67) is signed and dated in Ancona, but this date was crossed out. It is a parchment map produced from Spanish sources that outlines Atlantic navigation and shows discoveries up to 1513, including that of Florida by Ponce de Léon.[7]

The third phase of expeditions extended from 1514 to 1523. It began with the news of the discovery of the South Sea by Núñez de Balboa, in 1513, and of lands full of fabulous riches spreading to the south.

The geographic notions of the time had lead Balboa to believe that the land lying south of the Isthmus of Panama was a peninsula where the passage to India might be found. This is illustrated on a unique map, the *padrón* of the Antilles and of South America (see illustration 68), which includes Balboa's discoveries around 1518.[8]

This discovery led the Castilians to change their plans, and they abandoned their search for a passage to the Malukus, where the Portuguese had arrived in 1511. In 1515, therefore, Juan Díaz de Solís undertook

a voyage to El Maluco, but he went no further than the Río de la Plata, where he thought he might find the crossing.

In face of this failure, a new Spanish expedition comprising five ships launched in 1519, in order to look for the passage further to the south of the continent. It was under the command of the Portuguese Ferdinand Magellan, who managed to cross the strait that now bears his name, reach the Pacific Ocean and arrive at the Malukus 10 years after the Portuguese. Despite many difficulties and Magellan's death (on the Island of Cebus), the *Victoria*, the only ship left of the five that had begun the expedition, made it to Seville on September 6, 1522, having realized the first circumnavigation of Earth.

Magellan's voyage, which was completed by Sebastián Elcano, confirmed the theory that the Earth was indeed a globe. This had repercussions throughout Europe and stunned European intellectuals, who had to abandon their geographic conceptions and reconcile them with this new finding. Nuño García de Toreno's 1522 map of the Malukus was produced as an account of his trip for Emperor Charles Quint.[9] This big universal map, found in Turin and dated from around 1523, is the result of modifications to the *padrón real* following Magellan's voyage.[10]

The fourth and last phase of the expeditions extended from 1524 to 1530. The feats of the *Victoria* revived the diplomatic problem between Spain and Portugal, which had been resolved by the Treaty of Tordesillas. The political and geographical difficulties — caused by the technical impossibility of tracing the antemeridian of the Malukus, which would have assigned the archipelago to one nation or the other — resulted in a redoubling of efforts to find a northwest passage to Asia. This resulted in the entirety of the Atlantic coast of North America being surveyed.

In order to reach a political accord based on geographic terms, there was a series of conferences of learned men in Elvas and Badajoz. However, negotiations were unsuccessful, and open warfare broke out in the Asian seas. The 1525 worldwide map, said to be Castiglioni's[11] but attributed to Diego Robero, Salviati's worldwide map (of Nuño Garcia de Toreno, 1525)[12] and Vespucci's maps from 1524 and 1526[13] show, with somewhat uneven results, the Spajnish concepts outlined during the Elvas-Badajoz summit. An anonymous 1527 map and Diego Ribero's two 1529 maps were most likely attempts to validate Spain's interests in the European courts.[14]

Finally, in 1529, by virtue of the Treaty of Saragossa, the Malukus were assigned to Portugal (they were indeed in their zone of influence), and Spain received a compensation of 350 million ducats. It was also stipulated that the line of demarcation had to be provisionally drawn at 17 degrees east of the Maluku archipelago.

This ends our brief overview of the geopolitical conflicts that arose between the two Iberian monarchies, who competed by way of their Atlantic explorations.

We have observed the geographic discoveries of the time and the resultant cartographic representations. Two treaties framed these events, the Treaty of Tordesillas in 1494 and the Treaty of Saragossa in 1529, resulting in a peaceful conclusion to the rivalry between the two Iberian crowns that were united by strong family bonds. From then on, each country took hold and colonized their newly conquered territories: Portugal in Asia and Brazil, and Spain in the rest of South America and in the Philippines.

Luisa Martín-Merás Verdejo
Original text translated by Marie Noual

Works Cited

1. The Casa de Contratación de Indias was an institution that controlled everything to do with commerce and navigation involving the New World: levying taxes, control of crew and passengers and registering all territorial discoveries in order to perfect the maps.

2. Museo naval, No. 270, Madrid.

3. Biblioteca Estense Universitaria, C.G.A.2, Modena.

4. NLF, Maps and Plans, GE SH. ARCH-1, Paris.

5. Topkapu Saray Museum, R 1633, Istanbul.

6. Biblioteca Oliveriana, No. 1940, Pesaro.

7. Archivio di Stato, No. 15, Florence.

8. Herzog August Bibliothek, Aug. 103, Wolfenbüttel.

9. Biblioteca reale, OXVI-2, Turin.

10. Biblioteca reale, Turin.

11. Biblioteca Estense Universitaria, Modena.

12. Biblioteca Medicea Laurenziana, Florence.

13. Hispanic Society, New York.

14. 1527, 1529, Thüringische, Landesbibliothek, Weimar; 1529, Biblioteca Apostolica Vaticana, Rome.

65
Pirî Reis, Map of the Atlantic
1513

Set up in 1513 by an admiral of the Ottoman flotilla, this map, with its rich iconography (rulers, animals, buttresses and caravels), is the western portion of a long-lost planisphere. It relies on Iberian sources from the beginning of the 16th century, which are close to Christopher Columbus's conceptions. The author had access to one of the celebrated navigator's maps, which had been seized from a Spanish vessel.

Topkapi Sarayi Müzesi Kütüphanesi, Istanbul, R. 1633 mük.
Illuminated manuscript on parchment, 24¾ × 35½ inches (63 × 90 cm).

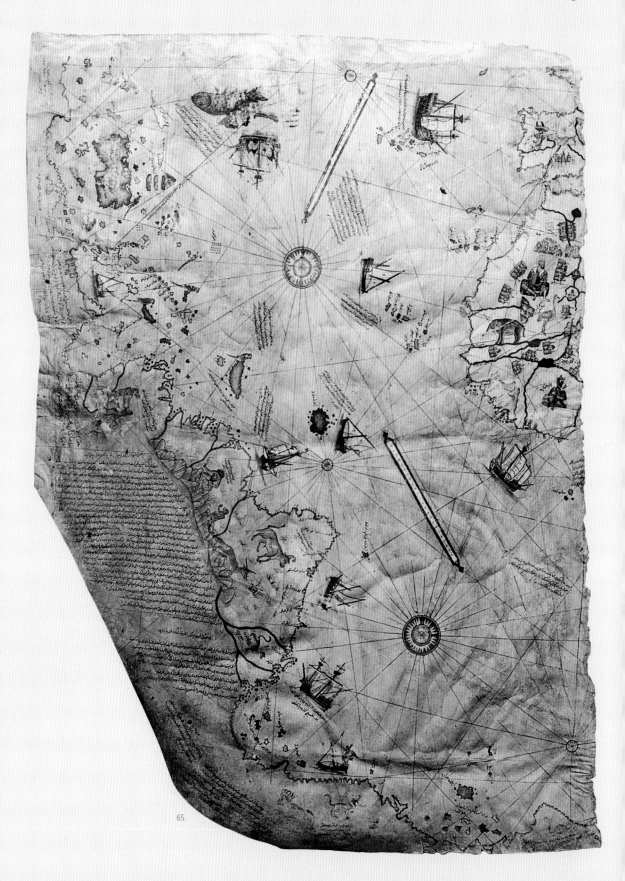

65.

66
Juan de la Cosa, Universal Map
Santa Maria (near Cadix), 1500

The Basque pilot Juan de la Costa accompanied
Christopher Columbus during his first two
voyages (1492–1494). This planisphere, drawn
in 1500, offers the oldest representation of the
East Indies, in the form of a circular arch around
the Antilles, from Nova Scotia up to the north of
Brazil. Was the cosmographer aware that he was
drawing an image of the "New World"?

Museo Naval, Madrid, No. 270.
Illuminated manuscript on parchment, 46 × 37½ inches
(117 × 95.5 cm).

66.

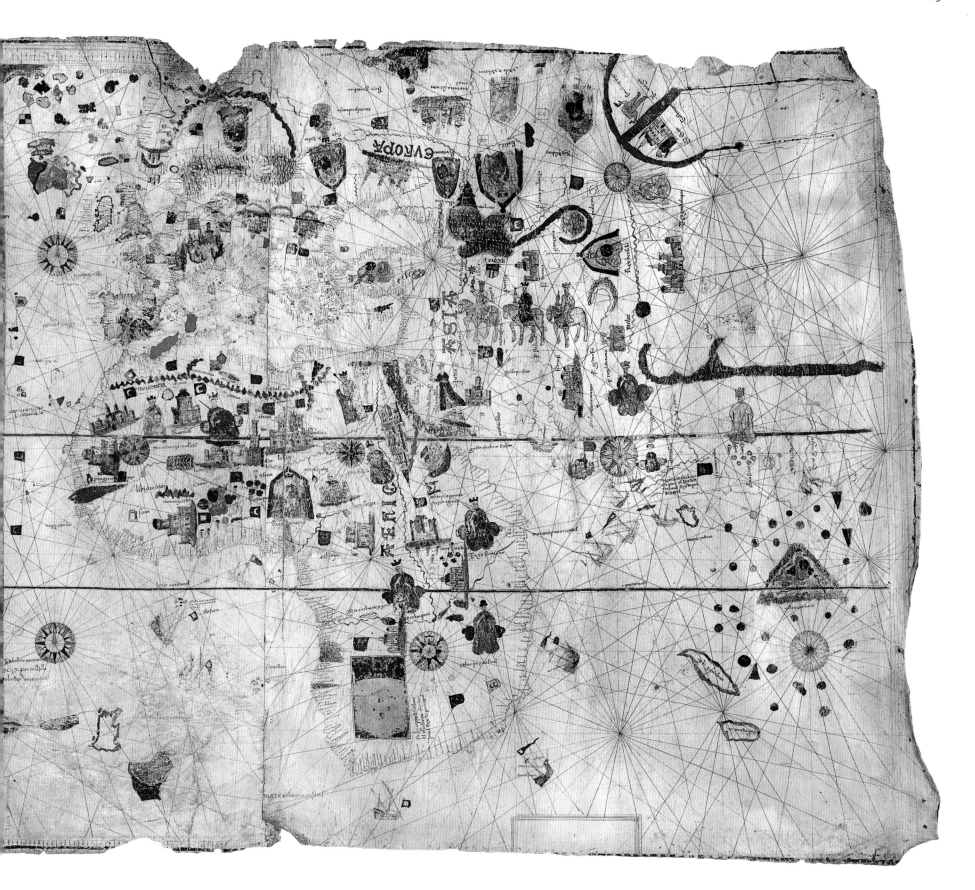

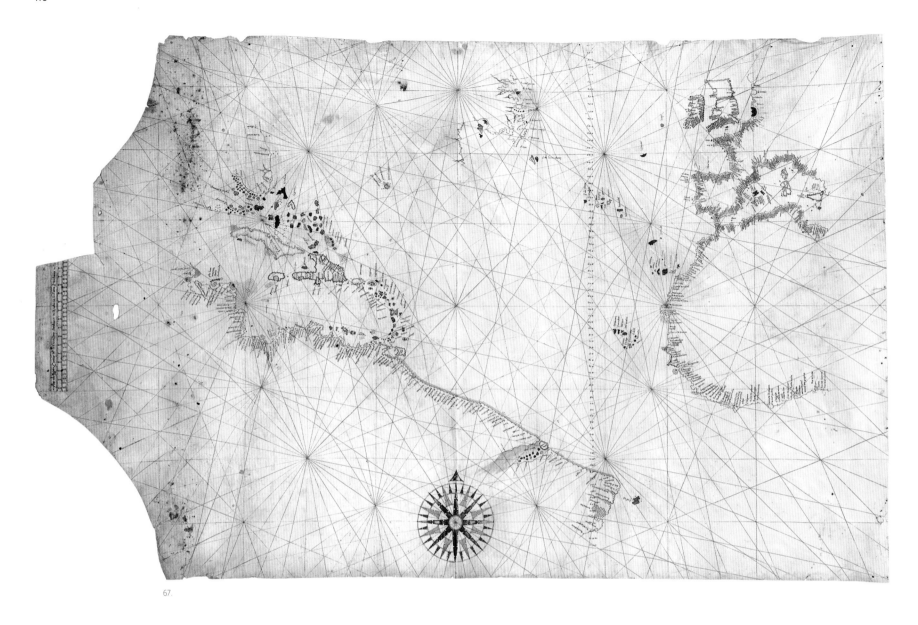

67.

67

Ottomano Freducci, Universal map
Ancône, post-1513

Ancône was a small Mediterranean commercial
production center active during the first half of
the 16th century. This map, which originates from
there, uses Spanish sources to present discoveries
made in Latin America before 1513. Even though
the concept of a new continent was widespread,
the main goal of the expeditions in this region
remained the search for a passage to Asia.

Archivio di Stato, Florence, Prat No. 549,
carta nautiche No. 15.
Illuminated manuscript on parchment,
48 × 30¾ inches (122 × 78 cm).

68

Padrón of the Antilles and South America
Spain, circa 1518

A network of rhumb lines with 16 secondary wind
roses that is centered around the equator is traced
on this anonymous map of Spanish and Portuguese
possessions between the Antilles and Cape Frio. The line
of demarcation, to the right of the mouth of the Amazon,
favors the Spanish interests. A Latin inscription evokes,
without naming him, Balboa and his 1513 discovery of the
South Sea, as well as the hypothesis of the insularity of
the lands to the south of the jj.

Herzog August Bibliotheck, Wolfenbüttel, Aug. 103.
Illuminated manuscript on parchment, 35½ × 26¾ inches
(90 × 68 cm).

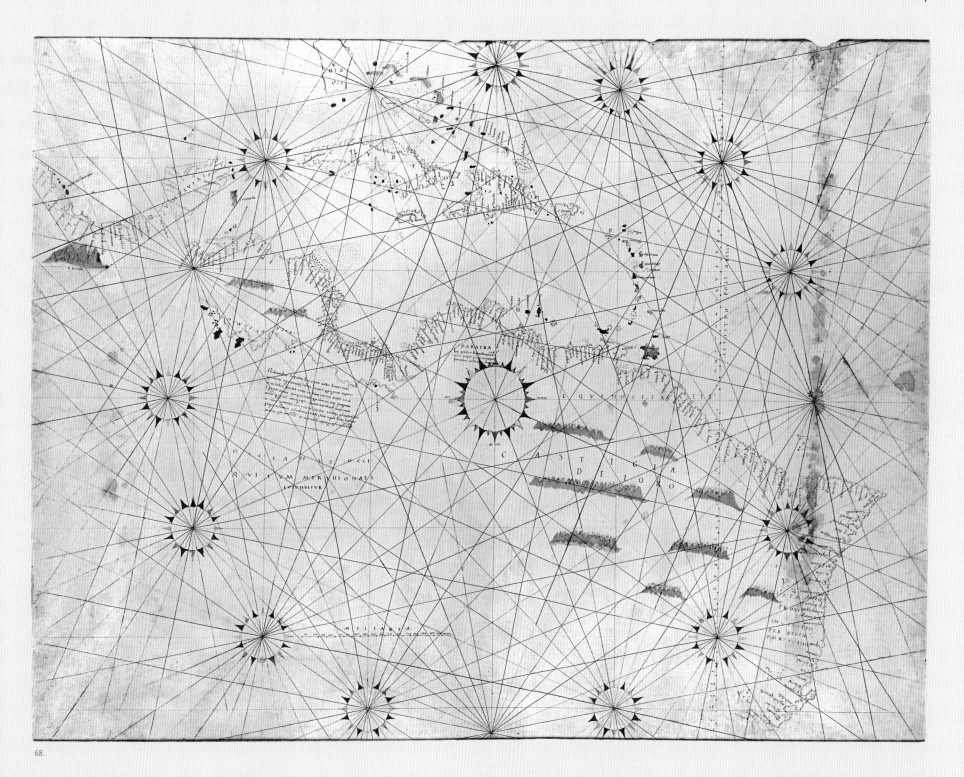

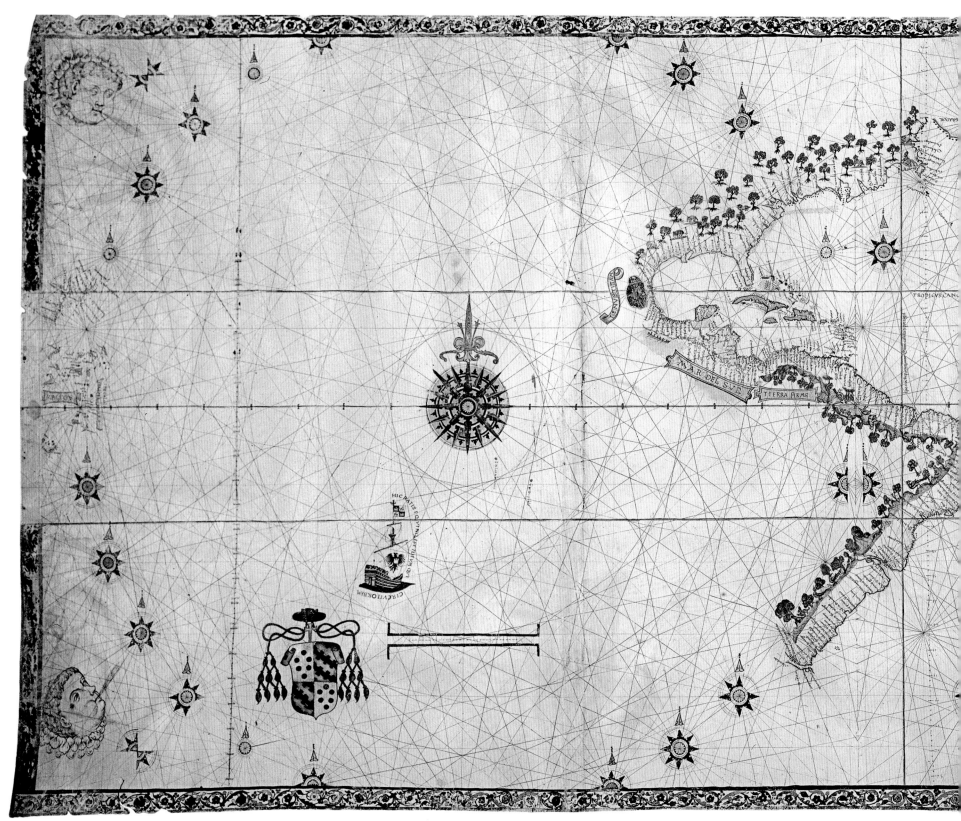

MAR DEL SVR

TIERRA FIRME

TROPICVS CAN

HIC PATIS EQVINOCTIVR PER
CIRCVITORVM

69
Nautical planisphere Known as Salviati's Map
Spain, circa 1525

This copy of the Spanish *padrón real*, undoubtedly due to Nuño García de Toreno, carries the coat of arms of Cardinal Salviati (1525–1530), a Spanish apostolic nuncio. While it erroneously situates the Malukus in the Spanish hemisphere, it credits the knowledge of the world acquired thanks to Magellan, whose circumnavigation is evoked in the legend. The coastlines of America and Asia are recognizable, and the Pacific Ocean, occupying nearly half of the planisphere, is revealed in all its amplitude.

Biblioteca Medicea Laurenziana, Florence, Med. Pal. 249. Illuminated manuscript on parchment, 80½ × 36⅜ inches (204.5 × 93 cm).

70

Andreas Homem, *Universa ac navigabilis totius terrarum orbis descriptio* (A Description of the Whole Navigable Territories of the World)
Anvers, 1559

Ten parchment sheets form this Lusitanian planisphere, which measures 115 ¾ × 59 inches (294 × 150 cm) and is the largest ever conserved. It provides a salient overview of the level of knowledge of Portuguese mariners at the middle of the 16th century. The Portuguese and Spanish hemispheres are clearly identified by the line of demarcation passing through the middle of the map and by the crowns of the two Iberian powers, which are featured in their respective zones.

NLF, Paris, Maps and Plans, GE CC 2719 (RES).
Illuminated manuscript on parchment, 10 sheets about 23⅜ × 29½ inches (60 × 75 cm).

70.

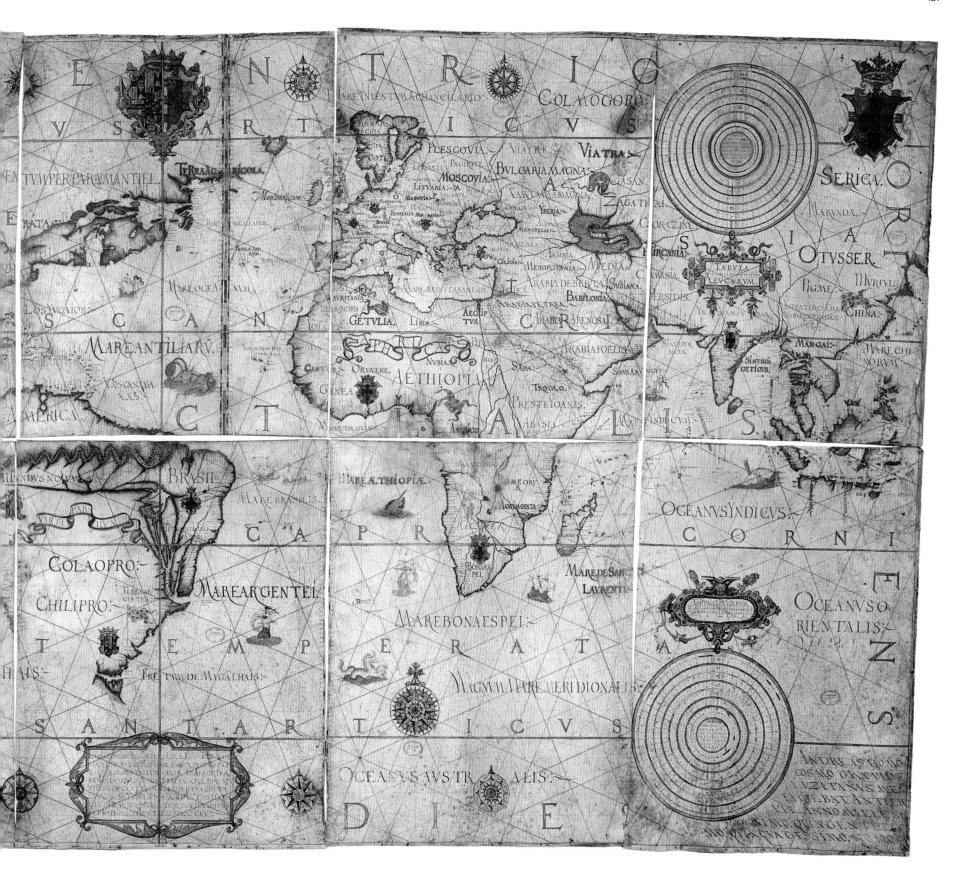

71
Gold Funeral mask
Nazca (Peru), 200 BC–600 AD

Originating from Peru, this funereal mask is made of a gold sheet cut and folded over. It is part of several precious objects that Spanish conquistadors discovered in South America and which fed the greed of Europeans.

Pier Branly Museum, Paris, Inv. 71.1930.49.1.
Folded and cut gold sheet, 9½ × 11½ inches (24.2 × 29 cm), 19¼ ounces (547 g).

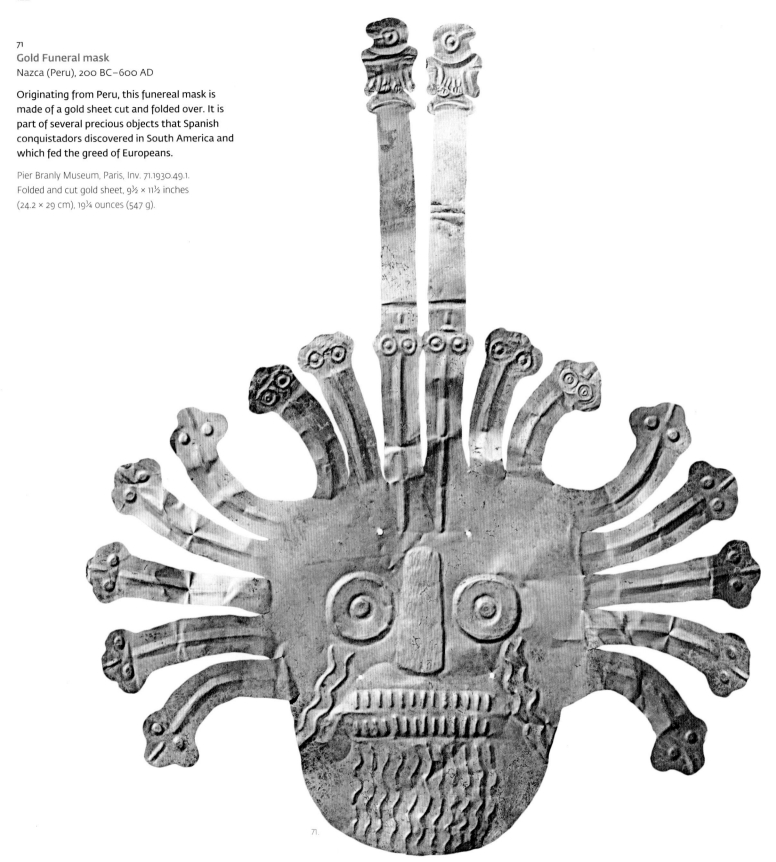

71.

72

Ivory Salt Dispenser
Benin, 16th century

Beginning in 1415 with the seizure of Ceuta, the Portuguese sought to explore and conquer Africa's shorelines in search of riches. Thanks to its position along the Portuguese's commercial routes, the kingdom of Benin developed commercial exchanges that flourished with each new arrival. This refined ivory salt dispenser, representing a Portuguese warrior topped with a ship, testifies to the blossoming trade in African arts and crafts destined for European nobility.

Pier Branly Museum, Paris, Inv. 70.2008.14.1.
Elephant tusk ivory, 10¼ × 3⅛ × 3⅜ inches
(26 × 8 × 8.5 cm).

73.

73
Domingos Sanches,
Map of the Atlantic Ocean
Lisbon, 1618

The only known work from this Portuguese
cartographer, this map with numerous
miniatures (coats of arms, ships, towns, saints)
displays the extent of the maritime and colonial
power of Spain and of Portugal at the beginning
of the 17th century under King Philippe III. The
south Atlantic routes are marked with patron
saints (Saint Benedict, Saint Joseph, Saint
Stephen, etc.), in a kind of geographical *ex-voto*.

NLF, Paris, Maps and Plans, GE AA 568 (RES).
Illuminated manuscript on parchment, 37⅜ × 33 inches
(95 × 84 cm).

FROM THE MEDITERRANEAN TO THE OCEAN: NEW PROBLEMS, NEW SOLUTIONS

Joaquim Alves Gaspar

74
Map of the Atlantic Coast
Circa 1471

This anonymous map is the oldest surviving Portuguese maritime map. Showing only rhumb lines and a graphic distance crossing, this very scantly decorated map is centered on the west coast of Africa, which is abundantly labeled with toponyms. The presence of the Rio do Lago, discovered in 1471, helps us date it.

Extension University Library, Modena, C. G. A. 5c.
Manuscript on parchment, 28¾ × 23⅜ inches (73 × 60 cm).

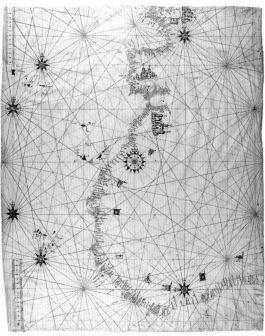

74.

THE SEA OF DARKNESS

In 1434, after many unsuccessful attempts by a number of navigators engaged by Prince Henry of Portugal over a period of 13 years, Gil Eanes finally succeeded in bypassing Cape Bojador. These coastal waters opposite the Canary Islands were dangerous and had many obstacles, including sand banks that were far from land, strong southern currents that stopped ships from the rear and arid soil where nothing living could exist, not to mention the sea monsters sailors thought populated the Sea of Darkness.[1] According to a saying brought back by Alvise Cadamosto, a Venetian navigator employed by Prince Henry, "he who crosses cape No will return or no".[2] However, these fears were mostly baseless, as it became quite clear that crossing Cape Bojador did not pose major difficulties. On the contrary, the progress of ships to the south was helped by trade winds that blow from the northeast and the Canary Islands currents, which paralleled the African coastline. The main problem was the return voyage, during which sailors encountered the same elements but from the opposite direction.

When Gil Eanes crossed Cape Bojador, the ships used for exploratory voyages could not sail against the wind. This deficiency resulted in long and arduous return trips, and it was sometimes necessary to resort to oars to travel north. However, the advent of caravels — which were equipped with Latin sails and were able to handle winds more effectively — marked significant progress. In addition, a better grasp of the wind systems and currents in this part of the world helped captains understand that it is better to plot their return trips at some distance from the African coast, so as to avoid the Canary Islands currents and the winds from the northeast. Captains took this preferable route at the cost of an extended western detour via the Sargasso Sea to the latitude of the Azores, and then they directed their ships toward Portugal. This ocean lane, which was used from about 1450 onward, was called the *volta da Guiné* (Guinean turnaround) and contributed greatly to the success of exploratory voyages along the African coast. A problem of a different nature, however, had to be resolved before this solution could be adopted in a safe and secure manner.

In Africa as in the Mediterranean, captains generally followed the coastlines, relying on the information available on their itineraries and the distances between sites that were carefully recorded on their route charts. However, a captain occasionally needed to distance himself from the coast in order to reach a faraway island, although such oceanic trajectories rarely lasted longer than a few days. To make such a journey, the captain determined his ship's position based on the last cape followed after his last-known position, the position indicated by his compass and by estimating the distance he had traveled. Portuguese captains referred to this method as the *ponto de fantasia* (imaginary point), a colorful expression that clearly reflects the uncertainties involved with such estimations. Any errors inherent in this method, however, were rarely a serious navigation problem since they were easily corrected once the coastline became visible again. However, this was not the case for ships that remained in open waters for several days or even weeks, such as when they left for the Azores or returned from the coast of Africa following the curve of Guinea. The more time passed between sightings of the coast, the more inaccurate positional estimates became, to the point of almost being useless, especially when the ship was forced to change direction many times in order to catch favorable winds. To confront this new problem, a new navigation method was needed.

TECHNICAL INNOVATIONS

The solution came in the second half of the 15th century. Astronomical navigation was created by adapting observation instruments that were used by astronomers on land, the quadrant and the astrolabe (see illustration 75), and by developing very simple procedures that were accessible to sailors. We do not, however, know how or where these methods were first introduced or who was responsible for their development. Initially, captains used the latitude of the North Star to verify the north–south displacement of their ship relative to a point of reference. Later on, captains were able to directly determine latitudes by establishing basic rules to correctly measure the height of the North Star above the horizon, both at sea and on land, in order to obtain their exact latitude. This method could not be used everywhere, however, since as one traveled further south, the North Star eventually disappeared below the horizon. A more general solution, introduced some 15 years before the end of the 15th century, was to observe the sun at high noon. At that point the observer could easily deduce his latitude based on the height of the sun above the horizon and by taking its declination into account. Navigators used ephemeris tables, which indicated the solar declination for each day of the year, to determine the latitude of any site.

The oldest historical source referencing astronomical observations at sea is a work Diogo Gomes wrote

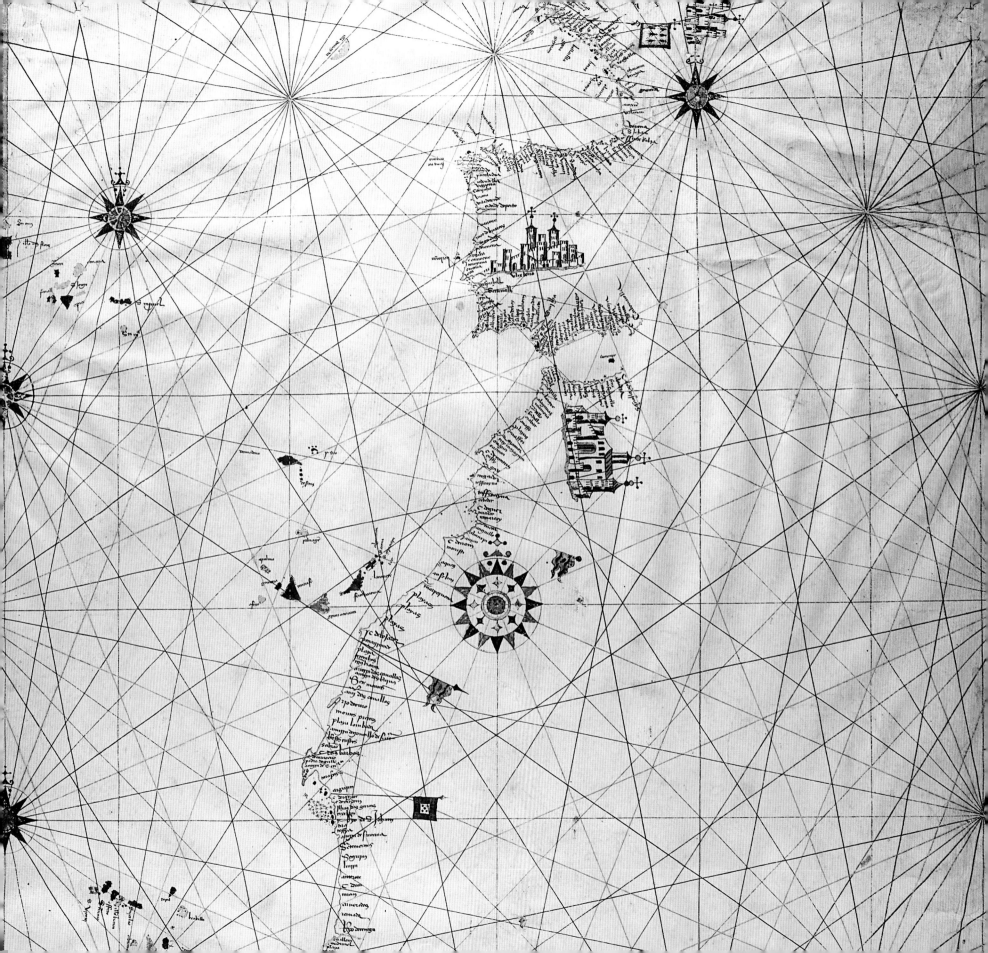

around 1460, which was translated into Latin by Martin Behaim. In it, the Portuguese captain explains how he measured the height of the North Star near the Cape Verde archipelago. Other sources mentioned the use of instruments and the practice of astronomical navigation during the voyages of Bartolomeu Dias (1487–1488), Vasco de Gama (1497–1498) and Pedro Álvarez Cabral (1500).[3]

CARTOGRAPHY'S SILENT REVOLUTION

When the systematic exploration of the African coastline began, the captains in these waters used nautical maps that were similar to the portolan maps they used in the Mediterranean. These maps were created based on information gathered at sea, and the sites were located according to the estimated distances and the magnetic courses plotted by compass. In the first stages, during the first half of the 15th century, all maps used by Iberian captains were imported from Majorca. Around 1443, Portuguese cartography of the Atlantic Ocean took its first steps, when Prince Henry of Portugal ordered that cartographers should add the recently discovered lands beyond the Cape of Bojador to their maps.[4] At the same time, Portuguese navigators had just scaled the Cap Blanc and were advancing to the south in their systematic exploration of the African coastline.

The oldest Portuguese map that we know of has been traced back to 1471 and represents the western coastlines of Europe and Africa, from the Ushant Island up to Lagos, in the Gulf of Guinea (see illustration 74). This map, quite plain and without decorations, only represents the Atlantic, excluding the Mediterranean and northern Europe, which suggests that it was specifically drawn for navigation along the African coastlines.

Drawn around 1492, Pedro Reinel's map, which is now conserved in the departmental archives of the Gironde in Bordeaux, is, according to itself, the oldest surviving Portuguese signed map (see illustration 76). It represents the Atlantic, from the British Isles up to the mouth of the Congo together with the eastern Mediterranean. Like the anonymous map drawn in 1471, the Reinel map was undoubtedly destined to be carried on board ships, judging from its somber decorations and evidence of its having been handled. A section of the African coastal region, to the east and south of the Gold Coast (present-day Ghana), is shown at the interior of the Sahara and Sahel zones. This ingenious approach was probably

taken because there was not an adequate model that covered this part of the world when this map was created. With the discovery of new lands to the south, the models that cartographers used for everyday production had to be redrawn at different scales, since the size of the animal pelts that were available could not change. The same solution was adopted for Jorge de Aguiar's 1492 map (conserved in the Beinecke Rare Book and Manuscript Library in Yale University, New Haven, Connecticut), which is the oldest known Portuguese map having not only a signature but also a date.

With the introduction of astronomical navigation methods, the imaginary point, which was established on a magnetic course, ceded its place to the *ponto de esquadria* (the "quadrangle point" or calculated point), where the observed latitude became the dominant element of information. None of the Portuguese maps of the 15th century presents the least trace of latitude observed by the astronomical method: no latitude scale appears, and the representative geometry is identical to that of the traditional portolan maps. However, since they belong to an era when astronomical navigation was already being practiced by Portuguese captains, it is likely that maps of the same type were used with the calculated point methodology. To accomplish this, captains had to superimpose a latitude scale on the map while keeping, as much as possible, the coastline in sight. However, this sleight of hand could only function in the areas where the magnetic declination was weak, so that the relative north–south positions were not affected. Such was the case for the Atlantic coast of Europe and Africa, from the British Isles to approximately Cape Verde, but not for the Gulf of Guinea and the south Atlantic, where the latitudinal distortions were much more pronounced. To represent these regions according to their latitudes and relative to the other shorelines, a new cartographical model became necessary. This evolution had to wait for an astronomical coverage of the areas that Portuguese explorers had already visited but for which the latitudes were not know with the necessary precision. We know, via a note in Christopher Columbus's manuscript, that such a statement was ordered for the African coastline by King Jean II of Portugal around 1485.[5]

The oldest map in existence on which the latitudes as observed by the astronomical method have indisputably been incorporated is the Cantino Planisphere, drawn by a Portuguese cartographer in 1502 (see illustration 78). While there are no explicit figures for the latitudinal graphic scale, the representations of the equator, tropics

and Arctic Circle allow us to conclude, despite minor latitudinal errors on the western and eastern coasts of Africa, that these sites are representative of the calculated point method, according to latitudes and the observed magnetic course.[6] For other sites, such as the Mediterranean, the Black Sea and northern Europe, the old portolan model continued to be used and was a common trait shared with the rest of the Iberian cartography of the 16th century and beyond. This can be explained by the fact that the representations of these zones continued to be copied from non-astronomical models for a long time.[7] The Cantino Planisphere is one of the most precious monuments of our cartographical heritage: it was already valuable at the time it was drawn, since it included the most up-to-date geographic data at a time when knowledge of world geography was progressing rapidly and could give one a strategic advantage. Today it is valuable because it provides unique historical insights into exploration missions and the technical evolution of maritime navigation and nautical cartography at a particularly interesting time, the end of the 15th century and the beginning of the 16th century. The Ptolemaic representation of the Indian Ocean was finally abandoned on this map, the Europeans' unknown territories in far-off lands (Newfoundland, Florida and Brazil) are represented in their correct geographic placement, and the contours of the Americas are shown in a manner that clearly identify them as a new continent, cleanly separated from India. Going against the official policy that forbade propagating any information regarding recently discovered territories outside of Portugal, Alberto Cantino, an agent of the duke of Ferrare, secretly acquired this map in Lisbon and brought it to Italy, where it is still kept today.

The Cantino Planisphere established a new cartographic model that was rapidly embraced for other world maps. The depiction of Africa's coastline on this map provided much geographic information concerning Madagascar and the Red Sea, which were to remain more or less unchanged in nautical cartography. The planisphere, drawn in 1504–1505 by the Genoan cartographer Nicolò de Caverio (see illustration 62), belongs to a rather important group of world maps that were drawn according to Portuguese prototypes at the beginning of the 16th century. This group included the King-Hamy Map (circa 1504), the portolan of Vicount Maggiolo (1504) and Pesaro's map (1505–1508). Caverio's Planisphere is thought to be one of the sources Waldseemüller used to realize his map in 1507; it is also thought to be a source for Cantino's map and several other even older maps.

75
Nautical Astrolabe Built
by Sancho Gutiérrez
1563

This astrolabe, destined to be used by mariners, was constructed in Seville and carries the year 1563. Contrary to Arabic astrolabes, which were used to calculate the positions of the stars, nautical instruments such as this one were used to measure the meridian height of the sun and to determine the latitude of the site being observed. They could easily be used at sea.

CNAM, Paris, Inv. 3864-001.

Pedro Reinel's map (circa 1504), which today is conserved at the Bayerische Staatsbibliothek in Munich, marks another significant step toward the adoption of a new cartographic model. It is the oldest nautical map in existence on which one can see a scale of latitudes (see illustration 77). Curiously, one can see two independent scales. The main one, which is oriented in a north–south direction, is an oblique scale located near Newfoundland and is solely applicable to that area. This hybrid system has a simple explanation: Newfoundland was drawn based on a magnetic course and its estimated distance relative to the Azores as calculated with the imaginary point method. This oblique latitude scale for Newfoundland is found on other Iberian maps of the 16th century, such as the 1550 Atlantic map of Diego Gutiérrez (see illustration 79) and the anonymous Portuguese map drawn around 1560 (see illustration 80), both of which are conserved at the National Library of France.

THE REIGN OF LATITUDE MAPS

Before the 1569 publication of the Mercator map, with its crisscrossing latitudes, all nautical maps were drawn by direct transfer and had a constant scale, since navigational data were gathered at sea and on land as though the Earth was flat. Ignoring the roundness of the Earth resulted in incoherent geometry: the geometry of each map depended on the collected itineraries that served as the basis of the map's design, and only these itineraries were represented with any accuracy. The invention of Mercator's projection in 1569 did not resolve this problem, since the navigational methods of the time were not adapted to the new model, which was based on latitudes, longitudes and real geographic directions. The latitude map continued to be used and was not supplanted by Mercator's projection until more efficient methods of determining longitude at sea were established, in the mid-18th century, and the spatial distribution of magnetic declination was discovered. Despite its limits and apparent simplicity, the latitude map was indeed a major progression in Renaissance nautical cartography and was widely used for two and a half centuries.

Joaquim Alves Gaspar
Original text translated by Laurent Bury

Works Cited

1. See Gomes Eanes de Zurara, *Crónica do Descrobimento e Conquista da Guiné*, c. 1448, Lisbon, Publicações Euro-American, 1989, 58–63.

2. Cape No is known today as the Cape Noun, or Cape Chaunar, and is along the southern Moroccan coastline.

3. One finds a good summary of the astronomical methods used during the 15th century in "Navigation astronomique" by Luís de Albuquerque in Armando Cortesão's and Luís de Albuquerque's *History of Portuguese Cartography*, Lisbon, Junta de Investigações do Ultramar, 1971, vol. II, 221–442. See also António Barbosa. *Novos subsídios para a história de ciência náutica portuguesa, na época dos descobrimentos*, 2nd ed., Porto, Instituto para a Alta Cultura, 1948.

4. See Charles Verlinden, *Quand commença la cartographie portugaise?*, excerpt from *Revista da Universidade de Coimbra*, vol. XXVII, Centro de Estudos de Cartografia Antiga, Coimbra, Junta de Investigações Científicas do Ultramar, 1979.

5. This note has been attributed to Columbus or his brother Bartolomeo in the margin of an excerpt from *Historia papae Pii*, Venice, 1447.

6. The equator and the Tropic of Cancer are also displayed in Juan de la Cosa's planisphere (1500). The distribution of the latitude errors along Africa's western coastline, measured by the map's implicit scale, nevertheless reveals that no data from astronomical observation had been incorporated.

7. For a detailed description of the Cantino Planisphere's geometry, which includes the results of a systematic cartometric analysis, see Joaquim Alves Gaspar, *From the Portolan Chart of the Mediterranean to the Latitude Chart of the Atlantic: Cartometric Analysis and Modeling*, doctoral thesis, Lisbon, Universidade Nova de Lisboa, 2010.

76

Pedro Reinel, Map of the Atlantic's Western Coast from the British Isles to the Congo
Circa 1492

The oldest signed Portuguese map that has reached us was discovered around 1960 in a notary's minutes. On the map, the African coastline extends into the continent's interior right up to the opening of the Zaire River, which was discovered in 1482 and is where explorers placed the first Portuguese padrao, the stone cross seen here.

Departmental Archives of the Gironde, Bordeaux, 2 Fi 1582 bis.
Manuscript on parchment, 37⅜ × 28 inches (95 × 71 cm).

76.

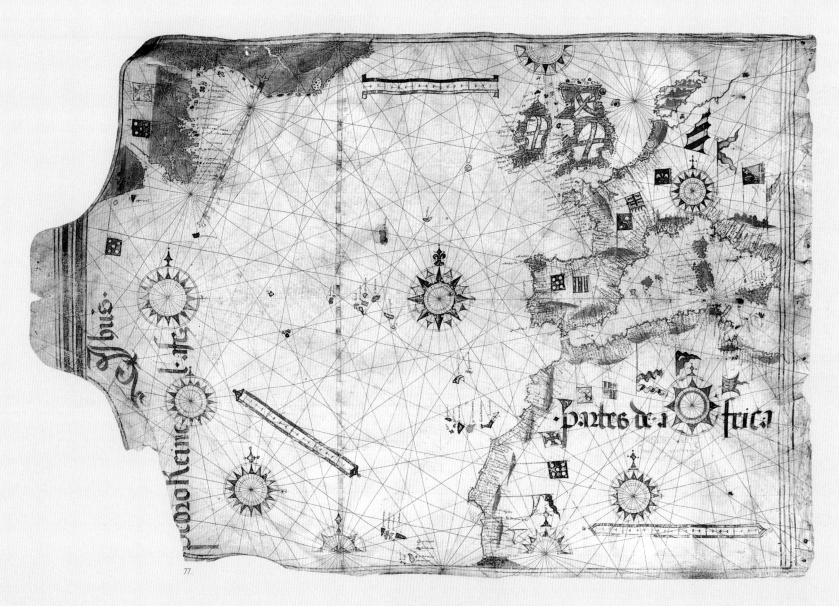

77

77
Pedro Reinel, Map of the Atlantic
Circa 1504

This map, along with Caverio's map, is one of
the oldest maps with a latitude scale, which is
situated in the middle of the Atlantic Ocean. For
the very first time, we can also see, in the area of
Newfoundland, a secondary latitude scale, which
runs along the magnetic north (with a 21-degree
declination). The lands are visibly well documented
in this area, which show the great interest the
Portuguese had in this area.

Bayerische Staatsbibliothek, Munich, Cod. Icon. 132.
Illuminated manuscript on parchment, 29 × 23⅜ inches
(73.5 × 60 cm).

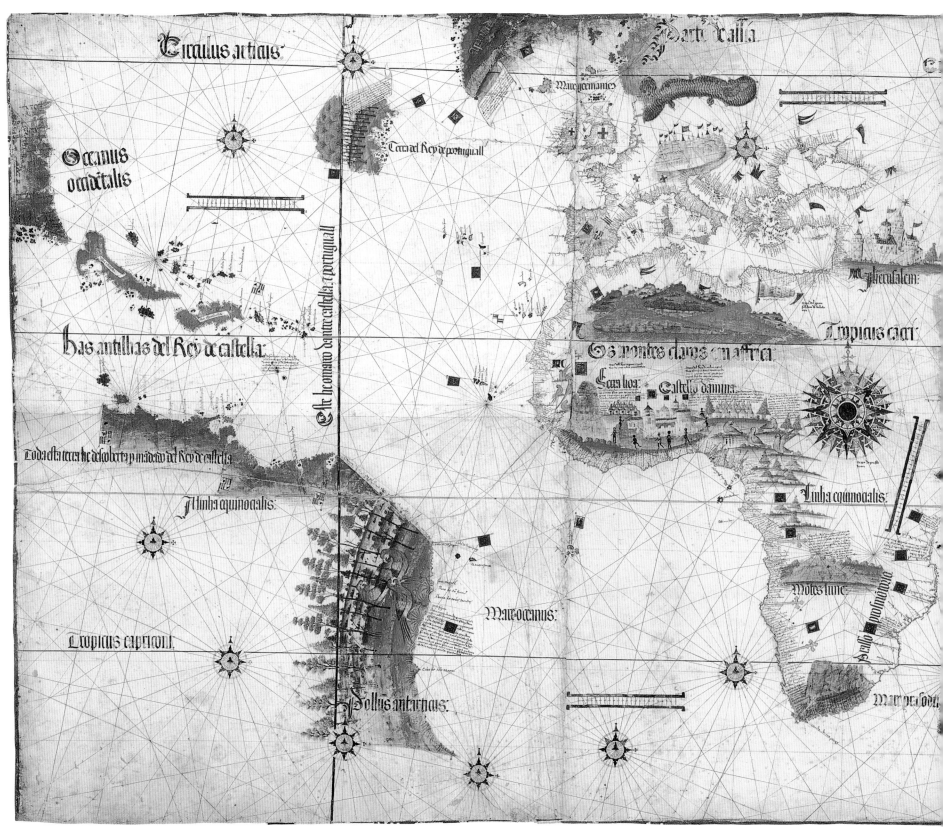

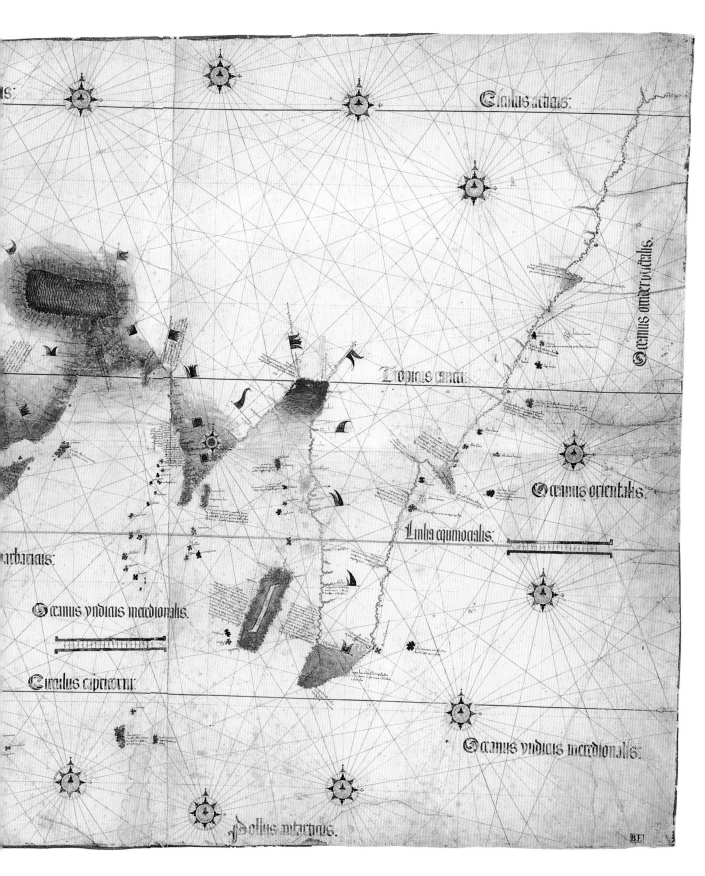

78

Planisphere Known as the Cantino Planisphere

1502

This anonymous planisphere was named after the person who purchased it, Alberto Cantino, representative of the duke of Ferrare at Lisbon. It does not have any latitudinal scales, though the presence of the equator, the tropics and the Arctic Circle attest to the fact that it was constructed with astronomical measurements of latitude. The new European discoveries (Brazil, Newfoundland, etc.) are there, as well as the line of the Treaty of Tordesillas, which separated the Spanish and Portuguese Empires.

Biblioteca Estense Universitaria, Modena, C. G. A. 2. Manuscript on parchment, 86⅝ × 41⅜ (220 × 105 cm).

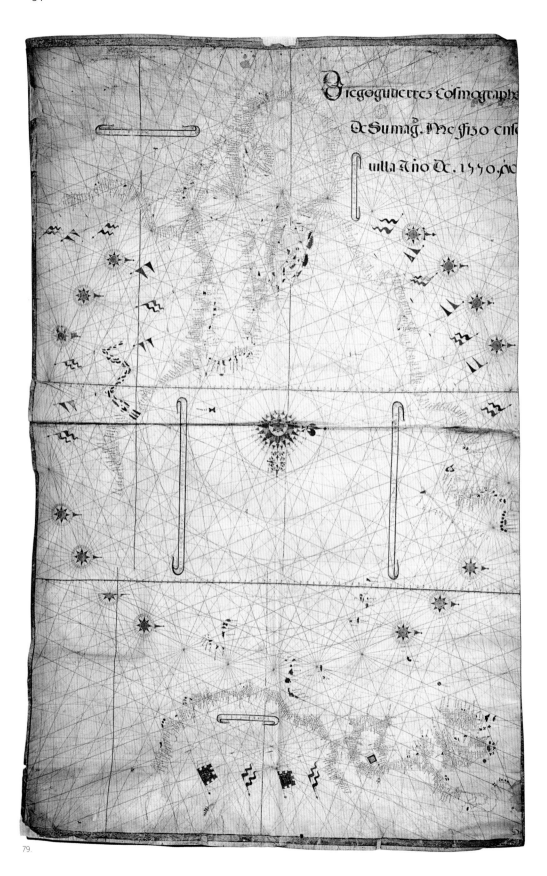

79.

79
Diego Gutiérrez, Map of the Atlantic
1550

This map is an official work of the Casa de contratación of Seville, and it combines the various cartographic systems of the 16th century. It displays three different latitudinal scales: one traverses the mouths of the Amazon; the other crosses the Azores, landing 2030' more to the south than the first one; and the third runs obliquely and to the east of Newfoundland, in order to take the magnetic declination into account.

NLF, Paris, Maps and Plans, GE SH ARCH 2. Manuscript on parchment, 33⅜ × 51⅞ inches (85.5 × 131.8 cm).

80
Map of the Atlantic
Circa 1560

The rich ornamentation of this Portuguese map still leaves room for the pavilions of different countries and representations of African and American cities. The course of the Amazon, descending via Orellana in 1542, is also well displayed. This map, as with those of Reinel and Guitiérrez, has an oblique latitude scale in the region of Newfoundland.

NLF, Paris, Maps and Plans, GE B 1148 (RES). Illuminated manuscript on parchment, 34⅝ × 28¾ inches (88 × 73 cm).

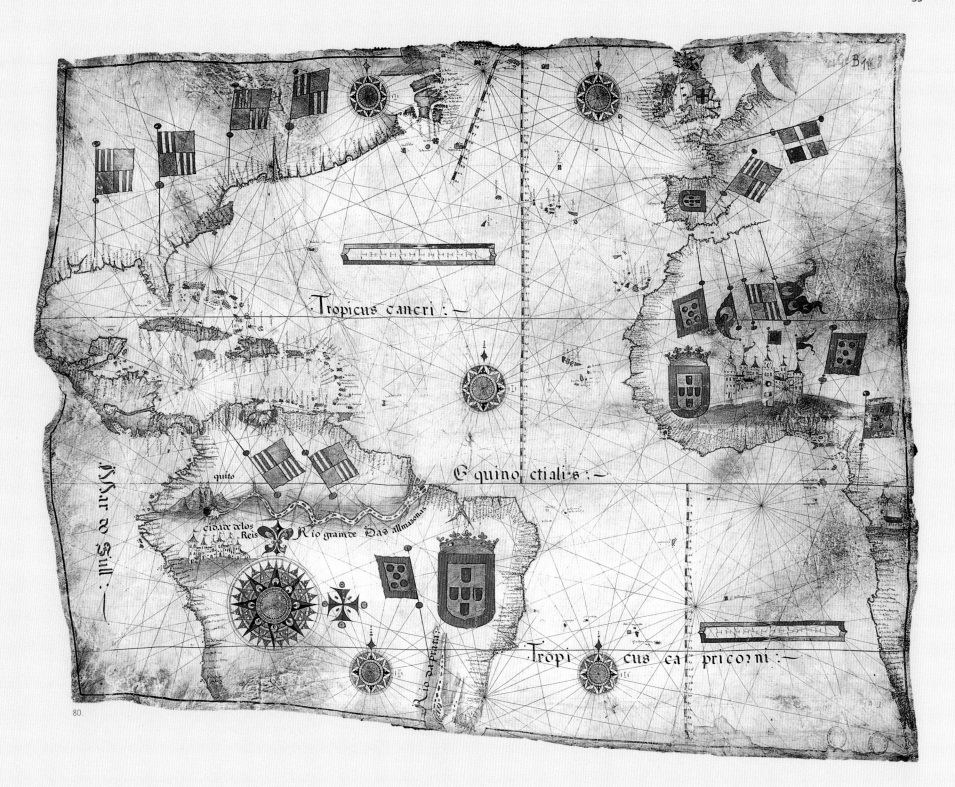

Tropicus cancri :—

Equino ctialis :—

Mar do Sull :—

quito

cidade dlos Reis   Rio grande das Almasonas

Tropi   cus   capricorni :—

NORMAN HYDROGRAPHERS 16TH AND 17TH CENTURIES

Sarah Toulouse

* Among the imaginary lands
represented by 16th-century
cartographers, "Big Java" is particular
to Brittany and Normandy. This vast
expanse of land that extends from
the south of Indonesia to join up
with Australia has been responsible
for much ink and is still debated
among historians of cartography.

81
Pierre de Vaulx,
Map of the Atlantic
(detail)

See full map on page 141.

Between 1480 and 1650, Normandy was without a doubt the most active French maritime province. It is not surprising therefore that, beginning in 1530, an indigenous school of hydrography and maritime cartography developed, from which about 20 names are still known and some 50 works remain. In the absence of any archives, the cartographers are not well known. Pierre Desceliers is often cited and identified by his compatriots as the "father of French cartography," and occasionally Jean Roze, who worked for Henry VIII and then Henri II, is also cited. Some cartographers are only known by their signatures on a few maps, such as Nicolas Desliens and Jean Cossin (see illustration 82). The maps, atlases and other navigational treatises that they left behind shed considerable light on their experience and knowledge.

The first trait shared among Norman cartographers is that they were practical men as well as men of science. Mariners or merchants produced tools for their fellows during the 16th century: flat portolan maps overlain with the traditional network of rhumb lines. However, they also wrote treatises that paralleled the work of mathematicians who were making advancements in their attempts to resolve the representation of the Earth's curvature on maps. Indeed, the first French map constructed along the Mercator projection system was created by the Norman hydrographer Guillaume Le Vasseur (see illustration 83) in 1601. Other cartographers also used these complex projections, such as Guillaume Le Testu (see illustration 90), who in 1566 drafted a very beautiful world map in a projection said to be "de Bonne" ("good"), which was a remarkable mathematical feat with curvilinear meridians and concentric and circular parallels.

With regard to which regions Norman cartographers represented, we likewise find a combination of motives: a wish to provide mariners with navigational instruments coupled with an intellectual curiosity to pursue discoveries. Consequently, cartographers focused on seas frequented by their compatriots, including the Atlantic Ocean (see illustration 85); Brazil, at the time when Norman expeditions were targeting this region (see illustration 83); and the northern European coastline, when Norman merchants were interested in Spitzberg (Jean Dupont's 1625 map and Jean Guérard's 1628 map). On the other hand, Desceliers's huge planispheres (see illustrations 98 and 99) and various other atlases and cosmographies described the entire known world as well as the imagined lands not yet discovered.*

The development of portolan maps could equally have been responding to the teaching needs and politics of the time. Several Norman maps are dedicated to princes. For example, Desceliers painted the coats of arms of King Henri II, Constable Anne de Montmorency and the French Admiral Claude d'Annebaut on his 1550 planisphere. Guillaume Le Testu dedicated his 1556 atlas to the admiral of Coligny, and Jacques de Vaulx placed his hydrography treatise of 1583 under the patronage of the duke of Joyeuse, the admiral of France (see illustration 26). These are richly illuminated works that create genuine scenes that were lessons in geography as well as in history and zoology, while also creating allegiances and garnering favors. Occasionally, cartography can also be seen as propaganda. The presence of heraldry carrying the French coat of arms in northern Brazil and Florida on the 1613 map by Pierre de Vaulx (see illustration 84) is informed by France's efforts to reconquer lands in the Americas in the early 17th century.

Just as they knew how to incorporate the work of mathematicians, Norman cartographers were familiar with the work of other European cartographers and found inspiration in them. They positioned themselves evenly between the Portuguese and Spanish maritime cartography of the 15th and 16th centuries — again close to medieval portolans — and the revival brought by the Dutch at the end of the 16th century.

At the beginning of the 16th century, the Portuguese were dominating European nautical science. Since their maps were widely circulated and served as models, Portuguese cartographers were equally at home in France. Consequently, one can readily observe the Portuguese influence on the first Norman cartographers, notably by the presence of several Portuguese names on their maps, including those of places in Normandy! This influence, however, was not limited to the nomenclature. It is also evident through the coastal outlines on some maps, such as the representation of Scotland as an island.

Toward the end of the 16th century and during the 17th century, the Dutch were flooding Europe with printed atlases, which were quickly translated and copied. In addition to appropriating the elements for coastal tracings and the nomenclature of the northern European coasts, Norman cartographers also adopted their hydrographic symbols, namely anchors to indicate ports and network of dots to signal shallows and reefs, together with indicators of

the nature of shallows, such as those that appeared on Jean Guérard's maps starting in 1625.

Norman maps also contained original characteristics, including their presentation of the North American coastline. Thus, Labrador is shown as a large landmass toward the east that ends in a point and is separated from the rest of the continent by a deep indentation north of the Saint Lawrence River. In addition, Newfoundland is shown as an archipelago and not as a peninsula, as on other maps of the time, and there is also the imaginary Bay of Norambègue, which brushes the coast of Nova Scotia.

Normandy was not the only French province interested in the art of navigation and cartography. During the same era, the port of Conquet in Brittany was home to two families of cartographers, the Brouscons (see illustration 88) and the Troadecs (see illustration 89), who both produced maps and small nautical guides, some of which were printed and widely distributed between 1540 and 1590. Unlike the Normans, the Bretons addressed themselves solely to mariners, producing practical notebooks that were composed mainly of quadrants and were specifically designed to calculate the amplitude of tides. The Normans were aware of the Bretons' work and reproduced some of those schematics in their hydrography treatises. For their part, the Bretons got their inspiration for their few marine maps largely from the Normans.

Generally, Norman hydrographers were successful at popularizing the nautical science of their time. They were rarely innovative, but they remained aware of the latest discoveries and were quick to relay them to sailors. After 1643, however, Normandy no longer produced maps or navigational treatises. Religious wars greatly affected this region, resulting in the decline of its ports. By 1630, the cartography workshops in Rouen, Dieppe and Honfleur were being supplanted by those in La Rochelle and Bordeaux. The end of the Norman school of cartography was undoubtedly also tied to the limited distribution of its products. Even if Norman cartographers had wanted to change their content and transition from the medieval portolan model to modern maritime maps, Norman products remained in manuscript form and could not, ultimately, compete with Dutch printed atlases.

Sarah Toulouse

82

Jean Cossin, *Carte cosmographique ou Universelle description du monde* (Cosmographic Map or Universal Description of the World)
Dieppe, 1570

Founded on a scientific projection in which the meridians are sinusoids and the parallels are equidistant straight lines, the world map of Jean Cossin testifies to the mathematical knowledge of the Norman hydrographers. At the bottom of the map we see a vast southern continent, which is meant to counterbalance the lands of the northern hemisphere.

NLF, Paris, Maps and Plans, GE D 7896 (RES)
Illuminated manuscript on parchment, 17¾ × 10 inches (45 × 25.5 cm).

82.

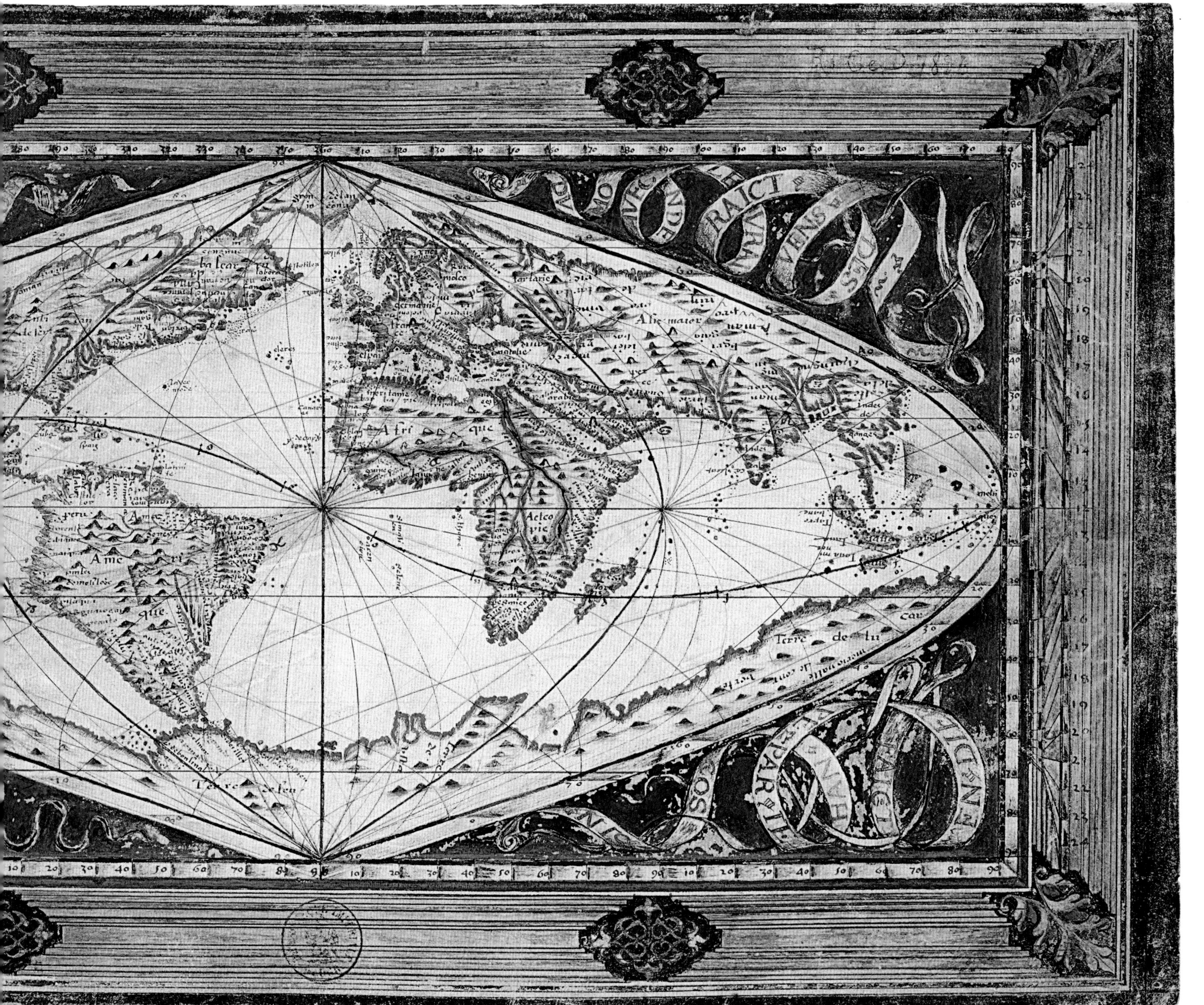

83

Guillaume Le Vasseur, *Traité de géodrographie ou Art de naviguer* (Treatise on Geodrography or The Art of Navigation)
Dieppe, circa 1608

Here, Guillaume Le Vasseur reviews the problems with the nautical science at the time, combining mathematical theory with concrete examples to facilitate understanding. It is one of the first navigational treatises to address in detail questions related to the construction and use of marine maps.

NLF, Paris, Manuscrips, French 19112. F. 86.
Manuscript on paper, 92 f., 6¼ × 13¾ inches (16 × 35 cm).

84

Pierre de Vaulx, Map of the Atlantic
Le Havre, 1613

Bursting with gold and colors, this map of the Atlantic reflects France's ambitions in America. The fleur-de-lis appears in New France, where the French toponyms and precision of the tracings attest to an old and renewed presence, and also in Brazil, where the map is nothing more than a remembrance of Villegagnon's expedition (1555) and other aborted colonization attempts. Near Lima, a deep blue wind rose enhanced with gold could very well symbolize the Incas' sun.

NLF, Paris, Maps and Plans, GE SH ARCH 6 (RES).
Illuminated manuscript on parchment, 37¾ × 27 inches (96 × 68.5 cm).

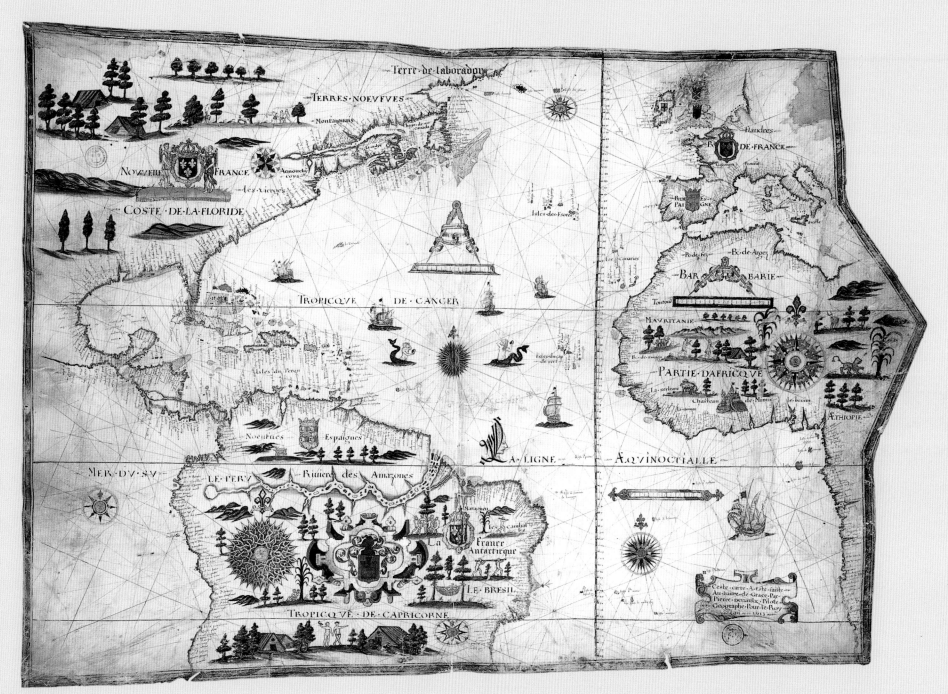

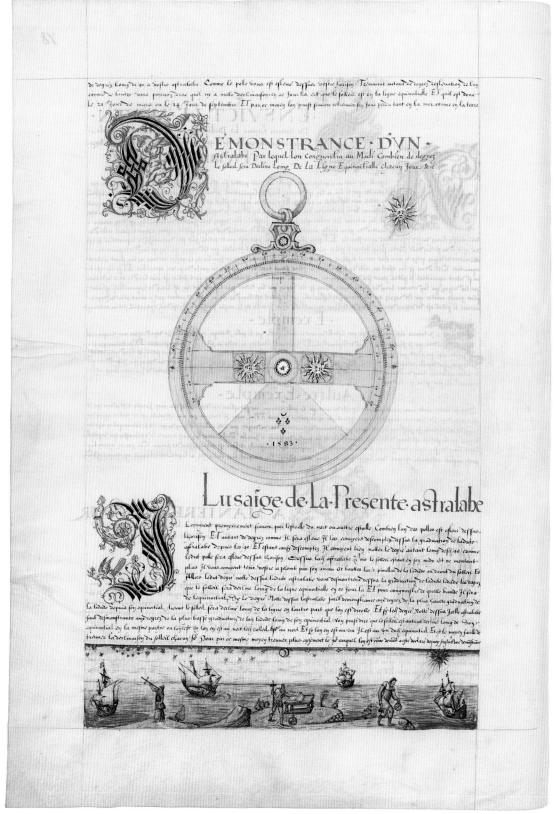

86.

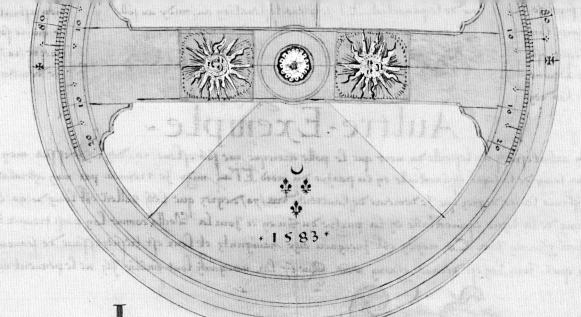

·1583·

Lusaige·de·La·Presente·astralabe

Il convyent premyerement scavoir par lestoille du nort ou aultre estoille Combien luy dit polles est esleue dessus
lhorison ET autant de degrez comme Il sera esleue Il les convyent descomptez dessus la graduation de ladicte
astralabe depuis les 90 ET estant ainsy descomptez Il convyent bien notter le degré autant long des 90 comme
ledict polle sera esleue dessus lhorison Dessus lad astralabe Puis le solleil estant en son midy Et ne montant
plus Il vous convyent tenir vostre a plomb par son aneau Et bouttez les 2 pinnulles de la sidade au droit du solleil Et
Allors ledict degré notté dessus ladicte astralabe vous desmontrera dessus la graduation de ladicte sidade les degrez
que le solleil sera declime long de la ligne equinoctialle en ce Jour la ET pour congnoistre de quelle bande Il sera
de lequinoctial Sy le degré Notté dessus lastralabe fait demonstrance aux degrez de la plus haulte graduation de
la sidade depuis son equinoctial Autant le solleil sera declime long de la ligne en lautre part que lon est dicelle Et sy les degré Notté dessus Icelle astralabe
fait desmonstrance aux degrez de la plus basse graduation de lad sidade long de son equinoctial lon puist dire que le solleil est autant declime long de son
equinoctial en la mesme partye ou lon est sy lon en est au nort les solleil Est au nort Et sy lon en est au su Il est au su dud equinoctial Et est le moyen facile de
trouver la derlinaison du solleil chacun Jo Pour par ce mesme moyen trouver plus aysement le Jo auquel lon est come deuant a este declaré dequoy sensuid une demonstrace

86 and 87
Jacques de Vaulx, *Fabrication et usage de*
l'astrolabe de mer et du nocturlabe
(Fabrication and Use of the Sea
Astrolabe and of the Nocturnal)
Le Havre, 1583

In his *Premieres Œuvres* (First works), a
sumptuously illustrated treatise on navigation,
captain Jacques de Vaulx was greatly inspired
by the learned works of the time (Petrus Apian,
Pedro de Medina, Oronce Fine, etc.). In this work,
a series of figures demonstrate the construction
and use of nautical instruments like the sea
astrolabe, which was designed to measure the
elevation of the stars and deduce a site's latitude,
and the nocturnal, which allows one to determine
the time at night.

NLF, Paris, Manuscripts, French 150. F. 7.
Illuminated manuscript on velum, 11 × 17¾ inches
(28 × 45 cm).

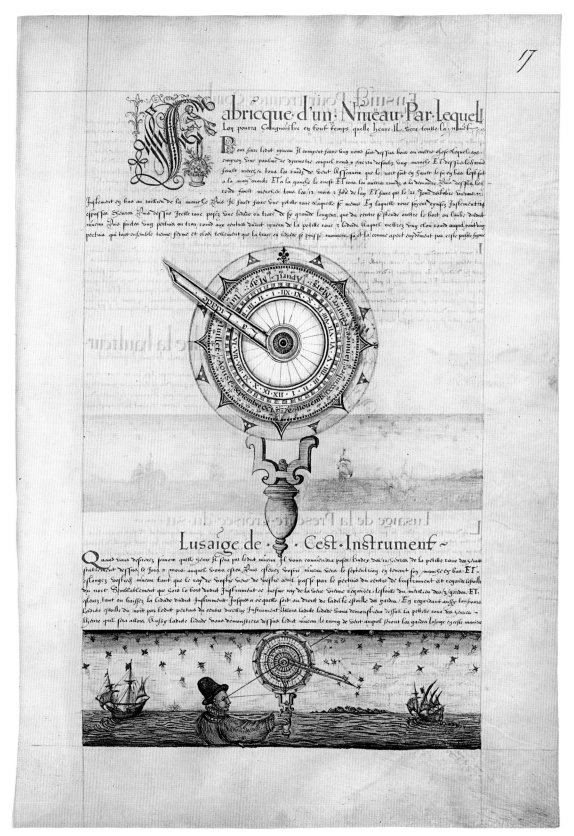

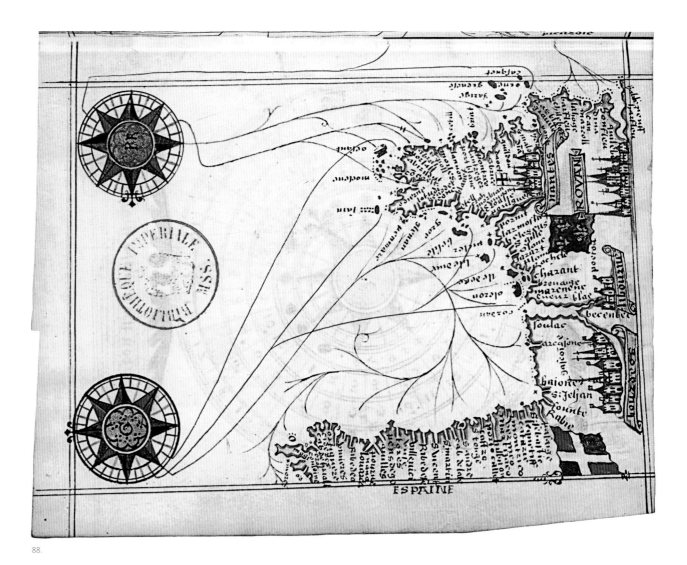

88.

88

Guillaume Brouscon,
Indexed Map to Calculate the Tides
Le Conquet, 1548

Combining data that is useful to navigation on the Atlantic coastline using figures, Guillaume Brouscon's *Manuel de pilotage* (Piloting manual) was helpful to many Ponant mariners, regardless of the language they spoke. A simple graphical system shows, for the main ports, the moon's position on the horizon on the 1st and 15th day of the month, when the sea is full, and, thanks to an included calendar, to estimate the hour of the tides for any particular day.

NLF, Paris, Manuscripts, French 25374, f. 25 vo-26, 1 map.
Illuminated manuscript on parchment, one map + 25 f.,
5½ × 6⅞ inches (14 × 17.5 cm).

89

J. Troadec,
Map of the Northeast Atlantic Ocean
Le Conquet, mid-16th century

Piloting guides from Brittany were distributed mainly in manuscript form but also in xylographic impressions. Issued from an almanac published by J. Troadec, this map, carved in wood and printed on velum, is overlaid with latitude scales and shows the maritime regions usually frequented by Breton mariners.

NLF, Paris, Maps and Plans, GE D 7894 (RES).
Xylographic impression on parchment with manuscript additions, 13⅜ × 11½ inches (34 × 29 cm).

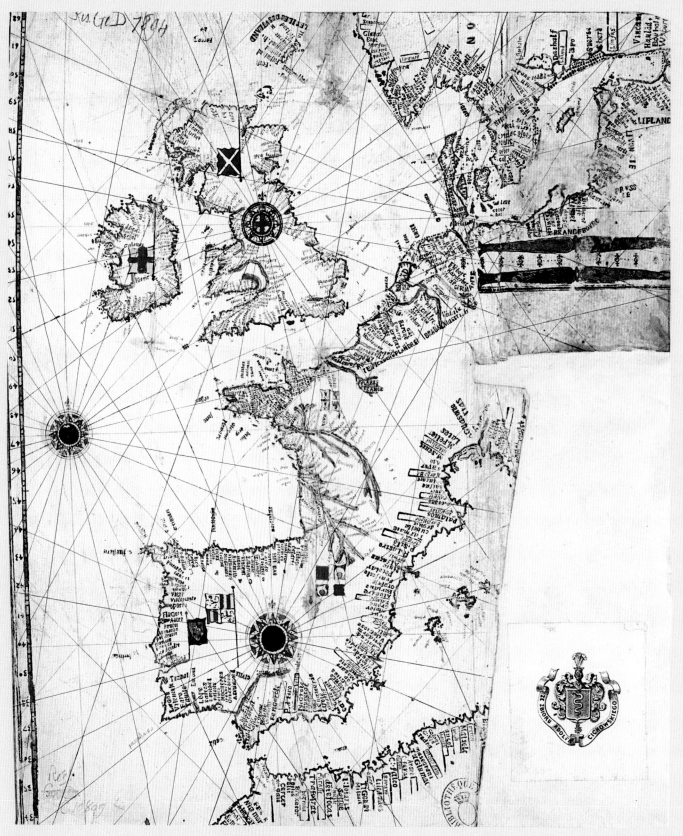

UNIVERSAL
COSMOGRAPHY
GUILLAUME LE TESTU

90
Guillaume Le Testu,
Cosmographie universelle
(Universal Cosmography)
Le Havre, 1556

Guillaume Le Testu's *Cosmographie universelle* is a magnificent world atlas drawn on paper. It's composed of six planispheres in scholarly projections and 50 regional maps equipped with rhumb lines and latitude scales. Each plank is accompanied by a commentary regarding geography, climate, inhabitants, human activities, etc. Le Testu unrolls before our very eyes an image of a fractioned world, making us travel from northern Europe to the Mediterranean, from Africa to the Eastern Indies and from the mythical southern lands to the Americas while offering us the most complete vision of the world and the most richly illustrated portolan ever seen.

A work of a royal captain from Le Havre, the *Cosmographie universelle* is akin to the maps from the Norman school of hydrography — the heir of Iberian cartography, particularly Portuguese cartography — and while it registers the progress of Norman hydrography, it does so with certain gaps. Thus, the Atlantic coast of the Americas is well defined, but the Pacific cost is rather vague. Like his fellow cartographers, Guillaume Le Testu was a well-established navigator who participated in diverse maritime voyages in the New World. Thus, he joined Villegagnon's expedition to establish a colony in Brazil in 1555 and, according to his friend the cosmographer André Thevet, perished in Mexico in 1572 during an attack by a convoy of Spanish gold.

The cosmography was dedicated to the French Admiral Caspard de Coligny and is not without a political slant. Its main distinction, however, is that it devotes a quarter of its regional maps to the mythical southern continent, which was conceived by 16th century cartographers as a counterbalance to the landmasses of the northern hemisphere. It shows Tierra del Fuego, discovered by Magellan in 1519, and the "Big Java" imagined by Norman cartographers to the south of Sumatra. Divided into 12 planks, this cartographic fiction was designed by the imagination, as admits the author in his commentary, and relies on his partial knowledge of isles or islets that are quite real but among which he created artificial relationships. This cosmography is prospective, anticipating the future progress of geographic knowledge while warning navigators about a potential immediate danger. It's rich iconography is of a composite nature, the illustrator giving free rein to his imagination and juxtaposing fabulous fauna and monstrous races from ancient and medieval traditions with civilized Oriental peoples known from the writings of Marco Polo and naked savages inspired by the Brazilian Tupinamba.

C.H.

Historic Defense Service, Library, Vincennes, D.1 Z.14.
Illuminated manuscript on paper (118 pages)
14¼ × 20⅞ inches (36 × 53 cm).

90 a
The World

World map centered on the Atlantic Ocean
Third projection, f. 4 v°.

90 b.

90 b
The World

World map in four sections (sixth projection),
with the French crest and the coat of arms of the
admiral of Coligny.
f. 7 v°

90 c
Europe

Newfoundland, Western Europe and the Barbary
Coast, with naval combat and a marine tank
carrying the silver eagle of the House of Coligny
coat of arms.
f 8 v°

90 d
Northern Europe and Greenland

f. 10 v°

90 c.

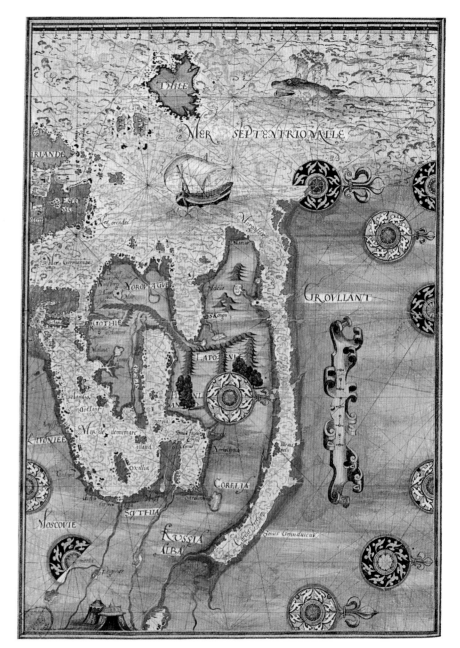

90 d.

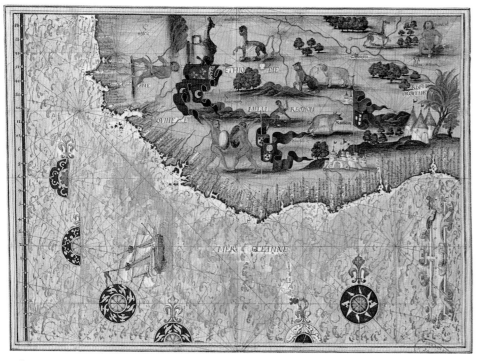

90 f.

90 g.

Africa

90 e
Western Africa from the Strait of Gibraltar to Cape Verde, with combat scenes between African warriors.
f. 17 v°

90 f
Western Africa from Cape Verde to the mouth of the Niger River, with combat scenery, wild animals and Cyclopes.
f. 18 v°

90 g
Southern Africa from the Gulf of Guinea to the mouth of the Zambezi, with Portuguese ports of call, camels and several wild animals.
f. 20 v°

90 h.

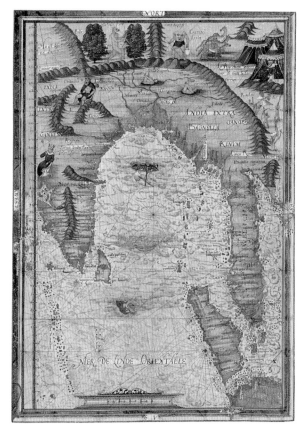

90 i.

Asia

90 h
The western Mediterranean and Middle East, with
Hebrews crossing the Red Sea.
f. 24 v°

90 i
The western Sea of Indi, from Ceylon to Sumatra,
with fabled creatures (cynocephalus, Blemmyes
and sciapods), two kings sitting on a throne and
the Great Tartar Khan in front of his tent.
f. 28 v°

90 j
The Red Sea and Persian Gulf, with naval combat
and the king of Persia on his throne.
f. 26 v°

MOLVQVES

petitte
Coste dangereuze

Rimerre de lille

Rimerre Roche

Baie Gamme

Terre de Offir

Rimerre du detroicet

des froles pacubeaz Lucaiangeloto et fessa

Guimape men araguanon cunbanne medame

Emsante Venche

fuggramme

Clere baie acacem Tubam

Mandalican

Capare

Rimerre basse Chambah

Riuierre de dom

Agaloman

Jlla des basses basses Comda

PETITE IAVE

Baie zonde

palmban

Trapbame Ante sarmatza

GRANDE IAVE

Rimerre de saint pierre

Coste langue

Rimerre Grande

Goultze

lac deaü

Rimerre mer

pracaillie

Goultze

Rimerre de perrles

longue baie

Goscap

montangne

Rimerre de lille des trois baies

90 m.

90 l.

Southern Lands

90 k
Big Java and Small Java to the south of the Maluku Islands.
f. 32 v°

90 l
Southern land facing the Cape of Good Hope.
f. 34 v°

90 m
Southern land, Tierra del Fuego and the Strait of Magellan.
f. 34 v°

America

90 n
New Spain, the Gulf of Mexico and the western
coastline of Central America, with the Spanish
two-headed eagle coat of arms, a mine, a forge
and several people in costume.
f. 53 v°

90 o
Florida, Canada and Labrador with Newfoundland,
the Saint Lawrence River, several aboriginal
villages (including Hochelaga) and the Saguenay
Kingdom.
f. 56 v°

90 o.

90 n.

90 p
The Giganton kingdom at the tip of South America,
with a scene of jubilation around an aboriginal
leader being carried on a chair.
[f. 43 v°]

THE ICONOGRAPHY OF THE NEW WORLD 15TH–17TH CENTURIES

Surekha Davies

The Mongol Khan of the Golden Horde,
Catalonian Atlas
(detail)
Majorca, 1375

Several sovereigns are represented in the *Catalonian Atlas*. The Christian kings are traditionally seated on thrones and shown crowned and carrying a hand scepter, but variations are introduced for the African and Asian princes. Installed on the edge of the Caspian Sea, this Mongol khan holds a scepter and a golden orb — symbols of wealth and power — though he is seated on the ground and is wearing a turban.

NLF, Paris, Manuscripts, Spanish 30, f. 3.
Illuminated manuscript on parchment, 12 half-sheets measuring 9⅞ × 25¼ inches (25 × 64 cm).

92

The Magi en Route to Bethlehem,
Catalonian Atlas
(detail)
See full caption above.

91.

From 1492, with the discovery of the Americas, and 1498, when Vasco de Gama reached India after having doubled around the Cape of Good Hope, navigators provided European cartographers new information regarding western Africa, the islands of the Atlantic Ocean and the Indian Ocean. Throughout the 15th century, thanks to those contributions, cartographers following the tradition of portolan maps in Portugal, Spain and France produced many well-illustrated maps. This chapter discusses the people who delivered the most detailed iconography on European maps during this time.

THE ANCIENT TRADITION OF MARVELS AND MONSTERS

Even before the age of discoveries, the Far East and southern Africa were associated with unbelievable peoples. Describing the world's habitants in his *Natural History* (circa 77–79 AD), Pliny the Elder notes that "Both India and Ethiopia are teeming with marvels."[1] These wonders include beings with extraordinary physical characteristics or customs, including the Astomes, who did not have mouths and fed exclusively on the odor of food; the Troglodites, who lived in grottos; the Anthropophages, who consumed human flesh; and the Sciapods, who had only one foot, which could also serve as a sun shade. Monstrous people still appear in world maps of the 13th century. Cartographers placed them as far as possible from Jerusalem, which was considered the center of the universe.[2] The idea that faraway parts of the world, both eastern and western, could shelter such marvelous — and monstrous — inhabitants was reinforced by Marco Polo's stories about Asia from the end of the 13th century as well as by Jean de Mandeville's book, the story of an imaginary voyage, which was widely distributed at the beginning of the 14th century. During the first two centuries of the printing press, European depictions of the peoples of Asia and Africa and, later, of the Americas were influenced by these books and by images of this type.

However, the iconography of faraway lands on the first portolan maps did not contain monsters, but rather rulers siting on thrones or cushions. Generally, these rulers held a scepter in their right hand and raised their left index finger, an attribute that painters and other artists from the Middle Ages traditionally used to denote a king.[3] These iconographic figures are also featured in the *Catalonian Atlas* (circa 1375), in which the author extends and adapts them to sovereigns from Africa to Asia while adding other elements to their

costumes (see illustrations 91 and 92). For example, Muslim and Tartar princes have local headgear instead of a European crown and a scimitar or mace instead of a scepter, are dressed in exotic gowns and sit on the ground instead of a throne. The author even added parakeets in the surrounding scenery to differentiate these kingdoms from their European counterparts.[4] The sovereign who figures most commonly on portolan maps is undoubtedly Prester John, a legendary Christian king who is thought to have lived in India or Ethiopia (see illustration 33).[5]

The 16th century saw the arrival of a new type of portolan map, one that was conceived to represent the world on either a single sheet or a collection of sheets. These maps lean heavily on earlier traditions in that they contain detailed information about coastal regions, but they were also inspired by iconographic traditions, blending aspects of medieval world maps, notably in the representations of monstrous peoples at the Earth's extremities. According to Sancho Gutiérrez's world map (1551; see illustration 93), we find living men with dogs' heads and others with a single gigantic foot on the northern fringes of Europe.[6] This conforms to the traditional Norman cartography, which held that both Africa and Asia sheltered monstrous peoples. The Norman world map known under the name "Rylands Map" depicts a gamut of creatures of this type in Asia (see illustration 96), notably beings with long ears and lips, Pygmies, a centaur and Blemmyes (people without a head or neck and with their eyes and mouths in their chests). They cohabitate as best they can with richly dressed kings of ancient civilizations: the "great cam of Kathay" (the great khan of China) accords an audience in his tent and, not far from that, a monarch with a dog's head and his hirsute subjects replicate the scene. The map drawn in 1550 by the Norman priest and cartographer Pierre Desceliers in turn offers different "African monsters," such as a headless man, a person with many arms and two black women (see illustration 98). The *Cosmographie universelle* of Le Testu situates in southern lands beings with ears so long that one is using an ear to cover himself and another is using one as his bed (see illustration 94a). In Patagonia, an area adjacent to the "Southern Lands," we find two individuals armed with bludgeons and shields (see illustration 94 b). These may very well be the giants described at the beginning of the 16th century by European voyagers, in particular Antonio Pigafetta, at the most southerly point of South America. Their muscular bodies and armaments suggest the mythical figure of Hercules. Beings like these were also mentioned in ancient Greek and Roman texts about faraway lands.

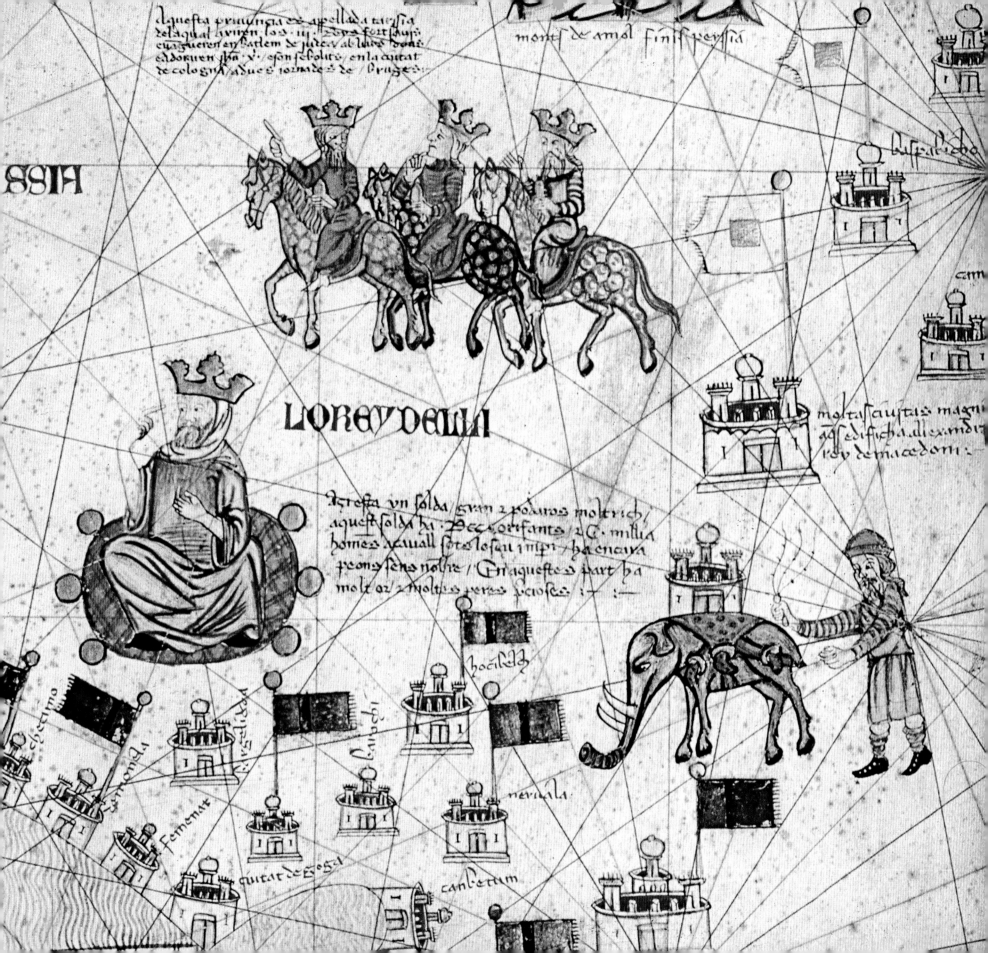

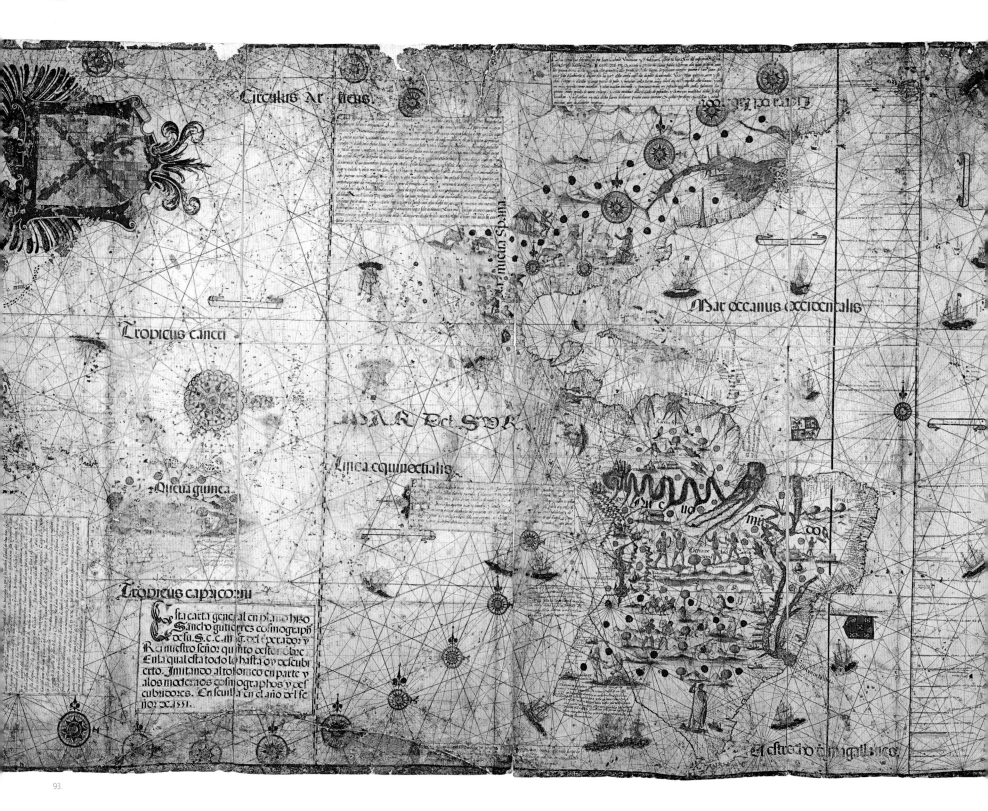

93.

See p. 165 for full caption.

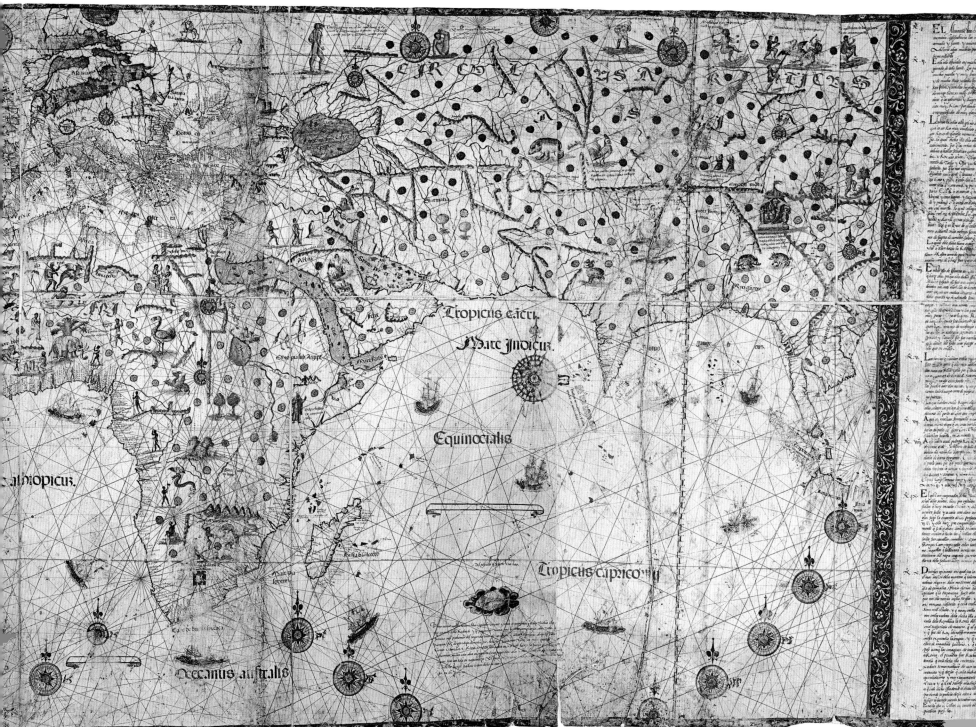

Tropicus cãcri.

Mare Indicus.

Equinocialis

Tropicus capricornus

Occeanus australis

93 a.

93 b.

93 c.

94 a.

94 b.

94 c.

94 d.

95 a.

95 b.

THE ILLUSTRATION OF GEOGRAPHIC EXPLORATIONS OF THE 16TH CENTURY

The most richly illustrated portolans maps were first produced in Normandy during the 16th century.[7] Norman cartographers often emphasized the results of French expeditions. For example, in Jean Rotz's 1542 atlas, one can see a Sumatran procession near a house of pylons (see illustration 97). The dwelling has a thatch roof and lattice walls, which was characteristic of many buildings from a large region of Southeast Asia.[8] As for the procession, in includes men holding long, gently curved sabers and, in the middle, a rider escorted by a servant on foot holding a parasol, attesting to his master's high status.[9] The procession is headed by a person holding a copper gong. Rotz was probably inspired by Jean and Raoul Parmentier's expedition, which, leaving from Dieppe, reached South Africa and then Sumatra in 1529. There was a painter on board, and he may well have brought back drawings that cartographers then consulted when illustrating their works.

The illustrations in Norman maps also testify to Cartier's expeditions to Newfoundland and Canada. The world map dedicated to the Dauphin (the future King Henri II of France), known as the "Harleian Map," shows the Saguenay leader sitting on a throne in the shape of a wooden chest and holding a lance in lieu of a scepter (see illustration 99). If the recourse to sovereigns on their thrones to illustrate nations is a throwback to the medieval cartographic tradition, this Norman representation of what is now Canada also uses information gathered during Cartier's voyages that was as yet unpublished at the time: in the illustration of Canada, cartographers sometimes draw from existing traditions and more recent information.

Thanks to these maps, we also have images of the relationship between Europeans and the peoples in faraway regions of the world, notably during the conquest of the Incan Empire by the conquistadors. In the *Cosmographie Universelle* by Guillaume Le Testu (see illustration 94 d),[10] a European — perhaps Francisco Pizarro — prepares to decapitate a semi-naked warrior, a fact we can surmise since there is another victim shown headless and dying nearby while his wartime companions vanish and others parade in front of a helmeted person brandishing a sword. The most important town, "Pachacalmy," was said to be larger than Paris. Pachacamac was the site of a pre-Incan temple that remained the site of rituals and sacrifices until the Spanish conquest.

THE REPRESENTATION OF BRAZIL: CANNIBALISM

Norman Cartographers were eager to represent the newly discovered region known as Brazil. Their maps and atlases often show the relationship between European merchants (undoubtedly Normans) and the indigenous population of Tupinamba. The most prominent representations evoke peaceful commercial exchanges between Europeans, likely Norman mariners, and Brazilians. The Tupinamba are shown felling trees with metal hatchets and removing the bark with a knife. The indigenous people trade wood for what appears to be mirrors or hatchets, suggesting they obtained their metallic objects from the merchants. They also transport the wood to the coast and assist the merchants as they load it aboard their ships. This iconography reflects the experience of Norman and Portuguese merchants, who traveled to Brazil in search of stainable wood.

The most detailed ethnographic representations of Brazil (see illustration 97) are those of John Rotz, who was a Scottish captain and manufacturer of maritime maps living in Dieppe. He reached Guinea and Brazil in 1539. In his atlas, several elements of this newly discovered area were drawn in situ or are at least based on quick sketches he took of the Tupinamba engaged in all kinds of activities. At the bottom of the map we see battle scenes between aboriginal groups, ceremonial dances and a vignette showing a man tied to a post who is about to be hit with a bludgeon. In the middle of the map, there is another stockade above which fires are lit. Rotz also included images of a less pleasant practice: cannibalism. In the middle of the right side of the map, a seated person cooks a human leg on a barbecue, and there is a dismembered body to the right of the enclosure.

Images of cannibals cooking their victims, both printed and on manuscripts, had been widely circulated since the beginning of the 16th century. In fact, cannibalism was the most cherished ethnographic subject with which to decorate maps of South America. In the *Miller Atlas* of 1519, a description of Brazilians as "savage and very brutal" tells us that they "nourish themselves on human flesh." In the northeast corner of the atlas, a small fire appears to indicate the preparation of humans for a meal (see illustration 95 a). A more explicit name appears in the Norman cartographer Guillaume LeTestu's *Cosmographie universelle* (Universal cosmography; 1555–1556), drawn for the Admiral Gaspard de Coligny, one of the main leaders of the expedition aimed at establishing a French colony in Brazil in the 1550s. In the atlas this section of the world is named the "Cannibal Area," and indeed, there is an illustration depicting a cannibal cutting up his victim on a table (see illustration 196 c). The wording explains that those who live near the equator are naked, eat human flesh and are very bad. Other violent scenes in this atlas are shown in the unknown regions of the southern hemisphere; there are two warriors in the "Southern Lands."

These few examples in traditional Norman, Portuguese and Spanish portolan maps clearly display the mores and appearances of faraway peoples as well as their relationship to European explorers. Many of these were current and firsthand observations, but they did not entirely replace the traditions and prior sources with which they coexisted up until the 17th century.

Surekha Davies
Original text translated by Laurent Bury

Works Cited

1. Pliny the Elder, *Natural History, book* VII-2 (trans. Ajasson de Grandsagne).

2. Asa Simon Mittman, *Maps and Monsters in Medieval England*, New York/London, Routledge, 2006, 34–42.

3. Ramon J. Pujades i Bataller, *La Carta de Gabriel de Vallseca de 1439*, Barcelona, Lumenartis/Biblioteca de Catalunya, 2009, 346.

4. For these observations on kings in the work of Cresques Abraham see: Ramon J. Pujades i Bataller *op. cit.*, 346.

5. Francesc Relaño, *The Shaping of Africa: Cosmographic Discourse and Cartographic Science in Late Medieval and Early Modern Europe+*, chapter 3.

6. Vienne, Österreichische Nationalbibliothek, Kartensammlung, K I 99.416.

7. For an iconographic study see Sarah Toulouse, "Trade, Empires and Propaganda: French Depictions of Brazilians on Sixteenth-Century Maps," *The Historical Journal*, 2012. For a global vision of the Norman cartographic tradition, see Sarah Toulouse "Marine Cartography and Navigation in Renaissance France," David Woodward (ed.), *Cartography in the European Renaissance*, series "The History of Cartography" (vol. 3), Chicago/London, University of Chicago Press, 2007, t. II, 1550–1568.

8. Jean Rotz, *Atlantique nord, boke of idrography*, 1542, Bonsecours, Point de Vues, 2010, 67 (facsimile).

9. *Ibid.*, 68.

10. CV-ADG, D.2z.14, f.50 vo. Vienna, Österreichische Nationalbibliothek, Kartensammlung, K I 99.416, f. 44 v°.

96.

96
Pierre Desceliers, Nautical Planisphere
Arques, 1546

With the coats of arms of the Dauphin and the king of France, this large world map, known as the Rylands Map, is the oldest map signed by Pierre Desceliers, a priest and hydrographer from Arques, near Dieppe. It offers a broad gamut of fabled creatures, including centaurs, Blemmyes and dog-headed men, cohabitating with actual historical figures.

John Rylands University Library, Manchester, French, MS 1.°
Illuminated manuscript on parchment, four assembled sheets measuring 100 × 50⅜ inches (254 × 128 cm).

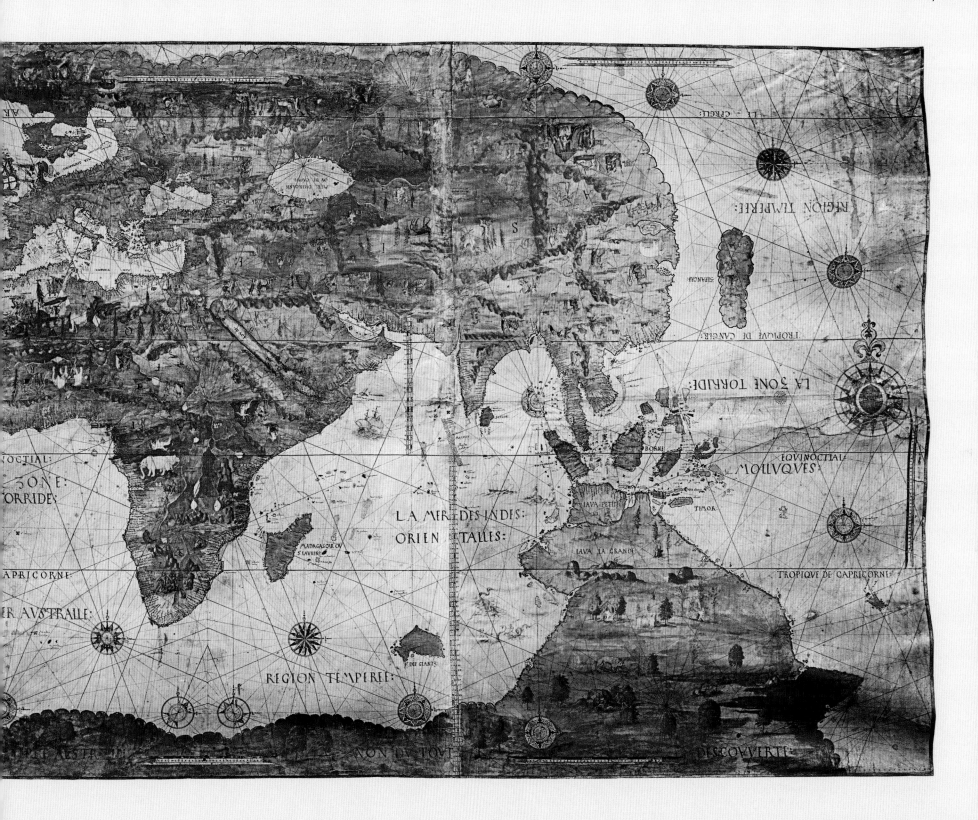

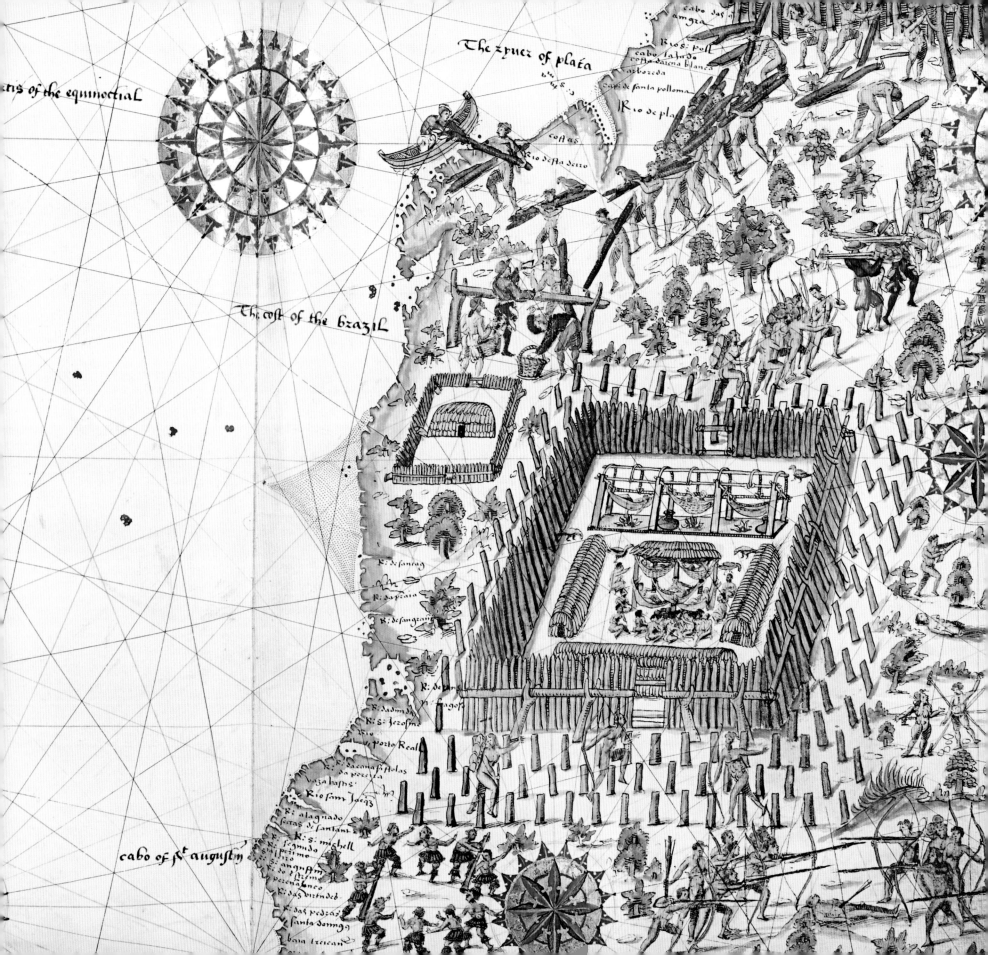

97
Jean Roze, *Boke of idrography*
(Book of Hydrography)
1542

From 1542 to 1546, Jean Roze, alias John Rotz, a captain from Dieppe who was originally from Scotland, was in the service of the British King Henry VIII, to whom he dedicated his *Boke of Idrography*, which was comprised of a world map and 11 regional maps. Once associated with the commercial activities of his father, at a very young age Roze experienced faraway navigations to Guinea and Brazil. Several scenes illustrated on these maps appear to have been drawn rather quickly.

97 a
Scenes from the lives of the Tupinamba aboriginals of Brazil.
f. 27 v°-28

97 b
A house on stilts and a procession in the Eastern Indies. f.9 v°-1

British Library, London, Royal MS 20 E IX.
Illuminated manuscript on parchment, 16 sheets measuring 30¼ × 23½ inches (77 × 59.5 cm).

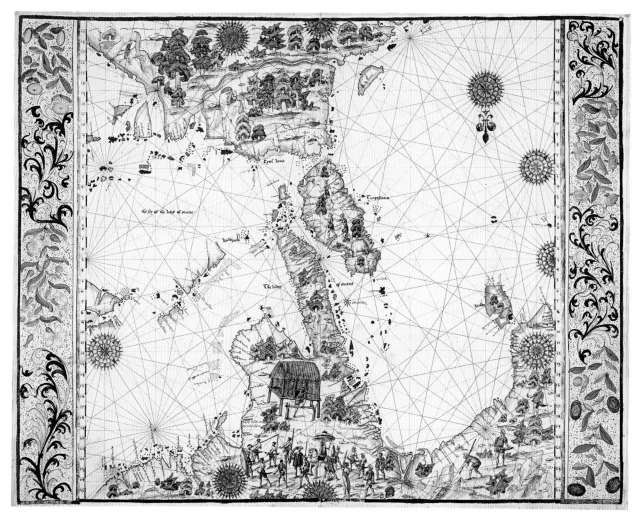

97 b.

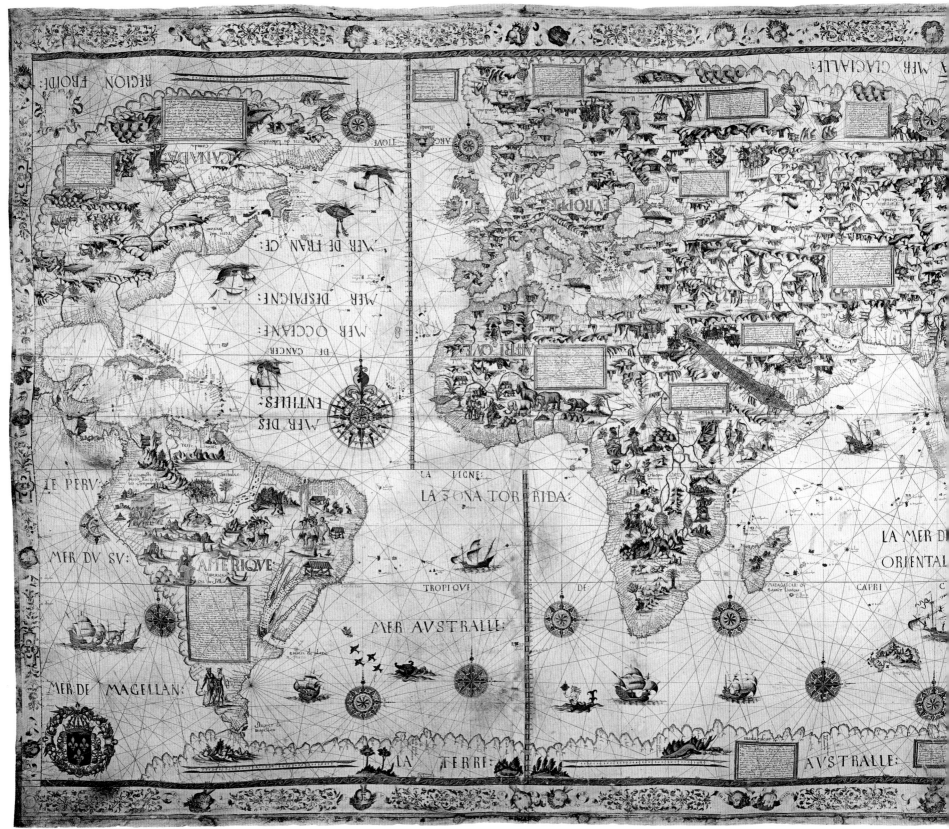

98
Pierre Desceliers,
Nautical Planisphere
Arques, 1550

Dedicated to a king (Henri II), a constable (Montmorency) and a French admiral (Annebaut), Pierre Desceliers's planisphere vaguely follows the Rylands Map. Of an exceptional iconographic quality, it offers several more or less fabled beings, such as, in Africa, headless men and men with several arms.

British Library, London, Add. MS 24065.
Illuminated manuscript on parchment, four assembled
sheets measuring 84⅝ × 53⅛ inches (215 × 135 cm).

99
Nautical Planisphere Known as Harleian Map
Dieppe, 1542–1547

Carrying the coat of arms of the Dauphin and the king of France, this world map bears the name of the first person known to own it, Edward Harley, count of Oxford, and is perhaps the oldest of the large Norman nautical planispheres. It interprets the results of Jacques Cartier's expeditions to North America and his discovery, in 1535, of the Saguenay River, at the end of which one would find, according to the tales of aboriginals, a kingdom where both gold and copper were abundant.

British Library, London, MS Add. 5413.
Illuminated manuscript on parchment, six assembled sheets measuring 96⅞ × 46½ inches (246 × 118 cm).

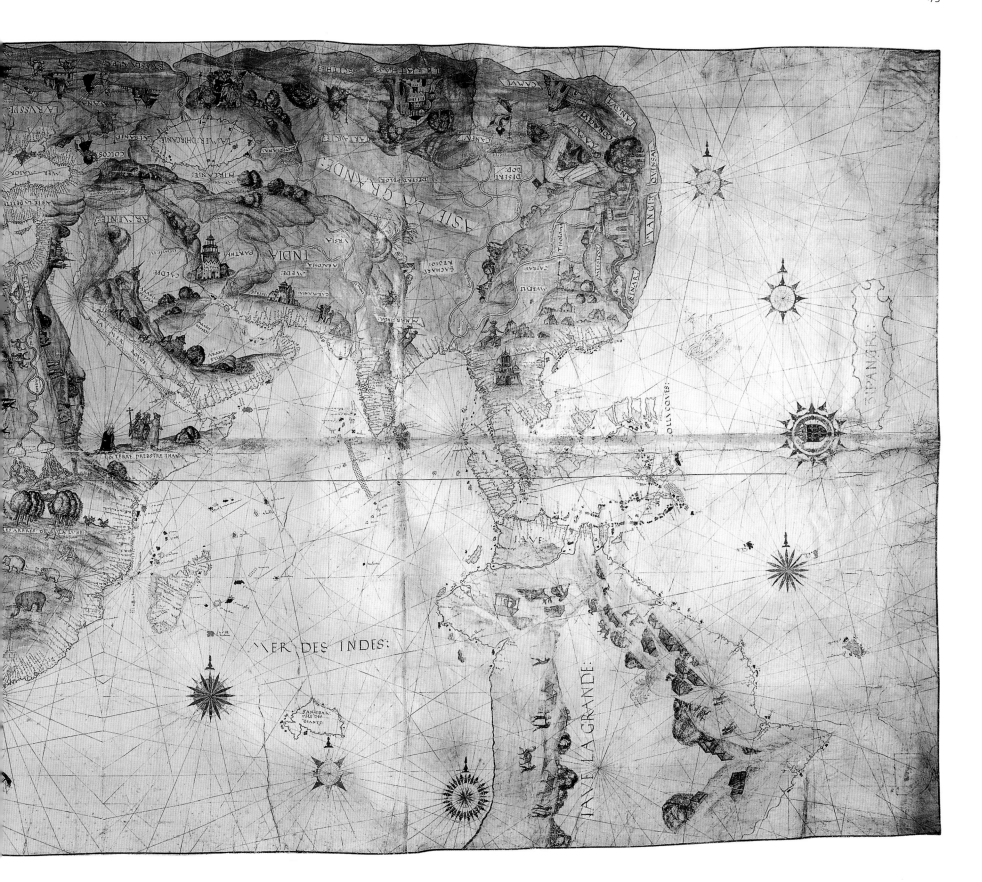

HYDROGRAPHERS ALONG THE THAMES 16TH AND 17TH CENTURIES

Sarah Tyacke

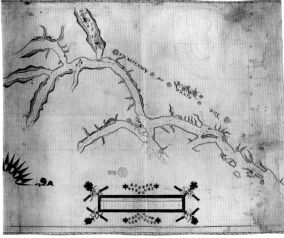

100.

100

Nicholas Comberford, Map of the Amazon River to the Confluence of the Tapajos

Circa 1626

This map, containing latitudes, quadrants and a graphic distance scale, has been attributed to Nicholas Comberford. It blends scientific elements, like the height of water and the shape of shorelines, with allegories, such as Amazons swimming in one of the river's tributaries.

The beginnings of hydrography in England date back to the middle of the 16th century.[1] Behind the Italians, Portuguese, Spanish and French, the English were obligated to explore the seas beyond their territorial waters for commercial, military or colonial ends. English maritime maps were produced almost exclusively in London, along the shores of the Thames, first by extending the cartographic traditions of continental Europe and then based on Dutch know-how. Artisans worked for ship's captains, in particular those of the British East India Company, and for the aristocrats and merchants who financed the voyages of commerce and exploration. The production of portolan maps began around 1560 and continued until about 1760. William Borough (1537–1598) was the first to produce British portolans, and he was followed by John Friend (who was active from 1703 to 1719) and then by his son Robert Friend (from 1719 to 1742). The Friends were the last hydrographers to be members of the Company of Drapers.

Drawn between 1568 and 1587, William Borough's maps cover British territorial waters, the Atlantic and the coastlines of North America, the Baltic, Norway and northern Russia. Having become the principal captain of the Muscovy Company in 1553, Borough sailed with Richard Chancellor in search of a northeast passage to Asia. He ended up reaching Novaya Zemlya and perhaps even the Ob River in Russia, and he told of these voyages in an annotated map that he drew around 1568 (see illustration 102). Borough also provided Anthony Jenkinson with information on the coastline from North Cape, Norway, to the Ob for the map by Abraham Ortelius published in 1570 in his *Theatrum orbis terrarium* (Theater of the Earth).

The number of English maritime maps remained small, and they were mostly used as a method to record geographic data rather than as navigational tools to be used at sea. In the 1590s, however, maritime maps began to illustrate England's oceanic ambitions in full growth, particularly their episodic wars with Spain between 1585 and 1604. They also showed the American coastline from the tip of Florida to Chesapeake Bay as well as the Atlantic and Pacific Oceans following the global circumnavigations of Francis Drake (1577–1580) and Thomas Cavendish (1591–1592). They also reflect privateers' intense interest in the Caribbean and the northern part of South America, the slave trade from western Africa and the various explorations, notably in Guyana, from the 1590s. Francis Drake's last challenge against the Spanish fleet (1595–1596), undertaken as a privateer, is described in the illustrated journal of his voyage (see illustration 101).[2] Drake was unsuccessful and perished from dysentery at sea. An anonymous English artist represented the main lands as well as the coastal scenery and included notes on hydrography and the approach to ports. In folio 13 he relates Drake's death as follows: "This morning, having finished the description of this land, the 28th of January 1595 [actually 1596], being a Wednesday, Sir Francis Drake died from the flow of blood, off the right shore of the Buena Ventura Island, about six leagues into the sea, he now rests with the Lord."

By 1600, English hydrography covered the seas surrounding the Cape of Good Hope as well as the Indian Ocean and Asia. In 1598, Martin Llewellyn (who was later the bursar of Saint Bartholomew's Hospital in London and who died in 1634) created the first known English copy of a Portuguese maritime atlas. This map showed the route to the East Indies, with additions most likely made following Cornelis de Houtman's first voyage (1595–1597). This interest in "oriental navigation" was maintained throughout the 16th century, with Gabriel Tatton (who was active from 1600 and died in 1621) producing a series of 17 maps (1620–1621) that represented a voyage to the coasts of Malaysia, China and the islands of the East Indies.

During this time, some practitioners established themselves as professional hydrographers, and they began to produce elaborate made-to-order maps based on original summaries. However, they were primarily copies of maps they already had on their premises bordering the Thames, according to Thomas Hood (1556–1620), a mathematician and physicist at Cambridge University who was also a mathematics teacher at Gresham College. The maps were drawn in a flat projection in colored ink on velum and featured a network of crisscrossing rhumb lines and wind roses, in the portolan style, as well as a latitude scale. Then known as Plane (or Plaine) charts, they were often mounted on hinged oak panels to help navigators more easily consult and store them while at sea. Up to the 1740s, 37 hydrographers are listed as masters or apprentices in the London Company of Drapers. The content and style of John Daniel's maps (who was active from 1612 and died in 1642) were passed down from master to apprentice. In this way, Daniel's apprentice Nicholas Comberford (active from 1626 to 1670) passed Daniel's maps down to such prolific practitioners as William Hack (who was active from 1680 and died in 1708). Hack copied maritime atlases spanning the Pacific and the Americas, which had been conquered by the Spaniards, as well

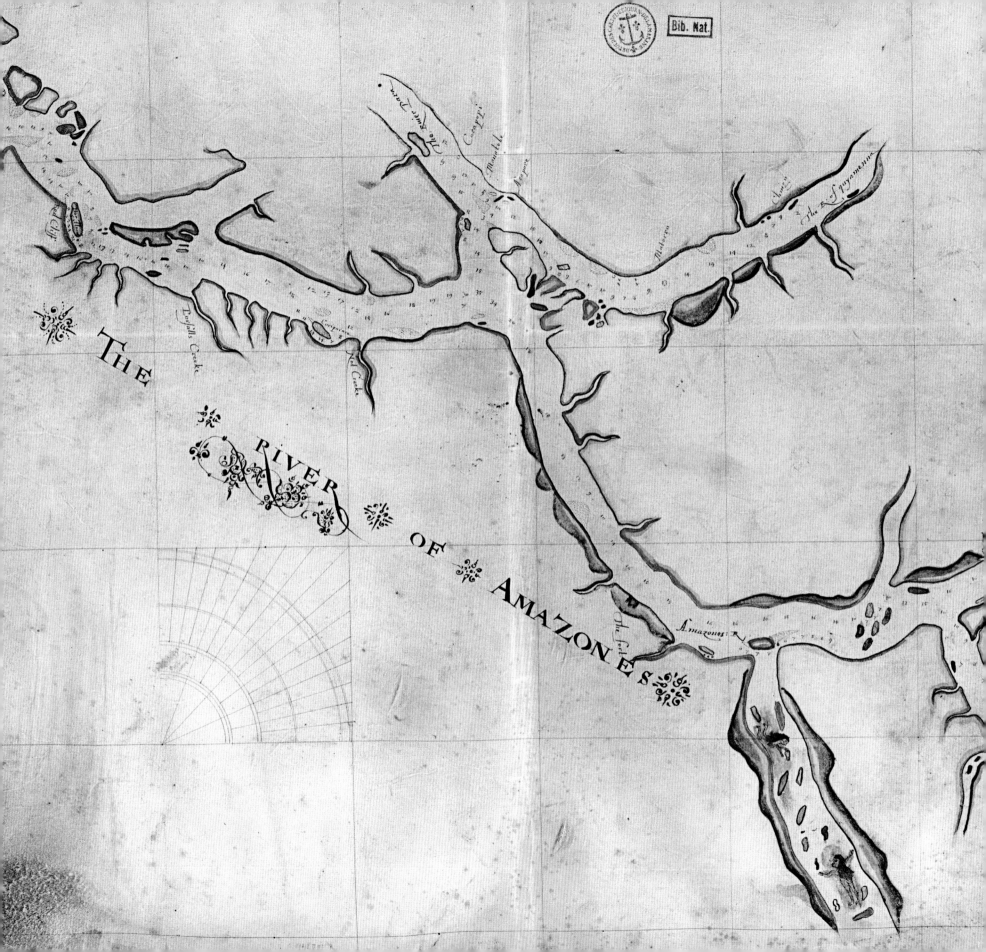

THE RIVER OF AMAZONES

many individual maps. Comberford is the probable author of a map of the Amazon up to its confluence with the Tapajos (see illustration 100), which was drawn around 1626. It retraced the explorations of Captain Thomas King, who sailed up the Amazon between 1611 and 1618, covering 350 miles (563 km) from its origin. We can even see the legendary Amazons swimming in the river! Comberford and his contemporary John Burston (active from 1638 to 1675) were the best hydrographers of their time and counted among their clients such personalities as Samuel Pepys (1633–1703), who was known to hang the beautifully decorated works of John Burston on the walls of his office.

At the end of the 17th century, as commerce and freighting were developing, the demand and production of maps grew. The English were mostly interested in maps for piloting along coastlines, particularly in the Indian Ocean, the Caribbean and North America. Without counting Hack's enormous output, at least 400 different maps from the second half of the 17th century survive, and we can tally eight hydrographers who earned their income from this trade.

During that time, we also see the beginning of the publication of printed maritime maps and atlases, which were produced based on manuscript maps, which were often copied from Dutch exemplars. These printed maps include Robert Dudley's *Arcano del Mare* (Florence, 1648) and the *English Pilot* (London, after 1671), which were printed by the compass-maker and hydrographer to King Charles II, John Seller (1632–1697). This enterprise reached its peak in 1703, with the maps for "oriental navigation" by John Thorton (1641–1708), whose contemporaries considered him to be the British East India Company's hydrographer. The maps of the Dutchman Joan Blaeu and his successors were obtained to make written copies or to serve as the basis for printed English atlases. John Seller, for example, created a map of the western coast of India, from the Persian Gulf to Malabar (see illustration 103), and also copied Dutch maps of the Cape of Good Hope and other places for the *English Pilot*. The east is oriented at the top of the map, which was done to help mariners, who would have been steering along the coast. This characteristic of English maritime maps borrows from the practices of the Dutch. Similar, though modernized, maps were published in the 1740s by Seller's successors. Thornton's maritime maps for the *English Pilot* were often direct copies of Dutch maps, with some improvements. For instance, his large-scale map of the Strait of Sunda (1699; see illustration 104), an

important passage between Java and Sumatra, is a tracing of a map by Jan Hendricksz that was produced in Batavia in 1662 and copied in Amsterdam by the Blaeus and their successors up until 1783.

Even after the publication of printed atlases, the number of manuscript maps, for "oriental navigation" in particular, appears to have grown considerably, paralleling the Dutch, English and French activities in these waters. This lasted at least until 1753, when the sixth part of the *Zee-Fakkel* by Van Keulen, which dealt with oriental navigation, was published. In 1758, William Herbert translated into English the *Neptune oriental* by the French hydrographer d'Après de Mandevillette under the title *A New Directory for the East Indies*. All the important maritime maps were based on this and included written plans of ports, river mouths, etc.

Sarah Tyacke
Original text translated by Laurent Bury

Works Cited

1. The science and practice whose main goal is to institute and bring forth maritime maps and the assembly of documents necessary for navigation.

2. An armed naval flotilla crossed the Atlantic Ocean once a year in order to bring gold, silver and other precious things from the diverse American colonies back to Spain.

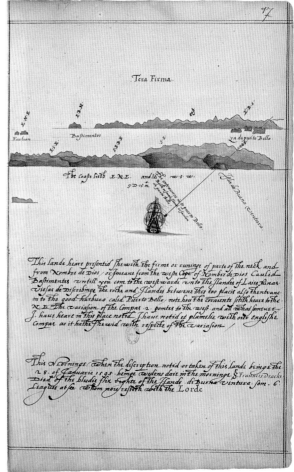

101.

101

Illustrated Journal of Francis Drake's Voyage to the East Indies
1595-1596

This anonymous manuscript relates the voyage Francis Drake undertook in Central America to harass the Spaniards. The journal is illustrated with coastal scenery that helps us note the alignments of notable landmarks as seen from the ship, as well as summary plans drawn from these observations. The death of Drake, on January 28, 1595, off Panama, is noted.

NLF, Paris, Manuscripts, English 51, f. 17.
Watercolor manuscript on paper, 7⅞ × 12¾ inches (20 × 32.5 cm).

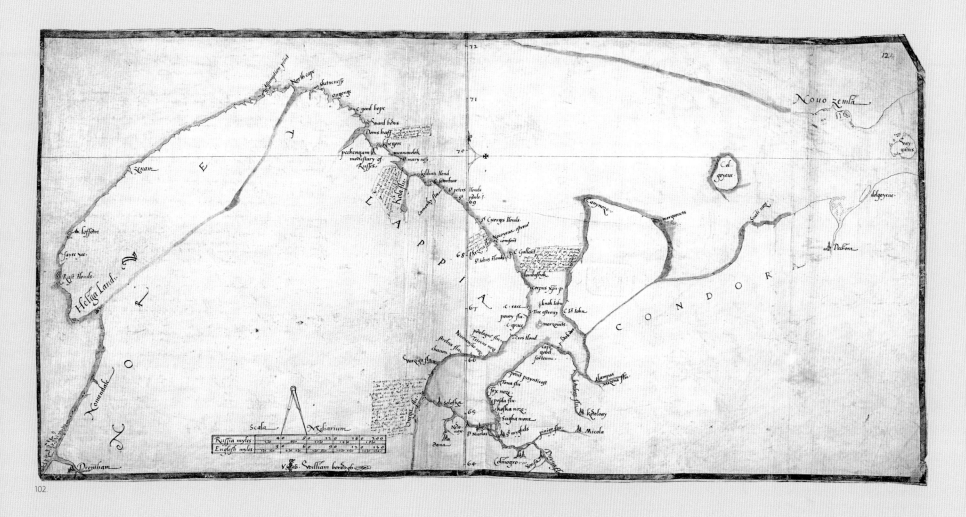

102.

102
**William Borough,
Map from Norway to Novaya Zemlya**
Circa 1568

This manuscript on velum is the work of William Borough, who is considered the founder of English nautical cartography. This map displays the results of a voyage made by the author with Richard Chancellor for the Muscovy Company in order to find the northeast passage and circumvent Russia by the north. The voyagers were stopped by ice.

British Library, London, Royal MS 18.D.iii, f. 124.
Manuscript on velum, 18⅞ × 12¼ inches (48 × 31 cm).

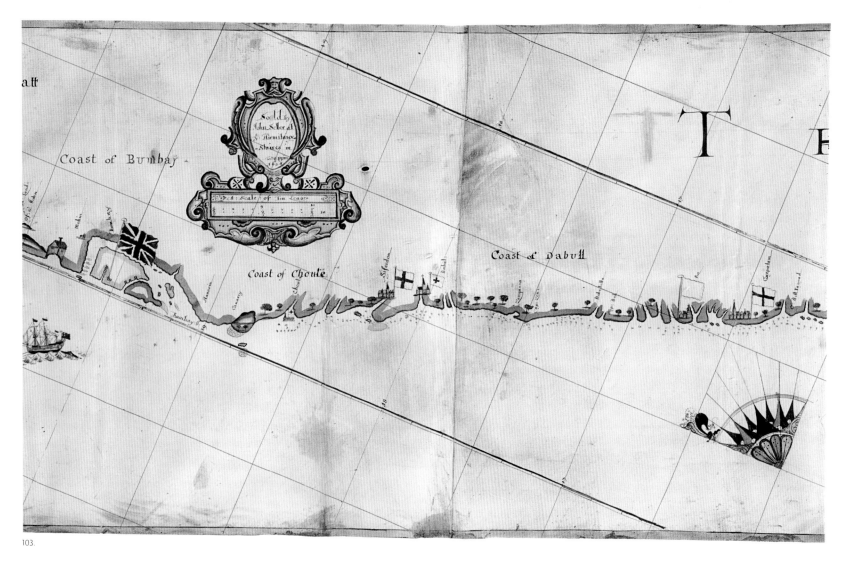

103.

103
A section of the Indian coastline
to the south of Bombay
**John Seller, Map of the Eastern Coast of India,
from Gujarat to Malabar**
(detail)
1684

We have here a section of a long map that was drawn
on a roll of parchment paper. We can see Bombay and
the coast that stretches to the south of the city. Flags
indicate trading posts installed along the coast by
Europeans (either the English or the Portuguese). Like
the Dutch map that inspired it, this map is oriented in
such a way that the entire coast faces the captain as
he approaches land.

NLF, Paris, Maps and Plans, GE SH 18 PF 206 DIV 2 P 1.
Illuminated manuscript on roll of parchment,
144⅞ × 23⅛ inches (368 × 58.8 cm).

104
**John Thornton,
Map of the Strait of Sunda**
1699

Thornton's use of Dutch maps is particularly evident
here. He copied the topology of a map drawn by
the Dutch East India Company at Batavia (see also
illustration 139). The Strait of Sunda, between Sumatra
and Java, was used regularly by the Dutch (for products
coming from the Maluku Islands), and the depth
measurements placed along it emphasize its importance.

NLF, Paris, Maps and Plans, GE SH 18E PF 194 DIV 2 P 4 (RES).
Illuminated manuscript on parchment,
31¾ × 27 inches (80.5 × 68.5 cm).

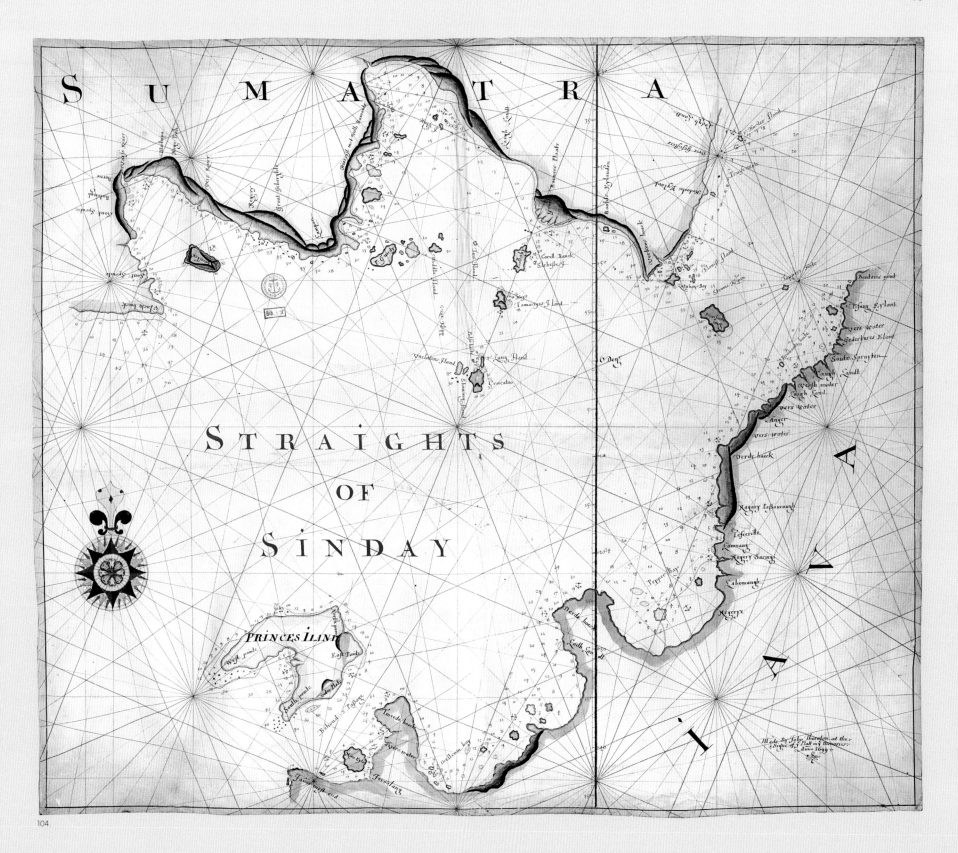

105

Lopo Homem (Pedro and Jorge Reinel and António de Holanda, *Miller Atlas*)

Portugal, 1519

The *Miller Atlas* is a collection of six recto-verso illuminated Portuguese maritime maps that were originally bound in one volume. The National Library of France acquired five of these maps in 1897 from the widow of the collector Emmanuel Miller; the library only acquired the sixth one in 1975. This sixth map represents the Portuguese sphere of influence in the form of a circular world map. A cartouche on the verso of the map carries the signature of the cartographer Lopo Homem (named "master of maps" in 1517), the document's date (1519) and the fact that it was made under the decree of King Manuel I of Portugal. The coat of arms of Catherine de Medici was added below the cartouche after 1559. The complete collection of maps was found in the library of the queen of France until the end of the 16th century, but thereafter they were distributed. The maps representing Africa were lost (and remain so).

A Portuguese work of cartographic art from the early 16th century, the Miller Atlas represents the world as Europeans knew it just before Magellan's famous expedition (1519–1522) and was the product of several artists. Indeed, specialists recognize the handiwork of Pedro and Jorge Reinel and of the illuminator António de Holanda, a Netherlands native who came to Portugal in 1510 and was related via marriage to the Homem family. Other artists may also have participated by drawing illustrations.

The atlas is based on contemporary documentation of the first Portuguese conquests in Asia and the Spanish discoveries in South America; if we count the pavilions displaying European colors, the Portuguese influence appears to dominate. The Indian Ocean is drawn from information gathered from Vasco de Gama's Indian expeditions (1498) and the military actions of Afonso de Albuquerque, who founded Portugal's Asian empire, from the Red Sea to the Strait of Malacca in Southeast Asia. The map of Brazil tells of the explorations of Pedro Álvares Cabral in 1500. On the map of the Atlantic Ocean, the Caribbean Sea's archipelagoes are already very well positioned; Spanish Florida (discovered in 1513) and Newfoundland, discovered by John Cabot in 1497, are represented as pastoral scenes, populated by bears and deer in the wilds of forests and mountains.

Constructed according to the portolan mapping tradition, these maps also follow Ptolemy's historical cartography. In fact, we see the mention of "climates" (latitudinal divisions), notably on the map of the Atlantic, where there are no wind lines. As for the maps of the China Sea and Indonesia, about which European navigators still knew very little, they are shown with the shapes and names attributed by Ptolemy. The abundant and quite varied iconography is at times based on realistic detail (the fauna and flora, the peoples of the New World, the ships, the shape of certain town, such as Aden), but it is also frequently from the artist's imagination.

E. V.

NLF, Paris, Maps and Plans, GE-D 26179 (RES), f. 1; GE-DD 683 (RES), f. 2–5; GE-DD 640 (RES), f. 6. Illuminated manuscript on velum, 23¼ × 16⅜ inches (59 × 41.5 cm), 23¼ × 16⅜ inches (59 × 41.5 cm) and 46½ × 24 inches (118 × 61 cm).

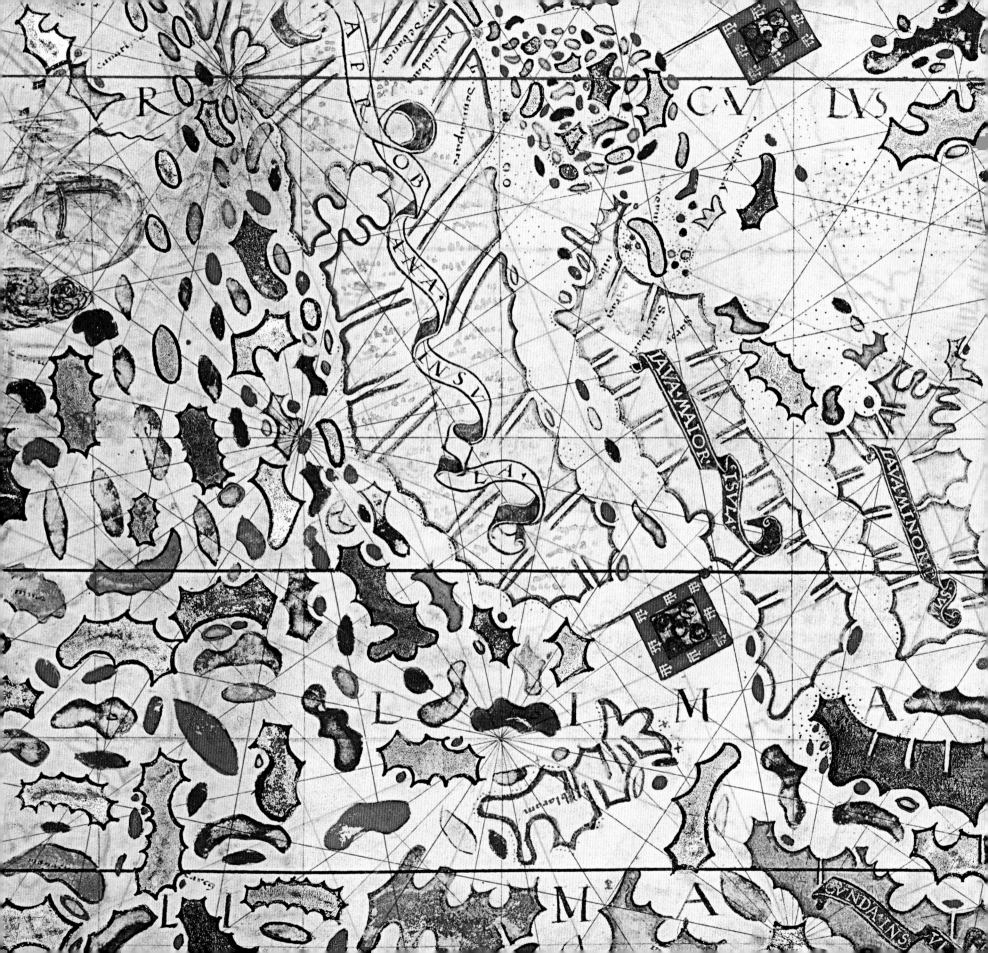

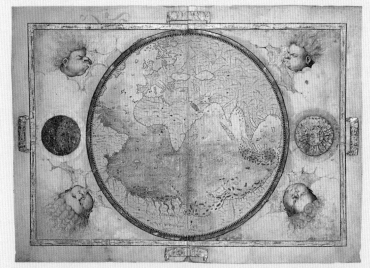

105 a.

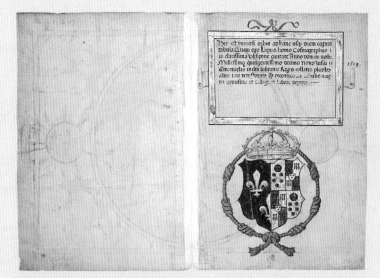

105 b.

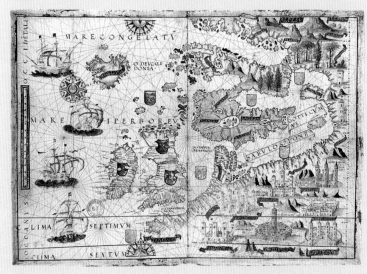

105 c.

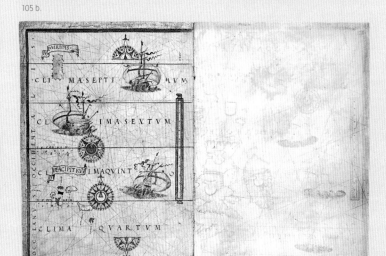

105 d.

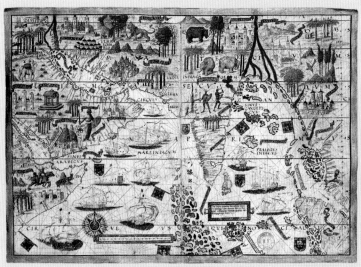

105 e.

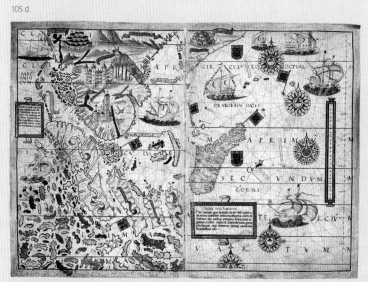

105 f.

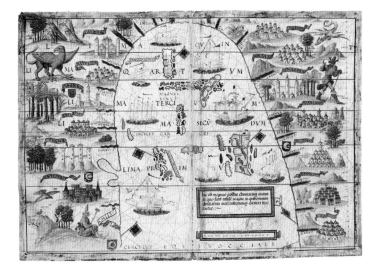

105 g.

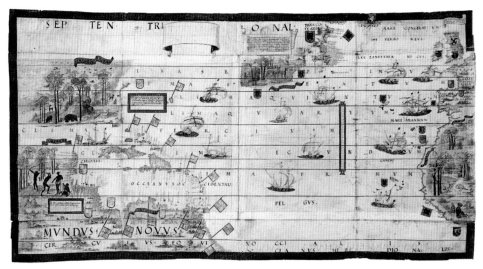

105 j.

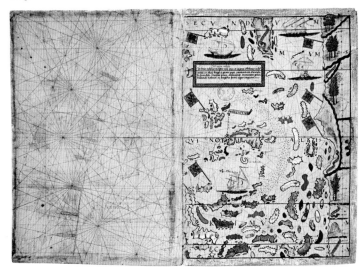

105 h.

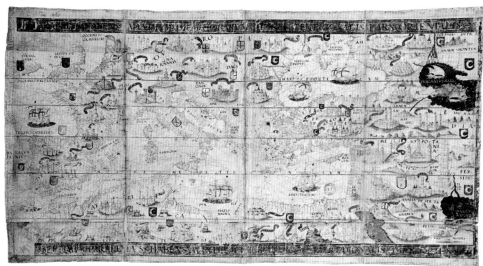

105 k.

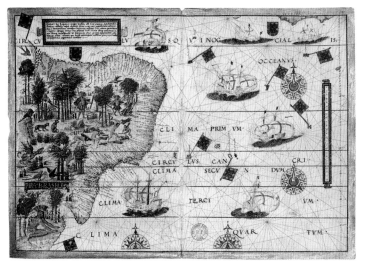

105 i.

105 a, b
Circular World Map of the
Portuguese Hemisphere
The title page and the coat of arms
of Catherine de Medici are on the verso.

105 c, d
Northern Europe
The Azores are on the verso.
See pages 184–185 for a detail of this map.

105 e, f
Indian Ocean, Arabia and India
See pages 186–187 for a detail of this map.

105 g, h
Ptolemy's *Magnus Sinus*
(Sea of Western China or Yellow Sea)
The Maluku Islands are on the verso.
See pages 192–193 for a detail of this map.

105 i
Brazil
The verso of this map is blank.
See pages 190–191 for a detail of this recto.

105 j, k
The Atlantic and the New World (Florida)
The Mediterranean and the Old World are on
the verso of this map.
See pages 188–189 for a detail of this map.

MARE IPERBOREV

OCCANVS

MARE

LIMA SEPTIMVM

OCCANVS BRITANICVS

AQTANIA

CLIMA SEXTVM

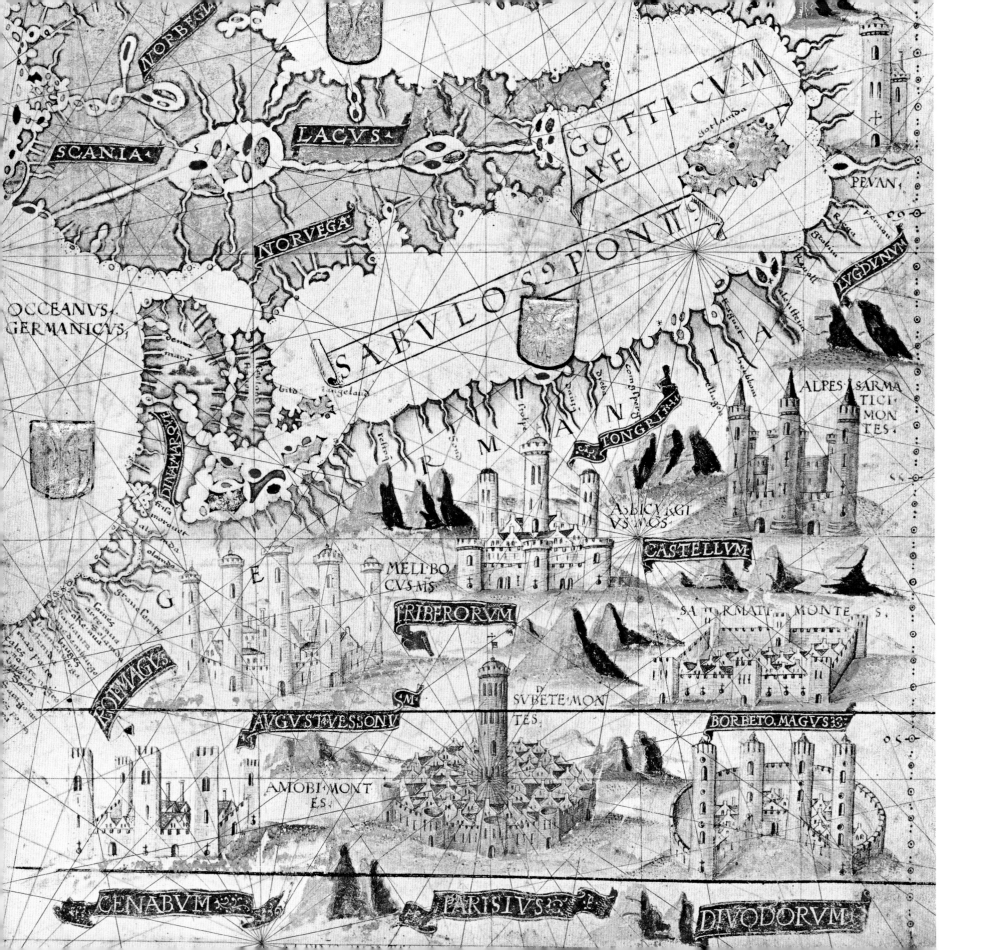

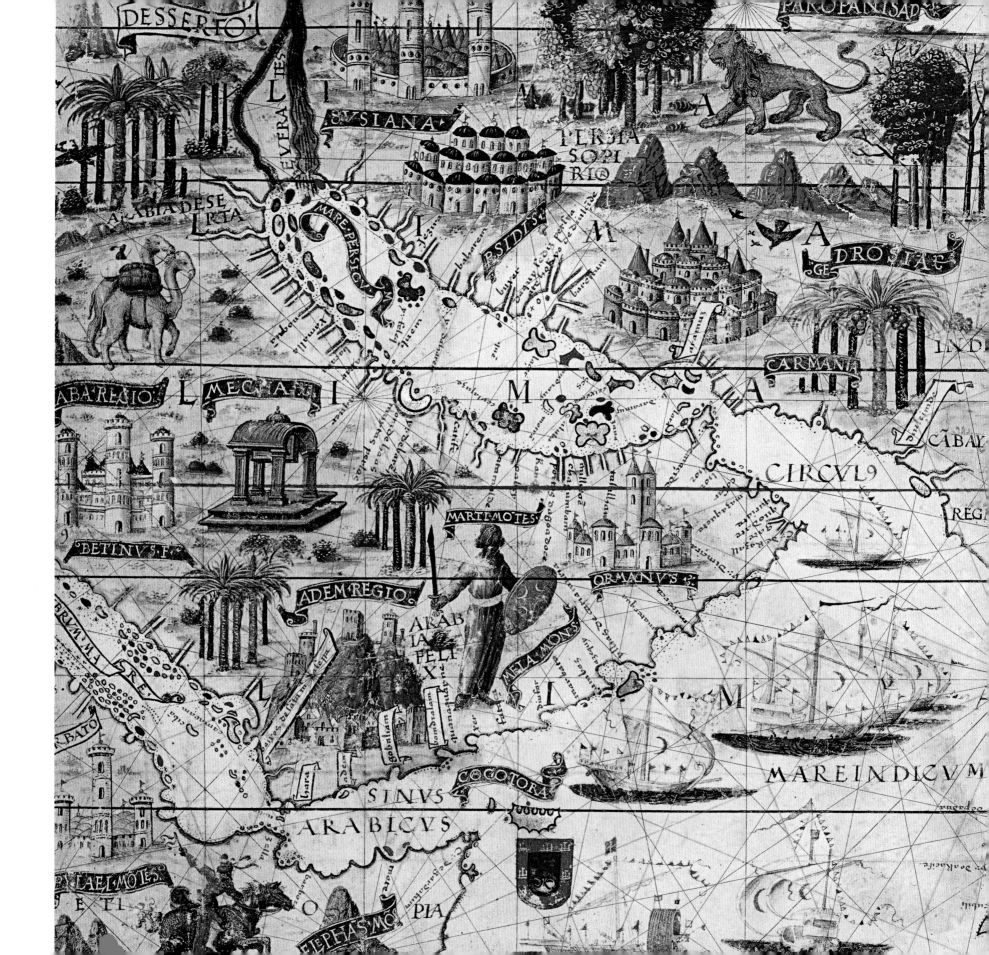

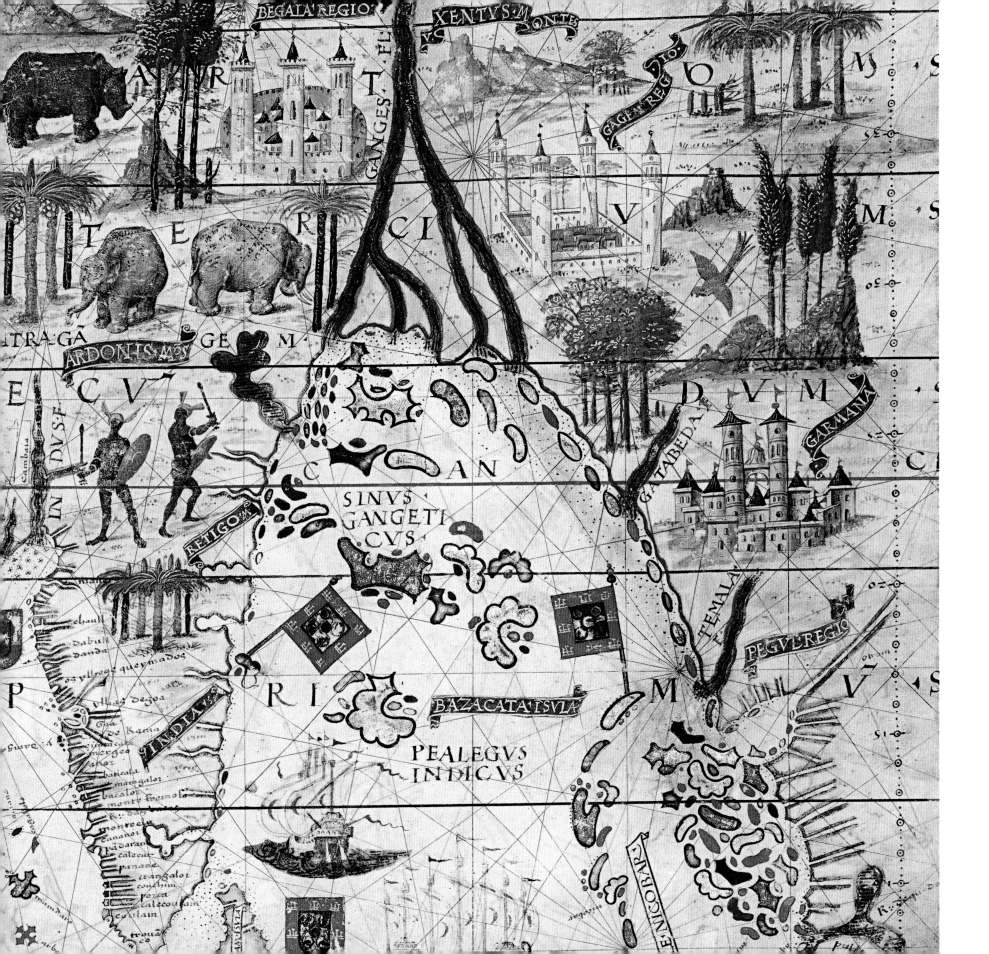

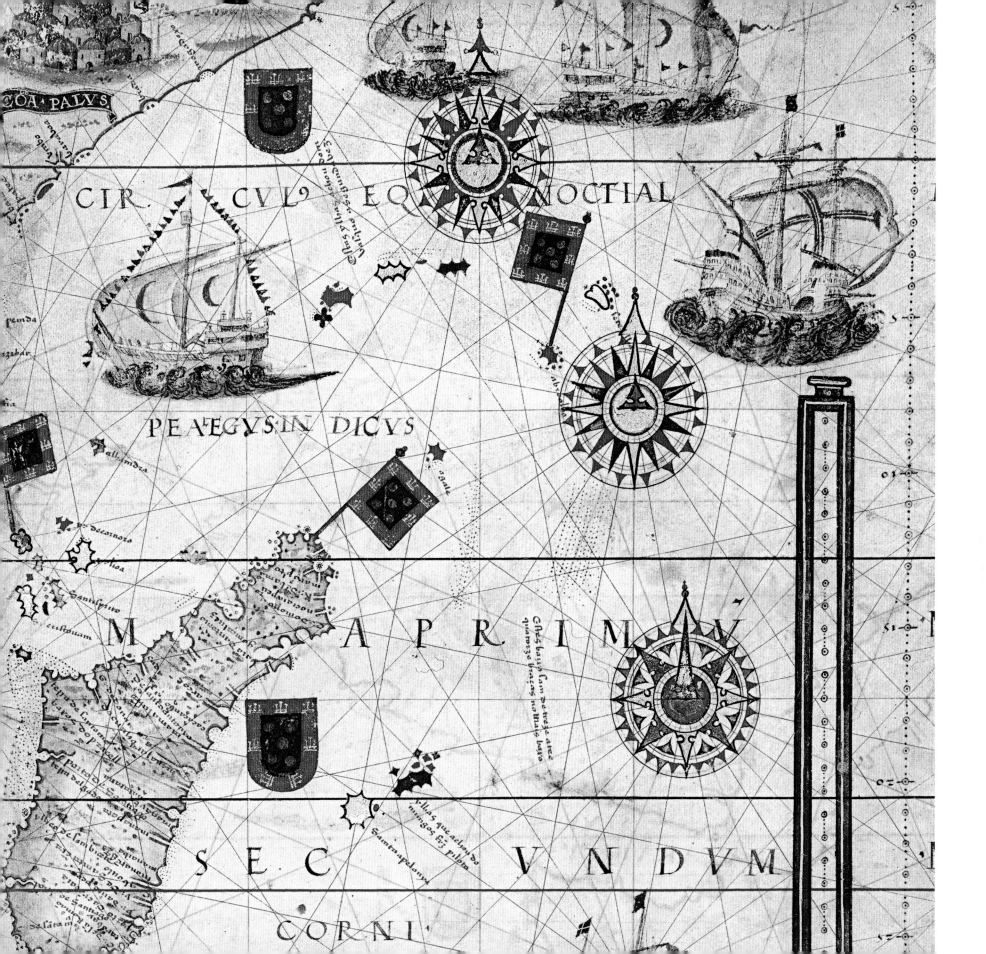

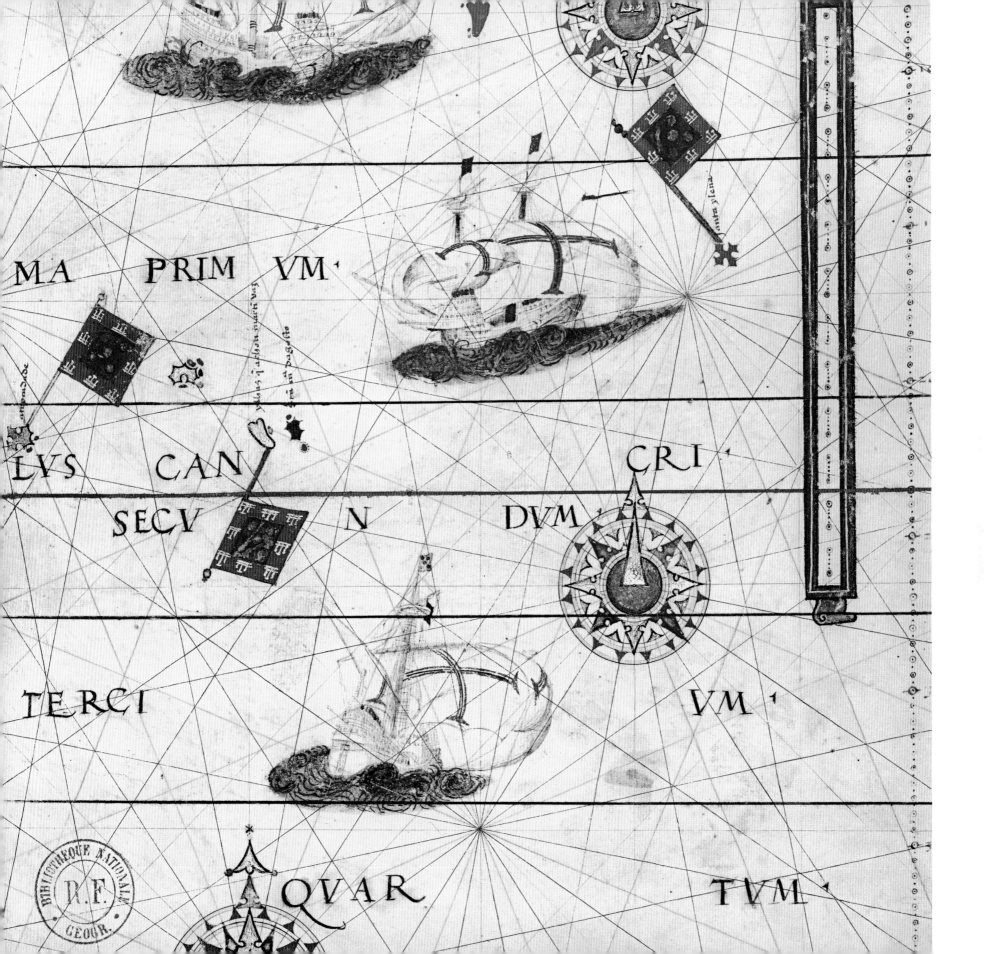

MA PRIMVM

LVS CAN CRI

SECV N DVM

TERCI VM

QVAR TVM

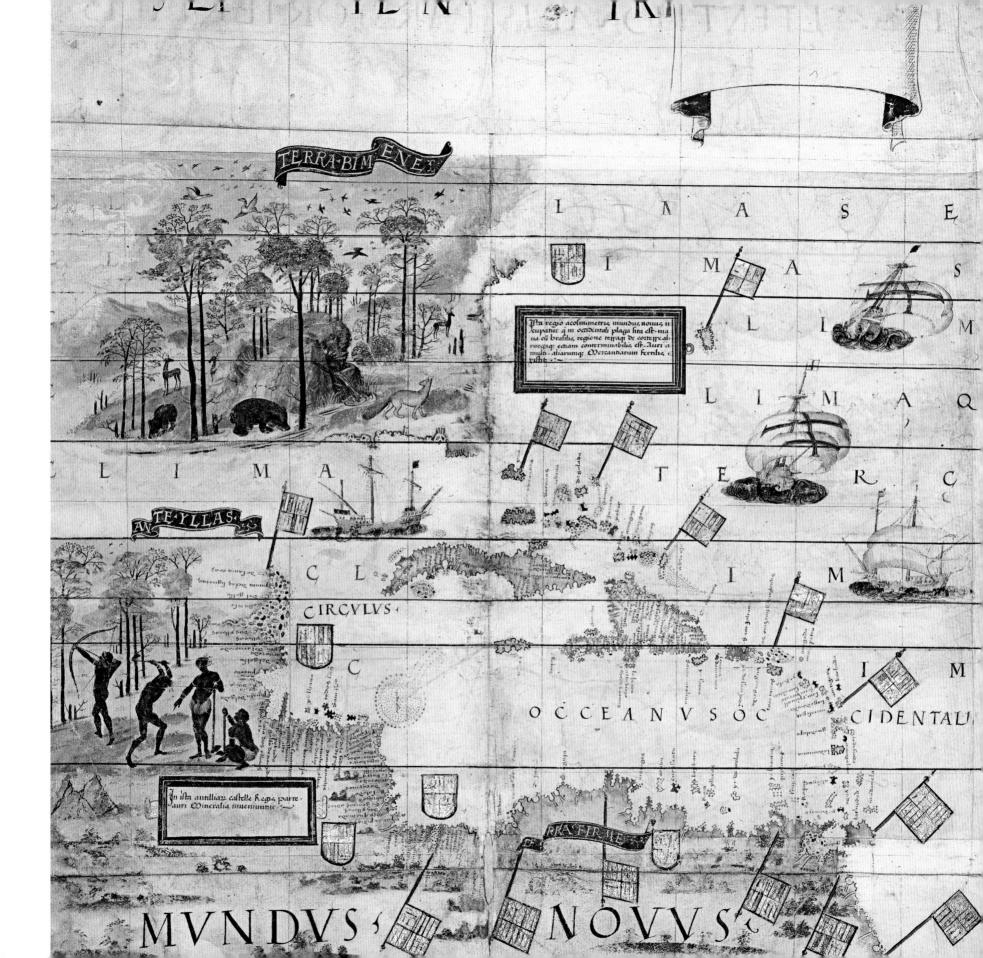

SEPTEN TRI

TERRA·BIM·ENES

L I N A S E

L I M A S

I M A L I M

LIMAQ

Ista regio acolimmetris, mundus nouus, n
scupatur q̃ in occidentali plaga hn est·ma
na eũ brasilie, regione tefraq de coterrealr
ruesqꝫ eciam conterminabilis, est·Auri a
multi·aliarũqꝫ Metcantarum fertilis e
rustit

L I M A

L I M A T E R Ç

ANTE·YLLAS

C L S

CIRCVLVS

C L I M

C

In ista antilliaꝝ castelle Regis parte·
auri Mineralia inueniuntur

OCCEANVSOC CIDENTAU

TERRA·FIRME

MVNDVS·NOVVS

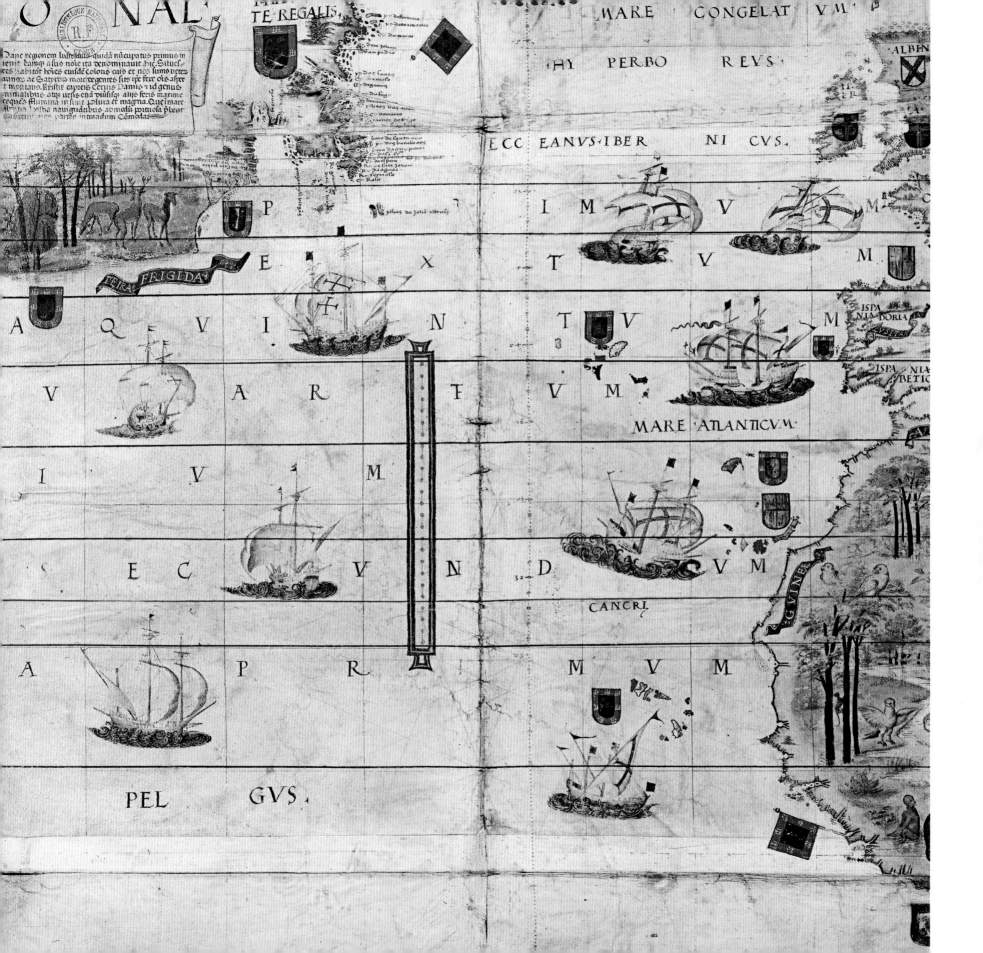

THE INDIAN OCEAN

THE DISTRIBUTION OF KNOWLEDGE

Emmanuelle Vagnon

It was not a "New World" but rather a very ancient region that Portuguese navigators invaded, sometimes brutally, when they rounded the Cape of Good Hope (Bartolomeu Dias, 1488), hugged the eastern coast of Africa and reached Calicut (present-day Kozhikode) in southern India (Vasco de Gama, 1498). From 1503 to 1515, Admiral Afonso d'Albuquerque attacked strategic ports of the Muslim maritime empire, including Aden on the Red Sea and Ormuz at the entrance of the Persian Gulf, paving the way for a European presence as far as Malacca and the spice islands in the Far East. The Portuguese thereby entered an active economic environment, with widespread networks and a multicultural space where trade in spices, ivory and textiles had taken place for many centuries. Arabic and Persian ships, having mastered the changing winds of the monsoons, met the merchants in Gujarat and southern India and frequented the cities of the African coast. Once they sailed beyond India, Islamic influences met up with Chinese civilizations and the merchant ships of Malaysia and Java.

The Western medieval world knew of the extensive economic activity in the Far East and hungered for the treasures to be found there. Since one of the Far East trade routes ended at the Mediterranean, having first passed through the Red Sea and the cities of Egypt, Western merchants were keen to find more routes. At the beginning of the 14th century, leaders of the Crusades were planning a blockade in the Red Sea by a Christian fleet in order to weaken the Sultan of Cairo. Portuguese mariners were well acquainted with these plans and were seeking and mapping new routes around Africa, thereby incorporating these same notions into the economics and ideology of medieval cartography. "We have come in search of Christians and spices," Vasco de Gama told the merchants of Calicut.

This is why the African maritime route to the Indian Ocean was labeled with markers and was supported by a detailed reading of ancient texts that were available in Europe, such as accounts from medieval travelers and Arab sources. Consequently, the cartography of the Indian Ocean from the Middle Ages to the Renaissance was based on these many sources. Similarly, the rich iconography of the "wonders of the Orient" was largely shared by both the Christian and Muslim worlds. From the 16th century, the activities of European mariners led to the gradual completion of portolan maps, though they were still mostly derived from ancient sources of humanist geography and illustrated through print production. The 17th and 18th centuries were the golden age of Western companies in India and Southeast Asia. The cartography that resulted from this commercial exploitation of Asia was more accurate and systematic than what had been produced previously. Better controlled and more widely distributed, the new cartography was firmly established: its ancient and medieval heritage, which was still apparent in the 16th century, finally disappeared from maps of the Indian Ocean.

106
Al-Harîrî, *Maqâmât*
(detail)

See page 205 for full caption.

MEDIEVAL CARTOGRAPHY OF THE INDIAN OCEAN
THE IMAGINED OCEAN

Emmanuelle Vagnon

107
Robinet Testard,
The Battle Between the Pygmies
and the Cranes
France, circa 1480

This illumination is taken from the *Secret de l'histoire naturelle contenant les merveilles et les choses mémorables du monde* (Secret of natural history containing the world's marvels and memorable things), which is a description of the countries and regions of the world, listed in alphabetical order and each illustrated with a miniature pictorial. It contains several anecdotes translated for the most part from Pliny and Solin, like this one of pygmies fighting cranes, whose iconography is similar to that in the *Catalonian Atlas*. Robinet Testard practiced his art in Poitiers and Cognac, in the court of Charles of Angoulême.

NLF, Paris, Manuscripts, French 22971, f. 47vo.
Illuminated manuscript on parchment, 8¼ × 12 inches
(21 × 30.5 cm).

The portolan maps of the 16th century are mainly associated with the discoveries of new lands as seen from the European point of view. With regard to the Indian Ocean, a center of ancient civilizations, its maps were based on a long tradition of cartography that relied on information from ancient voyages and vernacular knowledge, but also on new information exchanged along the commercial and exchange routes of the Mediterranean. It is these exchanges and transfers of knowledge that we will describe here.

THE TRANSFER OF ANCIENT KNOWLEDGE DURING THE HIGH MIDDLE AGES

Most of the medieval geographic knowledge about the Indian Ocean was derived from a heritage rooted in Greco-Roman times, as was the case in both the Latin and Arabic worlds. Alexander the Great's expedition (4th century BC) echoed loudly and profoundly in the literature and geographic descriptions of the East as well as the West. This ancient understanding of the East was integrated with the classical Latin geographies of Pomponius Mela and Pliny, which were then combined with more recent explorations of the coasts of India, such as the *Periplus to the Erythraean Sea*. These were subsequently summarized and edited by later Latin authors, such as Macrobe, Martianus Capella, Solin, Orose and Isidore of Seville. In contrast, ancient Greek cartography culminated in Alexandria in the 2nd century AD with the works of Ptolemy. His treatises on mathematics and his study of the stars, the *Almagest and the Tetrabiblos*, were completed in his *Geography*. The latter described measurements of the spherical Earth and gave the coordinates in both latitude and longitude of a large number of locations in the *oikoumenè* (the whole inhabited world), as well as how they can be displayed on world and regional maps. During the first centuries of Islam (the 7th and 8th centuries), learned men, who were mostly Syrians, began translating and adapting the main elements of this precious knowledge into Arabic. This literary and scientific geography, which flourished in Baghdad during the 9th century in the courts of the Abyssinian caliphs, was partly inspired by Ptolemy. Around the same time in the West, Ptolemy's works were known only by reputation and only among a few scholars, as none of his writings were readily available.

Hence, the ancient cartographic heritage varied greatly in the West and the East. While Europeans were concerned about the habitability of equatorial regions and the navigability of the Indian Ocean, in the Islamic world, by contrast, the Indian Ocean was well known during the Abyssinian dynasty. After leaving the Red Sea and the Persian Gulf, ships sailed the eastern sections of the Pacific and toward the coast of Africa, even as far as China. On many Latin medieval world maps (see illustration 109), the inhabited part of the terrestrial sphere is shown as being confined to the areas around the Mediterranean, which both unites and separates the shores of the three regions of the inhabited realm, namely Europe, Asia, Africa, all surrounded by a circular ocean from which emanates a seemingly limitless gulf. The Earthly paradise

is often placed on an island at the world's eastern extremity. By contrast, in the Abyssinian Empire, some manuscript maps of Istakhri's (see illustration 110) and Ibn Hawqal's — quite schematic even though they were sourced from Ptolemy — place the center of the inhabited world in a narrow isthmus that separates the Mediterranean Sea from the Indian Ocean. Arabia and Baghdad are symbolically located at the center of the map, at the heart of the Muslim world, with its two maritime borders mirroring each other. Thus, with just a few lines and geometric shapes (along with more elaborate shapes), the authors of these works offer a summary of their notion of the geographic equilibriums of their civilization.

Beyond these differences, however, the eastern horizon in maps of both cultures remained equally and similarly uncertain and immersed in the imagination. Sinbad's adventure, a popular tale later integrated into *A Thousand and One Nights*, retells the seafaring adventures of a mariner who reached the confines of the Indian Ocean. In this retelling of his sea voyages and islands populated with magnificent beings, we encounter legends derived from the history of Alexander the Great and echoes of Homer's *Odyssey*. The iconography in these Arab manuscripts ably illustrates their somewhat ambiguous familiarity with the Indian Ocean, as shown in the *Mâqamât* (see illustrations 106 and 112), and its status as a region of navigation and commerce but also a reservoir of legends.

THE INDIAN OCEAN OF THE 11TH TO THE 14TH CENTURIES

Things changed during the Crusades, which facilitated the exchange of knowledge between the East and the West.

During the 12th century, the Muslim scholar Al-Idrîsî (see illustration 111) composed the *Kitâb nuzhat al-mushtâq* (Book of pleasures), or the *Book of Roger*, while at the court of the Norman King Roger II of Sicily. This work was a vast geographic panorama of the entire habitable world and was accompanied by detailed maps founded on Ptolemy's works, the geographic tradition of Baghdad and new information provided by merchants and voyagers. This era also coincided with the appearance of the first portolan maps in the West and the first maps based on compass directions. In the 12th century, a text borrowing information from Arabic sources, the *De viis maris*, described a maritime itinerary going from Yorkshire to the northwest of India. Around 1320 in Italy, the

Genovese cartographer Pietro Vesconte associated portolan maps to a world map (see illustration 113) by using both Latin and Arabic models. While one part of "India" (the general term used to designate Asia) is still shown, as was traditionally done, near eastern Africa, both the Red Sea and Persian Gulf were from then on clearly identified as opening into the Indian Ocean toward the East. In addition, maps associated with a Crusader plan against the Sultan of Egypt helped, among other things, to visually explain the spice routes between the Mediterranean and Asia.

At the end of the 13th century, voyages into the Mongol Empire, particularly Marco Polo's land and maritime journeys to China, brought back to Italy and the rest of Europe previously unknown information about the locations and toponyms of the Far East that were more or less accurate. The *Livre des merveilles* (Book of marvels; see illustration 108), an extraordinary source of authentic information on the Far East, also includes many fables and anecdotes about Eastern legends linked to Alexander the Great and to the bestiaries of Solin. Marco Polo's story and his iconography were subsequently used in one of the most beautiful testaments to medieval cartography, the *Catalonian Atlas* (see illustration 25). Dated from 1375, this work came from the workshop of Jewish artists in Majorca and illustrates their new familiarity with Asia. This learned and luxurious piece belonged to King Charles V of France in 1380, and it is the sole preserved example of a portolan atlas of this era that shows the entirety of Asia. It represents a scholarly mix of the canons of world maps of the time and those of nautical cartography. At the Eastern limits of the atlas, where the Earthly paradise was usually shown, the artist presented Alexander the Great and the mythical people of Gog and Magog, an island populated by mermaids and, curiously, the Antichrist. The atlas's four Eastern planks also show a far more complete toponymy than was previously published, with India, for example, shown for the first time as a triangular shape pointing south. The regional powers and richness of Asia are also highlighted using illustrations of various figures and legends, including the Sultan of Delhi, the Great Khan and his capital, as well as a caravan of dromedaries, a Muslim pilgrim in Mecca, a pearl diver in the Persian Gulf and Chinese junks.

THE 15TH-CENTURY SYNTHESIS

Several decades later, around 1409, Ptolemy's *Geography* (see illustration 115) was finally translated into Latin from a Greek manuscript brought back to Florence from Constantinople. European humanists became extraordinarily infatuated with the works of the learned Alexandrian. Ptolemy was compared to other ancient authorities, including Pomponius Mela (known in the West from the 14th century) and Strabon (who was translated from the Greek by Guarino of Verona in the mid-15th century). However, scholars quickly asked themselves whether there was a manifest contradiction between the medieval tradition and the maps that accompanied the *Geography*, since Ptolemy was indeed the only author to represent the Indian Ocean as a sea, closed to the south by a southern landmass linking southern Africa to Asia. Most of the 15th century authors refuted Ptolemy on this point, beginning with Cardinals Pierre d'Ailly and Guillaume Fillastre in 1410. However, the Alexandrian's authority was such that, for most of the 15th century, cartographers vacillated among several hypotheses and produced world representations both varied and complex, all in order to reconcile contradictory information. At the same time, all new information about Asia was greeted with enthusiasm. Should an Ethiopian delegation visit Florence or Rome? Will Nicolò de' Conti, a voyager returning from the Indies, request an audience with the Pope? Returning explorers were immediately summoned and listened to by the learned men of the time, and their stories were reported and commented upon in correspondence between humanist authors like Flavio Biondo and Poggio Bracciolini. Around 1450, Fra Mauro (see illustration 116), a Camaldolese monk from Murano, near Venice, managed to produce a huge map of the world that was both a work of art and a scientific synthesis of all the available information. He used the same Greek and Latin sources that Marco Polo, Nicolò de' Conti and the Ethiopian tales had used, as well as the results of the first Portuguese explorations along western Africa and, when he could, Arabic and Asian sources. He justified his choices through short texts inserted within the map itself. In one famous legend, which was in line with the already widespread opinions of most scholars of the time, he refuted Ptolemy by citing Pliny and affirming that Africa could be circumvented via a southern sea. In depicting India's shape, on the other hand, he followed Ptolemy and represented it as a peninsula that was slightly elongated to the south.

Interest in the cartography of the Indian Ocean was not solely confined to Europeans, as clearly shown in other contemporary cultures, who depicted the ocean in a variety of forms. In the Arabic-Persian tradition, world map models remained schematic and always highly stylized, even beyond the 16th century. In Korea, Asian cartographic traditions, which were associated with information about the Indian Ocean from Arabic and Persian sources, were summarized into an imposing world map, called the *Kangnido*. In China, the *Wu Bei Zhi* (see illustration 117), a tome in many volumes that was printed at the beginning of the 17th century, contained copies of simple but effective drawings that showed maritime routes in the Indian Ocean. Their content celebrated the voyages of Zheng He (see illustration 118), who explored during the 15th century.

In the West, apart from the Catalonian Atlas, few portolan maps showed the Indian Ocean before the 16th century. Even in the atlas known as the *Médicis Atlas* (see illustration 119), which is conserved in Florence and contains some maps that can be dated to the end of the 16th century, the image of Africa pointing to the south and surrounded by an ocean is probably a later addition. Some beautiful, large maps created around 1450 pay explicit homage to marine cartography in their representation of the Indian Ocean. That was the case with the almond-shaped Genovese map (see illustration 120) as well as with the large world map fashioned in the Catalonian style and conserved in Modena, whose iconography resembled that in the Charles V atlas of 1375. Those, however, were only very few contemporary examples amid many copies of Ptolemy's Geography, which were timidly updated through minor modifications in the shape of maps or by the addition of "new tables." As a result, European cartography of the Indian Ocean was largely speculative and awaited decisive confirmation of ancient hypotheses. Those confirmations arrived in 1488, when Bartolomeu Dias rounded the Cape of Good Hope, an event that was integrated into the world map of the *Geography* by Henricus Martellus, in Florence, in 1489 (see illustration 121).

Consequently, due to the hazards of posterity, it was not these marine maps, which have undoubtedly since been lost, but a modernized Ptolemaic planisphere that best symbolizes the exploits of European navigators.

Emmanuelle Vagnon

108

Marco Polo, Disembarquement at Ormuz in
Le Devisement du monde ou Livre des merveilles
(The Description of the World or Book of Marvels)
France, circa 1410–1412

Destined for the Duke of Burgundy, this richly illustrated manuscript with 265 paintings brings together the core of early 15th–century knowledge on the Orient. The report of the Asian expedition of Venetian merchant Marco Polo (1254–1324) is recounted then followed by those of Odoric of Pordenone, John Mandeville, Hayton and other authors of the 13th and 14th centuries.

NLF, Paris, Manuscripts, French, 2810, f. 190.
Illuminated manuscript on parchment,
11¾ × 16½ inches (29.8 × 42 cm).

108.

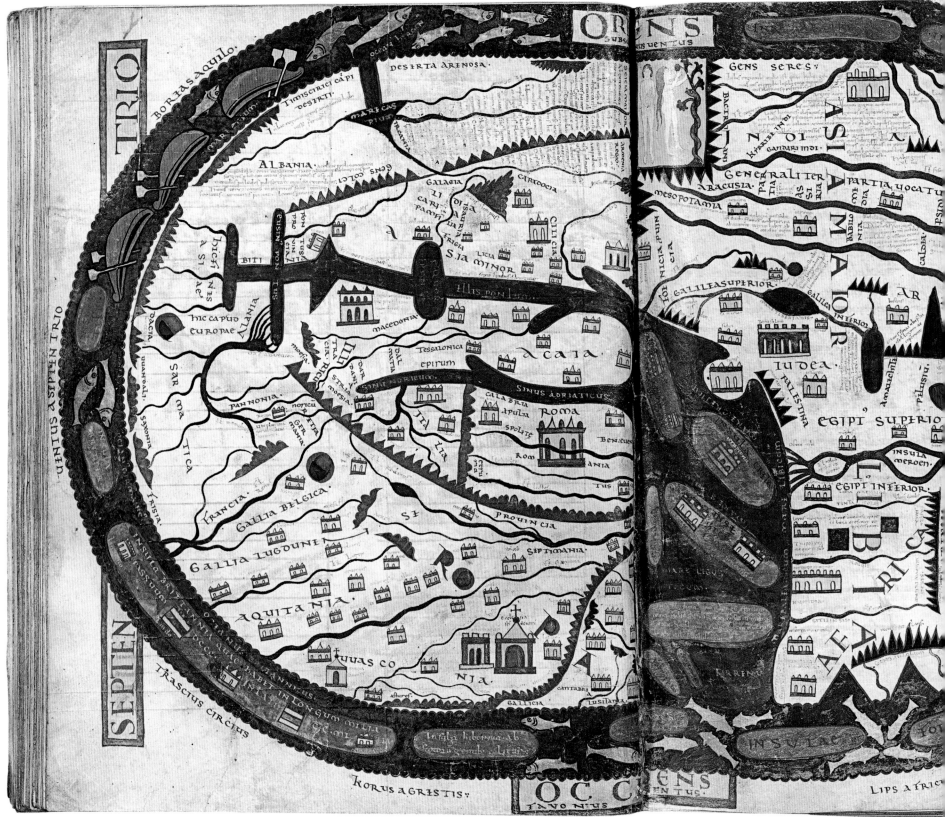

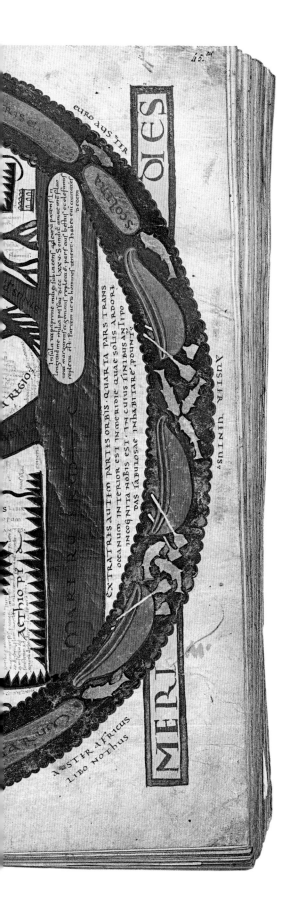

110.

109

**Beatus of Liebana, Commentary
on the Apocalypse**
Circa 1060

This manuscript, from the 11th century and issued
by the Saint Sever Abby in Gascony, reproduces
the work of Beatus of Liebana, an Austrian monk
(late 8th century). The world map represents the
inhabited regions in the shape of an oval with
the Mediterranean Sea at the center. The Indian
Ocean, confused with the Red Sea, occupies the
southern portion of the map.

NLF, Paris, Manuscripts, Latin, 8878, f. 45 v°-46.
Illuminated manuscript on parchment, 11¼ × 14½ inches
(28.6 × 36.7 cm).

110

Al-Istakhrî, World Map
Iran, 14th century

This work — a Persian translation of al-Istakhrî's
Masâlik al-mamâlik, which was written in Arabic
between 930 and 933 — deals with the geography
of the seven climates on Earth. The shape of
this world map stems from the cartographic
tradition of Baghdad in the 9th century: lands
and seas are represented as geometric shapes
within the circle, with the Arabian Peninsula in
the middle.

NLF, Paris, Manuscripts, suppl. Persian 355, f. 2 vo-3.
Manuscript painted on paper, 12¼ × 8⅝ inches
(31 × 22 cm).

111.

111
Al-Idrîsî, *Nuzhat al-mushtâq fî ikhtirâq al-âfâq*
Maghreb, copied circa 1300

This geographic treatise, whose name translates
to "an amusement for those who desire to travel
the different parts of the world," was written in
the mid-12th century for King Roger II of Sicily.
This circular world map, oriented to the south
and inspired by Ptolemy's works, was often
imitated in the Arab and Latin worlds. The work
contains very detailed regional maps.

NLF, Paris, Manuscripts, Arabic 2221.
Manuscript painted on paper, 8¼ × 10¼ inches
(21 × 26 cm).

112.

112
Al-Harîrî, *Maqâmât*
(Book of Séances)
Iraq, 11th century (copied circa 1237)

This famous collection of travel stories from
the Arab literary canon is richly illustrated with
scenes of daily life done by Al-Wâsitî in the 13th
century. Here, a boatful of Arabic merchants sails
in the Indian Ocean.

NLF, Paris, Manuscripts, Arabic 5847, f. 119 v°.
11 × 14½ inches (28 × 37 cm).

113
Pietro Vesconte, World map
Venice, circa 1328–1329

This map, attributed to the Genovese
cartographer Pietro Vesconte, is oriented toward
the east and was reproduced in the manuscripts
of the Crusade treatise by the Venetian merchant
Marino Sanudo and in the *Chronologia magna*
by the Venetian historian Paulin. It greatly
resembles Idrîsî's world map, particularly in the
representation of the Nile and the shapes of the
Indian Ocean and Africa.

NLF, Paris, Manuscripts, Latin 4939, f. 9.
Parchment, 16 × 20⅝ inches (40.5 × 52.5 cm).

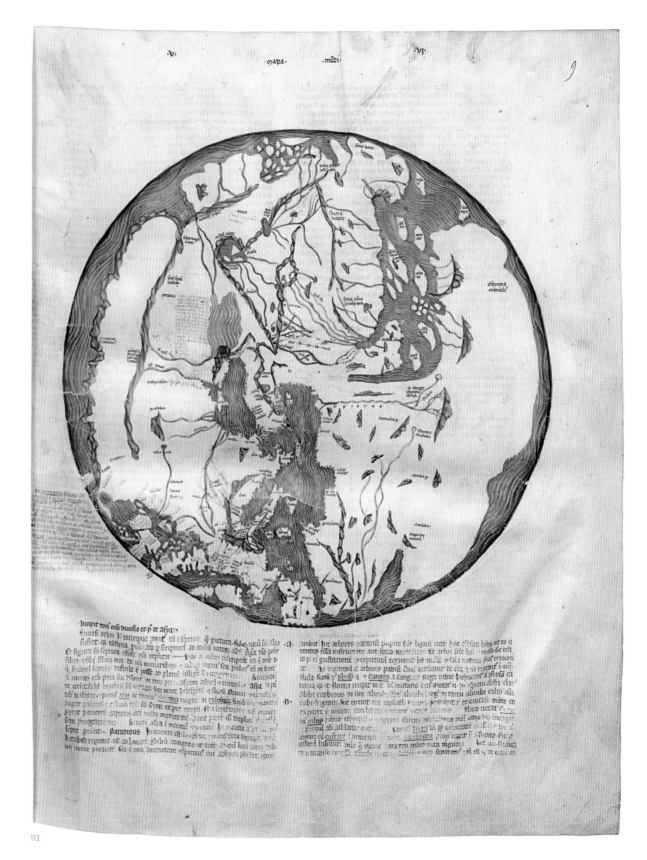

113.

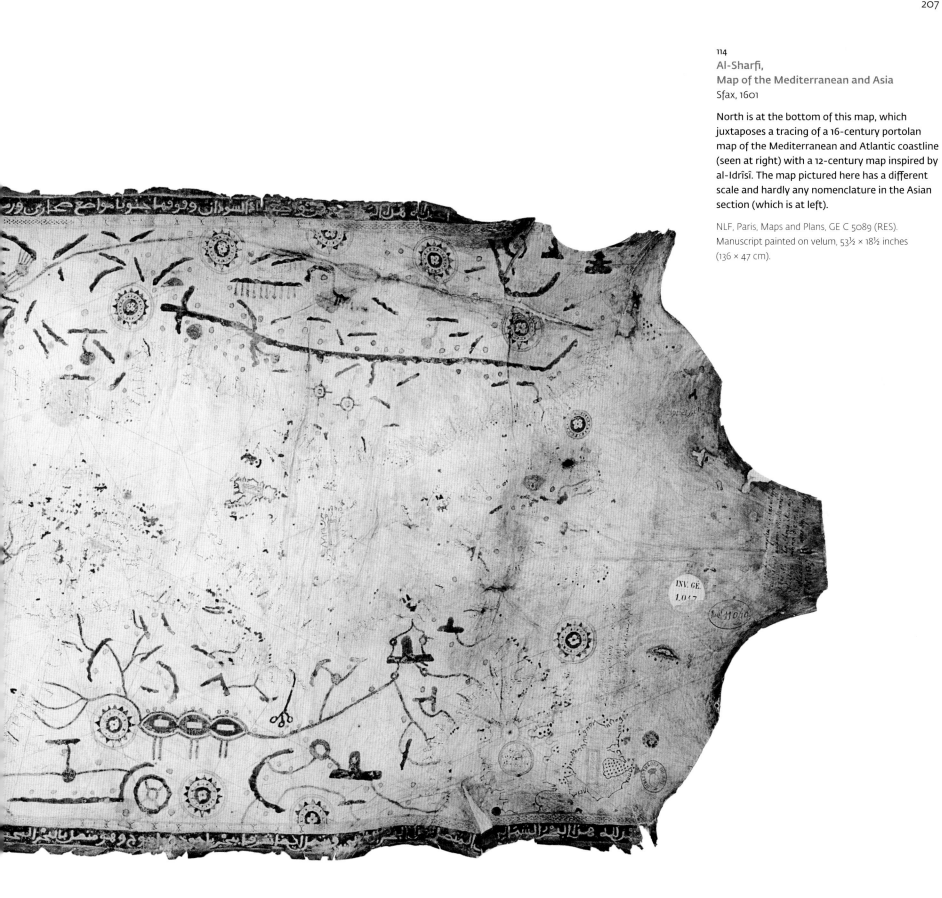

114
Al-Sharfi,
Map of the Mediterranean and Asia
Sfax, 1601

North is at the bottom of this map, which juxtaposes a tracing of a 16-century portolan map of the Mediterranean and Atlantic coastline (seen at right) with a 12-century map inspired by al-Idrîsî. The map pictured here has a different scale and hardly any nomenclature in the Asian section (which is at left).

NLF, Paris, Maps and Plans, GE C 5089 (RES). Manuscript painted on velum, 53½ × 18½ inches (136 × 47 cm).

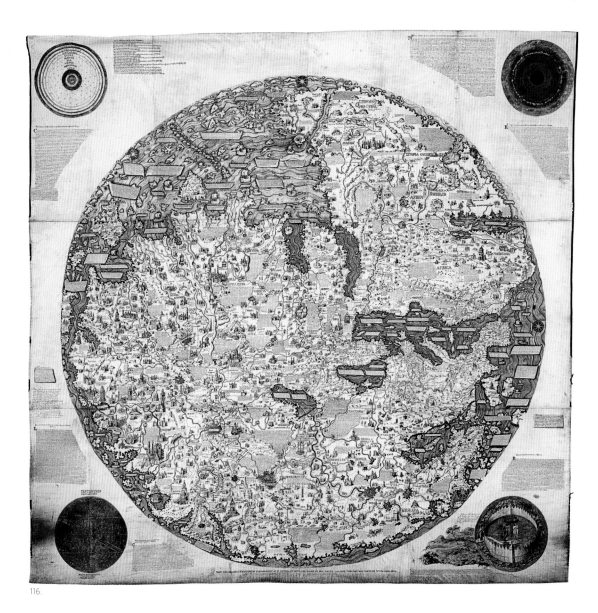

116.

115

Claude Ptolémée, *Geography*
Florence, circa 1475–1480

This luxurious example of the works of the
Alexandrian geographer Ptolemy (2nd century
AD) — translated at the beginning of the 15th
century by Jacopo d'Angelo — belonged to the
three Aragonese kings of Naples. It was copied
by Hugues Commineau of Mézières and the
cartographer Pietro del Massaio. In addition to
the ancient maps, it contains seven modern maps
and 10 city plans.

NLF, Paris, Manuscripts, Latin 4802, f. 74 vo-74 bis.
Illuminated manuscript on parchment, 17¾ × 24 inches
(45 × 61 cm).

116

Fra Mauro, World Map
Venice, circa 1459

The Venetian monk Fra Mauro gathered an
immense amount of information on this large
circular world map, which positions the south
at top and represents the totality of the known
world at the middle of the 15th century. The shape
of the Indian Ocean is based on sources from
antiquity but also on Marco Polo and Arab sources.
The big island close to Africa may be Madagascar.
(See pages 210–211 for a detail of this map.).

Biblioteca Marciana, Venice, facsimile from the British
Library, London, Add. MS 11267.
Illuminated manuscript on parchment, 90⅛ × 94 inches
(229 × 239 cm).

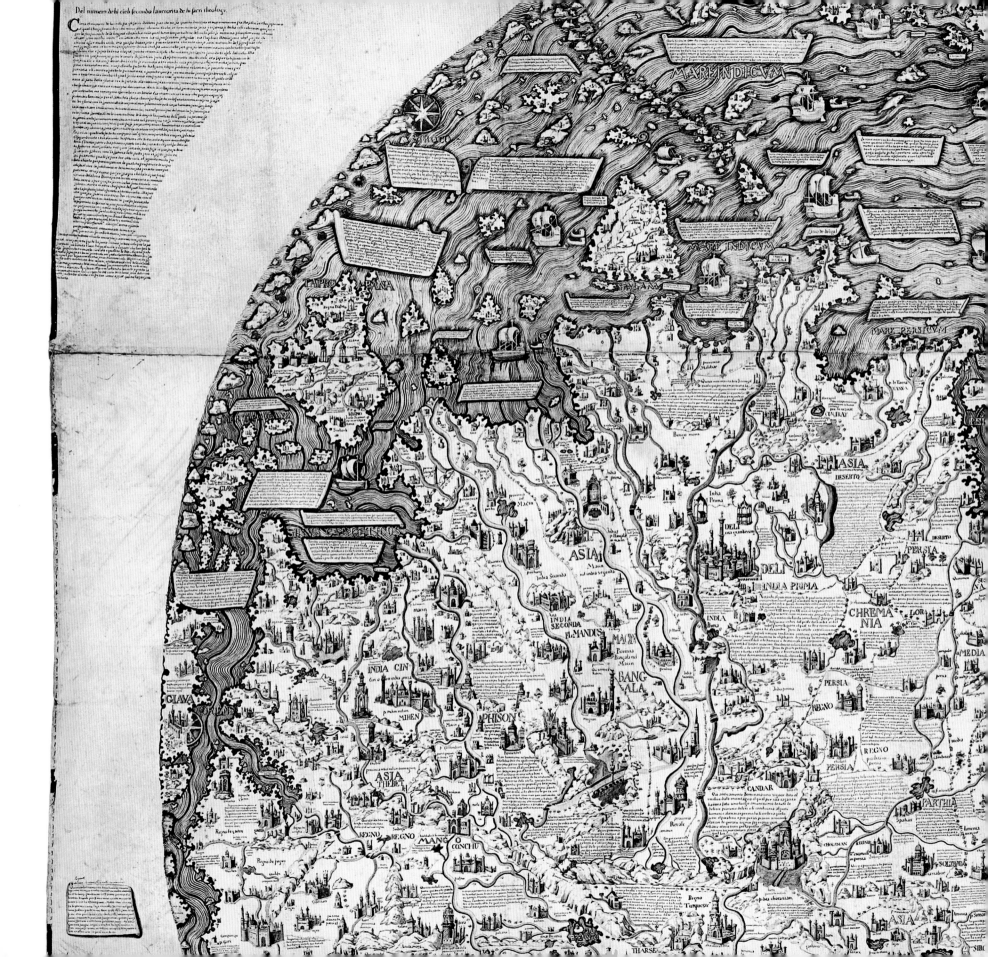

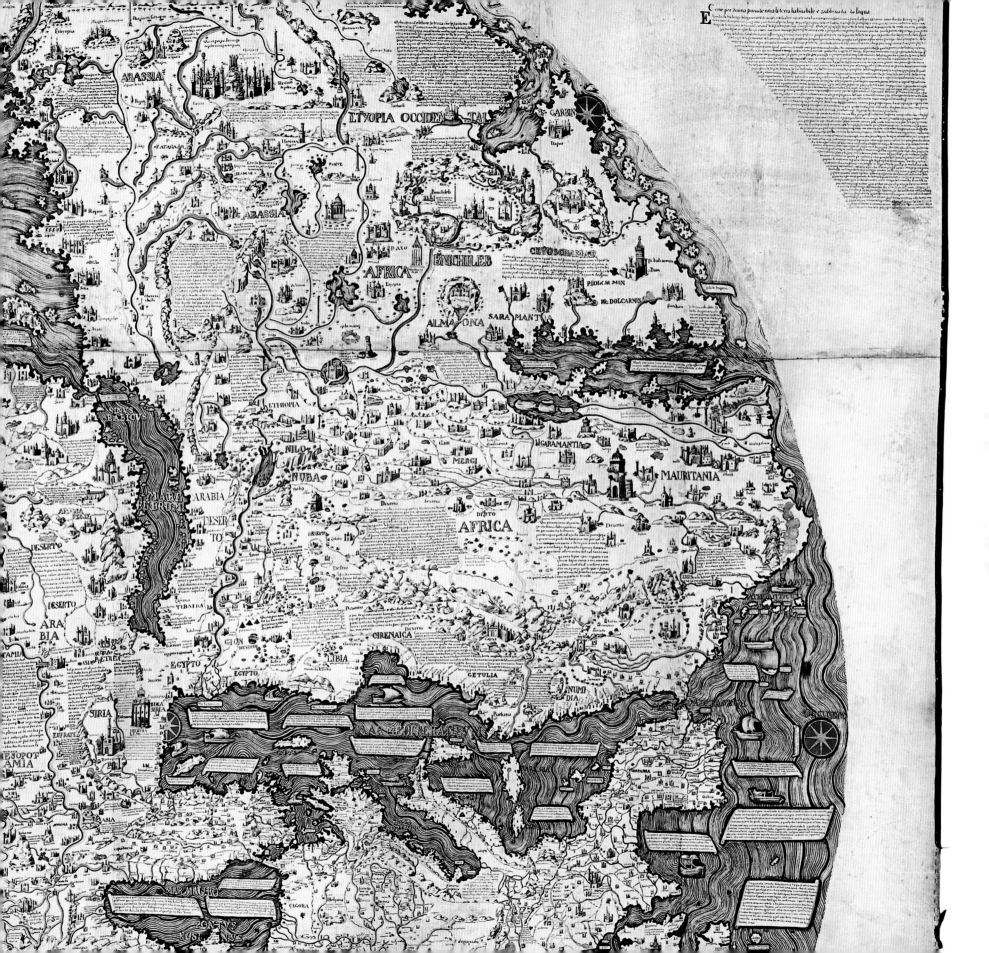

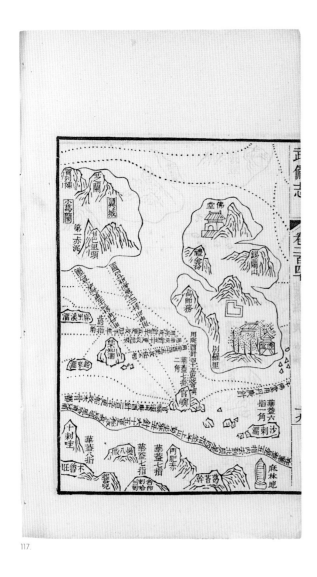

117.

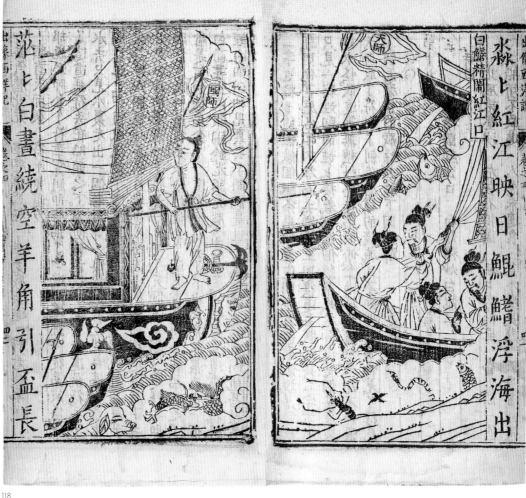

118.

117
Map of Sri Lanka in the
Wu Bei Zhi
China, 1621

The maritime atlas compiled by Mao Yuanyi (1594–circa 1644) appears in the 240th volume of the *Wu Bei Zhi* (1621) and recounts the tales of members of the expedition of Admiral Zheng He (1371–1433), such as the *Ying-yai shenglan* (1433). These maps reflect the state of knowledge of Chinese mariners around 1425–1430. The planks showing the Indian Ocean bear traces of exchanges with Arabic cartography.

NLF, Paris, Manuscripts, Pelliot B 1400, vol.8, chapter 240, f. 19 v0-20.
Xylographic print, 8¼ × 12 inches (21 × 30.5 cm).

118
The Descent Toward
the Asian Seas
China, 1597

This boat caught in a storm belongs to a Chinese adventure novel, *The History of the Occidental Voyage of the Eunuch San Bao*, which tells of the Indian Ocean expeditions made by Sheng He (who died around 1431) and was also known as San bao tai jian.

NLF, Paris, Manuscripts, Chinese, 4024, chapter 4, f. 41 v0-42.
Xylographic print, 6⅜ × 10½ inches (17 × 26.5 cm).

119
World Map
in the *Médicis Atlas*
Circa 1370–1380

In this atlas composed of eight maritime maps and a circular calendar dated 1351, the toponymy is identical to that in the *Catalonian Atlas*, particularly along the Indian coastline. Nevertheless, the world map with Africa surrounded by the ocean may have been retouched at a later date.

Biblioteca Laurenziana, Florence, Gaddi 9, tavola II.
Manuscript on parchment, 22 × 16½ inches (56 × 42 cm).

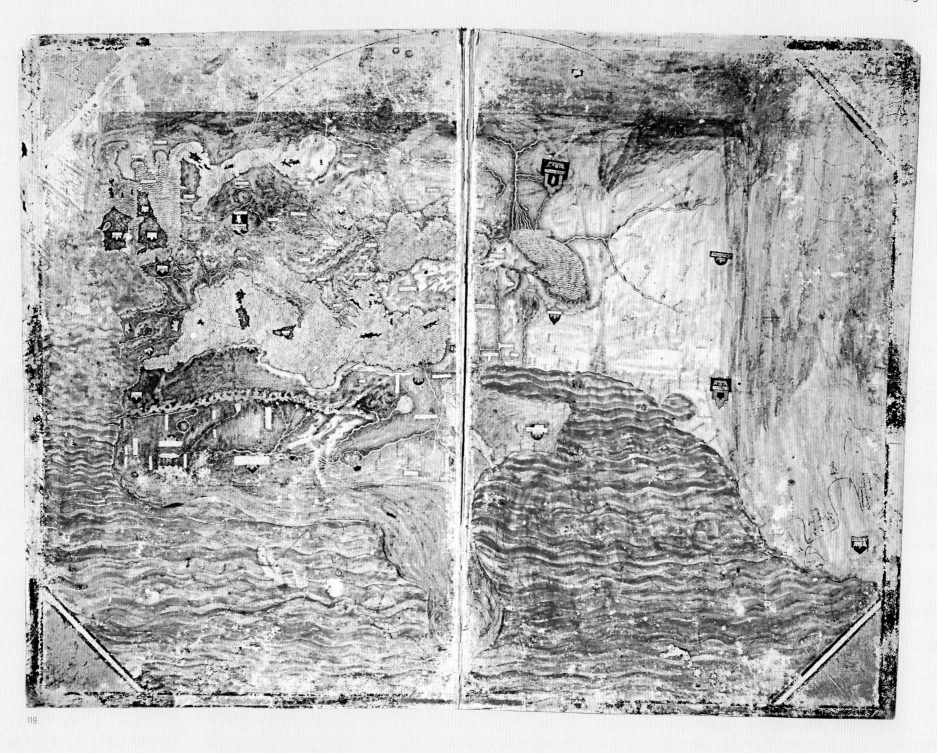

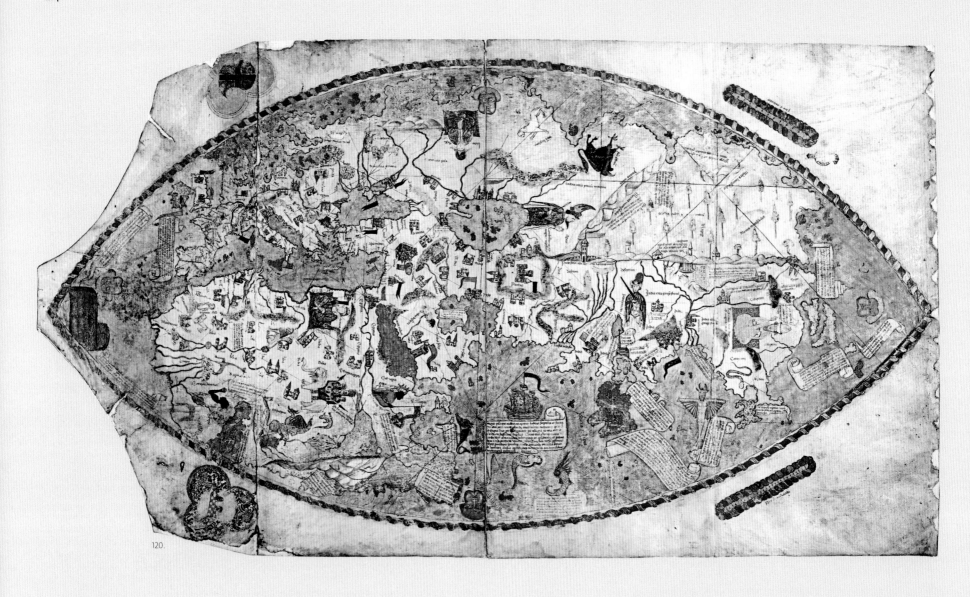

120.

120

Almond-shaped Genovese World Map
Genovese writing, circa 1450–1460

This planisphere has an original shape and is a synthesis
of the geographic knowledge of its time. Its design was
inspired by maritime maps of the Mediterranean and
Europe, medieval world maps and, for Asia, Ptolemy.
The iconography is similar to that in the *Catalonian
Atlas*.

Biblioteca Nazionale Centrale, Florence, portolano 1.
Manuscript on parchment, 32¼ × 16⅛ inches (82 × 41 cm).

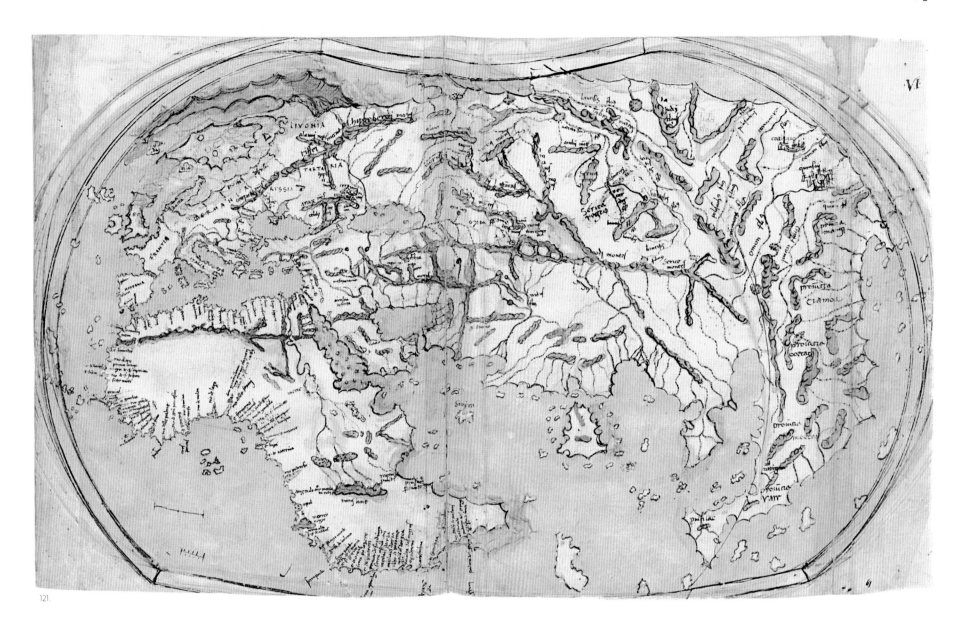

121.

121

Henricus Martellus Germanus,
Insularium illustratum
Florence, circa 1489

On this work-in-progress manuscript, the author
sketched a new world image based on very recent
information. Ptolemy's world map was modified in
order to integrate information gathered during the
Portuguese explorers' circumnavigation of Africa in
1488.

Biblioteca Medicea Laurenziana, Florence, XXIX-25, f.66 vo-67.
Manuscript on parchment, 8½ × 11½ inches (21.5 × 29 cm).

NAUTICAL AND HUMANIST CARTOGRAPHY OF THE INDIAN OCEAN 16TH AND 17TH CENTURIES

Zoltán Biedermann

122
Pedro Barreto de Resende,
Demonstraçao da ilha de Goa
(Demonstration of the Island of Goa)
(detail)

See page 225 for full map.

A Moorish warrior brandishing his saber, a fortified city at the edge of the Indian Ocean, palm trees, a pair of camels and, at the site of Mecca, a strange black building made of sacred stone suspended under an archway — this was the image of an Arab world still discreetly perceived by the Portuguese, who had been eager for commerce with the region from the 16th century. This image was derived from a map of countries bordering the Indian Ocean as portrayed in the extraordinary 1519 *Miller Atlas* (see pages 180–193). Let us review this tableau once more and find a red-hatted knight galloping on the horn of Africa, elephants in northern India, birds, cities in dream-like shapes and, in the north, the bluish scenery of faraway mountains. Let us follow the outline of this new Asia and note its differences with medieval maps, whether of Ptolemaic or Arabic inspiration, which preceded the arrival of Vasco de Gama in these waters in 1498. But to what degree are we dealing here with a maritime map, and what are the associations in this image between experience, imagination and knowledge?

Financed by King Manuel I of Portugal (1495–1521) — who was known as "the Fortunate" and proclaimed "Lord of the conquest, commerce and navigation of Ethiopia, Arabia, Persia and India"

after the return of de Gama to Lisbon — the *Miller Atlas* illustrates an extraordinary moment in history. Europeans began to see Asia not only through the region's own books and world maps or by relying on the stories of a few isolated travelers and echoes of Arabic texts, rather they also began to perceive it based on their own observations from Portuguese ships. It is also important to note that cartographers were only modernizing slowly and reluctantly and that cartography still remained, in many ways, attached to the traditions of more ancient times. Some of the most interesting aspects of the cartography of the 16th century arose from the tension between time-honored knowledge and new observations, between Renaissance humanist cartography and the new nautical maps, and between Western and Eastern knowledge.

MODERN NAUTICAL MAPS AND THE SOURCES OF KNOWLEDGE

In can also be interesting to compare an older image of Asia, of classical and Islamic origins, to the more modern one, depicted by the new marine cartography that conquered the world via Western Europe, which was in full expansion. This was indeed the case for the famous 1489 world map by Henricus Martellus Germanus (see illustration 121). On this map, an oriental sea that appears to be contoured in Ptolemaic fashion (a rectangular Persian Gulf in the northwest, a shapeless India and Taprobane Island oversized and in the middle, the "dragon tail" in the southeast) is overwhelmed at its western entrance by a totally different image, the coastline of western and southern Africa, which was drawn based on information from Portuguese explorers. This shows in great detail the route between the Atlantic and the Indian Oceans as explored by Bartolomeu Dias in 1488.. We do, however, have a tendency to see rather too profoundly the differences in the relationship between the "medieval" and "modern" image of the world.

Let us take for example the Portuguese planisphere known as the "Cantino Planisphere" (see illustration 78), which was made in Lisbon in 1502 and is undoubtedly one of the most important maps of the "big discoveries" era. At first glance, this map does indeed portray the Indian Ocean with outlines approaching those that we now consider accurate. Africa is fully formed and, though the Persian Gulf remains rectangular, following the Ptolemaic tradition, the Indian subcontinent finally emerges as a large

triangle, thereby making a clear distinction between the Arabian Sea on the one side and the Gulf of Bengal on the other. To the east, however, the stamp of the Alexandrian geographer still dominates, as it does in the map of Nicolò de Caverio (see pages 98–105). However, the Portuguese were quick to correct the drawings of this area on other nautical maps. From the 1511 conquest of Malacca, in the strait of the same name, the Malay Peninsula starts to take shape on maps. It was therefore not from ignorance that the authors of the *Miller Atlas* (1519) still drew this area with a "dragon tail," which indicates a deliberate choice and compromise between the new Portuguese cartography and the Renaissance humanist cartography based on readings of ancient texts. In the 1520s, a new image of Southeast Asia is evident in the Portuguese cartography of the Iberian Peninsula and, gradually, in the rest of Europe. Subsequent to that, the shape of the Far East was redrawn during the 1520s to 1550s, thereby providing a solid foundation upon which cartographers in the later centuries were able to develop new theories.

Several points must be made regarding these innovations, especially in regards to the Cantino Planisphere. Firstly, how did the Portuguese manage to produce such an accurate map of eastern Africa, the Gulf of Aden, India and the island of Ceylon in 1502, only a few short years after their first expedition, in 1498? Did they accomplish this entirely on their own, as Martellus's map implies, providing new cartographic concepts and techniques at a time when very ancient ideas were still dominating? Or had they simply copied Asian maps that are now lost but were circulated at the time, as claimed by the Chinese science historian Fuat Sezgin? It is quite possible that the Portuguese had access to maps or texts from African and Asian captains. In 1498, Vasco de Gama admitted to having seen a local map covering the Indian coastline, and in 1513, the cartographer Francisco Rodrigues, a colleague of Alfonso de Albuquerque (see illustration 118), referred to a Javanese map of excellent quality, in particular with regards to Southeast Asia. The pioneering texts of Tomé Pires (1515) and Duarte Barbosa (1516), which described the commercial geography of the Asian coastlines, contain elements that suggest an Islamic influence, notably their systematic references to the Muslim communities that resided in those ports. However, on the Cantino Planisphere, the areas that were still untouched by the Portuguese in 1502 were still drafted along the Ptolemaic model, notably the Red Sea, the Persian Gulf, the Gulf of Bengal and Southeast Asia.

Are we to conclude that these areas were not present on the maps that the Portuguese had supposedly copied? Or is it more plausible to consider complex transmission methods, whereby the Portuguese would have used Asian maps together with direct observation to create a new style of blended map?

Secondly, despite the marked progress in the maritime cartography of Asia after 1500, the iconography and other Ptolemaic or medieval elements (both Christian and Islamic) gradually disappeared from the panorama of Western cartography. It is obvious that the images that densely cover the *Miller Atlas* are of different origin and, occasionally, medieval. In the prologue to his trip log, Dom João de Castro (see illustration 124), an outstanding leader of marine expeditions in the Arabian and Red Seas (1539–1542), combined very precise empirical observations with erudite discussions of ancient authors, particularly Ptolemy. He thereby attempted to integrate the new information by way of many small contradictions and syntheses rather than a complete destruction of the classical authorities, which would not have been advisable at the time. It is also true that during the 16th century — as the works of Ptolemy and other Greco-Roman authors were gradually being transformed from authoritative sources to objects of curiosity and pure scholarship — the repercussions of Portuguese "discoveries" on the Western culture were kept at a distance from the ancient authorities. It is important to observe in detail the process of this progressive and often non-linear transformation.

NAUTICAL MAPS AND LAND MAPS

Several medieval portolans — often Italian — concentrate mostly on the representation of coastlines rather than of interior lands. It is generally understood that this lack of detail indicates a relative rather than absolute ignorance of the territories, quite different from the whiteness of the *terrae incognitae*. Mostly, when medieval cartographers left the interior of Italy, France or Spain white, it was not because they were not aware of the existence or location of Florence, Paris and Toledo. Rather, the methods they used to fill in details on maritime maps did not apply to land depictions and the language applied to land-based cartography was quite different, so it's use would create dissent.

That was also the case with the Italian portolans of the Mediterranean and certain Portuguese maps of the Indian Ocean. Francisco Rodrigues's nautical

maps (circa 1513) and those of Pedro Reinel (1517; see illustration 125) and Gaspar Viegas (the 1530s) are the most rigorous recordings and the most uncompromising in their use of whiteness on landmasses. A similar logic was applied to Dutch maps (see illustration 126) known as *paaskaarten*, as well as the maps of the English East India Company (see illustration 127). It is also reasonable to assume navigators on board Portuguese ships headed for Asia, most of which were lost during the 16th century, must have also used this restrained and economical type of map, which would have borne no resemblance to the extravagant specimens that have survived in libraries.

However, these "pure" nautical maps constituted only part of the panoply of maps of the Indian Ocean produced during the 16th century, when many cartographers were looking to create products that, in the end, had to please the eye rather than serve aboard ships. In fact, these maps became increasingly complex, analogous to the medieval Catalonian cartographic tradition, combining marine maps and paintings of continents. These maps presented a multiplication of strategies and a search for a complex cartographic language and technique rather than a reduction to a simple portolan "language." Let us not forget that the *Catalonian Atlas*, so richly illustrated, was described in its time as a "sea map" even though it represented terrestrial observations with great flair.

This blending of empirical and theoretical information, both European and Asian, and its incorporation into nautical and terrestrial cartography, both as science and as art, demonstrates the important role Portuguese maps played in the 16th century. Unlike most of the nautical, or "pure," maps, most of the maps that have survived to this day show lands full of all kinds of visual and textual information. Indeed, it is easy to imagine a division of labor between the *stricto sensu* (strict sense) cartographer and other people engaged in their workshops, often anonymously, who specialized in painting. The exact proportion between cartographic and iconographic work depended on the demands of the client and, primarily, on his monetary means. We also know that for the *Miller Atlas*, the cartographers in the king's service — Pedro Reinel, Jorge Reinel and Lopo Homem — were helped by one of the best illuminators of the time, António de Holanda.

However, the strictly cartographic works and those arising from the artistic domain or from humanist knowledge were often closely related. For example, there is an omnipresent legend, which refers equally to

the classic cosmography and new "discoveries." In the *Miller Atlas*, we can decipher the Latin words "*Clima Tercium*" (third climate), which refers to the Greco-Roman theory of climate zones, and *India Intra Gangem* (India at the interior of the Ganges), which evokes the ancient three-part division of Asia, namely the "first" (generally the Hindu region), the "second" (the area along the Ganges, also known as *India Interior*) and the "third" (the region beyond the Ganges, also known as *India Exterior*). Even in the far more sober maps of Diogo Ribeiro, a Portuguese cartographer in the service of the Spanish crown, we find classical names such as *Susiana*, *Gedrosia* and *Persia superior* next to more recent names, such as *Adem Regio*, a modern Latin designation for the region or kingdom of Aden, which was not known by that name in antiquity.

The situation is even more complex in maps produced during the 16th century in other European countries, notably Italy, Flanders and the Holy Roman Empire. Very often cartographers, like the Venetian Giacomo Gastaldi (see illustration 128), were inspired — often without much concern for accuracy — by Portuguese maps of coastlines and then filled in the land spaces with a very interesting mix of toponyms from classical and medieval sources as well as modern ones, including travel logs that are lost today. Thus, Gastaldi's Persia contains hundreds of cities that one would look for in vain on Portuguese maps, even though many diplomats and Lusitanian merchants had crossed this country. On the other hand, we also note an omission: the landscapes that embellished Portuguese maps — the turreted villages piercing a bird-filled sky, the animals and the flowers — have given way to simple names and conventional symbols.

Beyond Portuguese cartography, particularly among Gastaldi and his successors, iconography was only used in the spaces free of toponyms, like the oceans, where on some printed maps we still see sail-bearing ships and maritime creatures. Thus, the richest iconography was found in the spaces that the technical cartographers did not need. However, from the point of view of cultural history, the differences between cartography, iconography and traditional texts are not necessarily more important than the complex affinities that existed between the various knowledge domains, transfers, odd jobs, cross-fertilization and the roles played by these exchanges in the construction of a still-enchanted image of the world.

Zoltán Biedermann

123.

123

Francisco Rodrigues,
Profile of Indonesian Coastline
After 1521

Francisco Rodrigues was a captain in the fleet
that Afonso Albuquerque sent from Malacca to
search for the Maluku Islands in 1511. His journal
(1515–1517), which describes the voyage in fine
detail, is illustrated with maritime maps and
drawings of shorelines. The manuscript also
contains the *Suma oriental* (1521) of Tomé Pirès, an
ambassador to the king of Portugal in Peking. It is
a geographic description that covers the Red Sea
to the China Sea.

Library of the National Assembly, Paris, f. 60.
Manuscript on parchment, 10¼ × 15 inches (26 × 38 cm).

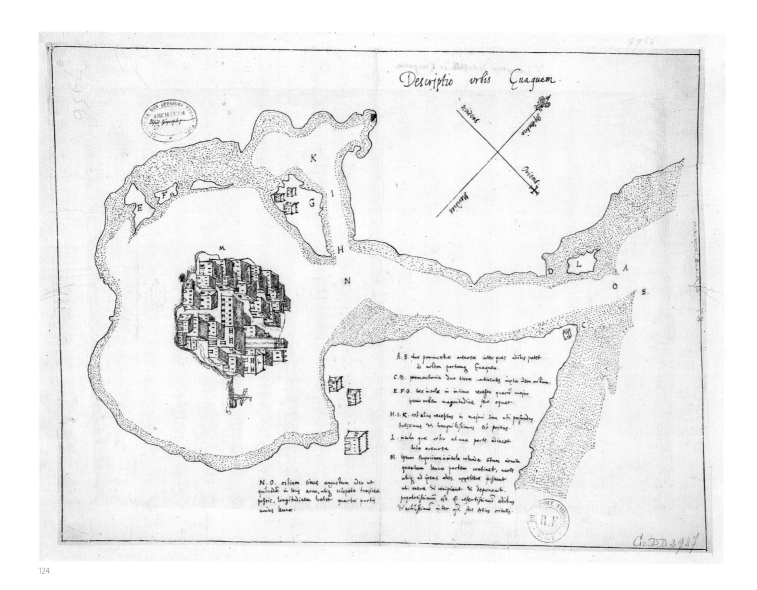

124.

124

João de Castro,
Descriptio urbis Cuaquem (View of Suakin)
1541

Conserved in the Jean-Baptiste d'Anville
collection, this map is from a copy of the *Roteiro
do Mar Roxo*, a log describing the maritime route
in the Red Sea taken by the 1541 Portuguese
expedition in which João de Castro participated.
Sketches of the main coastlines and ports
accompany the text. Suakin is on the present-day
Sudanese coast.

NLF, Paris, Maps and Plans, GE DD 2987 (7956).
Manuscript on paper, 17¾ × 13¼ inches (45 × 33.5 cm).

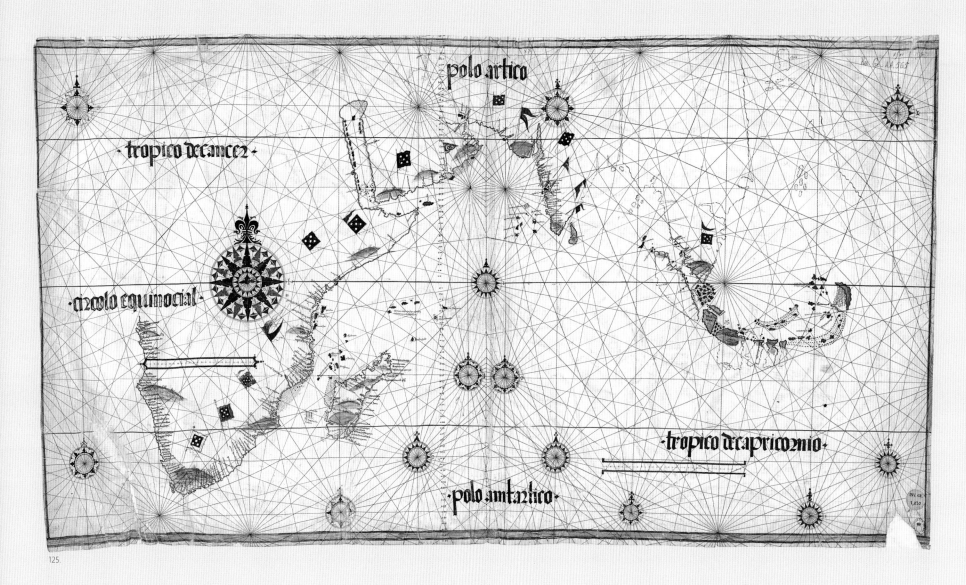

125.

125

Pedro Reinel, Map of the Indian Ocean
Lisbon, circa 1517
(facsimile by Otto Progel, 19th century)

At the beginning of the 16th century, the cartographers of the Reinel family of Lisbon were benefitting from the most recent information from the Portuguese expeditions in the Indian Ocean and Persian Gulf. Pedro Reinel and his son Jorge also participated in the production of the *Miller Atlas* in 1519. The original version of the map above was destroyed during the Second World War.

NLF, Paris, Maps and Plans, GE AA 565 (RES).
Facsimile manuscript on velum, 50¼ × 27½ inches
(127.5 × 70 cm).

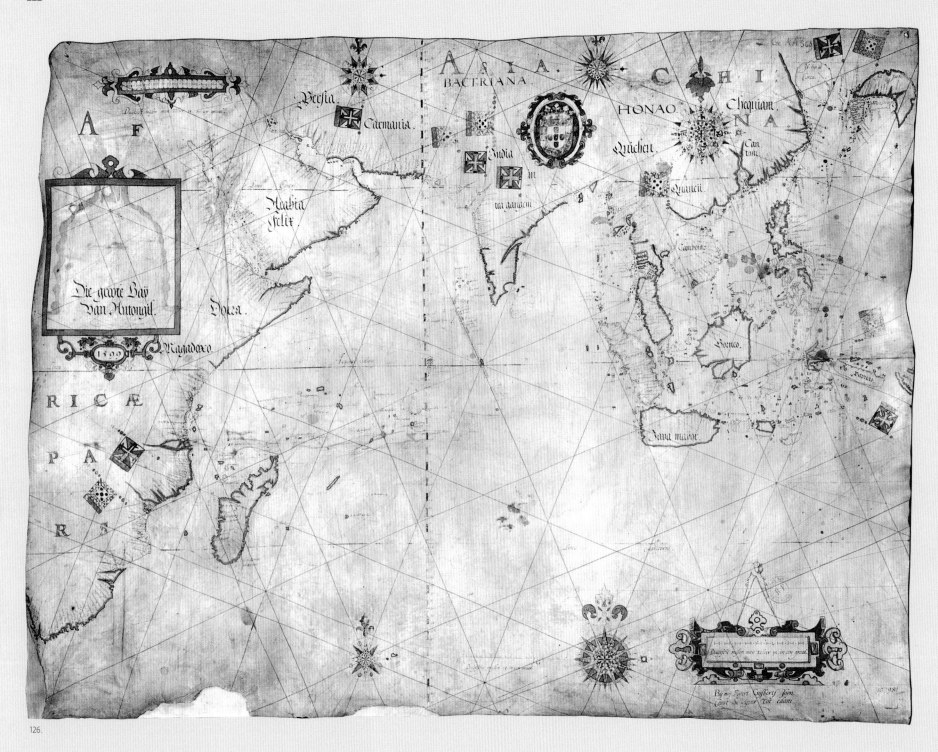

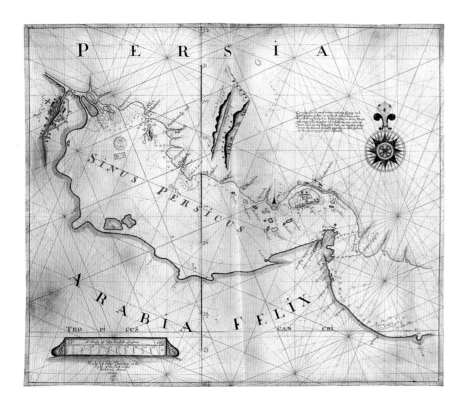

127.

128.

126
Evert Gijsbertsz., Nautical Map of the
Indian Ocean and China Seas
Edam, 1599

The first Dutch maritime map of the Indian
Ocean, this map was directly inspired by
Portuguese sources. It is signed in Dutch "by me,
Evert Gysbertszoon, draftsman of maps at Edam,"
and it carries the coat of arms of Portugal (at
the north of India) as well as 12 other Portuguese
pavilions. It is similar to the maps illustrating the
Itinerario of Jan Huygen of Linschoten (1596).

NLF, Paris, Maps and Plans, GE-AA 569 (RES).
Illuminated manuscript on velum, 39⅜ × 29⅛ inches
(100 × 74 cm).

127
John Thornton, Map of the Persian Gulf
London, 1699

Characterized by an English style enhanced with
vivid colors and a beautiful wind rose, this map
belongs to a series of copies based on Dutch
models that depicted the Persian Gulf region
quite accurately.

NLF, Paris, Maps and Plans, GE SH 18 PF 209 DIV 2 P 5.
Illuminated manuscript on velum, 29⅜ × 25 inches
(74.5 × 63.5 cm).

128
Giacomo Gastaldi,
Il Designo della terza parte dell'Asia
(The Design of the Third Part of Asia)
Venice, 1561

Closely related to the work of the Venetian
publisher Giovanni Battista Ramusio, whose
works he illustrated, this cartographer created
engraved maps based on a compilation of
multiple sources. Often less exact than the
contemporary manuscript maps of Asia and the
Indian Ocean, they nevertheless had a significant
distribution.

NLF, Paris, Maps and Plans, Ge DD-1140 (73 RES).
Impression on paper, 33⅜ × 26⅜ inches (77 × 67 cm).

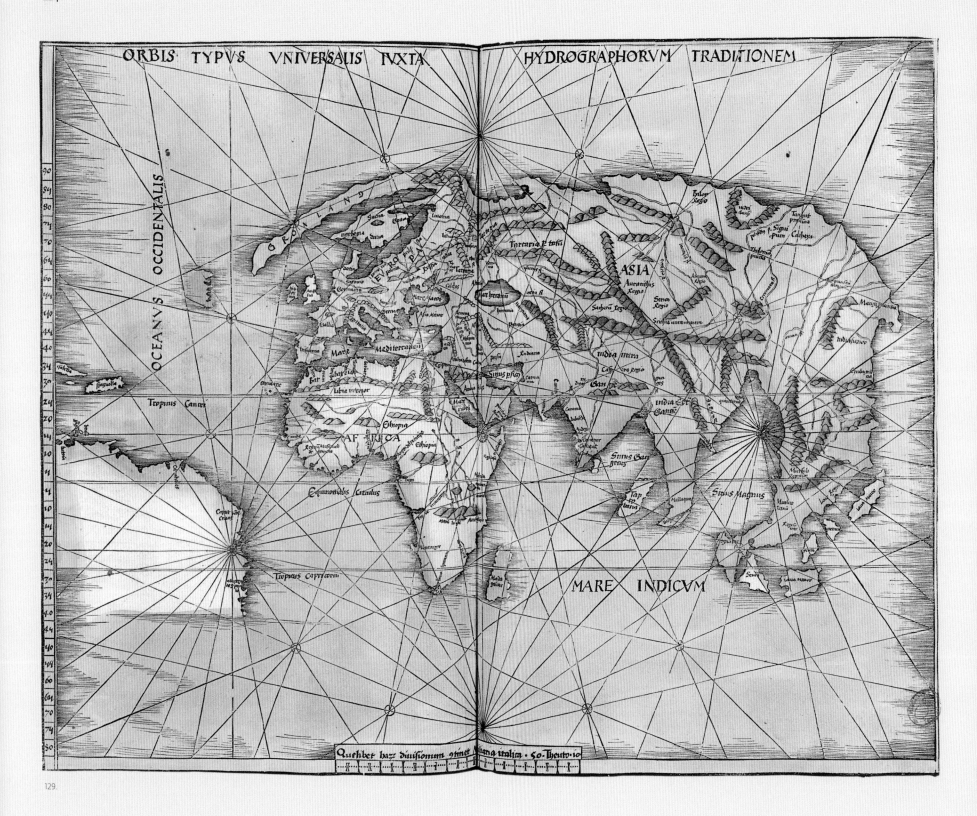

129
Martin Waldseemüller, Planisphere
Strasbourg, 1513

A member of the Saint Dié School, the author of this map also created a modernized edition of Ptolemy's *Geography* based on recent manuscript maps for Duke René II of Lorraine. For the world map, Waldseemüller used Nicolò de Caverio's planisphere, designed between 1502 and 1506, as his model for Europe, Africa, the New World and India, but he remained faithful to Henricus Martellus's 1490 world map for the rest of Asia.

NLF Paris, Maps and Plans, GE-DD 1009 (RES), map 29.
Engraved maps on wood and printed on paper,
13 × 18⅛ inches (33 × 46 cm).

130.

130
Pedro Barreto de Resende,
Demonstraçao da ilha de Goa
(Demonstration of the Island of Goa)
After 1635

This manuscript from the *Relacion da India* contains portraits of Portuguese navigators and views of cities and ports along the Indian Ocean. The island of Goa, in the northeast of India, was the administrative capital and port of the Portuguese empire in Asia from the time of its conquest, in 1510, by Afonso de Albuquerque.

NLF, Paris, Portuguese 1, f. 267.
Illuminated manuscript on velum, 13 × 17 inches
(33 × 43 cm).

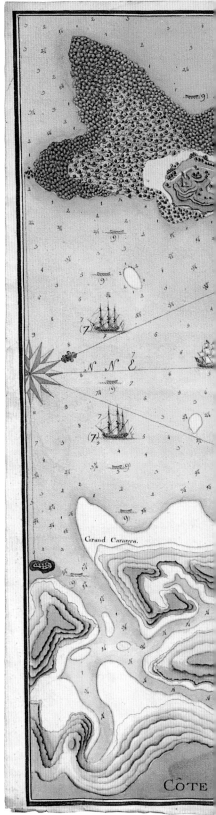

131

Louis François Grégoire Lafitte de Brassier,
Plan de l'isle de Bombay
(Plan of Island of Bombay)
1777

This plank, extracted from the *Atlas des cartes géographiques principalement des plans des villes les plus considérables, appartenant aux différentes nations européennes ainsi qu'aux princes indiens de l'Asie* (Atlas of geographic maps, principally plans of the largest towns belonging to different European nations as well as to the Indian princes of Asia), is a large-format album that highlights French ambitions in India during the 18th century. The author, an engineer-geographer, drew views of cities and plans distinguished for their precision and colors.

Service historique de la Défense, Vincennes, Marine, Ms. 203, pl. 5.
Watercolor pen drawing on paper, 45¼ × 25¼ inches (115 × 64 cm).

131.

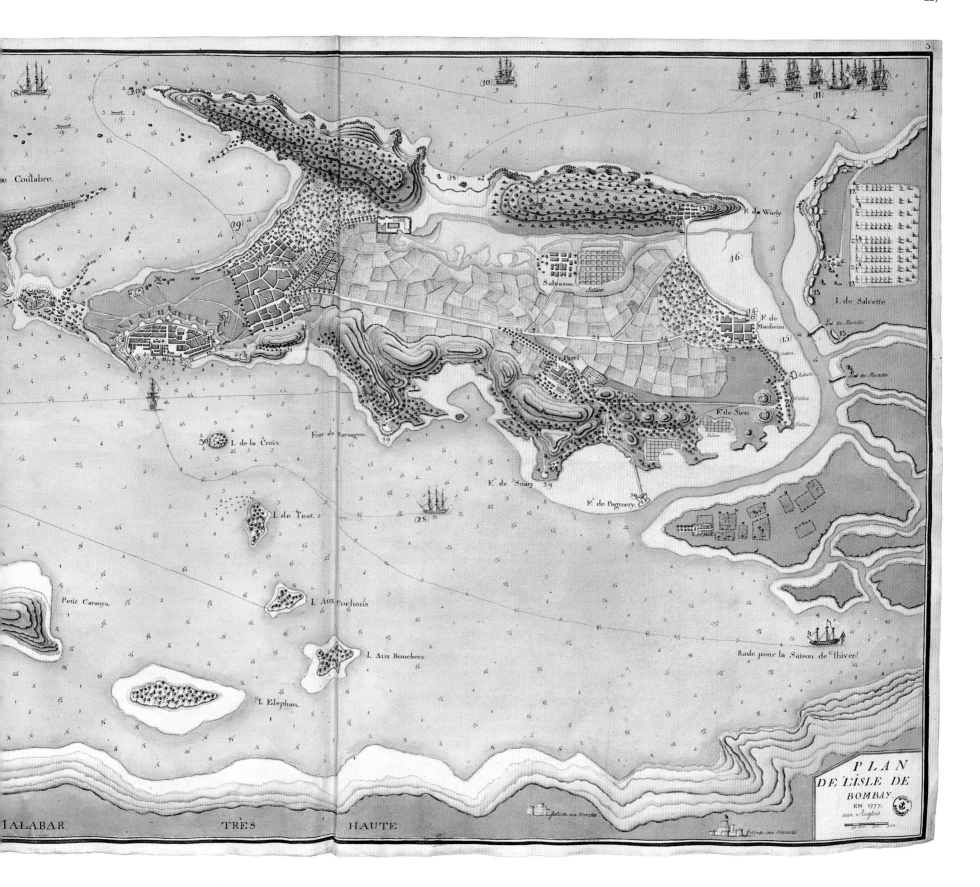

e Coulabre.

(19)

F. de Warly.

Salvason

16

I. de Salcette

13

N Blk

Fort de Karsagen.

I. de la Croix

F. de Manheim

(15)

13

F de Sion

I. de Test.

F. de Suary

F. de Pognery.

Petit Caranya.

I. Aux Cochons

I. Aux Bouchers

Rade pour la Saison de l'hiver.

I. Elephan.

MALABAR.   TRÈS   HAUTE

PLAN
DE L'ISLE DE
BOMBAY
EN 1777.
aux Anglois

CARTOGRAPHY OF THE DUTCH EAST INDIA COMPANY'S FAR EAST ROUTES

Hans Kok

The East India Company — or, in Dutch, the
Verenigde Oostindische Compagnie, hence the
acronym VOC — was to be the first anonymous
company in history, with shares listed in the stock
exchange. Founded in 1602, it became known
worldwide. A combination of poorly adapted financial
policies and international politics led to its demise in
1799. The VOC by then formed an integral part of
the Dutch economy, so the government was obliged
to scoop up the vestiges of this private commercial
empire and transform it into a colonial empire.

The 17 provinces of the Netherlands once belonged
to the Hapsburg Empire, which was overthrown
following the Eighty Years's War (also known as
the Dutch War of Independence), which began in
1568 and ended with the Treaty of Munster in 1648.
At that time, Spanish ports were closed to Dutch
ships, meaning the Dutch could no longer transport
merchandise coming from Hispano-Portuguese
colonies. Since they did not have access to other
routes, the Dutch ships were forced to sail around the
Cape of Good Hope. In the meantime, the union of
the 17 provinces had dissolved, with the northern ones
having seceded. After 1595, several small companies
had carried out expeditions, but the northern republic
lacked both commercial and political power, and they
realized that such enterprises would be in vain. This
forced a union in 1602 that resulted in the founding
of the East India Company. A charter registered the
company's commercial interest while still granting it
a degree of independence, particularly on the military
front, in order to allow it to defend its investments. Its
cartographically defined zone of operation extended
from the Cape of Good Hope eastward to the Strait of
Magellan.

THE ORGANIZATION OF THE VOC

The East India Company consisted of six houses,
each representing different cities, whose influence
was tied to the proportion of their invested capital.
Consequently, eight directors were from the
Amsterdam house, four were from Middelburg and
the other houses had one director each; together
with a supplementary "rotating" director, they
formed the famous *Heren Zeventien*, the Council
of the Seventeen. Each house armed its own ships,
with expenses and receipts managed according
to a specific process. Since communications with
the Far East took a considerable amount of time,
local authority was exerted by the *Raad van Indië*,
a council presided over by the governor general of
Batavia (present-day Jakarta). However, the Dutch
directors were required to come to an agreement
for the more important decisions. The VOC had a
vertical structure that controlled the entire chain of
production, from the purchase of merchandise to
transport to commercialization. This global structure,
unlike with the British East India Company,
entailed the standardization of ships, maps and
instruments; during its two centuries of operation,
all modifications to instruments were listed in a
document called the *Lijste van de Boeken Kaarten en
van Stuermansgereetschappen* (see illustration 133).

The VOC's main commercial ports of call were in
the Maluku Islands (spices), Ceylon (cinnamon),
Cambodia and Siam (deer pelts) and Japan (textiles
and ceramics); to these we can add manufacturing
sites in India (silks, textiles), Bengal, China, Malaysia
and the Red Sea and Persian Gulf. Several trading
posts on Indonesian islands moved merchandise to
Batavia for onward transport to the Netherlands.
Deshima Island (present-day Nagasaki) played a
special role, opening a unique window into Japan for
the West, and vice-versa, until Admiral Perry's flotilla
opened the country to other nations in 1853. The
establishment in 1652 of a port of call at the Cape
of Good Hope, one without commercial purposes
but simply as a rest stop for ships and their crews,
facilitated the resupply of returning ships, since their
cargo of food could be adjusted for much shorter
voyages (see illustration 137).

THE VOC'S CARTOGRAPHIC SERVICES

From its onset until its demise, the VOC had its own
exclusive cartographic and hydrographic service.
An official cartographer was located in Amsterdam,
and a complimentary service, in charge of regional
routes and return trips, was located in Batavia, where
the registry and building of fortifications made for
a busy local economy. Copies of all maps produced
in Batavia (see illustration 134) were sent to the
Netherlands, where more than 50 cartographers
resided around 1745. First supervised by an *equipage-
meester*, who was responsible for armaments, and
then by a *baas-kaartenmaker*, a chief cartographer,
the main operations in Batavia were focused on
expeditions to the "Unknown Southern Lands" in the
1620s, with Maarten Gerritsz. de Vries's expedition
to Japan and beyond as well as Abel Tasman's voyage
to Australia, Tasmania and New Zealand in 1643,
and with the new expedition by Willem de Vlamingh
along the Australian coast in 1697.

The VOC's maps were mainly manuscript copies
based on original maps that were constantly being
updated. The *Lijste* tells us which maps were on
board which ships and which captain was responsible
for them in case of damage or loss. The manuscript
copies, which were preferred to the mechanically
printed ones, also guaranteed a level of confidentiality,
which was initially considered necessary. In 1753,
however, Jan de Marre persuaded the *Here Zeventien* to
accept the printing of maps, which cost much less than
producing maps on velum. On board ships however,
the volumes of Van Keulen's *Zeefakkel* were still

133.

133

List of Maps and Navigational Material Furnished by Evert Caspersz., Captain of the *Ternate*
Amsterdam, 1673

The very structured organization of the Dutch East India Company entailed the standardization of both navigational and cartographic materials, which were produced in the company's workshops. The materials, books and maps supplied to the ships were consigned on lists, which were first in manuscript form and were later printed.

Nationaal Archief, The Hague, N° d'inv. 5017.
List printed on two pages.

134

**Reinier and Josua Ottens,
Plan and View of Batavia**
Amsterdam, circa 1740

Batavia — founded by Jan Pietersz. Coen, governor general of the VOC, on the ruins of Jayakarta in 1619 — was the company's capital in Asia. It had its own cartography workshop. This etching, published by Reinier and Josua Ottens, shows both Batavia's harbor and the manner in which the nearby fort could protect it.

NLF, Paris, Maps and Plans, GE DD 2987 (7653).
Engraving on copper, 25½ × 19½ inches (65 × 49.5 cm).

preferred, and more than one map on velum ended up as the binding for the company's books.

We also know the company's list of official cartographers. Before 1608 and the merging of several companies into the VOC, the role of cartographer was assigned to Petrus Plancius and the hydrographers of the Edam School. In northern Holland, Augustin Robaert was the cartograther from 1608 to 1617, and then Hessel Gerritsz. took over from 1617 to 1632. Following them there was a succession of Blaeus: Willem Jansz. Blaeu from 1633 to 1638, Joan Blaeu I from 1638 to 1672 and Joan Blaeu II from 1672 to 1705. After them, Isaac De Graaf was the official cartographer from 1705 to 1743, and then the Van Keulen family took over between 1743 and 1799.

The many anonymous maps we know of came either from Batavia or from local providers hired by the different houses; we also note complaints about the high prices charged by the cartographer of the Amsterdam house.

THE SELECTION OF ROUTES

Sailing routes were not chosen in relation to distance but rather in relation to travel time, since it was preferable to add miles in order to take advantage of favorable winds and currents. Among the potential dangers were political risks, pirates and meteorological and nautical hazards. After leaving the Netherlands, ships aimed either for the English Channel or the "service entrance" around Scotland and Ireland, depending on the political circumstances and dominant winds. The usual route then passed about 280 miles (450 km) to the west of Cape Finisterre then on to the Canary Islands and the Cape Verde islands. On approaching the equator, ships would enter the converging inter-tropical zone, where the winds lessened for prolonged periods of time and ships had to rely on marine currents, since they lacked the motoring strength to keep to any specific route. The VOC then advised its ships to follow the *Karrespoor* (see illustration 135), the "cart route," which was drawn on maps between the equator and the 12th parallel to the north, between Africa and Brazil, and where the strength of the currents was, at least in principle, weaker. Ships could also drift along the west African coast or in the open seas of the northern coast of South America, which would lengthen the voyage considerably. They would continue this trajectory along the South American coastline until

they encountered west winds, which would allow them to quickly cross the ocean to the trading post set up by the VOC at the Cape of Good Hope. This particular trading post became what is now known as South Africa. In order to cross the Indian Ocean, the route was diverted considerably from the equator due to strong head winds. The passage by the Roaring Forties assured a fast crossing thanks to both westerly winds and the favorable marine currents.

On the way back, winds and currents were unfavorable, and return trips were sailed on different routes. It was possible to go directly from Ceylon or from the Strait of Sunda to the Cape of Good Hope while passing to the south of Madagascar, in the direction of Table Bay or False Bay, and then continue toward Saint Helen Island.

Routes between Batavia and the regional trading posts were subject to the same considerations. A ship heading for Ceylon, where the VOC had considerable interests, would leave in a western direction from Cape Sunda then turn to the north up to Galle's latitude while crossing the Maldives. These routes are known today thanks to the maps registering the position of the ships. To reach Siam, ships would pass by Malaysia before heading up to Chao Phraya near Ayutthaya, while on the return trip they would skirt the eastern shores of the Gulf of Siam, one of those passages said to be *geode* (good), while the other was said to be *quade* (bad). These routes are shown on VOC maps.

CHARACTERISTICS OF THE MAPS

The VOC maps were mainly in the form of manuscripts either on paper or velum, the latter being more resistant to a marine environment, though its size was limited to that of the animal used to make it. These portolans usually showed a primary wind rose and 16 secondary roses, some of which were very ornate and were used instead of the cartographer's signature. The maps of the VOC bore a standard scale according to the zone in question. Others were drawn on the length of half pelts (see illustration 136), for example for the north coast of Java, "from Bantam to Java," and the central rose consequently became a half wind rose and was placed above or below the half pelt and surrounded by six secondary roses.

Two types of maps were available. The maps with a constant scale in all directions are what we refer to as "flat maps." These maps were convenient enough

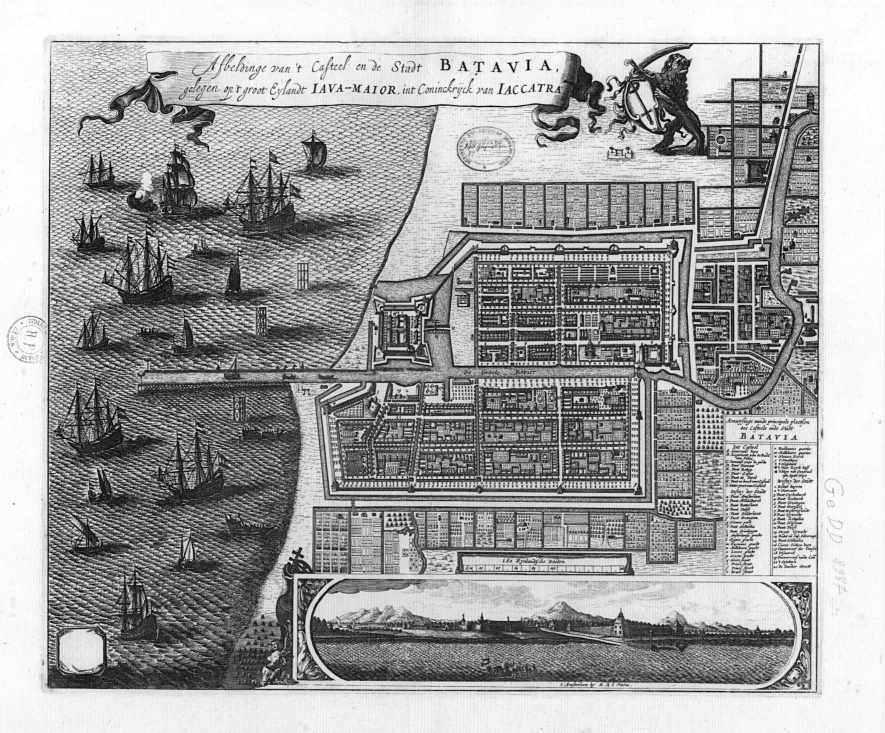

Afbeeldinge van 't Casteel en de Stadt BATAVIA, gelegen op 't groot Eylandt IAVA-MAIOR, int Coninckryck van IACCATRA

De Groote Revier

Aenwysinge vande principale plaetsen des Casteels ende Stadt BATAVIA

180 Rynlandsche Roeden

't Amsterdam by R. & I. Ottens.

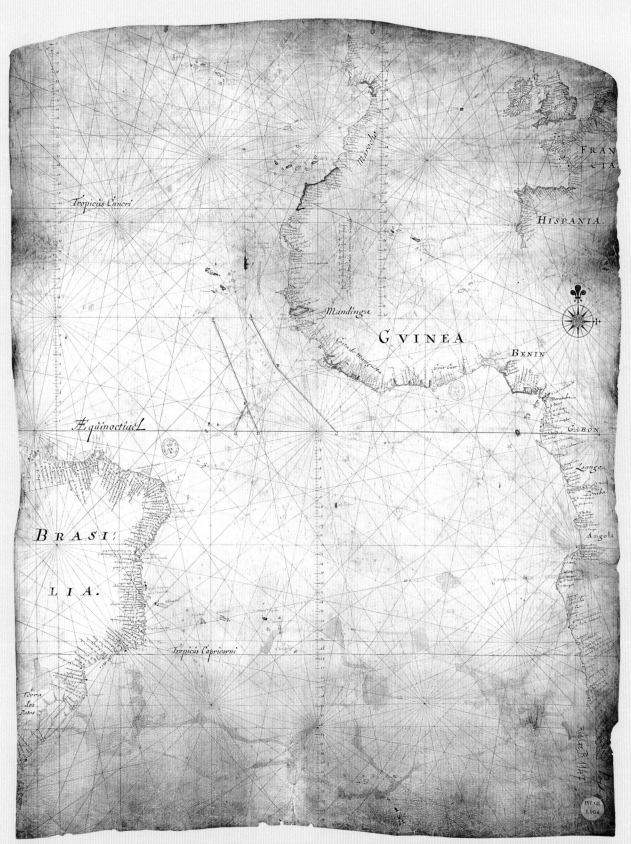

135.

135

Joan Blaeu, Map of the Atlantic Ocean
Amsterdam, circa 1655

Among the routes followed by VOC ships in the Atlantic, the "cart route," between western Africa and northern Brazil, was a zone of weak currents that was used to avoid the doldrums north of the equator. By placing Western Europe in the interior of Africa, this map shows the entire route on one sheet, from the English Channel to the Cape of Good Hope.

NLF, Paris, Maps and Plans GE B 1147 (RES).
Manuscript on parchment, 28⅜ × 36⅝ inches
(72 × 93 cm).

for short distances, but for longer journeys, especially while moving away from the equator, distortions due to the spherical shape of our planet became apparent. Mercator's projection partly resolved this problem, since it avoided the convergence of meridians and also increased the distance between parallels as one moved toward the south or north. The use of Mercator maps was not feasible, however, for mariners without an adequate education, and many pilots still preferred their flat maps. It is easy to distinguish between these two types of maps, since flat maps did not include a longitude scale, due to the lack of reliable methods (clocks) to locate the islands at their correct longitude, but they did have a distance scale. Flat maps of the Indian Ocean display a number of lowlands, islands, reefs and rockeries, whereas Mercator's version appear more "empty," since these elements could not be placed at a dependable longitude (see illustration 137). For Madagascar, only its southernmost point is shown; the same is true for Cape Comorin at the southern extremity of India and for the tip of Galle in Ceylon. With respect to the coasts of Africa, flat maps only showed discontinued coastlines, exclusively devoted to capes and promontories. Still, as larger-scale maps became more readily available (for the Strait of Sunda, for example, see illustration 139), flat maps began to include coastline profiles and information on sea depths, such as "bottomless," "small white pebbles" or "large corals." Local maps were occasionally presented lengthwise, with north indicated diagonally so as to better fit the coasts on paper or velum.

VOC maps for long-distance voyages consisted of groups of two flat maps or three Mercator maps. Since the flat maps had constant distance scales, their east-west and north-south dimensions corresponded to their latitude/longitude coverage in degrees at the equator. Consequently, the sizes of such maps were limited by the dimensions of the pelts used to make the vellum, and thus the number of degrees they could cover in latitude/longitude was also limited. For maps covering the distance from the Netherlands to the Cape of Good Hope, the north-south direction was placed along the velum's longest dimension; for routes going from the cape to the Strait of Sunda, maps were turned 90 degrees, so that the east-west axis was thereby situated along the longest dimension of the velum. For the first part of the route, flat maps either only showed the route from Spain to the cape, due to a lack of space, or contained a separate box that showed the section from the Netherlands to Spain with its own specific latitudinal scale. Since sailors occasionally followed the route passing to the north

of Scotland, the box could cover up to 63 degrees north. On the *wassende graden* (a Mercator projection) map, the north-south axis could not be contained on a single sheet of velum, due to the stretching of the latitudes away from the equator. It was necessary, therefore, to use two separate maps for the first part of the journey leading to the cape, for a total of three maps. In terms of the journey around Scotland, it was possible to use two velum pelts for the maps and not include a separate box. When it came to crossing the Indian Ocean, the latitudinal distortion was not a problem since ships remained close to the equator, and a single sheet of velum sufficed. When the route taken was further south, the cartographic surface had to be extended to 43 degrees south in order to include a larger portion of the southern part of ocean. Consequently, the coastline of the Bay of Bengal was omitted, and, again, the size of the velum became critical to show the north-south axis. If the size of the velum allowed it, the map's network of lines could be extended to the edges of the pelt, but rarely was any supplementary information added to that. If necessary, the "neck" of the pelt was also used, sometimes still showing the animal's blood vessels.

Flat maps of the Atlantic and Indian Oceans were drawn on the same scale, with distance scales corresponding to 2¾ inches (72 mm) for 100 Dutch miles. Minor distortions were often caused by the map crinkling or the velum contracting. Some of the anonymous maps and those of Abraham Anias had scales of less than five percent. We are not aware of any VOC instructions concerning this matter; however, this number is just outside of the distortion level that is deemed acceptable by today's standards. Scales of coastal maps varied considerably, depending on their uses. By design, Mercator maps had variable scales that were linked to the latitude and include no mention of distance scales.

MAPS OF THE INDIAN OCEAN

These maps reflect the routes approved by the VOC. In 1615, the Brouwer Route was explored by Commander Brouwer, future governor general of Batavia. This southern voyage led to the discovery of *Nagtegaels Eylandt* and use of the islands of Saint Paul and Amsterdam as anchors for the Strait of Sunda, a route favored by southeast winds. It was crucial to be able to identify these islands visually, since they were uninhabited and often missed at night or when visibility was otherwise poor, in order to locate the east-west axis. This was often the cause of

136.

136
Chinese Plate with
Ship Motif
China, 1756

Porcelain imported from Japan and China was one of the VOC's commercial interests. These goods were produced in China for export, complete with Chinese or other Oriental designs. This plate recalls the 1756 Chinese campaign of the *Vrijburg*, under the command of Captain Jacob Ryzik.

Guimet Museum, Paris, coll. Grandidier G. 106.
Porcelain, 15-inch (38 cm) diameter.

accidents, with ships sailing too far east and finishing ashore on the Australian coast, as was the case with the *Batavia* in 1629 and the *Zeewijk* in 1727. These mishaps were duly noted on maps and also noted in *Tryall's Rudsen*, a history of the sinking of the English ship *Tryall* in 1622. The discovery of the islands Dina and Maarseveen in the Indian Ocean was announced in 1663. They were named after ships but today are known as Marion Island and Prince Edward Island. Their exact location was initially contested but then verified and ultimately validated. For ships running short on supplies, the maps of these islands provided information such as where to find pigs, coconuts and potable water (*soute spruyten*) from coastal rivers. A *negorij* (local village) could be a source of revitalization, and it was better still where the coast was *al met volck bewoont* (populated everywhere). The final eastward turn at the *Vierde Hoeck* (fourth cape) of Java indicated the final leg of the journey, directly to Batavia. The port was bad but the harbor was good, since ships were protected by the *Casteel* (Batavian fortress), which was the main commercial and administrative center of the VOC in the Far East.

The VOC velum maps can be considered to be the last portolans. Exceeding the initial production of Mediterranean maps, they eventually covered the whole world, something Portuguese and Spanish cartographers had already begun. The appearance of these maps also changed. Artistically decorated maritime maps became quite rare, as priority was given to unadorned maps that were intended only for navigation, in line with the Calvinist mores of the Dutch. The organizational rigor of the VOC allowed cartographers to adapt their products to common norms maintained over 200 years. The production of these maps was based on the accounts provided by sailors, on information from scientific explorations and from various other sources. Several tens of thousands of maps were then produced, of which only a few hundred have survived. The National Library of France's collection occupies a special place in this history, since it has amassed a sizeable collection.[*]

Hans Kok
Original text translated by Laurent Bury

137.

137
Joan Blaeu, Map of Java's North Coast,
Between Bantam and Batavia
Amsterdam, 1688

Joan Blaeu II, who succeeded Joan I in 1672, created this map on a half-sheet of parchment, on which the primary rose, at bottom, is also cut in half. To facilitate the pilot's task, the coast is shown facing him, like the shoreline he is approaching, thereby placing south at the top of the map.

NLF, Paris, Maps and Plans, GE SH PF 192 DIV 3 P 4 (RES).
Manuscript on parchment, 40½ × 16⅜ inches
(103 × 41.5 cm).

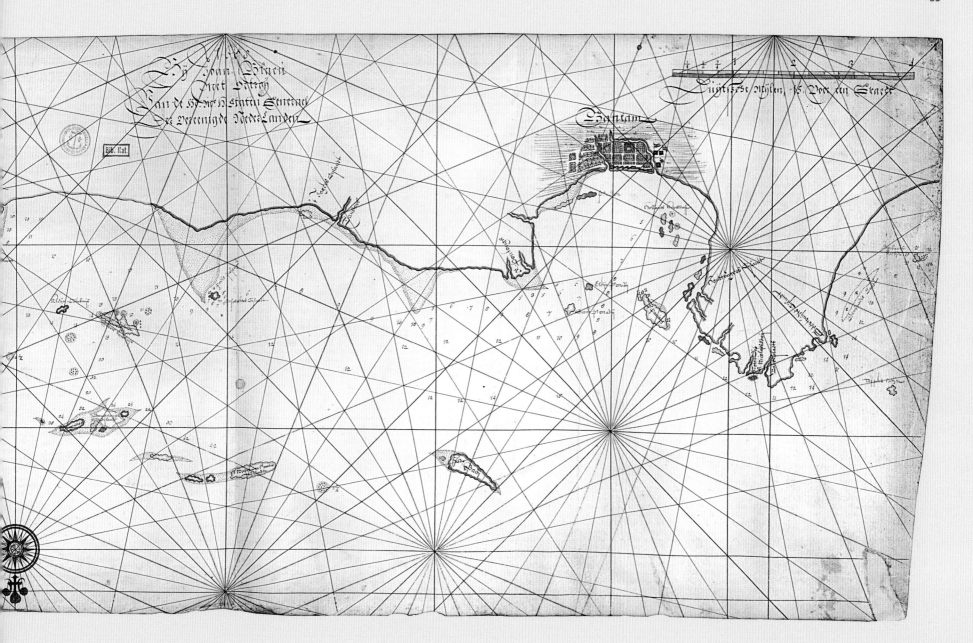

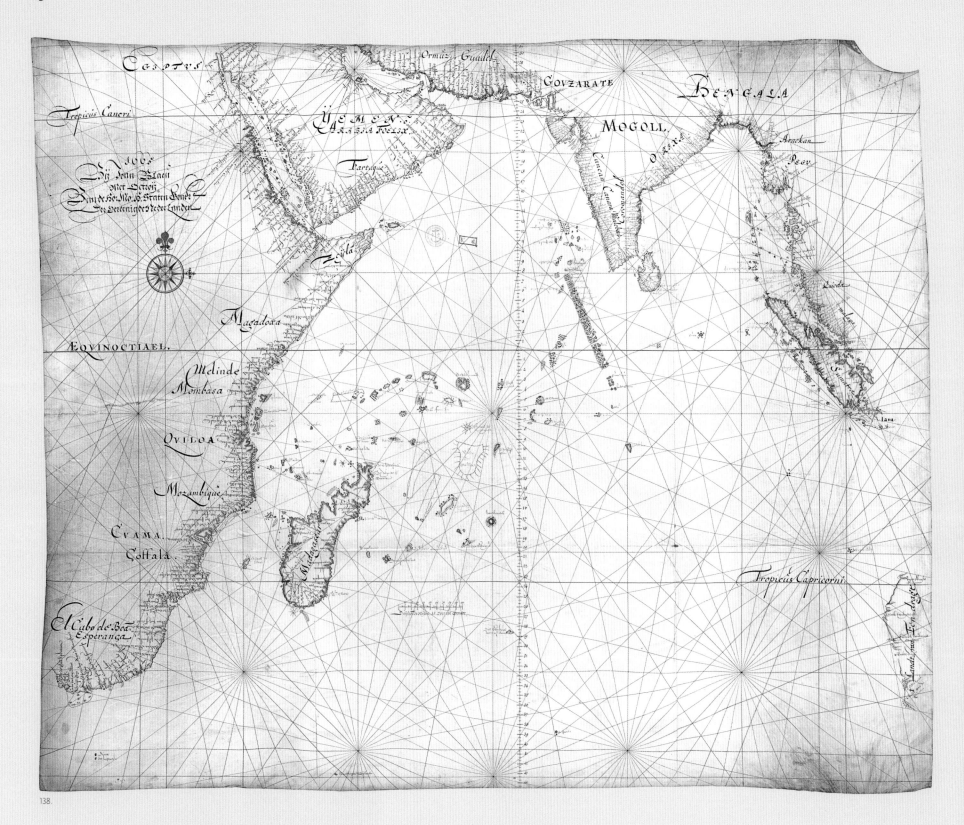

138
Joan Blaeu, Map of the Indian Ocean
Amsterdam, 1665

We see here the totality of the Indian Ocean, where the VOC's commercial sites could be found, including the stopover at the Cape of Good Hope, which was founded in 1652. This map is the work of the second member of the Blaeu dynasty to hold the position of the company's official cartographer.

NLF, Paris, Maps and Plans, GE SH 18 PF 213
DIV 3 P ½ (RES).
Manuscript on parchment, 35 × 28 inches (89 × 71 cm).

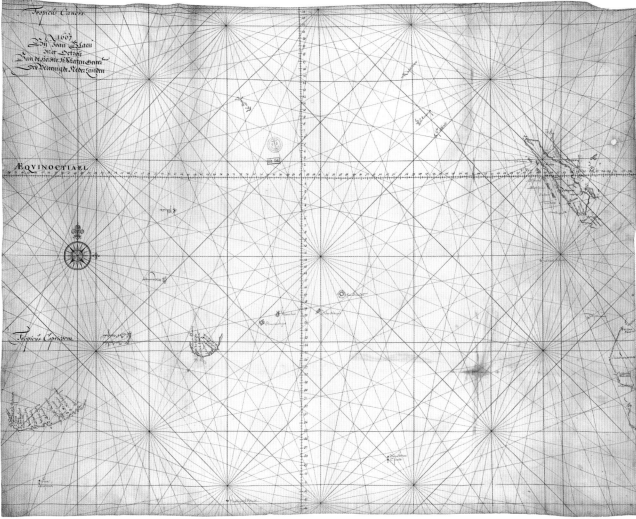

139.

139
Joan Blaeu, Map of the Indian Ocean, from the Cape of Good Hope to the Sunda Strait
Amsterdam, 1667

Built according to the Mercator projection, this map displays longitude and latitude scales. Unfortunately, this method, with the uncertainty of its longitude measurements, made it nearly impossible to locate some lands, hence here, many islands, reefs and coasts are absent. Only the southern point of Madagascar is shown...

NLF, Paris, Maps and Plans, GE SH 18 PF 213 DIV 3
P 3/1 (RES).
Manuscript on parchment, 38¼ × 30¼ inches
(97 × 77 cm).

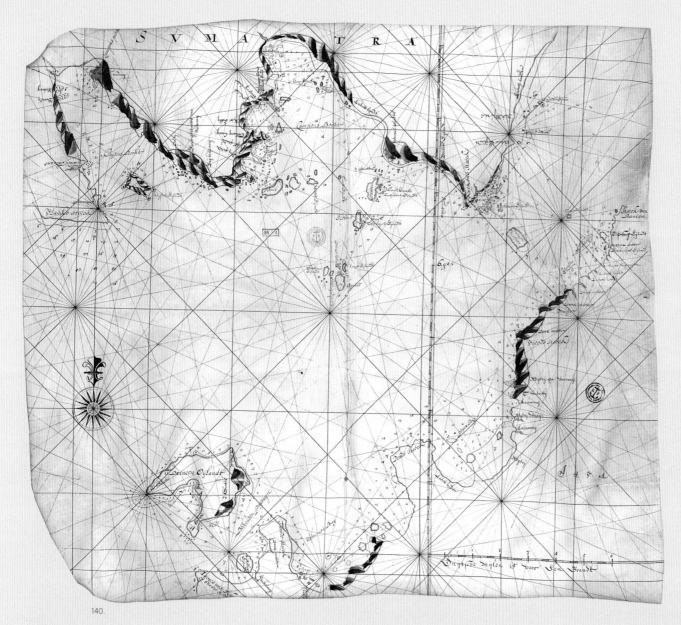

140.

140

Dutch Map of the Sunda Strait
Circa 1690

On this anonymous map, the Dutch toponymy uses an anchor to indicate places where one can drop anchor and blank ink to indicate places where one can find water. One can easily see the relationship between this map and the one produced by Thornton in 1699 (see illustration 104).

NLF, Paris, Maps and Plans, GE SH 18 PF 194 DIV 2 P ⅛ (RES).
Manuscript on parchment, 30¾ × 26¾ inches (78 × 68 cm).

141

Fred Woldemar, Makassar Harbor
1660

On June 12, 1660, the Dutch attacked the trading post of Makassar, founded by the Portuguese in the Celebes Islands in 1525. An insert provides the legend for the entire scene, with the names of the ships and vessels engaged in the battle. The loss of Makassar (and then of Bantam, in 1682) marked the fall of the Portuguese empire in Asia.

NLF, Paris, Maps and Plans — Geographic Society, SG BON Y 832 (RES).
Illuminated manuscript on parchment, 35½ × 27¾ inches (90 × 70.5 cm).

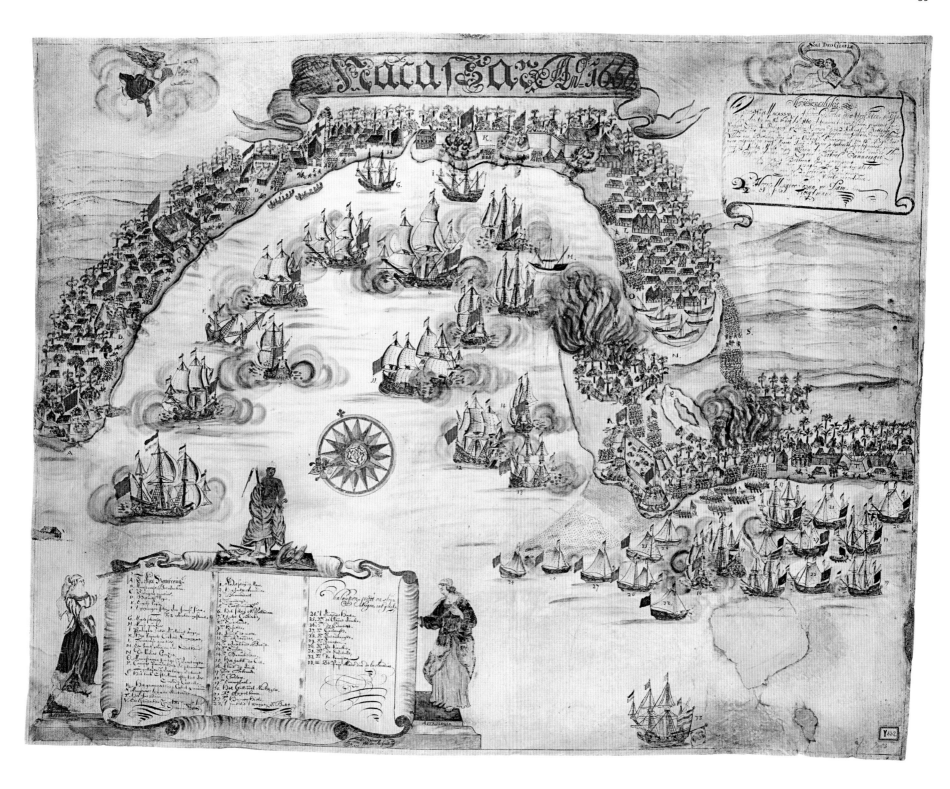

MAP OF THE PACIFIC OCEAN

HESSEL GERRITSZ

142

Hessel Gerritsz., Map of the Pacific Ocean
Amsterdam, 1662

This large manuscript map on parchment is the work of Gerritsz., the official cartographer of the Dutch East India Company between 1617 and 1632. Unlike the bulk of his works, it is not an unadorned portolan intended for navigation, but a luxurious map made for the directors of the VOC.

In order to combine all of the current information about the Pacific, this map evokes the history of its discovery, with portraits of Balboa, Magellan and Lemaire. It also includes the most up-to-date discoveries in this part of the world: under the name Nueva Guinea, we can see a section of the north coast of Australia, discovered by Jansz. in 1606. With very novel iconography, this map indicates the navigational conditions in the Pacific Ocean. Even though the Dutch seemed to have mastered the Pacific, the VOC must take the navigational and meteorological conditions, and the risks they entail, into consideration when choosing which route to take and where to develop their activities: strong but regular winds from the north, doldrums that immobilize ships in the torrid zone and storms in the South Pacific, where ships, under reduced sails, are shaken by a hostile sea, as seen in the tales of earlier voyages.

The map was subsequently corrected, undoubtedly by Gerritsz.'s successor, whereby the date was changed (1634) and an insert with a small planisphere with crisscrossing latitudes was added, underscoring more recent cartographic notions, such as California's insular character.

H. R.

NLF, Paris, Maps and Plans, GE SH ARCH 30 (RES). Illuminated manuscript on parchment, 55½ × 42⅛ inches (141 × 107 cm).

142 a
Ships Caught in the Roaring Forties

See pages 242–243.

142 b
Dutch Ships in the North Pacific

See pages 244–245.

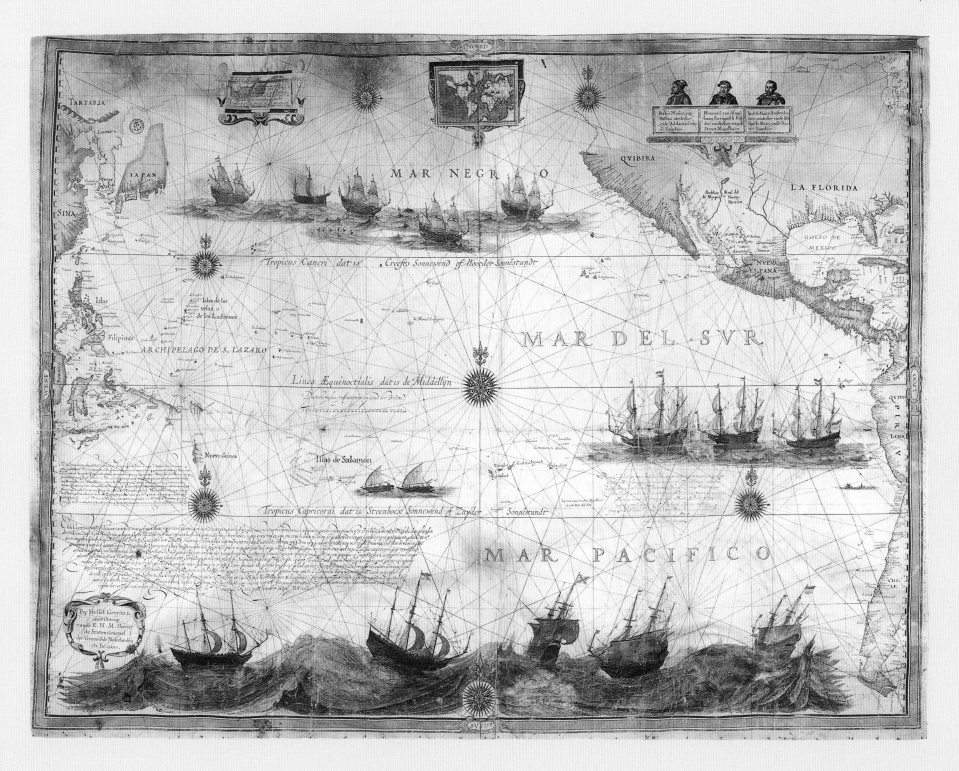

Wereylant   Eylandt zonder grondt   Honden eylandt

Vliegh eylandt

San Blas   la primera que descubrio Magallanes
                            en este mar del sur

l of Zuyder   las vyrgines   Sonnestandt

M A R   P A C I F

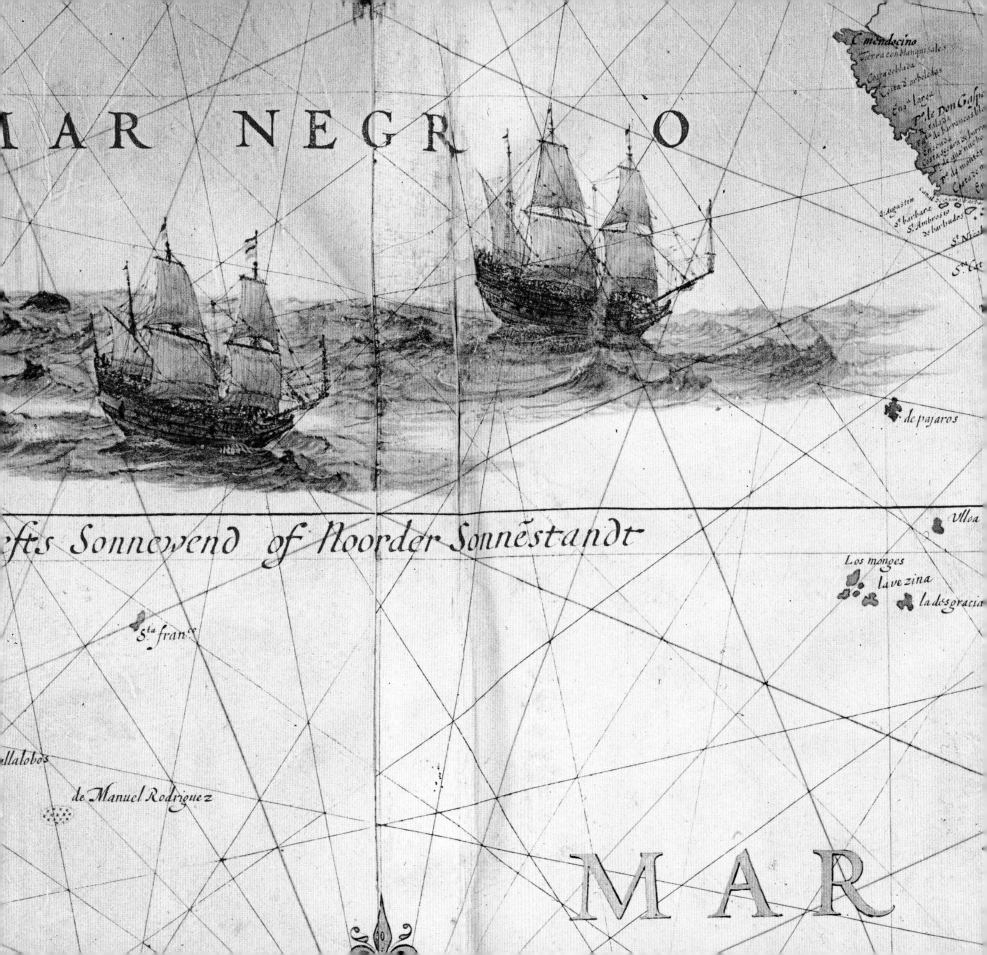

MAR NEGRO

Mendocino

Tierra con blanqui sales
Cap. a coblada
Costa d'arbeledas
En.a larga
P.te de Don Gaspa

S.Augustin S.barbara
S.Ambrosio
de bar.ludos

S.Nico

S.Cat

de pajaros

Ulloa

efts Sonnewend of Noorder Sonnestandt

Los monges
la vezina
la desgracia

S.ta franc.e

llalobos

de Manuel Rodriguez

MAR

142 C
Dutch Ships in the Tropical Doldrums Zone

See pages 244–245.

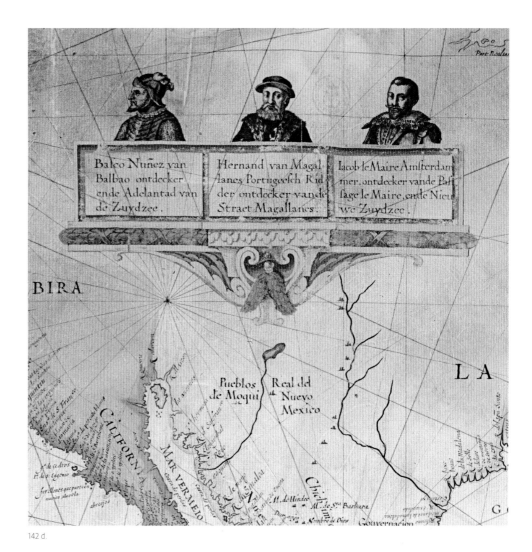

142 d.

142 d
Portraits of Pacific Ocean Explorers: Balboa, Magellan and Lemaire

BIBLIOGRAPHY

Alegria, Maria Fernanda, Suzanne Daveau, João Carlos Garcia, Francesc Relaño, "Portuguese Cartography in the Renaissance." In *Cartography in the European Renaissance.* Edited by David Woodward. Vol. 3 in *The History of Cartography.* Chicago/London: University of Chicago Press, 2007.

Amalgià, Roberto, *I lavori cartografici di Pietro e Jacopo Russo*, 301–320. Rome: Academia Nazionale dei Lincei, 1957. (Excerpt from *Rendiconti della classe di scienze morali storiche e filologiche.* Series VIII, vol. XII, facsimile 7–10, July-October 1957.)Alves Gaspar, Joaquim. "From the Portolan Chart of the Mediterranean to the Latitude Chart of the Atlantic: Cartometric Analysis and Modeling." PhD diss. Universidade Nova de Lisboa, 2010.

Astengo, Corradino. *La Cartografia nautica mediterranea dei sesoli XVI e XVII.* Genoa: Erga, 2000.

Astengo, Corradino. "The Renaissance Chart Tradition in the Mediterranean." In *Cartography in the European Renaissance*, 174–241. Edited by David Woodward. Vol. 3 in *The History of Cartography.* Chicago/London: University of Chicago Press, 2007.

Barbosa, António. *Novos subsídios para a história da ciência náutica portuguesa, na época dos descobrimentos*, 2nd ed. Porto, Portugal: Instituto para a Alta Cultura, 1948.

Bertrand, Romain. *L'Histoire à parts égales: Récits d'une rencontre Orient-Occident (XVIe–XVIIe siècles).* Paris: Seuil, 2011.

Besse, Jean-Marc *Les Grandeurs de la Terre: Aspects du savoir géographique* à la *Renaissance.* Paris: ENS Éditions, 2003.

Biedermann, Zoltán Dejanirah Couto, Jean-Louis Bacqué-Grammont and Mahmoud Taleghani. *Atlas historique du golfe Persique, XVIe–XVIIIe siècle.* Terrarum Orbis 6. Turnhout, Belgium: Brepols, 2006.

Boucheron, Patrick, dir. *Histoire du monde au XVe siècle*, coord. by Yann Potin, Pierre Monnet and Julien Loiseau, Paris: Fayard, 2009.

Bouloux, Nathalie. *Culture et savoirs géographiques dans l'Italie au XIVe siècle.* Terrarum orbis 2. Turnhout, Belgium: Brepols, 2002.

Brincken, Anna-Dorothee Von Den. *Kartographische Quellen Welt-, See- und Regionalkarten.* Typologie des sources du Moyen Âge occidental 51. Turnhout, Belgium: Brepols, 1988.

Campbell, Tony. "The Drapers' Company of Chart-Makers." In *IMedited by Sarah Tyacke and Helen Wallis.* London: Francis Edwards and Carta Press, 1973.

Campbell, Tony. "Portolan Charts from the Late Thirteenth Century to 1500." In *Cartography in Prehistoric Ancient and Medieval Europe and the Mediterranean*, 371–463, Edited by John Brian Harley and David Woodward. Vol. 1 in *The History of Cartography.* Chicago/London: University of Chicago Press, 1987. Caraci, Giuseppe. "Il cartografo messinese Joan Martines e l'opera sua." In *Atti della Reale Accademia Peloritana*, 619–667. Vol. 37. 1935. Cattaneo, Angelo. *Frau Mauro's Mappa Mundi and Fifteenth Century Venice.* Terrarum Orbis 8.Turhout, Belgium: Brepols, 2011.

Cavallo, Guglielmo, ed. *Cristoforo Colombo e l'apertura degli Spazi. Mostra storico-cartografia*, Exhibition catalog for the Commitato Nazionale per le celebrazioni del V centenario della scoperta dell'America, Palazzo Ducale, Genoa. Rome: Instituto poligrafico e Zecca dello Stato, 1992.

Cordier, Henri. "L'Extrême-Orient dans l'Atlas catalan de Charles V, roi de France." In *Bulletin de géographie historique et descriptive*, 19–64. Paris, 1895.

Cortesão, Armando, and Luís de Alburquerque. *History of Portuguese Cartography.* 2 vols. Lisbon: Junta de Investigações do Ultramar, 1969–1971.

Cortesão, Armando, Avelino Teixeira da Mota and Alfredo Pinheiro Marques. *Portugaliœ Monumenta Cartographica* (facsimile). 6 vols. Lisbon: Imprensa Nacional — Casa de Moeda, 1987.

Davies, Surekha. "French Depictions of Brazilians on Sixteenth-Century Maps." *The Historical Journal* 55-2 (2012): 217–238.

Davies, Surekha. "The Wondrous East in the Renaissance Geographical Imagination: Marco Polo, Fra Mauro and Giovanni Battista Ramusio." *History and Anthropology* 23-2 (2012): 215–234.

Destombes, Marcel. "François Ollive et l'hydrographie marseillaise au XVIIe siècle." *Neptunia* No. 37 (June 1954): 1–4.

Donattini, Massimo. *Spazio e modernità: Libri, carte, isolari nell'età delle scoperte.* Bologna, Italy: Clueb, 2000.

Edson, Evelyn. *Mapping Time and Space: How Medieval Mapmakers Viewed Their World.* London: British Library, 1997.

El Atlas catalán de Cresques Abraham: El primer atlas del Mundo. Primera edición completa en el sexcentésimo aniversario de su realización, 1375–1975. Barcelona: Diafora, 1975.

Falchetta, Piero. *Fra Mauro's World Map, With a Commentary and Translations of the Inscriptions.* Terrarum Orbis 5. Turnhout, Belgium/Venice, Italy: Brepols/Biblioteca Nazionale Marciana, 2006.

Ferretto, Arturo. "I cartografi Maggiolo oriundi di Rapallo." In *Atti della Società Ligure de Storia Patria*, 53–83. Vol. 52 in *Miscellanea geo-topografica.* 1924.

Foncin, Myriem, Marcel Destombes and Monique de La Roncière. *Catalogue des cartes nautiques sur vélin conservées au département des Cartes et Plans.* Paris: National Library, 1963.

Gautier Dalché, Patrick. *Carte marine et portulan au XIIe siècle: Le Liber de existencia riveriarum et forma maris nostri Mediterranei (Pisa, circa 1200).* Rome: École Française de Rome, 1995.

Gautier Dalché, Patrick. *Du Yorkshire à l'Inde: Une géographie urbaine et maritime de la fin du XIIe siècle, Roger de Howden?* Geneva: Droz, 2005.Gautier Dalché, Patrick. *La Géographie de Ptolémée en Occident (IVe–XVIe siècle).* Terrarum Orbis 9. Turnhout, Belgium: Brepols, 2009.

Gautier Dalché, Patrick. "Un problème d'histoire culturelle: Perception et représentation de l'espace au Moyen Age." *Medievales* No. 18 (1990): 5–15.

Gentile, Sebastiano. *Firenze e la scoperta dell'America: Umanesimo e geografia nel'400 Fiorentino.* Florence: L.S. Olschki, 1992.

Harley, John Brian, and David Woodward, eds. *Cartography in Pre-historic, Ancient and Medieval Europe and the Mediterranean.* Vol. 1 in *The History of Cartography.* Chicago/London: University of Chicago Press, 1987.

Harley, John Brian, and David Woodward, eds. *Cartography in the Traditional East and Southeast Asian Societies.* Vol. 2 in *The History of Cartography.* Chicago/London: University of Chicago Press, 1994.

Hoogvliet, Margriet. *Pictura et Scriptura: Textes, images et herméneutique des Mappæ Mundi (XIIIe–XVIe siècle).* Terrarum Orbis 7. Turnhout, Belgium: Brepols, 2007.

Kamal, Youssouf. *Monumenta cartografica Africæ et Ægypti*, rev. ed. 16 vols. Cairo: Royal Egyptian geographic Society, 1987.

Kok, Hans, and Günter Schilder. *Sailing for the East: History and Catalogue of Manuscript Charts on Vellum of the Dutch East India Company VOC, 1602–1799.* Utrecht Studies of the History of Cartography 10. Houten, the Netherlands: Hes and De Graaf Publishers, 2010.

La Roncière, Monique de, and Michel Mollat du Jourdin. *Les Portulans: Cartes marines du XIIIe au XVIIe siècle.* Fribourg, Switzerland/Paris, France: Office du Livre/Nathan, 1984.

Le Carrer, Olivier. *Océans de papier: Histoire des cartes maritimes des périples antiques au GPS.* Grenoble, France: Glénat, 2006.

Lestringant, Frank. *Le Livre des îles: atlas et récits insulaires de la Genèse à Jules Verne.* Geneva: Droz, 2002.

Lestringant, Frank. *L'Atelier du cosmographe ou l'image du monde à la Renaissance.* Paris: Albin Michel, 1991.

Llompart Moragues, Gabriel, Ramon J. Pujades i Battaler and Julio Samsó. *El Mon i els dies: l'atles català, 1375.* Barcelona: Enciclopèdia Catalana, 2005.

Martín-Merás, Luisa. *Cartografía marítima hispana: la imagen de América.* Madrid: Lunwerg, 1993.

Martín-Merás, Luisa. *Cartografía marítima hispana: la imagen de América.* Madrid: Lunwerg, 1993.

Martín-Merás, Luisa. "La expansión atlántica de la corona de Castilla." In *Juan de la Cosa y la época de los descubrimientos*, 33–49. Madrid: Sociedad Estatal de Conmemoraciones Culturales, 2010. Milano, Ernesto. *La Carta del Cantino e la rappresentazione della Terra nei Estense e Universitaria.* Modena, Italy: Il Bulino, 1991.

Miller, Konrad. *Mappæ Arabicæ.* Stuttgart, Germany: self-published, 1926.

Pastoureau, Mireille. *Voies océanes. Cartes marines et grandes découvertes.* Paris: National Library, 1992.

Pelletier, Monique, dir. *Couleurs de la Terre: Des mappemondes médiévales aux images satellitales*, catalog for the exhibition of the same name, National Library of France, 1998–1999. Paris: Seuil/NLF, 1998.

Pflederer, Richard. *Census of Portolan Charts and Atlases.* Williamsburg, Virginia: self-published, 2009.

Pujades i Bataller, Ramon J. *La carta de Vallseca de 1439/Gabriel Vallseca's 1439 Chart.* Barcelona: Lumenartis, 2009.

Pujades i Bataller, Ramon J. *Les Cartes portolanes: la representació medieval d'una mar solcada.* Barcelona: Institut Cartogràfic de Catalunya/Institut d'Estudis Catalans/Institut europeu de la Mediterrània, 2007.

Raup Wagner, Henry. "The Manuscript Atlases of Battista Agnese." *The Papers of the Bibliographical Society of America* 25, 1931: 1–110.

Relaño, Francesc. *The Shaping of Africa: Cosmographic Discourse and Cartographic Science in Late Medieval and Early Modern Europe.* Aldershot, England: Ashgate, 2002.

Rey Pastor, Julio, and Ernesto García Camarero. *La Cartografía Mallorquína.* Madrid: Consejo Superior de Investigaciones Científicas, 1960.

Roselló i Verger, Vicenç M. *Portolans procedents de collecions espanyoles.* Barcelona: Institut Cartogràfic de Catalunia, 1995.

Sandman, Alison. "Spanish Nautical Cartography in the Renaissance." In *Cartography in the European Renaissance*, 1095–1142. Edited by David Woodward. Vol. 3 in *The History of Cartography*, Chicago/London: University of Chicago Press, 2007.Schilder, Günter, and Marco Van Egmond. "Maritime Cartography in the Low Countries During the Renaissance." In *Cartography in the European Renaissance*, 1384–1432. Edited by David Woodward. Vol. 3 in *The History of Cartography.* Chicago/London: University of Chicago Press, 2007.

Sezgin, Fuat. *Mathematical Geography and Cartography in Islam and Their Continuation in the Occident.* 2 vols. Frankfurt: Institute for the History of Arabic-Islamic Science, 2005.

Smith, Tom. "The Thames School." In *The Compleat Plattmaker: Essays on Chart, Map and Globe Making in England in the Seventeenth and Eighteenth Centuries*, edited by Norman J.W. Thrower. Berkeley, California: University of California Press, 1978.

Subrahmanyam, Sanjay. *Vasco de Gama: Légende et tribulations du vice-roi Indes*, Translated by Myriam Dennehy. Paris: Alma editor, 2012. (Original edition: *The Career and Legend of Vasco da Gama.* Cambridge: Cambridge University Press, 1997.)

Thomaz, Luís Filipe, and Alfredo Pinheiro Marques. *Atlas Miller.* (Commentaries on the facsimile.) Barcelona: Moleiro, 2006.

Tolias, Geoge. "Isolarii, Fifteenth to Seventeenth Century." In *Cartography in the European Renaissance*, 263–284. Edited by David Woodward. Vol. 3 in *The History of Cartography.* Chicago/London: University of Chicago Press, 2007.

Toulouse, Sarah. "Marine Cartography and Navigation in Renaissance France." In *Cartography in the European Renaissance*, 1550–1568. Edited by David Woodward. Vol. 3 in *The History of Cartography.* Chicago/London: University of Chicago Press, 2007.

Tyacke, Sarah. *Before Empire: The English World Picture in the Sixteenth and Early Seventeenth Centuries.* London: Hakluyt Society, 2001.

Tyacke, Sarah. "Chartmaking in England and Its Context, 1550–1650." In *Cartography in the European Renaissance*, 1722–1753. Edited by David Woodward. Vol. 3 in *The History of Cartography.* Chicago/London: University of Chicago Press, 2007.

Vagnon, Emmanuelle. "Les rivages africains de l'océan Indien: cartographies occidentales du XIVe au XVIe siècle." *Cartes et géomatique* No. 210 (December 2011), acts of the Cartographier l'Afrique colloquium (2–3 December 2010): 63–78.

Verlinden, Charles. *Quand commença la cartographie portugaise?* In *Revista da Universidade de Coimbra* vol. XXVII, Coimbra, Portugal: Junta de Investigações Científicas do Ultramar, 1979.

Waters, David. *The Art of Navigation in England in Elizabethan and Early Stuart Times.* New Haven, Connecticut: Yale University Press, 1958.

Woodward, David, ed. *Cartography in the European Renaissance.*Vol. 3 in *The History of Cartography*, Chicago/London: University of Chicago Press, 2007.

Zandvliet, Kees. *Mapping for Money: Maps, Plans and Topographic Paintings and Their Role in Dutch Overseas Expansion During the 16th and 17th Centuries.* Amsterdam: De Bataafsche Leeuw, 1998.

Zandvliet, Kees. "Mapping the Dutch World Overseas in the Seventeenth Century." In *Cartography in the European Renaissance*, 1432–1433. Edited by David Woodward. Vol. 3 in *The History of Cartography.* Chicago/London: University of Chicago Press, 2007. Zurara, Gomes Eanes de *Crónica do Descobrimento e Conquista da Guiné* (1448). Lisbon: Publicações Europa-América, 1989.

GLOSSARY

References to glossary entries are set in *italics*.

Astronomical Navigation: A navigational technique that consists in determining a ship's position by observing the position of stars and measuring their height (i.e., the angle between the star's direction and the horizon).

Bearings, Take the Ship's: To determine the ship's position with the help of navigational instruments.

Borda's Reflecting Circle: Circle that allowed mariners to take repeated measurements of angles for astronomical observations (meridian heights, lunar distances, etc.). Handheld and very malleable, this instrument was used at sea and provided very reliable observations for hydrographic works.

Cabotage: A type of navigation practiced along coastlines or for short crossings, generally done without losing sight of land. Compare *long-distance navigation*.

Cartouche: A more or less decorative frame that contained the document's title and necessary information in order to identify it.

Casa de contratación de las Indas: An independent Spanish institution that was founded in Seville in 1503 and controlled all the commercial and financial transactions between private or government entities and the Spanish colonies in America. It had its own administration, custom services, court and pilots who taught the art of navigation and how to direct flotillas. They also produced maps of the newly conquered territories. One of the most celebrated "pilotos mayores" engaged by the Casa de contratación was Amerigo Vespucci.

Clock and **Marine Watch**: Referred to as a clock in its fixed format and a watch in its mobile format, these were highly precise instruments that measured time. They were developed in England and France between 1760 and 1770 and were used to preserve a ship's original meridian hour, thereby allowing mariners to more easily and rigorously calculate *longitudes*. During the 19th century, marine watches became known as maritime chronometers.

Compass: Navigational instrument consisting of a magnetized needle that aligns itself with the Earth's magnetic field. Compare *mariner's compass*.

Cross-staff or **Jacob's Staff**: An instrument that measures the height of a celestial body (such as a star or the sun) and thus provides the observational *latitude*. Used between the 14th and the 17th centuries, it looked like a wooden ruler, graded in degrees, on which runs a cursor called a hammer.

Dead Reckoning: A navigational technique that consists of deducing the ship's position based on its route and the distance it has traveled since its last-known position. This method relies on instruments that measure the ship's heading (i.e., *compass*), its speed (i.e., speed log) and the amount of time passed (i.e., hourglass); it depends as well on the estimated environmental influences (e.g., currents, winds) on the ship's advance.

Graphic (or **Bar) Scale**: A graduated segment that is divided in equal parts and allows navigators to gauge the distances represented on a map. The graphic scale may be found in the map's title, margin or frame.

Hydrography: The section of physical geography that deals with salt and fresh waters; the cartography of seas and rivers.

Insular: A translation from the Italian "isolario," this term designates a literary genre created in the 15th century in Italy. It refers to a geographic collection composed mainly of descriptions of islands that are accompanied by maps.

Latitude: One of the coordinates of any point on the Earth's surface. It is defined as the angular distance from this point to the equator and is measured in degrees. Compare *longitude*.

Latitude Scale: A graduated graphic scale that indicates *latitudes*, that is, a point's angular distance from the equator, measured in degrees and along a meridian.

Long-Distance Navigation or **Ocean-Going Navigation**: Open-sea navigation, far from coastlines, which forces the pilot to observe the stars and to measure their height above the horizon in order to deduce the ship's *latitude*, hence the name ocean-going navigation.

Longitude: One of the coordinates of any point on the Earth's surface. It is defined by the angular distance from this point to the prime meridian and is measured in degrees. Compare *latitude*.

Loxodromy: A curve at sea that one follows to go from one point to another and that cuts all meridians at the same angle; it is shown as a straight line on *Mercator projection* maps.

Magnetic Declination: The difference between the Earth's actual pole and the magnetic pole indicated by a *compass*. This difference varies according to the time of day and the location.

Magnetic Route: In navigation, a route is the angle between the direction the ship is following and the direction of true north (the true route) or the magnetic north (indicated by the *compass* or *sea compass*). In days gone by, this angle was expressed in relation to the cardinal points, in quarters of the compass's rose (or *wind rose*). For example, a route could be "one quarter northeast."

Mariner's Compass: A navigational instrument that is equipped with a magnetized needle that always points to the magnetic north; it had a graded quadrant on which the cardinal points are inscribed.

Mercator Projection: Established at the end of the 16th century, this projection allows a navigator to easily transcribe a route onto a canvas of meridians and orthogonal parallels; the parallels are positioned at crisscrossing intervals moving away from the equator. It can represent loxodromic routes with straight lines that cut the meridians at constant angles. A pilot thereby need only follow these lines to guide his route and keep a constant angle in relation to the direction of the meridian, determined by the *compass*'s needle, corrected by the *magnetic declination* and the fixed point of the departure.

Nautical (or **Sea) Astrolabe**: Simplified astrolabe that was perfected during the 15th century and served exclusively to measure the height of the sun above the horizon and to determine the ship's *latitude*.

Nautical Instructions: A book destined for mariners that contains the necessary navigational information, such as descriptions of the ports and coastlines, the principal navigational routes, a calendar of lunar phases and tides, etc.

Padón Real: In the 16th century, this was the official general reference map from which all maps on board Spanish ships were drawn. It was conserved in the *casa de Contratación* in Seville.

Pavillion: On a map, it is a flag that flies on a ship or a near port, particularly above a *vignette*.

Periplus: A tale of circumnavigation or, more generally, of any maritime journey.

Pilot Book: A book or manual of nautical instructions gathering the knowledge of mariners. Called a "routier" in French, prominent examples include *Le Grant Routier et Pilotage et enseignement pour ancrer tant es portz, havres que autres lieux de la mer* (The big pilot book and piloting and teaching for anchoring in ports, harbors and other places at sea) by Pierre Garcie-Ferrande (which was reprinted several times from 1483 onward).

Planisphere: A map that represents the Earth's two hemispheres on a flat surface.

Portolan: A text that describes the coasts, ports and navigational conditions in a specific maritime space. Extended to cartography, from the 19th century onward the term designates a collection of plans of ports and, more improperly, an ancient maritime map.

Projection: A method of representing the Earth's surface on one plane as well as the image obtained from this method.

Quadrant: A navigational instrument that measures the angular distance between two celestial points. It took the ship's *bearing* at sea along its *latitude* position. The name of the instrument was derived from the fact that it measured along a 90-degree arc, which represents a quarter circle.

Rhumb Lines: An angular space (of 11°15′) that separates two of the 32 directions on a *wind rose* (synonymous to "quarter winds"). By extension, we often call the lines that indicate the direction of winds drawn on ancient maritime maps rhumb lines. Compare *wind lines*.

Roteiro: From the Portuguese for "route," it is the name given to navigational journals of 16-th century Portuguese sailors (which included descriptions and listings of coasts and maps), for example, the roteiro of Dom João de Castro (1541).

Scale (Map's): The relationship between the linear distances as measured on a map and the corresponding linear distances as measured on the terrain.

Sea-mark: A prominent point that is visible at sea; it can be either natural (peak, rock, cape, islet...) or artificial (spire, lighthouse, tower...).

Vignette: On a map, these are drawings of a city's profile.

Wind Lines: Lines that indicate the main directions of the *wind roses* on a maritime map. See also *rhumb lines*.

Wind Rose: A geometric figure in the shape of a star that indicates the four cardinal points (north, south, east and west) and the intermediary orientations, up to 32 directions. The roses on Mediterranean maritime maps traditionally carry the ancient names of the eight main winds (or their equivalents in other languages): tramontane (north), gregale (northeast), levanter (east), sirocco (southeast), ostro (south), libeccio (southwest), ponente (west) and mistral (northwest).

Windward: A maneuver consisting of setting the sails to navigate in a direction as close as possible to the wind's axis (sail upwind).

World Map: Called "mappemonde" in French, during the Middle Ages these were figurative, detailed or schematic representations of the totality of the inhabited world. They were usually designed in a conventional geometric shape (either a circle or an oval).

LIST OF EXHIBIT PIECES

National Library of France (NLF)

NLF, Arsenal Library

ARS, 4°S 3476 and 3477: F. Berthoud, *Traité des horloges marines*, 1773.

ARS, 8°H 1464: Jean Paulmier de Courtonne, *Mémoires touchant l'établissement d'une mission chrestienne dans la troisième monde appelé la Terre Australe, méridionale, antarctique et inconnue*, 1663.

ARS, 8°NF 5082 bis (2nd part): *Relation du voyage fait à la Chine sur le vaisseau l'Amphitrite*, 1700.

ARS, RESERVE Fol S 266: Michel de Montaigne. *Les Essais*, 1595, chap. XXX: "Les Cannibales," pp. 118–119.

[fig. 22] ARS, Fol S 1295: Georges Fournier, *Hydrographie contenant la théorie et la practique de toutes les parties de la navigation*, 1643.

ARS, Ms. 3221: *Déclaration du véyage du Captaine Gonneville et ses compagnons ès Indes*, 1502–1658.

[fig.42] ARS, Ms. 8323: Joan Martines, *Nautical Atlas of the World*, 1583.

NLF, Department of Maps and Plans CPL, GE A 275 (RES): Arnold Floris van Langren, Terrestrial Globe, 1612–1616

CPL, GE A 276 (RES): Martin Behaïm, Terrestrial Globe, 1492 (facsimile from 1847).

CPL, GE A 335 (RES): Green Globe, circa 1507.

[fig. 45] CPL, GE A 850 (RES): François Ollive, *Special Map of the Mediterranean Sea*, 1662.

CPL, GE A 1064 (RES): Gerardus Mercator, World Map with Crisscrossing Latitudes. 1569

[fig. 13] CPL GE AA 562 (RES): Map said to belong to Christopher Columbus, after 1488.

[fig. 11] CPL, GE AA 564 (RES): Jorge Reinel (attributed to), World map, circa 1519 (1843 facsimile).

[fig. 125] CPL, GE AA 565 (RES): Pedro Reinel (attributed to), Map of the Indian Ocean, circa 1517 (19th century facsimile).

[fig. 32] CPL, GE AA 566 (RES): Mecia de Viladestes, Marine map of the Mediterranean, 1413.

[fig. 54] CPL, GE AA 567 (RES): Anonymous, Map of the Aegean Sea, 16th century.

[fig. 73] CPL, GE AA 568 (RES): Domingos Sanches, Map of the Atlantic Ocean, 1618.

[fig. 126] CPL, GE AA 569 (RES):

Evert Gijbertsz., Nautical Map of the Indian Ocean and China Seas, 1599.

[fig. 43] CPL, GE B 550 (RES): Alvise Gramolin, Marine *Map of the Aegian Sea and the Marmara Sea*, 1624.

[fig. 30] CPL, GE B 696 (RES): Angelino Dulcert, Marine map of the Mediterranean, 1339.

[fig. 7] CPL, GE B 1118 (RES): Pisan map, late 13th century.

CPL, GE B 1132 (RES): Gaspar Luis Viejas, Map of the Atlantic Ocean, 1534.

[fig. 135] CPL, GE B 1147 (RES): Joan Blaeu (attributed to), Map of the Atlantic Ocean, circa 1655.

[fig. 50] CPL GE B 1148 (RES): Portuguese, Anonymous, Map of the Atlantic Ocean, 1549.

CPL, GE BB 246, vol.17, f.97: Open sea battle offshore from Bantam between the Portuguese and the Dutch, engraving, 1603.

[fig. 114] CPL, GE C 5089 (RES): Al-Sharfi, Maritime Map of the Indian Ocean and the China Sea, 1601

[fig. 44] CPL GE C 5093 (RES): Francesco Oliva, Marine map of the Mediterranean, 1603.

CPL, GE C 5110 (RES): M.F. Gérard, Map of the Gulf of Mexico, 1746.

CPL, GE CC 1128: *Neptune français*, 1693.

CPL, GE CC 1551 (6): *Ebstorf's world map*, circa 1300 (facsimile from 1898).

[fig. 70] CPL, GE CC 2719 (RES): Andreas Homem, Planisphere, 1559.

[fig. 89] CPL, GE D 7894 (RES): J. Troadec, Xylographed map of the Atlantic Ocean, 16th century.

CPL, GE D 7895 (RES): Nicolas Desniens, Planisphere, 1566.

[fig. 82] CPL, GE D 7896 (RES): Jean Cossin, World map, 1570.

[ig. 85] CPL, GE D 13871 (RES): Jacques de Vau de Claye, Map of the Brazilian coast, 1579.

CPL, GE DD 326: Giovanni Ramusio, *Navigazioni e viaggi*, 1550, Tome I.

[fig. 129] CPL, GE DD 1009 (RES): Ptolemy's *Geography*, ed. by Martin Waldseemüller, 1513.

CPL, GE DD 1297: J. Van Keulen, *De Groote Niewe Vermeerderde Zee-Atlas*, 1695.

CPL, GE DD 1302: Jean-Batiste Nicolas Denis d'Après de Mannev-

illette, *Neptune orientale*, 1775.

CPL, GE DD 1398: André Thevet, *Universal Cosmography*, 1575.

CPL, GE DD 1605–1607: Braun and Hogenberg, *Civitates orbis terrarum*, 1572, pl. 21: Amsterdam.

CPL GE DD 1605–1607: Braun and Hogenberg, *Civitates orbis terrarum*, 1575, pl. 54: Aden, Cefala, Monbaza, Quiloa.

CPL, GE DD 1831: Melchisédech Thévenot, *Relations de divers voyages curieux*, 2nd part, Paris, 1664, pl. depl.: eastern coast of Africa.

CPL GE DD 1988 (RES): Grazioso Benincasa, Nautical atlas, 1467.

[fig. 60] CPL, GE DD 1989 (RES): Bartolomeo da li Sonetti, *Isolario*. 1485.

CPL, GE DD 2013 (RES): J. Teixeira Albernaz (attributed to), *Plantas das cidades, portos e fortalezas da conquista da India Oriental*, 17th century.

CPL, GE DD 2987 (63) (RES): Oronce Fine, Cordiform world map, 1536.

CPL, GE DD 2987 (6813): Huych Allard (ed.) *India quæ orientalis dicitur et Insulæ adiacentes*, 17th century.

[fig. 124] CPL, GE DD 2987 (6700): João de Castro (attributed to), Map of the Arabic coast, from Moka to Aden, 1541.

CPL, GE DD 4796 (140): Charles Beautemps-Beaupré, *Atlas du voyage de Bruny-Dentrecasteaux*, 1807, pl. 14: map of the Archipelago of the Recherche.

CPL, GE FF 2036: J.H. de Linschoten, *Histoire de la navigation... aux Indes orientales*, 1638.

CPL, GD FF 3500 (RES): Henry Michelot, *Portulans de la Méditerranée ou le vray guide des pilotes costiers*, 1709.

CPL, GE FF 8183 (a3): Théodore de Bry, *Brevis narratio eorum quæ in Florida Americæ provincia Gallis acciderunt, secunda il illam navigatione, duce Renato de Laudonnière*, 1591.

CPL, GE FF 8340: Charles de Brosses, *Histoire des navigations aux terres australes*, 1756.

[fig. 55] CPL GE FF 9351 (RES): Cristoforo Buondelmonti, *Liber insularum Archipelagi*, 15th century.

CPL, GE FF 14409 (RES): Joao Teixeira (attributed to), Nautical atlas, circa 1640.

CPL, GE FF 14410 (RES): Battista Agnese, Nautical atlas, 1543.

[fig. 62] CPL, GE SH ARCH 1 (RES):

Nicolò de Caverio, Planisphere, circa 1505.

[fig. 79] CPL, GE SH ARCH 2 (RES): Diego Gutiérrez, Map of the Atlantic Ocean, 1550.

CPL, GE SH ARCH 3 (RES): Domingos Teixeira, Nautical Planisphere, 1573.

[fig. 20] CPL, GE SH ARCH 6 (RES): Pierre de Vaulx, Map of the Atlantic Ocean, 1613.

[fig. 10] CPL, GE SH ARCH 7 (RES): Joris Carolus, Map of the Arctic Ocean, 1614.

CPL, GE SH ARCH 15 (RES): Jean Guérard, *Carte universelle hydrographique*, 1634.

[fig. 142] CPL, GE SH ARCH 30 (RES): Hessel Gerritsz., Map of the Pacific Ocean, 1622.

CPL, GE SH 18 PF 16 P 10 (RES): Pieter Blaeu, *Pascaarte van alle de Zeecusten van Europa*, 1677.

[fig. 100] CPL, GE SH 18 PF 166 DIV 1 P 4 (RES): Nicholas Comberford (attributed to), Map of the mouth of the Amazon, circa 1626.

CPL, GE SH 18 PF 177 DIV 2 P 1 (RES): Teixeira Albernaz, Map of the Pacific Ocean, 1649.

CPL, GE SH 18 PF 179 DIV 9 P 3 (RES): Map of the Canton River, drawn during Étienne Marchand's expedition, 1792.

CPL, GE SH 18 PF 179 DIV 10 P 3 (2) D: Plan of the Canton River surveyed by Captain Nuddart, 1787.

CPL, GE, SH 18 PF 179 DIV 9 P 9: *Carte plate d'une partie de la coste de la Chine*, circa 1752.

CPL, GE SH 18 PF 181 P 04 (RES): John Thornton, Map of the China Sea, circa 1700.

CPL, GE SH 18 PF 181 P 6 (RES): John Thornton, Map of the Gulf of Siam, Cochinchine and Borneo, 1699.

CPL, GE SH 18 PF 187 DIV 3 P 1 (RES): Dutch map of a section of the northern coastline of New Guinea, 1705.

[fig. 137] CPL, GE SH 18 PF 192 DIV 3 P 4/1 (RES): Joan Blaeu, Map of Java's north coast, between Bantam and Batavia, 1688.

CPL, GE SH 18 PF 193 DIV 6 P 1 (RES): View of Bantam, late 17th century.

[fig. 104] CPL, GE SH 18 PF 194 DIV 2 P 4 (RES): John Thornton, Straights of Sinday, 1699.

[fig. 103] CPL, GE SH 18 PF 206 DIV 2 P 1 (roll) (RES): John Seller, *Coast*

of India from Gujarat to Malabar, including Bombay, 1684.

CPL, GE SH 18 PF 209 DIV 2 P 5 (RES): John Thornton, Map of the Persian Gulf, 1699.

CPL, GE SH 18 PF 213 DIV 3 P 2 (RES): Teixeira Albernaz, Map of the Indian Ocean, 1649.

[fig. 139] CPL, GE SH 18 PF 213 DIV 3 P 3/1 (RES): Joan Blaeu, Map of the Indian Ocean, 1667.

CPL, GE SH 18 PF 213 DIV 3 P 4 (RES): John Burston, Map of the Indian Ocean, 1665.

CPL, GE SH 18 PF 213 DIV 3 P 12 (RES): Pieter Goos, Indian Ocean, 1660.

CPL, GE SH 18 PF 213 DIV 3 P 13 (RES): Theunis Jacobsz., *Pascaerte van Oost-Indien*, 1630–1640.

CPL, GE D 26179 (RES): *Miller Atlas*, 1519; Portuguese hemisphere (recto) and signature and coat of arms of Catherine de Medici (verso).

CPL, GE AA 640 (RES): *Miller Atlas*, 1519, Atlantic Ocean (recto).

CPL, GE DD 683 (RES) (f. 2): *Miller Atlas*, 1519; Northern Europe (recto) and the Azores (verso).

CPL, GE DD 683 (RES) (f. 3): *Miller Atlas*, 1519, Indian Ocean, Arabia and India (recto) and Madagascar and Southeast Asia (verso).

CPL, GE DD 683 (RES) (f. 4): *Miller Atlas*, 1519; *Magnus Sinus* (recto) and China Sea and Malukus (verso).

CPL, GE DD 683 (RES) (f. 5): *Miller Atlas*, 1519; Brazil.

NLF, Library of the Geographic Society

SG BON 8°H 57 (RES): André Thevet, *Les Singularitez de la France antarctique*, 1558.

[fig. 141] SG BON Y 832 (RES): Fred Woldemar, Makassar harbor, 1660.

SG GLOBE No. 17 (RES): Didier Robert de Vaugondy, Terrestrial globe, 1773.

[fig. 41] SG Y 1704 (RES): Jacopo Maggiolo, Map of the Mediterranean, 1563.

NLF, Engraving Department

EST, Ec7 d 2 fol. (p. 127): cannibals, Théodore de Bry, *Grands voyages, terres australes*, 1590.

EST, Ec7 d 3 (f.2.): black slaves working in Spanish mines in South America, Théodore de Bry, *Grands Voyages*, part 5, *Americæ pars quinta*, 1590.

EST Ja 31 in-fol (f.17 v°-18): Nutmeg, natural history, excerpt from the marshal of Richelieu's collection, 1733.

EST, Jd 13 (6) pet. fol. (f.585): Black slave and *Cardamomum minus*, 1773.

EST, Jd 48 pet. fol. (book 3, p.152) India and Indigo in a factory where the workers are black slaves, from *Histoire générale des drogues*, 1695.

EST, Li 72 (6) fol.: Optical view of the warehouse of the Dutch East India Company in Amsterdam, 1760.

EST, Md 43 (14) fol.: *Cosmographer in his workshop*, Philipe Galle engraving, 1580.

EST, Od 59 pet. fol.: *French Mission to the king of Siam*, 1688, pl. 7: solar eclipse in 1688.

EST, B 6 fol.: Bird with landscape, cabins and North American canoe by Desmon, offered to the marquis of Turgot, 1763.

EST, Rés. Ca 4b fol.: Albrecht Durer, Rhinoceros, 16th century.

EST, Rés. Ja 25 box fol.: Strawberry, American species introduced in Europe in the 17th century pl. 97 in *Florilège de Nassau*, 1662.

EST, Rés. Ja 25 box fol.: Jasmine, American species introduced in Europe in the 17th century pl. 79 in *Florilège de Nassau*, 1662.

EST, Rés. Ja 25 Box (4): Barbary (or Berber) fig tree introduced in Europe in the 16th century. pl. 96 in *Florilège de* Nassau, 1672.

EST. Td 24 vol. 15 (M21101): *Allégories des quatre parties du Monde*, 17th century.

EST, Td mat 1a.: Collaert, *Allégorie de l'Afrique*, 17th century.

EST, Td mat 1a.: Collaert, *Allégorie de l'Amerique*, 17th century.

EST, Td mat 1a.: Collaert, *Allégorie de l'Asie*, 17th century.

EST, Td mat 1a.: Collaert, *Allégorie de l'Europe*, 17th century.

EST, Vd 25 4 fol.: Braun and Hogenberg, *Calicut Calechut celeberrimum Indiæ emporium*, 17th century.

EST, Vd 25 6 fol.: Goa Bay, Dutch siege, 1638.

NLF: Manuscripts Department

[fig. 101] MSS, English 51: F. Drake's West Indies journal, 1595–1596.

MSS, Arab 2188: Ibn al-Wardî, The Pearls of Wonders *and the Uniqueness of Things Strange*, cosmographic treatise, 15th century.

MSS, Arab 2214: Ibn Hawqal, Geographic treatise accompanied by maps, copied in the 15th century.

[fig. 111] MSS, Arab 2221: Al-Idrîsî, "Amusement for those who desire to travel the different parts of the world," 13th century.

MSS, Arab 2278: Al-Sharafi, Portolan of the Mediterraean Sea, 1551.

[fig. 118] MSS, Chinese 4024: *The History of the Occidental Voyage of the Eunuch San Bao*, 1597.

[fig. 25] MSS, Spanish 30 (RES): Abraham Cresques (attributed to), *Catalonian Atlas*, circa 1375.

MSS, French 1378: *Secrets de l'histoire natural*, circa 1428; f.11 v°: Aboriginal widow on a log.

[fig. 86 and 87] MSS, French 150: Jacques de Vaulx, *Premieres Œuvres*, 1583.

MSS, French 12201: Hayton, *The Flower of Oriental Histories*, 15th century; f.17 v°: "History of the Tartars." MSS, French 12223: *Traitté des animaux à quatre pieds terrestres et amphibies, qui se trouvent dans les Indes occidentales, ou Amérique septentrionale*, 18th century.

[fig. 83] MSS, French 19112: Guillaume Le Vasseur: *Traité de géodrographie*, 1608.

[fig. 9] MSS, French, 20122: Augustin Roussin, Nautical atlas, 1633.

[fig. 107] MSS, French 22971 *Secret de l'histoire naturelle ou Livre des merveilles du monde*, circa 1480 (illuminations by Robinet Testard)

[fig. 61] MSS, French 24224: Antonio Pigafetta, *Navigation et discovrement de la Indie supérieure*, 16th century.

MSS, French 24225: M. L. N, P., *Histoire naturelle ou la fidelle recherche de tout ce qu'il y a de rare dans les Indes Occidantalles*, circa 1675.

MSS, French 24269 (f. 53–54): *Glossaire franco-indien (tupi) du Brésil*, 1540.

[fig. 88] MSS, French 25374: Guillaume Brouscon, *Manuel de pilotage à l'usage des marins bretons*, 1548.

MSS, French 2700 (f.11 v°, No. 201) Inventory of the Royal Library where the *Catalonian Atlas* is mentioned, 14th century.

[fig. 108] MSS, French 2810 (RES): *Livre des merveilles*, which contains, among things, the voyages of Marco Polo and John Mandeville, 15th century.

MSS, French 5589: Jacques Cartier, *Seconde navigation faicte pour le commandement et vouloir du très chrestien roy Françoys Premier de ce nom*, after 1536.

[fig. 37] MSS, French 9669: Angelus, Nautical atlas, 1575.

[fig. 39] MSS, Latin 18249. Battista Agnese, Nautical atlas, circa 1550.

[fig. 28] MSS, Latin 3123 (f. 134 v°) Roger de Howden (attributed to), *De viis maris*, 2nd quarter of the 15th century.

MSS, Latin 4798: Strabon, *Geography*, circa 1470 (illuminated manuscript by Francesco di Antonio del Chierico).

[fig. 115] MSS, Latin 4802: Ptolemy, *Geography*, 15th century.

MSS, Latin 5565 A, f.101: Diverse representations of ships (here, caravels and galleys), 1465–1474, illumination.

MSS, Latin 6142, f. B v°: Ship or caravel, 15th century, illumination.

[fig. 109] MSS, Latin 8878 f. 45 v°-46: *World map* of Beatus of Liebana (Saint-Server's manuscript), 11th century.

MSS, Moreau 770, f. 60–62: Contract for the chartering of three ships destined for the voyage to the Indies, 1526.

MSS, NAF 9256: Tale of the voyage of Samuel de Champlain, 1599.

MSS, NAL 1180: Pomponius Mela, *Cosmographiæ liber*, mid-15th century.

[fig. 40] MSS, NAF 1465: Roussin, *Atlas nautique de la Méditerranée*, 1672.

[fig. 117] MSS, Pelliot B 1400, vol. 8, fac. 73: *Wu Bei Zhi*, 17th century.

[fig. 130] MSS, Portuguese 1: Pedro Barreto de Resende, *Livro do estado da India oriental*, after 1635.

MSS, Portuguese 41: Gomes Eanes de Zurara, *Cronica da Guiné*, 1453.

MSS, Rothschild 1954: Martin Waldseemüller, *Cosmographiæ introductio... Insuper quattuor Americi Vespucii navigationes*, 1507.

[fig. 58] MSS, suppl. Turkish 956: Pirî Reis, *Kitâb-i bahriyye*, 1525–1526.

NLF, Department of Currencies, Medals and Antiques

MMA, bab 593: Cameo representing an African sovereign, 16th century.

MMA, bab 595: Cameo representing an African king with a quiver, 16th century.

MMA, bab 604: Allegories of the African and European continents, 16th century.

NFL, Rare Books Reserve

RLR, ZZ-3769: *Lettre du sieur de Lozier-Bouvet... à Messieurs de la Compagnie des Indes. À Lorient, le 26 juin 1739*, 1758.

RLR, Rés. G. 345: Pierre d'Ailly, *Tractatus de imagine mundi*, 1483.

RLR, Rés. G. 46 (1): Lucas Jansz. Waghenaer, *Speculum nauticum super navigatione maris occidentalis*, 1586.

RLR, Rés. O²k5: Francisco Alvares, *Ho Preste Joam das Indias*, 1540.

RLR, Rés. P V 128: Pierre Garcie, *Grand routier et pilotage*, 1531.

Other French Institutions

Écouen, National Renaissance Museum

Inv. E. Cl. 22254 a and 22254 b: silver fork and spoon, 16th century.

Dieppe, Musée-château

[fig. 34] Inv. 964.4.1: Sailor's trunk, Nuremburg, 17th century.

ijon, Municipal Library

Ms 550: Portuguese, anonymous, Map of the Mediterranean, circa 1510.

La Rochelle, New World Museum

Gregor Brandmuller, Allegory of the four continents, 1682.

Lyon, Municipal Library

Ms. 172, f.5: Jean de Sacrobosco, *Tractatus de spera*, 15th century.

[fig. 17] Ms. 175: Pietro Vesconte, Nautical atlas, 1319.

[fig. 8] Ms. 179: Cornaro atlas, second quarter of the 14th century.

Marseille, Municipal Library

[fig. 24] Ms. 2104: Atlas of the Mediterranean, late 17th century.

Nice, Departmental Archives of the Maritime Alps

[fig. 23] 01 Fi 1534: Baldasaro da Maiolo Visconte, Map of the Mediterranean, 1589.

Paris, Library of the National Assembly

[fig. 123] No. 1248 (1907 catalog): Francisco Rodrigues's journal, Tomé Pires's *Suma oriental*, after 1521.

Paris, Library of the Institut de France

Ms. 1288, No. 21: Map of the Atlantic Ocean drawn up for the VOC, circa 1650.

Paris, Sainte-Geneviève Library

S fol sup 43 rés: Indian rooster in Pierre Belon's *Histoire de la nature des oiseaux*, 1555.

Paris, Gulbenkian Foundation

Treaty of Tordesillas in Portuguese (facsimile).

Paris, Mobilier national

GMTT 185/1: New Indies, 1740.

Paris, National Museum of Arts and CraftsInv.

22590: Divider to record distances, 18th century.

[fig. 75] Inv. 3864-001: Sancho Gutiérrez, Nautical astrolabe, 1563.

Inv. 8952-0017: Nocturnal, 16 century.

Paris, National Maritime Museum

[fig. 18] Inv. 1 NA 10: sea compass fabricated by Manoel Ferreira, 1744.

Cross-staff or Jacob's staff, 1732.

Padrao of Saint-Augustine, mold of an original conserved in Lisbon, 20th century.

Paris, Louvre Museum

[fig. 132] Inv. 1921: Willem II Van de Velde, *Navy with Admiral's Vessel*, oil on canvas, the Netherlands, 17th century.

Paris, Branly Pier Museum

[fig. 71] Inv. 71.1930.49.1: Gold funeral mask, Peru, 200 BC–600 AD

Inv. 71.1936.48.64.2: Mato Grosso's feather diadem , Brazil, 20th century.

[fig. 33] Inv. 74.1994.9.1: Ethiopian processional cross, 15th century.

Inv. 78.32.265: Iroquois moccasins from the Saint-Lawrence, fabricated in the aboriginal tradition, Canada, 20th century.

Paris, Guimet Museum

[fig. 136] Coll. Grandidier G 106: Plate decorated with ship motif, porcelain, Qianlong period, 1756.

MA 2042: Chinese lettering mural fresco on terra-cotta, 13th or 14th century.

MA 3055: two statuettes with Chinese lettering, varnished terra-cotta, lead glaze, 13th or 14th century.

MA 3341, MA 3210, Ma 4229, Ma 3368, Ma 3273: six spice pots, small and medium sized, blue and white, even blue background, 14th century.

MA 5513: Jarre Guan, with painted decoration, 16th century.

MA 6519: Jarre Guan, pottery with altered surface due to time at sea, 16th century.

Paris, Private Collection

Brazilian bird, 21st century.

Rouen, Model-makers Club

Model of the *Dauphine* ship, conforming to the circa-1525 type. Made in 2003.

Vincennes, Defense Historical Service

Library D1. Z 14: Guillaume Le Testu, *Cosmographie universelle*, 1556.

Matine, Ms. 203: Lafitte de Brassier's atlas of, circa 1778.

Other European Institutions

London, British Library

[fig. 116] Add. Ms. 11267: Fra Mauro, World Map, circa 1459 (facsimile from the 19th century).

[fig. 99] Add. Ms. 5413: Nautical planisphere known as the Harleian Map, 1542–1547.

Add. 27376: Marino Sanudo, *Liber secretorum fidelium crucis*, 14th century.

[fig. 102] Royal Ms. 18. D iii (f. 124): William Borough, *Mapt from Norway to Novaya Zemlya*, circa 1568.

[fig. 4] Royal ms 20 E IX: Jean Roze, *Boke of idrography*, 1542.

Florence, Medicea Laurenziana Library

[fig. 119] Gaddi 9: *Médicis Atlas*, circa 1380.

[fig. 69] Med. Palat. 249: Nautical planisphere known as Salviati's Map, circa 1525.

[fig. 56] Plut. Latinus XXIX-25: Henricus Martellus, *Insularium illustratum*, circa 1489.

Venice, Marciana Library

[fig. 14] Cod. Marc. Ital. IV 170 (5379): Pietro di Versi, *Raxion de marineri*, portolan text, 15th century.

INDEX OF NAMES

A

Abreha, Saint: 69
Aeneas: 90
Agnese, Battista: 74, 78, 81, 90, 93, 248
Aguiar, Jorge de: 128
Ailly Pierre d': 62, 200
Albuquerque, Alfonso de: 180, 196, 218, 219, 225, 248
Albuquerque, Luís de: 130, 248
Alexander the Great: 198, 200
Alexander VI, Pope: 110
Al-Harîrî: 205
Al-Idrîsî: 198, 204, 205, 207
Al-Istakhrî: 198,203
Al-Wâsitî: 205
Andreu, Nicolau: 60
Angelo, Jacopo d': 209
Angoulême, Charles d': 198
Anias, Abraham: 233
Annebaut, Claude d': 136, 171
Anthiaume, Albert: 26
Anthony, Saint: 62
Anville, Jean-Baptiste d': 220
Apian, Petrus: 145
Après de Mannevillette, Jean-Baptiste Nicolas Denis d': 176
Aristotle: 13
Asbeha, Saint: 69
Avezac, Marie Armand Pascal d': 18

B

Baldacci, Osvaldo: 78, 81
Barbosa, António: 130, 248
Barbosa, Duarte: 216
Barceló, Maria: 65
Barreto de Resende , Pedro: 216, 225
Beatus of Liebana: 203
Behaim, Martin: 128
Benincasa, Adrea: 81
Benincasa, Grazioso: 30, 32, 70, 81
Benedict, Saint: 125
Bertelli, family: 93
Blaeu, family: 176, 230, 237
Blaeu, Joan I: 176, 230, 232, 234, 237
Blaeu, Joan II: 230
Blaeu, Willem Jansz.: 230, 240
Blondo, Flavio: 200
Bordone, Benedetto: 93
Borough, William: 174, 177
Boschini, Marco: 93
Brémond, Estienne: 81
Brémond, Jean-André: 81
Brouscon, family: 138
Brouscon, Guillaume: 146
Brouwer, Hendrick: 233
Buondelmonti, Cristoforo: 90, 93, 95, 97
Burston, John: 176

C

Cabot, John: 112, 180
Cabot, Sébastien: 93
Cabral, Pedro Álvares: 32, 98, 112, 128, 180
Cadamosto, Alvise: 126
Caloiro et Olivia, Placidus: 81
Camocio, Francesco: 93
Campbell, Tony: 24, 26, 62, 65, 248
Cantino, Alberto (planisphere): 34, 98, 112, 128, 130, 133, 216, 218, 248
Capella, Martianus: 198
Carolus, Joris: 22
Cartier, Jacques: 165, 172
Caspersz., Evert: 230
Castiglioni (map): 112
Castro, João de: 218, 220, 249
Catherine de Medici: 143, 180, 183
Cavallini, Giovanni Battista: 78, 81
Cavallini, Pietro: 78, 81
Cavendish, Thomas: 174
Caverio, Nicolò de: 7, 34, 98, 112, 128, 131, 216, 225
Chancellor, Richard: 174, 177
Charles II, King of England: 176
Charles V, King of France: 24, 42, 200, 248
Charles VI, King of France: 42
Ciribert, Jaume: 60
Coen, Jan Pietersz.: 230
Coligny, Gaspard de: 13, 16, 136, 148, 150, 151, 165
Collbató, Lluís de: 60
Colomb, Jasques: 74
Columbus, Bartolemeo: 130
Columbus, Christopher: 24, 26, 28, 110, 112, 113, 114, 128, 130, 248
Comberford, Nicholas: 174, 176
Commineau de Mézières, Hugues: 209
Conti, Nicolò de: 90, 200
Corcós, Samuel (a.k.a. Macià de Viladesters): 62
Cornaro, family: 18, 22
Coronelli, Vincenzo Maria: 93
Corte-Real brothers: 112
Cortés, Martin: 40
Cortesão, Armando: 130, 248
Cosa, Juan de la: 112, 114, 130, 248
Cossin, Jean: 136, 138
Cotrugli, Benedetto: 65, 72, 81, 86
Crescenzio, Bartolomeo: 81
Cresques, Abraham: 42, 86, 166, 248
Cresques, Jafudà (a.k.a. Jaume Ribes): 62

D

Daniel, John: 174
Datini (company): 62, 65
De Graaf, Isaac: 230, 240
De Houtman, Cornelius: 174
Desceliers, Pierre: 136, 160, 166, 171
Desliens, Nicolas: 136
Dias, Bartolomeu: 28, 110, 128, 196, 200, 216
Díaz de Solís, Juan: 112
Drake, Francis: 174, 176
Dudley, Robert: 176
Dulcert, Angelino: 65, 86, 89
Dupont, Jean: 136
Duval, Pierre: 18, 26

E

Eanes, Gil: 126
Elcano, Sebastián: 112

F

Fassoi, Marco: 81
Fernandes, Valentim: 90
Ferreira, Manoel: 34
Ferrer, Jaime: 52
Fillastre, Guillaume: 200
Fine, Oronce: 145
Fournier, Georges: 36, 38
Freducci, Angelo: 81
Freducci, Conte: 81
Freducci, Ottomano: 112, 116
Friend, John: 174
Friend, Robert: 174

G

Gabriel (archangel): 69
Gama, Vasco de: 128, 160, 180, 196, 216, 218, 248
Garbi, Rafel: 65
García de Toreno, Nuño: 112, 119
Garcie-Ferrande, Pierre: 249
Gastaldi, Giacomo: 218, 233
Gerritsz., Hessel: 230, 240, 247
Gijsbertsz., Evert: 223
Gomes, Diogo: 126
Gramolin, Alvise: 58, 80
Guarino of Verona: 200
Guérard, Jean: 138
Guidalotti, Nicolò: 81
Gutiérrez, Diego: 130, 134
Gutiérrez, Sancho: 129, 160, 165

H

Habsburg family: 228
Hack, William: 174, 176
Hamy, Ernest Théodore: 26, 248
Harley, Edward: 172
Harley, John Brian: 26, 65, 248
Hayton: 200
Henry, Prince of Portugal: 126, 128
Henri II, King of France: 16, 136, 165, 171
Henry IV, King of Castile and Léon: 110
Henry VIII, King of England: 16, 134, 169
Herbert, William: 176
Hercules: 160
Hervé, Roger: 16
Holanda, António de: 14, 180, 128
Homem, Andreas: 120
Homem, Diogo: 24, 93, 95
Homem, family: 180
Homem, Lopo: 14, 180, 218
Homer: 198
Honorius, Augustodunensis: 42
Hood, Thomas: 174
Hoogvliet, Margriet: 16, 248
Huchon, Mireille: 16

I

Ibn Hawqal: 198
Isabella of Castille: 110
Isidore of Seville, Saint: 198

J

Jenkinson, Anthony: 174
Joanna of Castile: 110
John II, King of Portugal: 110,128
John, Duke of Burgundy: 200
John, Prester see Prester John
John the Baptist, Saint: 62
Jomard, Edme-François: 21, 24, 26
Joseph, Saint: 125
Joyeuse, Duke of: 136
Julian, Saint: 62

K

King, Thomas: 176
King-Hamy (map): 128
Kuntsmann, Friedrich: 18, 26

L

Lafitte de Brassier, Louis François Grégoire: 226
Le Testu, Guillaume: 13, 16, 36, 136, 148, 160, 165
Le Vasseur, Guillaume: 38, 136, 140
Lelewel, Joachim: 18, 26
Lemaire, Jacob: 240, 247
Leu, Tomas de: 93
Linschoten, Jan Huygen van: 223
Llewellyn, Martin: 174
Louis XIII, King: 22
Louis XIV, King: 87

M

Macià de Viladesters see Corcós, Samuel Macrobe
Magellan, Ferdinand: 14, 25, 97, 112, 119, 148, 180, 240, 247
Maggiolo, Cornelio: 78
Maggiolo, Cornelio II: 78
Maggiolo, family: 39, 78, 81, 248
Maggiolo, Jacopo: 76, 78, 108
Maggiolo, Nicolò: 78
Maggiolo, Vicount: 78, 128
Malanima, Paolo: 65
Mandeville, Jean de: 160, 200
Manuel I, King: 180, 216
Maria Levanto, Francesco: 81
Marot, Clément: 10, 16
Marre, Jan de: 228
Martellus Germanus, Henricus: 90, 95, 200, 216, 225
Martin I, King: 65, 66
Martines, Joan: 78, 79, 81, 248
Massaio, Pietro del: 209
Mauro, Fra: 200, 209, 248
Mecia de Viladestes: 24, 60, 69, 86, 89
Medina, Pedro de: 10, 16, 145
Meilleraye, Charles de la: 13
Mercator, Gerardus: 26, 34, 36, 38, 130, 136, 230, 233, 237, 249
Micali, Giuseppe: 21
Michel de Rhodes: 30
Michael (archangel): 69
Michelot, Henry: 81
Miller, Emmanuel (Miller Atlas): 7, 14, 16, 24, 86, 89, 165, 180, 216, 218, 221, 248
Millo, Antonio: 81, 93
Miquel, Juan, Matilde: 65
Mittman, Asa Simon: 166
Mollat du Jourdin, Michel: 16, 248
Monno, Giovanni Francesco: 78, 81
Montmorency, Anne de: 136, 171

N

Napoleon I (Bonaparte): 24
Nordenskjöld, Adolf Erik: 26, 58
Núñez de Balboa, Vasco: 112, 116, 240, 247

O

Odoric of Pordenone: 200
Oliva, Bernat: 60
Oliva, Francesco see Ollive, François
Oliva, Giovanni: 78, 81
Oliva, Salvatore: 81
Olives-Oliva, Domingo: 81
Olives-Oliva family: 81, 83
Olives-Oliva, Jaume: 81
Olives-Oliva, Juan Riczo: 81
Ollandois, Jaques Anthoine: 74
Ollive see Oliva and Olives-Oliva
Ollive, François: 40, 72, 78, 81, 83, 85, 87, 89, 248
Orange-Nassau, House of: 22
Orellana, Francisco: 134
Orlandi, Angela: 65
Orose, Paul: 198
Ortelius, Abraham: 26, 174
Ottens, Josua: 230
Ottens, Reiner: 230

P

Palsky, Gilles: 26
Parmentier, Jean: 10, 16, 165
Parmentier, Raoul, 16, 165
Pastoureau, Mireille: 26, 248
Paulin: 205
Paulmy, Antoine-René d'Argenson: 79
Pelletier, Monique: 26, 248
Pepys, Samuel: 176
Perry, Mathew C.: 228
Pesaro (map): 112, 113, 128
Petti Balbi, Giovanna: 65
Peutinger, Konrad: 90
Pflederer, Richard: 24, 26, 234, 248
Phillip II, King: 93
Phillip III, King: 125
Phillip IV, King: 22
Pigafetta, Antonio: 97, 160
Pinargenti, Simon: 93
Pires, Tomé: 216, 219, 253
Pizarro, Francisco: 89, 165
Plancius, Petrus: 230
Pliny the Elder: 16, 160, 166, 198, 200
Poggio Bracciolini, Gian Francesco: 200
Polo, Marco: 13, 42, 52, 90, 148, 160, 200, 209, 248
Pomponius Mela: 110, 198, 200
Ponce de Léon, Juan: 112
Porcacchi, Thomaso: 93
Porro, Girolamo: 93
Prester John: 69, 160
Progel, Otto: 24, 25, 221
Ptolemy, Claudius: 13, 78, 90, 95, 98, 110, 112, 180, 183, 198, 200, 204, 209, 214, 218, 225, 248
Pujol, Domingo: 62

Q

Quint, Charles: 112, 165

R

Rabelais (François): 13, 16
Ramusio, Giovanni Battista: 223, 248
Reinel family: 36, 221
Reinel, Jorge: 14, 24, 25, 180, 218, 221
Reinel, Pedro: 14, 24, 128, 130, 131, 134, 180, 218, 221
Reis, Pirî: 93, 96, 112, 113
Relaño, Francesc: 166, 248
René II, Duke of Lorraine: 225
Ribeiro, Diogo (a.k.a. Diego Ribero): 112, 218
Ribes, Jaume see Cresques, Jafudà
Richard I, King: 62
Richelieu, Armand Jean du Plessis: 18, 22
Robaert, Augustijn: 230
Rodrigues, Francisco: 218, 219
Roger de Howden: 62, 200
Roger II, King: 198, 204
Rogerio di Camera: 65, 66
Roncière, Charles de la: 24, 28
Roselli, Francesco: 93
Roselló, Guillem: 65
Rotis, Denis de: 36
Rotz, John see Jean Roze
Roussin 74
Roussin, Augustin: 18, 22, 81
Roussin, Jean-François: 81
Roze, Jean (a.k.a. John Rotz): 16, 136, 165, 166, 169
Russo, Jacopo: 78, 81, 248
Russo, Pietro: 78, 81, 248
Rylands (map): 160, 166, 171
Ryzik, Jacob: 233

S

Salama, Saint: 69
Salviati, Giovanni (map): 110, 112, 119
Sanches, Domingos: 125
Santa Cruz, Alonso de: 93
Santarém, Viscount of: 18, 24, 26
Sanudo, Marino: 205
Schilder, Günter: 248
Seller, John: 176, 178
Serra, Joan: 60
Sezgin, Fuat: 218, 248
Sideri, Giorgio: 81, 93
Sivestri, Domenico: 93
Solanes, Francesc: 60
Soler, Guillem: 62
Soler, Joan: 62
Soleri, Guillermus: 86
Solin: 16, 198, 200
Sonetti, Bartolomeo da li: 93, 97
Stephen, Saint: 125
Strabon: 200
Strozzi, Phillippe: 143

T

Tasman, Abel: 228
Tatton, Gabriel: 174
Testa Rossa, Battista: 81
Testard, Robinet: 198
Thevet, André: 93, 97, 148
Thornton, John: 176, 178, 223, 238
Tim, Jan Hendricksz.: 176
Tissot: 24
Tornil, Bartomeu: 60
Troadec family: 138
Troadec, J.: 146

V

Vallseca, Gabriel de: 62, 65, 89, 166, 248
Van de Velde, Willem: 228
Van Keulen family: 230
Van Keulen, Johannes I: 176, 230
Vau de Claye, Jacques de: 143
Vaulx, Jacques de: 10, 136, 140
Vaulx, Pierre de: 38, 136, 140
Verlinden, Charles: 130, 248
Versi, Pietro di: 30
Vesconte, Pietro (or Petrus): 10, 33, 62, 200, 205
Vespucci, Amerigo: 112, 249
Viegas, Gaspar Luis: 218
Vigliarolo, Domenico (a.k.a. Domingo de Villaroel): 81
Viguié, Cristol: 72
Villaroel, Domingo de see Vigliarolo, Domenico
Villegagnon, Nicolas Durand de: 140, 143, 148, 165
Virgil: 90
Vivien de Saint-Martin, Louis: 18
Vlamingh, Willem de: 228
Volcic, Vicko see Volcio, Vicenzo
Volcio, Vicenzo (a.k.a. Vicko Volcic): 81
Vries, Maarten Gerritsz. de: 228

W

Waldseemüller, Martin: 98, 128, 225
Waters, David: 249
Woldemar, Fred: 238
Woodward, David: 24, 26, 65, 166, 248, 249

X

Xenodocos, Johannes: 81

Y

Yuanyi, Mao: 212

Z

Zandvliet, Kees: 26, 249
Zheng He: 200, 212
Zurara, Gomes Eanes de: 130, 248

THE AUTHORS

Under the guidance of Catherine Hofmann, Hélène Richard and Emmanuelle Vagnon, exhibition curators.

Joaquim Filipe Figueiredo Alves Gaspar, a retired officer in the Portuguese navy, specializes in the history of cartography and navigation. A post-doctoral researcher at CIUHCT — Faculty of Sciences at the University of Lisbon, he is the author of *From the Portolan Chart of the Mediterranean to the Latitude Chart of the Atlantic: Cartometric Analysis and Modeling* (thesis, ISEGI — Universidade Nova de Lisboa, 2010), "The Myth of the Square Chart" (*e-Perimetron*, vol. 2, No. 2, 2007, pp. 66–79) and "Dead Reckoning and Magnetic Declination: Unveiling the Mystery or Portolan Charts" (*e-Perimetron*, vol. 3, No. 4, 2008, pp. 191–203).

Corradino Astengo is a graduate of law, geography and political sciences. He was a visiting professor at the University of California, Los Angeles (UCLA), and he currently teaches the history of geography and explorations, cartography, travel and tourism at the University of Genoa. His many publications include *Il Libro della Conoscenza* (Genoa: Erga, 2000), *La Cartografia nautica mediterranea dei secoli XVI e XVII* (Genoa: Erga, 2000).

Zoltán Biedermann is a professor in the Departent of Iberian and Latin American Studies at London University (Birkbeck College). He works on the history of the Portuguese Empire and spatial representations. He coordinated l'*Atlas historique du golfe Persique (XVIᵉ–XVIIIᵉ)* (Historical Atlas of the Persian Gulf [16th–18th centuries]), edited by Dejanirah Couto, Mahmoud Taleghani and Jean-Louis Bacqué-Grammont (Turnhout, Belgium: Brepols, 2006) and authored "Quelques remarques sur les sources de la cartographie portugaise de l'océan Indien," (A few remarks on the sources of Portuguese cartography of the Indian Ocean), which was a contribution to *Transferts de savoir dans les cartographies de l'océan Indien* (Exchanges of knowledge on cartographies of the Indian Ocean), edited by Emmanuelle Vagnon and Éric Vallet).

Surekha Davies specializes in European cultural and scientific history. She has a particular interest in world exploration and cartography from the 16th to 18th centuries. She was a Leverhulme Early Career Fellow in the Department of History, Classics, and Archaeology (beginning of the modern era) at the University of London (Birkbeck College); she is now an assistant professor in European history at Western Connecticut State University. She has published "French Depictions of Brazilians on Sixteenth-Century maps" (*The Historical Journal*, 55-2, 2012), "The Wondrous east in the Renaissance Geographical Imagination: Marco Polo, Fra Mauro and Giovanni Battista Ramusio" (*History and Anthropology*, 23-2, 2012) and *Mapping the Peoples of the New World: Ethnography, Imagery and Knowledge in Early Modern Europe*, (Cambridge University Press, to be published in 2014).

Catherine Hofmann is an archivist-paleographer and the head conservator in the Department of Maps and Plans at the NLF. A board member of *Imago Mundi* journal, she is also the secretary of the "history" commission of the Comité français de la cartographie (French committee of cartography). She has published a dozen articles on the history of cartography of the modern era, and she has notably contributed to *Cartography in the European Renaissance*, vol. 3 in the project led by David Woodward, The History of Cartography (University of Chicago Press, 2007). She also headed *Artistes de la carte, de la Renaissance au XXIᵉ siècle* (Map artists from the Renaissance to the 21st century; Autrement, 2012).

Hans D. Kok, a retired airline pilot and navigator, is a collector of 17th- and 18th-century maps and currently presides over the International Map Collectors' Society (London). He co-edits *Caert-Thresoor magazine* (Utrecht) and has published, with Günter Schilder, *Sailing for the East* (Utrecht, the Netherlands: Hes & De Graaf Publishers, 2010), vol. 10 in Utrecht Studies of the History of Cartography.

Frank Lestringant is professor of Renaissance literature at the University of Paris-Soronne (Paris IV). He is the author of several articles, among them *L'Atelier du cosmographe ou l'Image du monde à la Renaissance* (The cosmograph's workshop or The world image during the Renaissance; Albin, Michel, 1991), *Le Livre des îles : atlas et récits insulaires, de la Genèse à Jules Verne* (The book of islands: Atlas and insular tales from Genesis to Jules Verne; Geneva: Droz, 2002) and, in collaboration, *Les Méditations cosmographiques à la Renaissance* (Cosmographic meditations during the Renaissance; University of Paris-Sorbonne Presses, 2009).

Luisa Martín-Merás Verdejo headed the Department of Cartography of the Museo naval of Madrid. She is a specialist in the history of maritime cartography and has published *Cartografía marítima hispana: la imagen de América* (Hispanic maritime cartography: this image of America; Madrid: Lunwerg, 1993), "*Las cartas portulanas: origen y desarrollo*" (Portolan letters: origin and development) in *Investigación, conservación y restauración de materiales y objetos cartográficos* (Research, conservation and restoration of cartographic materials and objects; Madrid: Misterio de Cultura, 2011) and "La Casa de la Contratación: escuela sevillana de cartografia" (The Casa de la Contratación: Sevillian school of cartography) in *Andalucía: la imagen cartográfica hasta fines del siglo XIX* (Andalucia: the cartographic image until the late 19th century; Seville: Instituto de Cartografia de Andalucia, 2010).

Ramon Pujades i Bataller is currently the archivist at the Archivo de la Corona de Aragón in Barcelona. A doctor in Medieval history he main area of interest is the written culture of the Middle Ages, particularly the cartography and publication of texts and maps of the medieval era. He is the author of *Portolan Charts: The Medieval Representation of a Ploughed Sea* (bilingual Catalan/English edition; Barcelona: Institut Cartogràfic de Catalunya/Institut d'Estudis Catalans/Institut europeu de la Mediterrània, 2007) and of *The 1439 Portolan Chart by Gabriel de Vallesca* (trilingual Catalan/Spanish/English edition with facsimile; Barcelona: Lumenartis, 2009).

Hélène Richard is an archivist-paleographer and was the director of the Maps and Plans Department of the French National Library between 1999 and 2009. She is currently the inspector general of libraries. In additional to her research on the history of books and of libraries, she has published works on the history of maritime exploration of the 13th and 19th centuries (d'Entrecasteaux, Dumont d'Urville) and on the associated nautical sciences. She was the curator of the catalog for the exhibition entitled La Mer, terreur et fascination (The sea, fear and fascination), which she oversaw with Alain Corbin (NLF/Seuil, 2004).

Jean-Yves Sarazin is an archivist-paleographer, a general conservator of libraries and, since 2010, has led the Department of Maps and Plans of the National Library of France. Initially a specialist in the diplomacy of private acts and the history of notaries from the Ancien Régime, he then directed works on the history of urban cartography. He was associated with the publication of Jean Boutier's book *Les plans de Paris: des origines (1493) à la fin du XVIII*e *siècle, étude, carto-bibliographie et catalogue collectif* (The Paris Plans: from the origins

(1493) to the end of the 18th century, study, carto-bibliography and collective catalog; NLF, 2002). He is also the author of *Rêves de capitale* (Capital Dreams; NLF, 2002), *Villes de France* (Cities of France; Assouline, 2007) and, with Alfred Fierro, *Le Paris des Lumières* (The Paris of the Enlightenment, RMN, 2005). Since 2007, he has collaborated regularly to enrich the articles in Wikipedia.
Research Director, Institute for Historical Research, National Hellenic Research Foundation
Institute of Historical Research, Department of Neohellenic Research
National Hellenic Research Foundation, Institute of Neohellenic Research
Department of Neohellenic Research/Institute of Historical Research, National Hellenic Research Foundation

Georges Tolias is research director of the Department of Neohellenic Research/Institute of Historical Research, National Hellenic Research Foundation and holds a doctorate from the University of Paris IV and an Habilitation à Diriger des Recherches (Ability to direct studies) from the University of Nice, Sophia Antipolis. He recently published *Mapping Greece, 1420–1480: A History, Maps in the Margarita Samourkas Collection* (New castle: DE/Athens, Oak Knoll Press for the INR/NHRF, 2011), "The Isolarii, Fifteenth to Seventeenth Centuries" (*Cartography in the European Renaissance,* vol. 3 in *The History of Cartography*, edited by David Woodward, Chicago/London: University of Chicago Press, 2007) and *The Greek Portolan Charts: A Contribution to the Mediterranean Cartography of the Modern Period* (Athens: NHRF/Olkos Publications, 1999).

Sarah Toulouse is an adjunct director of the Rennes Metropolitan Library. As a specialist in maritime cartography of the 16th century, she has published "L'hydrographie normande" (The Nor-

man hydrography) in *Couleurs de la terre: des mappemondes médié*vales *aux images satellitales* (Colors of the Earth: from medieval world maps to satellite images), an exhibition catalog (Paris: Seuil/NLF, 1998), and "Maritime Cartography and Navigation in Renaissance France" in *Cartography in the European Renaissance* (vol. 3 in *The History of Cartography*, edited by David Woodward, Chicago/London: University of Chicago Press, 2007).

Sarah Tyacke was the director of the National Archives of England and Wales. A former professor at the University of London, she now hosts an annual seminar on the history of maps at the London Rare Book School in collaboration with Catherine Delano Smith. She is the director of *Imago Mundi* and a founding member of the International Society for the History of Map (ISHM) and a specialist in English marine cartography (1550–1750).

Emmanuelle Vagnon, a former student of the École Normale Supérieure, is an *agrégée* and doctor in history and specializes in Western medieval cartography. Since 2009 she has been directing research in the National Center for Scientific Research's MeDIan program, and she is the chair of Cultural Dialogues Department at the University of Paris 1. Her publications include "Les rivages africains de l'océan Indien: cartographie occidentale du XIII*e* au XVI*e* siècle" (The African coastlines of the Indian Ocean: occidental cartography from the 13th to 16th centuries) in *Cartographier l'Afrique* (No. 210, December 2011) and *Cartographie et repré*sentations *occidentales de l'Orient méditerranéen, du milieu du XIII*e *à la fin du XV*e *siècle* (Cartography and Occidental representations of the Eastern Mediterranean, from the middle of the 13th to the end of the 15th centuries) to be published as part of the Terrarum Orbis series (Turnhout, Belgium: Brepols).

Photographic Credits

Unless noted otherwise, the works reproduced in this book are conserved at the National Library of France and the plates were done by its Reproduction Department.

All iconography from the NLF's collections is available for consultation in the image bank, http://images.bnf.fr and http://gallica.bnf.fr, and for sale from the Reproduction Department at reproduction@NLF.fr .

(The numbers refer to the illustration numbers.)

With the amiable authorization of the Geographic Society: 41, 141.
© Album/Oronoz/Akg: 66.
© akg-images: 65.
© British Library/Robana/Leemage: 97 b, 98, 99, 102, 116.
© The British Library Board: 4.
© RMN-GP (Guinet Museum, Paris)/Richard Lambert: 136.
© RMN-GP (Louvre Museum)/René- Gabriel Ojéda: 132.

With the authorization of the Minestero per i Beni e le Attività Culturali: Archivo di Stato , Florence: 67;
Biblioteca Medicea Laurenziana, Florence: 56, 69, 119, 121;
Biblioteca Nazionale Centrale, Florence: 120;
Biblioteca Estense Universitaria, Modena: 74, 78.
Biblioteca Nazionale Marciana, Venice: 14.
Departmental Archives of the Gironde, Bordeaux: 76.
Château-musée, Dieppe cl. Jean-Louis Leibovitch: 34
Archicio de la Corona de Aragón, Ministerio de Cultura, Spain: 31.
Nationaal Archief, The Hague: 133.
Municipal Library, Lyon, cl. Didier Nicole: 8, 17, 29.
The John Rylands University Library, Manchester (with the authorization of the university librarian and director): 96.
Municipal Library of Alcazar, Marseille: 24 a and 24 b.
Bayerische Staatsbibiothek, Munich: 77
Departmental Archives of the Maritime Alps, Nice: 23.
Library of the National Assembly, Paris: 123.
Museum of Arts and Crafts, Paris/cl. P. Faligot: 75.
National Maritime Museum, Paris/cl. P. Dantec: 18.
Branly Quai Museum, Paris, photo Thierry Ollivier/Michel Urtado/Scala, Florence: 72;
Photo Patrick Gries/Valérie Torre/Scala, Florence: 71;
Photo Scala, Florence, 2012: 33.
Österreichische Nationalbibliothek, Vienna: 93.
Historical Defense Service, Vincennes: Library: 90 a–p, 94 a–d.
Centrales Archives of the Marine Department: 131.
Herzog August. Bibliothek, Wolfenbüttel: 68.

Typography: Plantin and Fedra
Photoengraving: Planète Couleurs, Paris